The Life Journey
of a
Joyful Man of God

The Life Journey of a Joyful Man of God

The Autobiographical Memoirs of Adrian van Kaam

Edited with
Forewords and Afterword by Susan Muto

Preface by Joop Bekkers

RESOURCE *Publications* • Eugene, Oregon

THE LIFE JOURNEY OF A JOYFUL MAN OF GOD
The Autobiographical Memoirs of Adrian van Kaam

Copyright © 2011 Epiphany Association. All rights reserved. Except for brief quotations in critical publications or reviews, no part of this book may be reproduced in any manner without prior written permission from the publisher. Write: Permissions, Wipf and Stock Publishers, 199 W. 8th Ave., Suite 3, Eugene, OR 97401.

Resource Publications
An Imprint of Wipf and Stock Publishers
199 W. 8th Ave., Suite 3
Eugene, OR 97401
www.wipfandstock.com

ISBN 13: 978-1-60899-481-6

Manufactured in the U.S.A.

Epiphany Association
820 Crane Avenue
Pittsburgh, PA 15216-3050
www.epiphanyassociation.org

Contents

Acknowledgments / vii

PART ONE: WINTER OF MY SOUL

Foreword to Part One by Susan Muto / ix
Preface by Joop Bekkers / xv

1. The Beginning of My Journey / 1
2. Formative Fruits of My Early Friendships / 12
3. From Education to Formation / 21
4. From Enclosure to Exposure / 27
5. From Freedom to Captivity / 35
6. Knowledge from Experience / 40
7. A Terrible Toll / 47
8. Longing for Peace Amidst the Chaos of War / 51
9. Mad Tuesday / 56
10. The Price of Survival / 60
11. Compassion with Competence / 68
12. Splitting of Simplicity / 72
13. Fighting for Integrity / 76
14. Prophetic Envisioning / 84
15. Grace and Terror / 89
16. Agony of Deportation / 94
17. Message of the Sea / 98
18. Everyday Heroism / 102
19. Winter of Women / 106

20 Miracles of Survival / 111
21 The Cosmic Epiphany / 115
22 Clandestine Drama of Christmastide in Conquered Holland / 121
23 In Hiding, Open to Our Inmost Call / 128
24 Quest for Wisdom in Wild Times / 132
25 One Heart and One Soul / 135
26 Blessed Calamity / 140
27 Terror and Transformation / 145

PART TWO: SPRINGTIME OF MY HEART

Foreword to Part Two / 155

28 Return to Normalcy / 161
29 Long Range Influence of the Dutch Life Schools / 168
30 Discovering the Centrality of Formation Theology / 179
31 Events in Paris / 185
32 On to America and University Life / 197

INTERMEZZO 1: FIDELITY TO MY CALL / 209

33 Founding of the Institute of Formative Spirituality / 225

INTERMEZZO 2: BLESSINGS OF A CORONARY / 239

34 Fruits of Formative Thinking / 287
35 Remembering a Blessed Benefactor / 296
36 Fulfillment of Our Epiphany Mission / 307

Afterword / 312
Appendix 1: Poetry of the Winter of My Soul / 319
Appendix 2: Christmas Night in Ravaged Holland / 340
Appendix 3: Editorials by Adrian van Kaam in Cor Unum et Anima Una / 358
Appendix 4: Poetry of My Crucifying Epiphany / 394
Appendix 5: Biographical and Bibliographical Review / 416

Acknowledgments

Father Adrian van Kaam, CSSp, PhD (1920-2007), lived long enough to review the first draft of this remarkable set of memoirs. He entrusted their final production to me as his editor and to all of us at the Epiphany Association as his most trusted colleagues. He died as he had lived, yielding wholly to the Divine Forming Mystery, who guided his life. I and other close friends were at his bedside on November 17, 2007. There in his room in the presence of the Little Sisters of the Poor he took his last breath, receiving to the end the skilled, dignified care his frail health required. I was privileged to be with him almost daily during the last two and a half years of his life and to engage in the preparation of this blessed work of remembrance with a truly gentle and joyful man of God.

I thank in Father's name our Epiphany staff, notably Mary Lou Perez and Vicki Bittner who typed the manuscript, and our dear friends in the Netherlands, Joop Bekkers (Dutch translator) and Father Adrian's nephew Han van Gemert, for their help with the Dutch part of this story. Father and I were and are deeply indebted to the Board of Directors of the Epiphany Association for their support of this project and to the people here and in Holland whose passion for Father's work brought it to its completion. We dedicate this book to his memory and entrust its dissemination to the Divine Mystery that embraced Father Adrian van Kaam from birth to death. May his spirit of peace and joy remain with us always.

PART ONE

Winter of My Soul

Foreword

EACH OF US IS on a voyage into the unknown. Countless events invite us to give form to our lives. Not everything that happens has the same effect. Remembering our past, some episodes stand out more than others. Striking for Father Adrian van Kaam was the Hunger Winter (*De Hongerwinter*) that afflicted his life and all of occupied Holland from 1944 to 1945.

Few know what happened to Western and Northern Holland after the defeat of the Allies in spite of their heroic combat in the famed battle of Arnhem. The Allied troops and their commanders felt compelled to press eastward from Holland into Germany. They had to leave behind this part of the Netherlands whose population became cut off from the

rest of liberated Europe, only to be left at the mercy of their vengeful oppressors. Surviving in a kind of limbo, harassed by a foreign regime and its small quota of Dutch collaborators, short of food, clothing, shoes, fuel, and medicine, many starved to death, succumbed to illness or tottered on the verge of despair.

Born twenty-four years earlier, on April 19, 1920, in The Hague to Charles and Anna van Kaam, neither Adrian nor his three sisters, Bep, Lia, and Leonie (now deceased), could have imagined how this event would change the course of their lives. As this remarkable memoir will reveal, these years found Father van Kaam alternating between two emotional polarities—extreme gladness and equally extreme sadness. Gladness about the divine invitations this horrific time of loss allowed into his life and sadness because of how easy it might have been to miss the meaning of what God intended for his destiny and that of countless others. Happily for us, Father van Kaam opted for searing honesty in tracing the origins of his formational concepts not to abstract reasoning or idle curiosity but to deeply felt experiences that cut a trail through the dense underbrush of humanity's need to grasp life's meaning at the marrow of the bone. He traces his thoughts about the vicissitudes of life to their roots in the harshness of the reality of the Hunger Winter when failed expectations gave way to the brilliant light of building a new science, anthropology, and theology of human and Christian formation.

In Part One, *Winter of My Soul*, he traces the origins of his ideas concerning formative spirituality from his youth to the time shortly after World War II when he knew what his life's mission would be and how he would work under obedience to his religious superiors to fulfill it. Part Two, *Springtime of My Heart*, presents the main story of how his life's mission continued in the United States, together with an account of our shared mission in the Epiphany Association. His war experience taught him that if we are to enjoy any peace on this small planet of ours, we must begin by overcoming our self-centeredness and begging for the grace of true conversion of heart. In an era of worldwide struggle, where terrors threatened him and his peers wherever they turned, we find this young candidate for the priesthood living through harassed days with only one thought: how to understand humanity's meaning and purpose for today and tomorrow. He felt drawn to ponder not only the meaning of the war to which he was exposed in his disheartened city of birth but all wars from the beginning of time, of the killing and maiming of millions by their own people, of the scourge of infidelity that has deformed our destiny as the children of God.

His main discovery during the Hunger Winter was that he had to find better ways to prepare humankind for peace, for healing the rifts within us and between us. What kind of approach would it take to teach us how to give form to what is most noble in our nature? What discipline might help us to highlight in our different traditions anything that could bridge our divisions, heal the hates that tear us apart and in the end destroy us? Were these the utopian dreams of a young student lost in a ransacked city or was there a way to give form to life and world in the light of a mystery that is without beginning or end? As he said to me on October 26, 1966, the day we first met on the campus of the university where for the next twenty years we would teach and work together, first in the Institute of Man and then in the Institute of Formative Spirituality:

> I could not shake the feeling, indeed the certitude, that there had to be a new science of meaning aimed at disclosing the causes that create the dissonance that leads to war, a science that helps us to transcend our differences before they destroy us. Otherwise these divisions may immobilize the last remnants of faith, hope, and love. Then anger, resentment, and frustration may lead anew to desperate outlets in war-like strife for the dominance of one race or nation over another.

His prophetic vision prompted my personal "*Yes, Lord,*" to this mission, but it would take many more years of work in our co-founded Epiphany Association and several authored and co-authored books for the dream of this science, anthropology, and theology of formation to become a reality. Thanks be to God, Father van Kaam lived long enough to see our combined one hundred years of work bear fruit throughout the world. Instead of pointing only to the divisions between women and men, parents and children, neighbors and strangers, employers and employees; instead of only emphasizing what sets culture against culture, race against race, country against country, tradition against tradition, our goal has been to seek, find, and teach foundational directives that bind us together in full respect for our differences. We believe that our common aim must be to build with others an edifice for justice, peace, and mercy in the light of our distinctively human transcendence dynamic. The set of constructs designed by Father van Kaam and initiated during the Hunger Winter would eventually become the ingredients of the science of human and Christian formation.

As this first part of his life journey will show, the insights he gained in the seminal years from 1944 to his ordination to the priesthood on July 21, 1946, would never be lost. In the end, they empowered him to sacrifice whatever God asked of him to be faithful to his formative mission in full fidelity to his commitments as a religious priest and an always inspiring educator. As I witnessed personally when I came to teach with him, he gave up a brilliant career as a professor of psychology for the chance to keep alive his love for the new fields of formation science, anthropology, and theology he initiated during this winter of his soul. No matter the misunderstanding to which such a decision might lead, it was the one God called him to make. All those who knew and loved him see that he gladly gave his all to fulfill what he came to discern and what was consequently confirmed as his unique-communal life call in Christ. The enlightenment that flooded his mind during these seminal years would stay with him for a lifetime. Hints and guesses grew into convictions and these blossomed in turn into unshakeable pledges to open hearts to a new way of being, thinking, and acting.

My service to Father van Kaam as the editor of this book is one small way of thanking God for our partnership in the mystery of redemption for over forty years. My gratitude to this priest, friend, and mentor goes beyond words. He guided with grace my own call, vocation, and avocation in the field of formative spirituality. He taught me never to refuse the kind of service God asks of us, to always say *yes*. What mattered to Father was to tell this story not as a strict autobiographical account of his life, with what he humbly admitted were its countless failings, but to reveal in these episodes as honestly as possible the origins of his teachings and, by the grace of God, their significance for the lives of others. This work is not only a chronology of major events but a formational theology of his providential response to them. The episodes that comprise his life's journey during the period of time, presented in Part One, from his early upbringing in The Hague to his ordination, reveal the soil into which the seeds of his contributions to humankind in general and Christianity in particular have been planted. All of us owe this saintly man a profound debt of gratitude for being, like Christ, a beaming blade that allows us to see trails of light in the wilderness of fading hope. With his help, the divine beam in all our lives may continue to grow brighter. I know it has done so time and again in mine.

[Editor's Note: *In respect for the first person style of these memoirs, I have left them in the autobiographical mode in which, for the most part, they were written in various unpublished notes and journals as well as in some previously published materials in our former journal,* Envoy, *which first appeared in press when we directed the Institute of Formative Spirituality at Duquesne University.*]

Susan Muto, PhD

Preface

ORIGINS

THE ORIGINS OF THE van Kaam family lie in the Southwest of the Netherlands, in the village of Halsteren, a few miles north of the town of Bergen op Zoom. From perusing Father van Kaam's archives, it appears as if there may still be a cousin of his in that neighborhood, living on the Belgian border. Others in his ancestry came to live in the village of Uitgeest, about fifteen miles north of Haarlem, where Adriaan's father, Charles Louis was born on February 9, 1896. About the origins of his mother, Elisabeth Johanna Franke, I have no information; I only know she was born in The Hague on January 18, 1892. Both of Adriaan's parents became orphans at a young age, and they lived at an orphanage for some years. The orphanage was called RK Wees-en Oudeliedenhuis and the address was War noezierstraat 89–91, The Hague. There they got to know one another and married in The Hague on January 8, 1919. They remained in that city for the rest of their lives.

Early Years

Adriaan (the Dutch spelling of his name) van Kaam was born on April 19, 1920. It was and is still customary with most children, certainly with Catholics, to receive two or three official Latin names of saints, one of which, usually the first, was shortened for daily use. In this case, Adriaan Leo was the first-born of four siblings. After him came his three sisters. Elisabeth Julia, or Bep in daily use, was born on July 17, 1925; Julia Elisabeth, or Lia, on April 7, 1930; and Leonarda Jacoba, or Leonie, on July 17, 1935.

Adriaan's address at birth was Alberdingk Thijmplein 20, a square in the Southeastern most outskirt of the town. This neighborhood was at the time very small and just being developed. At a certain moment the family moved to the nearby Alberdingk Thijmstraat 8, where Adriaan's parents remained for most of their lives; his father was only in a nursing home for six weeks before his death.

This neighborhood was called Spoorwijk. In fact, it was more like a village than part of a town. At the time it was isolated from the rest of the city by a railway. It was and remained a respectable but poor section and

in the aftermath of the Wall Street crash (which not only hit America heavily but also Western Europe) it became extremely poor. His father drove a streetcar—and he was lucky insofar as buses and streetcars were an official service of the local government, so he was not fired during the Depression years. It meant a permanent job, however poorly paid.

In this new neighborhood a parish, too, was founded, named Saint Jeroen—a regional martyr and a parish priest, who was killed around the year 850 by the invading Vikings, who ravaged most of Western Europe for two centuries.

This is the neighborhood (which I, too, have known, having grown up there myself) where Adriaan spent his youth. His parents, though not rich at all due to these depressed economic circumstances, did the best for their children and in some ways it was a good time to be alive. Spoorwijk was adjacent to an agricultural district with ample vegetable and fruit growing. The food we ate was more wholesome than it is now with artificial means of preservation and the effect of acid rain. Dutch food is quite plain, but it is and was at least wholesome; its only specialty resides in the great variety of vegetables we produce, more than in any other European country.

The neighborhood had another advantage: it was at the edge of the town. When we walked down the streets, we were in the fields; there was also a park and some woods, so we had plenty of fresh air. The primary school was called Sint Jozefschool. The reports of Adriaan's grades, as found in the archives at the Epiphany Academy in Pittsburgh, are excellent. He was also a member of the boys' choir in his parish.

The school was new in a new neighborhood. We had some really good, enthusiastic teachers, who managed to stimulate their pupils and who also organized clubs and a singing group. The same can be said of the parish: it was more than an organization where one could attend religious celebrations; it was a meeting center where all kinds of clubs came into being, stimulated by the priests: acting and youth clubs, music clubs, and all this in spite of the reigning poverty. Whenever something was organized, lots of people volunteered to help.

At the age of twelve, Adriaan went to the junior seminary of the Holy Ghost Fathers at Weert. This seminary was popular in Spoorwijk among candidates for the priesthood: the parish priest favored it, and

besides, these fathers did not turn away candidates who could not pay the seminary fees. Sometime during these six seminary years, Adriaan must have been ill enough to be sent to a sanatorium—which in those years was usually for tuberculosis patients. I do not know exactly when this happened, but for sure he recuperated and completed his seminary years, inspired by his soul-friend, Marinus Scholtes. Their correspondence can be found in *Become Jesus: The Diary of a Soul Touched by God,* translated by Joop Bekkers, PhD and edited with an Introduction and Afterword by Adrian van Kaam and Susan Muto (Pittsburgh, PA: Epiphany Books, 1998).

Novitiate and Major Studies and the Hunger Winter

So far I have not mentioned the political situation in Europe. I do not know to what degree Adriaan was informed about it. The Second World War broke out in September 1939, about the same time he entered the novitiate at Gennep. It was when he was there that our country was invaded by the Germans. Gennep is situated only three miles from the German border. There used to be a railway station quite close to the novitiate where in the days before the war daily boat-trains from Germany passed to the port of Vlissingen from where there was a daily service to England. The railway ran close to the garden at the back of the novitiate, and it crossed the river Maas a few hundred yards from there. At the outbreak of the war the daily boat-train must have stopped. During the night, from May 9 to May 10 at daybreak, a German armed train entered the railway station, while German commandoes, disguised as Dutch policemen, took the bridge by surprise. In this disguise they could approach the sentries at both ends of the bridge and walk across it, and then the German train could pass. All this must have happened when the inhabitants of the novitiate were asleep. When they rose at their usual hour they must have been surprised to notice that the village with its station was in German hands. I have never heard Adriaan speak of this event, but he no doubt remembered it.

He must have made his profession in August or September of 1940; his novice master was Father Henri Strick, CSSp, who later was to become his provincial superior. Adriaan moved on to Gemert for his philosophical and theological studies. Rinus Scholtes had been there for two years already. The illness he contracted (cf. *Become Jesus*) proved to be fatal and he died on January 31, 1941 with his soul-friend, Adriaan, at his bedside.

About the course of studies he followed there are no details, but he must have been an excellent student or he would never have become a professor at Gemert. There was a debating club in Gemert, the "SOOS," and in 1944 he became its chairman. These were the years of the German occupation and, while the students in those days did not see any newspapers, he must have known what happened. The prestige of the Catholic Church in the Netherlands was never higher than in those years, also among Protestants and Socialists, because of its clear stand against the fascist ideology of Nazism. The Archbishop was the true leader of moral resistance. The Germans never dared to arrest him or the other bishops, not even after the letter they issued against the persecution of the Jews. The Nazis retaliated by more measures against the Jewish people. (It appears that Pope Pius XII, who was himself preparing a condemnation of Nazism, dismissed this idea because he expected the same kind of reprisals against Jews. His Christmas broadcast of 1942 left, however, no doubt about his concern for people suffering for reasons of racism. The Nazis were furious about this papal message and prevented its publication in Germany.)

Then came the summer of 1944. The students were at home on vacation when the sudden breakthrough of the Allies in France and later in Belgium made it impossible for many of them to return to Gemert. They remained at home, scattered throughout the country. After the Allies failed to administer a final defeat—at the Battle of Arnhem—the situation throughout most of the Netherlands became desperate. The Germans were responsible for the famine in the country and they wanted every able-bodied male to be transported to Germany to work for them. Many men, including many seminarians, went into hiding.

Adriaan managed to "dive under" in the village of Nieuwkoop, some thirty miles northeast of The Hague, from where he could arrange to transport food to his parents and sisters. Later on he arranged for his three sisters to stay in the same village. A graphic description of these months is to be found between the lines in *Cor Unum et Anima Una*, a bulletin that Adriaan set up, edited, and managed to distribute among his confrères (see Part One: Appendix Three). It was illegal, though it was not meant to be political, only to inspire his fellow community members, not to lose courage or give up hope. Some time after the German surrender in May of 1945, probably in July or August, Adriaan managed to return to Gemert.

Early Years of Priesthood (1946–1954)

Ordained a priest in the summer of 1946, he celebrated his first Holy Mass in the parish church in Spoorwijk on July 28. It was then that I first met him. After the war youth work in the parish, which had been forbidden during the German occupation, started again. There were a few hundred boy scouts, girl guides, and youth workers. Adriaan's first Holy Mass was the first great event in the parish, so he was welcomed with double rows of youngsters and their leaders. That summer, there were camps for the youngsters, which involved the curate who was in charge of youth work; he had to be at camp for some five or six weeks. Adriaan volunteered to take over for a week. It was a tremendous success. Though not sportsmanlike by nature, he joined in all the activities of the youngsters. He was liked very much; he appeared to be a born teacher, who could get on well with the most difficult teenager. He finished his seminary training in the summer of 1947 and was appointed to be a professor in Gemert, his subjects being, among others, philosophy and psychology. In the summers of 1947, 1948, and 1949, he went to camp again with the Spoorwijk boys.

The elder boy scout group, the Rovers, would go to some monastery or abbey every year during the Holy Week to attend celebrations there. One new member of the Rovers, an ex-seminarian of the Holy Ghost Fathers, suggested early in February of 1948: "Why not write to Father van Kaam at Gemert and ask him to get permission for us to camp there during Holy Week?" That is what happened. The Gemert superior gave his permission, and during these days Adriaan gave us (I was one of the Rovers there) two daily lectures explaining all the liturgical ceremonies, including Tenebrae. After the service of Easter Saturday, which in those days was not at night but in the early morning, Adriaan gave a guided tour through the buildings (an old castle) and the gardens of the seminary.

The same happened during the Holy Week in 1949. In that week I also had a longer talk with Adriaan and from then on we wrote to one another occasionally. I do not always remember the exact chronological order of events nor do I know the complete background of the years between 1949 and the summer of 1954. Some of my knowledge is based on oral reports, but I will try to be as exact as possible.

In those years, Adriaan also got involved in courses for older working girls, especially factory girls, at the "Life Schools" or the "Mater Amabilis" schools, a type of school founded by a Belgian educator, Maria Schouwenaars. Somehow the Papal Secretary of State (later Pope Paul VI), Giovanni Baptista Montini, got to know about this work and arranged for Adriaan to be given full permission to continue it.

In 1950 he was transferred to the community at Gennep, where the novitiate also was, and made free for his Mater Amabilis work. Gennep is only twelve miles from Nijmegen and had better connections to other places in the country. That appointment meant the end of his professorship at Gemert. It seems as if not everybody, especially at the Mother House, was in favor of practical psychology. Be that as it may, while he was at Gennep he was allowed to follow courses in psychology and education at Nijmegen University. At the same time he gave lectures in Holy Scripture, mainly on the Gospels, to the novices there as well as to his confrères. His lectures, which included Matthew, Chapter 1, and the Farewell Discourse of Saint John, were done in the same formative way as he would later write in books like *The Woman at the Well* and *Looking for Jesus*. He also preached the sermon in September 1951 on the occasion of the novices taking their first temporary vows.

Some time during those years he must have submitted his name for consideration for the missions in the Belgian Congo or in the Amazon region of Brazil, but nothing came of this request since, at the medical examination, it was determined that frail health made him unfit for living in tropical climates.

At the time practically everybody in the Holy Ghost Fathers, certainly in the Netherlands (and other parts of the world as well) adhered to the conviction that their founder, the Venerable Francis Libermann, had intended it to be mainly, if not exclusively, devoted to missionary work in foreign lands. Some members (who had studied the entire body of Libermann's writings more closely) had a different, broader interpretation, to which Adriaan no doubt felt an affinity, especially in regard to their educational intentions. (On the whole, most Dutch members of the

Congregation were broad-minded enough on the subject, even if they did not always agree with one another.)

To research the matter further may have been one of the reasons Adriaan was happy to have been sent to the motherhouse in Paris in 1952 with the task of collecting material and writing a biography of Libermann. Some members of the congregation thought this task to be something of a punishment, but not Adriaan. He stayed in Paris for almost two years and was fortunate to have the company of another Dutch Holy Ghost Father, Cor Neven, who was there studying modern catechetical methods. Cor proved to be a good friend and supporter of his as was the then Dutch provincial superior, Father Strick, his old novice master.

When in Paris, where many members of all the provinces came to visit, certainly all the provincial superiors, Adriaan met the American superior, Reverend Vernon Gallagher, the person who invited him and a few other Dutch priests to come to Pittsburgh to Duquesne University to teach there. (Some Dutch University professors, for example, the scientist-philosopher, Andrew Van Melsen (1912–1994), had been there already as guest professors.) Adriaan was given permission to go to the States on the condition that he would first finish his biography of Libermann.

In 1953 and early in 1954, Adriaan was back in the Netherlands where, for a short time, he served also as editor of the monthly magazine published by the Dutch Holy Ghost Fathers, the *Bode van de H. Geest* (Holy Ghost Messenger). Its quality, which had been below average, rose enormously in those few months! Adriaan finished his work on Libermann, revealing in *A Light to the Gentiles*, the full vision he lived by and inspired others to follow. When it was published (some time after he had already left for Duquesne) several confrères said, "He has defended—and proved—his thesis."

On July 11, 1954, the yearly date when appointments in the Dutch province were made known, it became official that Adriaan was appointed to go to Pittsburgh. He must have known of this trip for some time to make his arrangements. That summer he left for America, which was to be his home and his place of citizenship from then on. Adriaan became Adrian and English, in due time, became his first language. Reading the memoirs of this dear friend of mine was a touching experience. I continue to thank God for his life, his vision, and his remarkable, highly original work.

Joop Bekkers, PhD

1

The Beginning of My Journey

LET ME START WITH my mother Anna, the woman to whom I credit the most influence on my life and my calling to the priesthood. Because of the death of her parents and because she was so much younger than her other siblings, who had married lives of their own, they decided that she would be sent to an outstanding orphanage in The Hague, which was more like a boarding school. Sad as this decision might have seemed to an outsider, it was God's providential means of safeguarding her own and, by extension, my future calling. There she received an outstanding education in the Catholic faith, which could not be said of most other members of her family. All of them, especially my Uncle Ferdinand, her brother, were fine human beings with many religious traits but no formal affiliation with the Church. Thank God for my mother Anna. She made it possible for me to be a good Christian, a faithful Catholic, and, in response to God's grace, a priest for life.

My father Charles was in a worse predicament. His father was a strict but kind man, the head of a company of builders. He was quite well-to-do, but he had to travel a lot to find work. My father never knew his mother because she died in childbirth. He was cared for by his older brothers and sisters and for the first part of his life enjoyed great freedom and economic stability. After the death of my grandfather, his siblings sold the company and began to go their own way. What were they to do with this youngster? They decided to send him to the boy's division of the same orphanage where my mother was. He was absolutely heartbroken and cried for days and days. He missed his happy-go-lucky life and the attention he was used to receiving at home. This parting of the ways put a stamp on his life that may have accounted for what struck me as a certain sadness in his constitution. He had a special relationship to one of his older sisters, a good Catholic woman, who tried to be his second mother, but he lost contact with her while he was in the orphanage. The rest of his extended family more or less drifted away from the faith. In retrospect I also believe that God protected his call to lead a good Christian life by bringing him to the orphanage and assuring his religious formation. I am deeply grateful to my father for the strong witness to the meaning of commitment and fidelity he gave to me and my sisters.

My parents met one another by chance in the orphanage. Dating other boys and girls was out of the question so couples more likely than not found their future partner there. In every sense Charles and Anna appeared to be a good match. Their love for one another grew, even though they were quite different. My mother was a refined woman of delicate taste—traits that radiated through her whole personality. A priest-mentor whose guidance she received in her formative years at the orphanage nurtured her spiritual leanings and educated her in the meaning and mystery of the faith. Years later she presented me with the treasure box of beautiful religious pictures this priest had given her to awaken her love for the Lord and his mother. This sensitivity to faith was a virtue she fostered in me. Slowly I came to see what a lonely walk she had to make. Since most of her family no longer shared her faith, visits with them could be difficult. They made her feel uneasy. I surmised as I grew up that her loneliness might have accounted for her love of the *hidden life*. Having grown up in the orphanage and then having to adapt to the outside world made her feel slightly estranged from others. In a sense both of my parents were "always in the orphanage"—and not quite of this world. They made a kind of cocoon in our immediate family where we felt protected and cherished. Until the age of five, when my first sister was born, I was the apple of their eye.

Since their choice of a mate for life was not done in the normal way, my parents had to grow through and beyond their differences. Their relationship manifested a creative tension between two distinct persons: Anna, a refined, warm, emotional woman, educated traditionally by the priests and nuns, and Charles, a strong, organized man, a bit rough and outspoken but with a generous heart, resistant to imitating his own father's touchy temperament but not always successful. If a coffee mug was chipped my grandfather would simply toss it away. He ate alone, not with the children who had to dine in another room and who had to keep quiet. He was the boss. Life in the orphanage modified these traits in my father, but there was also in him an inclination to milder but still explosive outbursts of anger of which I am not innocent! He, however, had great technical skills, which I do not.

When the Great Depression hit Europe, he was married and had to make a living. Though he had studied to be an electrician, he had to take a job as a streetcar conductor because he could find no position in his field of choice. He worked in public transportation until retirement to support our family, but I always sensed what he felt: that his freedom was gone. In public he had no choice but to be nice! To relax he smoked cigars and enjoyed buying little gifts for me, my sisters, and especially his dear wife.

When he sought permission to marry my mother, he had to ask her oldest brother, Uncle Ferdinand (Ferry), for her hand. Since she was not physically strong, my father promised him that he would take a lot of the heavy household work out of her hands—a promise he kept with great integrity. He was a man of his word, always doing laundry, dishwashing, cleaning, and repairs. My mother was a skilled lace-maker, a hobby she loved. Her way of dressing and acting was so exquisite and precise that before she married she was hired by outstanding families to care for their household and be a traveling companion. Her aesthetic way of being was as highly developed as were my father's work-a-day skills.

Uncle Ferry and his wife were exceptionally kind and good to me. Though they were not Catholic, they saw to it that I got to the parish preschool. My aunt picked me up and took me to their home to take a nap and have a snack. I remember feeling perfectly joyful there. The family festivity that thrilled me most as a little boy was the Dutch Christmas festivity of Saint Nicholas Day. Lights glittered throughout the house. They gave me baskets of goodies, but what I loved most were books. I was crazy about them! This love puzzled my parents, who thought I'd like toys and candy more, but I wanted to read everything. Over the course of life I noticed from these earliest days two prevailing traits: *an enormous need to read* and *a deep desire for the hidden life.*

My choice of reading materials was quite varied. For instance, I enjoyed perusing the comic strips with my father. Around the age of five or six, I had the sudden revelation that I could read them on my own! This moment opened up a new world for me. Providentially, since unlike my father I was neither handy nor hardy, reading and writing became the basis of my life's calling. I was born left-handed, but to be so was forbidden in school. I had to use my right hand, which made me even more awkward. This aberration turned out to be providential, too, since it caused me to be less fit for other jobs.

By the age of seven or eight, I began to write small poetic verses, which encouraged me even more to find my life in books. I wrote good compositions in school, where I was told I had a talent for expressing myself. Socially, I felt a bit awkward. My extraordinarily Catholic parents had taught me a morality the other children did not make so central. They did not know what to think of me. I was nicely dressed, pious and polite, not a loud jokester or a purveyor of pranks. No wonder I felt a little lonely. When I was naughty my father would flare up, but I would usually flee to my mother for protection. I got the usual spankings, of course, but I could count on my mother to intervene. She sensed with compassion when my father came home from work irritated and depressed. His income, though adequate, was not great. Still he insisted on giving a *guilder* to the church every week. Most of our family entertainment was confined to walking in the woods on the outskirts of our village and visiting our uncles, aunts, and cousins. It was fun for all of the children to sleep in the same big bed. We had to be quiet and, if we would stop crying, we would get some chocolate.

Although most of my relatives did not share our faith, they impressed me by the care they showed for friends and family, for neighbors and passersby. As a young boy, I appreciated how well we got along together and how much we learned from one another. Passed on to me, more by example than by words, was the loving kindness and compassion I associated with the Gospel. All of these people and the way they lived awakened in me a lifelong curiosity about what makes us who we are.

The suburb of The Hague where we lived bordered on the lovely historical town of Delft, which was so near to us I could walk to its center in about fifteen minutes. I loved going there because this was the town where the great Dutch artist, Jan Vermeer, had lived and where he created contemplative masterpieces that would inspire the world.1 As memory serves me, my Mother had hung in our living room two reproductions of his works that were the same size as the original paintings. Every time I saw them it was as if they filled the room with the stillness and luminescent beauty that orients us to the transcendent. I believe the peaceful atmosphere they created had an indelible influence on me as a child and an adult. Vermeer's use of light—his "epiphanic style," his attention to detail—all had later implications for my insights into the Divine Forming Mystery and its manifestations in daily life.2

Lest I get too far ahead of my story, I recall having had the benefits of both public and private education. I attended kindergarten and the early grades in the public school across the plaza from our house. At age twelve, I entered the Catholic school system under the auspices of the Junior Seminary of the Holy Ghost Fathers in Weert, a town south of Eindhoven.

Having been born at the end of one world war and about to live through another, politics were certainly not a foreign topic to me. Many demonstrations for one or the other socialist, communist, or Catholic cause took place in the plaza in front of our house. The only oasis of stability for us was the beautiful old church where I made my First Holy Communion. What impressed me most was not the organizational or juridical side of the Church but the fact that here was the place where I could meet Christ experientially. The pastor who taught religion had a devotion to the Sacred Heart of Jesus and the Immaculate Heart of Mary. Both images touched me. Venerating them gave me an initial and intensely memorable experience of God's presence. When the day to make my First Communion finally came, I was so excited I stood up when I should have knelt down. I still remember saying to my mother after the ceremony, "I think I would like to be a priest." From a neighbor I received the gift of a statue of the Sacred Heart. Everyone came to my party and congratulated me. Though in 1927 remnants of the Great Depression could still be seen everywhere, we were able to purchase breads and cakes from luxurious restaurants. That day they tasted especially delicious.

The unity that bound our family together in the midst of these religious, social, and political upheavals planted in my soul the seeds of cooperation with others without compromise of our own beliefs. My immediate family made me feel at ease with everyone in my school and neighborhood, whether or not we shared the same background or belonged to a common faith grouping. Many in our vicinity were adherents of non-Christian religions, including Islam, Hinduism, and Buddhism. They had come to our country from different colonies in the East and West Indies. Having served on the ships of our merchant fleet, they decided to settle down in Holland and raise a family there. We were a country composed mostly of Christians belonging to the Dutch Reformed Church, but we were known for welcoming in our midst many immigrants. I met the children of these settlers in the public school I attended. When our parish was able to open its own Catholic school, I tried to keep in touch with the friends I had made. This interest deepened when one of my uncles, a prison administrator in present-day Indonesia, stayed at our home over the holidays and brought an international flavor to our family gatherings.

Most of all, I attribute my dispositions of gentleness, respect, and openness to my mother. I hold in my mind's eye the lovely silhouette of her gentle face and beautiful head, bowed in prayer before a white statue of the Blessed Virgin with bright sunlight shining on it. Dimly, in a childlike way, I sensed a peace in her that pervaded her words and movements as she prepared our meals and cleaned our house. Even after my three sisters were born and she was extremely busy, hand washing their diapers in a bucket, she sang while doing so. I found her "spirituality of diaper changing" extraordinary. The statue she most loved, as I later learned, was an image of Mary as she appeared to the humble children at Lourdes in southern France. Mother gave this representation of her appearance a place of honor in our home. She always kept a devotional light burning at the feet of our Lady. Often she brought her fresh flowers, purchased from a hand cart pushed by a door-to-door vendor. I loved his manly voice singing loud praises to God for his freshly cut bouquets. With them and her vigil candles, Mother created an in-house shrine to celebrate this tender apparition of the Blessed Mother. As a family, she insisted that we gather around Mary to honor her presence among us with simple prayers and the devotion of saying the Rosary.

Thanks to my mother, there was instilled in me a deep love for the Gentle Woman I later named Our Lady of Epiphany. In our parish church, in a side chapel adjacent to the sanctuary, the pastor had built a shrine to her as Our Lady of Lourdes. Her lovely figure towered above us. Prior to and after Mass we would kneel before her in veneration and light candles that produced a blazing sea of dancing flames. Holding my mother's hand, I stared in wonder. Suddenly I realized that the love of Our Lady went beyond the privacy of our home or the shrine in our church. Her motherly presence embraced people everywhere in the world. In due time I heard about the apparitions of Mary in Portugal and Mexico, in Poland, Japan, Ireland, and Holland. She became for me the Lady of all these appearances, no matter where or when they happened. In Dutch, I called her "Onze Lieve Vrouw van de Verschijiningen," meaning "Our Lady of the Appearances" or, better still, "Our Lady of Epiphany."

By the age of twelve, a decisive change occurred that would seal my vocation to the priesthood. That was the year I left home to attend the junior seminary. What I remember missing the most was not only being at home with my family but being able to bicycle to Our Lady's chapel. Whenever I had the chance, I would go there to pray and to visit the Blessed Sacrament. One day in particular stands out for me because it had such an impact on my calling. The church was almost empty, except for a few muffled footsteps and the steady ticking of the clock. The atmosphere was mysteriously soundless. My mother had given me some coins to light a candle of my own. Mary seemed to tell me to light one for her in my heart where she also longed to appear. At that moment I seem to have become less bound to her outer apparitions and more aware of her presence in the inner depths of my soul. It seemed to me that her divine appearances over the ages pointed to the awesome truth that God is with us and that the incarnation of his Son is the highest manifestation of this truth. I prayed to Mary, to Joseph, to the shepherds, to the three visitors from far away lands, and to the baby himself that his presence as the Son of the Eternal Father would radiate like a shining star lighting up earth and sky and helping me to find my vocation. I asked the Spirit to descend into my waiting heart. How else could I become aware of such appearances except by opening myself to the grace of faith? Only then might I be able to see the appearances of God in whatever happened to me.

This realization of God's presence in every finite manifestation of the mystery instilled in me an appreciation of Our Lady's care for the children of God. All of us are in some way "inmates" of the Trinity. Several years later, when rumors began to spread about the intolerable hatred heaped on Jewish people and other "outsiders" by fast-rising fascist forces, I was horrified. Though racism began to rule with an iron fist in Nazi Germany, no one could conceive that it would lead to the Holocaust. Most of my teenage years were spent in study and prayer, begging Our Lady of Epiphany to save us from the threat of a war that would engulf civilization as we had known it.

I also credit my mother for enabling another seminal event that profoundly influenced my life. Perhaps it was woman's intuition that guided her to get me a subscription to a children's journal published by the Dutch province of the Holy Ghost Fathers titled *Vriendje (The Little Friend of the Missions)*. Father Jan van der Zandt, the main editor of this monthly, stated that his mission was to help us to align our youthful idealism with the life of Jesus of Nazareth. A counsel of his that stays with me to this day was *niet klagen*, meaning "Do not complain." Be like the boy Jesus, who was not a complainer. Live as he did in appreciation. Look always for what you can find in life that fills you with gratitude.

It was "Uncle John's" custom to use the centerfold of the journal to draw for us, under the banner *niet klagen*, the figure of a child any one of us could be. He placed him in his drawing at the beginning of a series of increasingly difficult life situations in which one could choose between complaining about them or appreciating them in and with Jesus. The child figure could be removed and placed in a slot under the picture of what it would look like to deal with this happening with a grateful heart. Our "uncle," as he preferred to be called, asked us to write him a letter about any progress we might have made in our life of appreciation with Jesus. He always answered our letters and, on the last page of the journal, printed a reply or two to cheer us on and, if we had a relapse, to fire us up again.

When I came to the end of my seventh year of elementary school, he sent me, to my immense surprise, a personal letter that was like a missive from heaven. He told me that he had gleaned from my letters to him over the past few years that I might be eligible to start the six-year junior seminary program in Weert at the boarding school of the Spiritans. I asked my parents what they thought of this invitation and without hesitation they confirmed it, as did several of my teachers, as a gift from God. Soon thereafter, Father van der Zant asked if he could visit me at home and my parents agreed. He was a charming, wise and prayerful soul. He sat with the three of us for some time and helped us to reach the decision that I should go to Weert. He discussed particulars like what clothing to bring and the cost of this first-class education; it represented a great sacrifice on the part of my parents despite the modest tuition remission I was eligible to receive. The curriculum would be classical, consisting less of the "sciences of measurement" like chemistry and biology and more of the "sciences of meaning" like liberal arts, language and literature, history and philosophy and, of course, theology as preparatory for the priesthood. There was little stress on competitive sports but a good exercise program with soccer every afternoon was the rule. Home visits would be few because of the long trip by train. One would be at Christmas, the other at Easter for a few weeks and a month-long summer vacation.

The bellicose atmosphere escalating in Europe enabled us to see later on that one purpose of this religious schooling had been to quell prejudice of any sort. The aim of such an education was to teach us to appreciate one another's gifts and any sign of good will in other human beings. This respectful approach did not deny the reality of the differences between us. Already at Weert we had to cope with the contrast between poorer boys from the South and those of higher status from the North from towns like Amsterdam. We had no choice but to open up to influences beyond those to which we had become accustomed while trying to preserve the truth of our own faith and formation traditions. There had to be a way to come to better understanding among religions, cultures, and nations, despite the bloody wars and bitter conflicts our parents had to endure in the First World War. We junior seminarians, young as we were, wanted to inspire one another to live in the light of the *love* and *respect* asked of us by the Lord. Such ideals might sound preposterous to those still enclosed in prisons of prejudice, but they were the directives that sustained us.

It was not easy for me to leave the security of my familial setting and go to the seminary. I had much to learn and, being a physically weak person to begin with, I did not find it easy to change so rapidly everything from eating to study habits. When I came home for my first visit, my parents said I looked like death warmed over! Idealistically I wanted to be in Weert—the food was good, the courses challenging—but the one drawback for me was the lack of privacy. We each had a "chambret" or small cubicle to which we could return at day's end. When I got there at last I heaved a sigh of relief and said, "Thank God, I'm alone." We had assigned chores and mine was to clean a high set of stairs. I had the same sensation of relief when I reached the top one: "Alone again, thank God!" Still I persevered, loving especially my study of Dutch, English, French, and German.

By the time I was ready to move on to higher studies in philosophy and theology I knew that the quest for truth would be the ground of my calling. To communicate with one another across the lines that threaten to divide us, to fulfill our longing for solidarity, we must allow the mystery to awaken within our humble hearts an *implicit* knowledge of God's saving design for all humanity. Faith in this mystery of divine guidance, already in the beginning stages of my life's journey, strengthened me to shun the "false gods" and "forces of fanaticism" that showed no respect for human dignity. My prayer was that God would give me and my fellow seminarians, young as we were, the courage to halt the depreciation, intolerance, and extremism that fueled all wars. I intuited then what I know now: that our interformational dialogues must be guided by respect for the unique-communal call given by God to each and every person we encounter; that propagandistic self-promotion is the breeding ground of untruth; and that we need to accept with heartfelt sincerity the obligation of charitable outreach to the physically and spiritually abandoned.

In the turmoil that soon overtook us, we realized that these youthful pledges of fidelity to God and country could only amount to a small step in the right direction. Everyone agreed that we had to do what we could to foster personal and cultural freedom and to counter the onslaught of Nazism about to engulf Western Europe. It was our duty to heal in some way the pain arising from religious and ideological prejudice and persecution cut off from the living treasures of truth revealed by our faith and formation traditions.

Notes

1. The book on Vermeer most loved by Father Adrian van Kaam and perused almost to the day of his death was: *Jan Vermeer van Delft: In de Spiegel Van Zijn Tijd* by Hajo Duchting (Lisse, Nederlands: Rebo Productions, 1996).

2. See C. Kevin Gillespie, SJ, "Similarities and Differences: The Psychologies and Spiritualities of Henri Nouwen and Adrian van Kaam," *Theoforum* 33 (2002), 105–121, Reprinted in *Epiphany International,* Volume 9:1 (Spring, 2003), 10–21. Gillespie concludes: "Van Kaam's systematization of spiritual formation has enabled us, like Vermeer, to see the spiritual in the ordinary. Nouwen's universalization of personal insights and struggles has helped us, as did Rembrandt, to see light in human darkness" (*Epiphany International*, 20).

2

Formative Fruits of My Early Friendships

UNDERNEATH THE MORE EVERYDAY remembrances of where we are in the plan of God is the deepest ground of our identity preformed by God from all eternity. No matter what happens we retain and return to this awareness in the depth of our being. The reality of this "I am I" experience, which I consider God's greatest gift to me, is always with me.

[Editor's Note: *I recall an episode pertaining to this very experience when Father Adrian and I visited my mother in 1998 when she was in the last stages of Alzheimer's disease. She had for the most part lost all capacity for recognition of me or anyone else and yet Father said, "I see that she is still she—I mean her Helenness, her essence despite what has happened to her existence, is still there." In the same way, Father van Kaam's Adrianness and yours and mine will never disappear.*]

From these early experiences I came to understand that our existence is secondary; our essence is primary or, to say the same, our existence follows from and is an expression of our essence.1 Our being is not of our own making; it is God who creates us according to his image. This belief in our essence as the beginning of our always changing and changeable existence was one of the undercurrents of our education in the junior seminary. By the time I completed my program there I was already an implicit opponent of the philosophy of atheistic existentialism that would eventually sweep across the continent. It reversed the "essence-existence" structure typical of great Christian thinkers like Thomas Aquinas to whose works we were introduced at Weert and later in the senior seminary were obliged to study from start to finish.

Another discovery I could not avoid as a result of this "I am I" experience was that of becoming aware of my poetic soul. Poetry was no longer something I wrote; it was part of my being. It surprised me to admit in the rough-and-ready atmosphere of the junior seminary that my deepest essence was poetic and that to express it in poetry brought me great joy. I remember a rather remarkable point of self-recognition in this regard. It happened to me in elementary school. One of our teachers took time to explain the use of "alliteration" in the writings of a Flemish-Dutch priest-poet, whose works had been underestimated and who had even been persecuted in his time for writing them. I felt the music in this sentence, translated from the Dutch: "The rustling of the slender reeds." Hearing this line was a revelation. I repeated it for days on end. It made me aware in my inmost soul, in my essence, *there was in me the possibility for poetic expression and that this gift would play a great role in my life* [See Appendix 1 and Appendix 2, for confirmation of this facet of Father Adrian van Kaam's calling].

This poetic ability was nourished in the junior seminary's language-oriented curriculum, which included extensive reading of classical literature, but poetry, to my disappointment, did not occupy a central place. The priest appointed to be our professor told me years later that he had been advised in no uncertain terms by the then provincial superior to teach literature—but "under no condition to make the students enthusiastic for this subject." He was to offer it as an obligation only. Because of my interests, I always received at the end of the year the prizes in literature, art, and history. These were not the most popular prizes, but I liked them and they made my parents happy since at home this controversy was unknown. In all honesty, this love for literature became a leading theme in my life. I accepted it as linked indelibly with the soul that was mine. No misunderstanding ever eroded this conviction. For it I thank in great measure my father Charles, an avid reader who really appreciated the liberal arts education he received in the orphanage. Though not an emotional man, he sought religious inspiration in the books, journals, and other publications he always had on hand. My mother preferred to talk, but I was a reader like my father. This love of literature may also have been related to the weak state of my health. As a young boy, for example, I would get involved in childish fights, but, if I did, I always lost. In the seminary, I met rough guys from farms, one of whom I could not stand. He beat me black and blue, and, believe me, I did not try to fight with him a second time!

Because my health worsened, I got to go to a kind of "rest home" run by the Holy Ghost Fathers. My diagnosis was "enlarged heart." I went there twice during summer vacations for four or five weeks. I gained weight, drank lots of milk, and had the luxury of ample time to read. These summer vacations also gave me a chance to be in contact with my three younger sisters. The older I got, the more grateful I felt to them, especially for the way they and my parents willingly made many sacrifices to pay for my travel costs and tuition. I knew my oldest sister Bep best of all. She was as outspoken as my father and we liked the disposition of candor we saw in each other. My sister Lia was more like my mother so it was easy for us to talk and laugh together. The youngest Leonie struck me as most feminine and beautiful. The girls told me I was a mixture of father and mother, both tough and tender.

Friends and mentors were as important to me at this time as were my family members. Before I went to the junior seminary, when I was in the seventh grade and in my eleventh year, I was blessed with an unforgettable teacher, Jan van Rooijen. Every week, before another Sunday was upon us, he made sure that we would rise, stand next to our desks, and listen attentively as he read in his beautiful diction the Gospel we would hear again at Mass. He then asked us to share what it meant for our lives; he encouraged us to think about it, especially from the perspective of how we might apply its meaning to our daily lives.

One day he asked a few of us, after singing class, if we might like to join the new choir being assembled in our parish church. Its director and organizer was the gifted musician and organist, Anton Toneman.[2] Though my singing was nothing to brag about, I agreed to join the group. Toneman was an outstanding liturgist and a former novice of the Benedictine Monastery in Oosterhout in the South of Holland. Mister Rooijen, who assured him that I was of good will, if not of outstanding voice, said to the choirmaster, "You will not be sorry if you take him." Much later I learned that because Toneman had such an artistic temperament the Benedictines thought it would be difficult, if not impossible, for him to fit into the enclosed life of a strict community of contemplatives. His directors were sure that Anton was called to live a spiritual life in the world. The conclusion was that he would do much better serving the church not as a monk but by sharing his ministry as a full-time musician. Time revealed that this was the right decision. Life took its destined turn for him when he began the music ministry in my parish. He agreed to start the choir on the condition that it would maintain the highest professional and liturgical standards. For instance, he insisted that we dress uniformly in surplices and cassocks, sing the age-old psalms and chants of the Church either in the choir stall or on the altar, and most of all, absorb the music not only with our voices but also with our hearts. At that time, being on the altar was considered a liturgical innovation of sorts and that made it all the more awesome for us.

The Church's liturgical life and its classical expression in the Benedictine tradition were so nourishing for Toneman that he felt no ambition to pursue a secular musical career. He relished the task of initiating us into the formative or experiential meaning of the texts we would be singing during Holy Mass and on other solemn occasions, such as benediction and adoration of the Blessed Sacrament.

What I remember most about being in that group was that Toneman gave us our first introduction to spiritual reading. He would stop in the midst of rehearsals and invite us to consider both ecclesiastically and experientially the words we were singing. "What did you just intone?" he would ask, and "How does it make you feel?" He would encourage us to dwell on the text: "Don't simply sing it, live it. Dive as deeply as you can into its meaning." His suggestions were aimed at helping us to immerse our whole selves in these classical compositions.

The practice was as informative as it was formative. From the first moment we entered the choir, we were immersed in the art and discipline of meditative reflection. During our rehearsals, Toneman took the time to connect the ecclesial frame of reference of each text we sang to our everyday life. From the choir loft he would direct our eyes to the tabernacle in reverence for the real presence of Jesus Christ for whom we were singing "like angels." How near this directive made me feel to my Lord!

After his marriage to a lovely French woman of the Byzantine Catholic rite, Toneman set up a prayer chapel in his home. This rich tradition was so inspiring to him that he tried until his death to obtain permission from Rome to be ordained as a married priest in the Eastern rite. In the meantime, he created in our church an excellent choir guided by gifted and well-trained cantors and sub-cantors.

Besides youngsters like myself, there were also older members of the group who became good friends of mine for life. One of them was Adriaan Langelaan, a director of the Amsterdam Bank in The Hague.3 Interested as he knew I was in the spiritual dimensions of life, he became another beloved mentor of mine whose commitment to Christ I admired more with each passing year. Another friend and choir member was Gerard Bol, who had been a novice in the Society of Jesus.4 Upon re-entering lay life, he became a doctoral student in Dutch literature, with a special interest in the classics. His professor, Pieter Nicolaas van Eyck, was a poet, critic, and essayist of national fame, a beloved expert in spiritual and mystical literature and a man of unusual depth and re-

Missiehuis Paters v. d. H. Geest, Weert

ligious inspiration. His writings and courses were highly regarded. We had access to them through Gerard, who was our contact person with van Eyck and his other more spiritually-minded students.

I was fortunate enough to be able to meet with Gerard a few years later during my vacations from the junior seminary. Toneman had allowed me to remain an honorary member of the choir. This privilege included access to the loft with its special seating from whence to view the liturgical events held in our parish. Many a time Gerard and I sat next to one another, conversing about our common interests in literature and the liturgical life. In many ways he made up for what I missed in the seminary. Despite the difference in our ages, he shared with me his lecture notes from the classes he attended at the University of Nijmegen.

Our friendship grew through participation in the choir itself, through our love for poetry and art, and through our commitment to the pursuit of Christian excellence in the working places of family, church, and society. Though Gerard, like Anton, accepted that his calling was to lay life and ministry in the world, both friends encouraged my vocation to the priesthood. They confirmed my hope that I would have much to contribute to our growing understanding of human and Christian formation, reformation, and transformation.

These friendships became my mainstay at home and in the seminary. There I met the soul-mate who was to become during his short life span (1919–1941) my dearest companion on the way to becoming more like Jesus, Marinus Scholtes. Both of us were born and raised in The Hague though we only met in the junior seminary. He was two years ahead of me and an amazing mentor and friend from the time of my initial formation in the religious life, until his early death at the age of 22.[5] Rinus not only nurtured my vocation; he also released in me the freedom to speak about the spiritual life, its traditions, devotions, and foundations. From about the age of fourteen he kept a diary of his experiences of intimacy with Jesus and Mary in the context of his everyday life as an avid learner, a loving member of a large family, a player on the sports fields, and a loyal Spiritan confrère. Along with the lay people who mentored and befriended us, we formed for the sake of prayer and reflection, notably during our long summer holidays, what now strikes me as the prototype of our present-day Epiphany Association. We all seemed interested in fostering a formative approach to theology that would complement the catechetical information about the faith we knew so well from study and practice.

Returning to the seminary, we both felt blessed that our spiritual director and confessor approved of our friendship, confirming that it was not a so-called "particular friendship" that excluded others but that it was a "soul-friendship" that helped us on our journey to God and in our ministry to others. Rinus and I were by nature somewhat shy and prone to solitude, but we had no trouble relating to the choir members and others who shared our intellectual and spiritual concerns. Our real interest was not sentimental religiosity but the state of our soul. What I liked most about Rinus was the clear, candid, childlike openness of his character. What attracted him to me was my ease of making friends, my commitment to the spiritual life, my love for solitude, and my inclination to maintain joy in almost every circumstance. Since Rinus was older than me by two years, I always looked to him for advice and encouragement. When he died I lost my best friend and sojourner in the faith. The formative fruits of our togetherness in Christ will never be forgotten. Let me try to explain why.

Coming from The Hague and being in the seminary together added to the affinity Rinus and I felt. Our long walks and conversations during the holidays deepened the trust between us. I was privileged to share the spellbinding story of his graced journey from the beginning of the junior seminary to the end of his short life in the major seminary in Gemert. I was at his side for that final farewell. His death led to the promise that he would be with me in spirit, protecting my endeavors on earth and awaiting my coming to our eternal home. In the course of our friendship, both of us felt as if Holy Providence has been preparing us for some sort of mission and ministry in the realm of spiritual formation. We longed to foster a prayerful awareness of the shining forth in all people of the Divine Formator of humanity, the Holy Spirit, who enables us to live our Christian presence in the world as an epiphany of the mystery.

In the last weeks before his death, Rinus kept repeating joyously that the Holy Spirit had disclosed to him the mysterious mission of his own brief passage on earth. He felt that he would be empowered to spend his heaven in contact with all people anywhere who were in need of God's saving grace and who sought God's mercy, as Rinus did, in the unspectacular ups and downs of the day. The marks of his character that never failed to impress me were his combined courage and candor. His meditation notebooks contain boyish, colloquial expressions that hide a heart gifted with the grace of mystical ascent to God. His awareness of his bride-soul allows the feminine component of his male mysticism to draw him into the bridal intimacy of a relationship with God that moves from spiritual courtship to espousal to mystical marriage.

Another unique feature of his life was his unexpected, almost instantaneous inspiration to pray for the dying. During the novitiate I know for a fact that he began a fervent life of prayer and sacrifice to beg for God's merciful invitation to repentance and salvation for sinners dying anywhere in the world. Rinus witnessed to the universal outreach of this inspiration by literally naming different towns and nations where he believed dying people were most in need of prayer. Hardened of heart or despairing as they might be, all those who found themselves suddenly at the gate of eternity would find Rinus there, too, praying for them and interceding on their behalf.

At approximately the same time when Saint Faustina Kowalska (1905–1938) had been made aware by Christ that her mission in time and eternity would be to spread devotion to the mercy of God, Rinus Scholtes gained the insight that his mission would be to alert others to the epiphany of God's presence in and among them. He was convinced that each of us was to become a "little light" or "living manifestation" of the Most High.

Rinus' fascinating story of a soul traces the movement from outer to inner freedom. He taught me to look past the glaring imperfections that scar our personal and communal lives and to focus instead on the miracle that we are unconditionally loved and forgiven by God. Rinus' simple yet profound quest for union with the Father's will challenged all of us in the Epiphany group we referred to as the Pioneers of Mary to flow with the graces beckoning us to the highest reaches of spiritual maturity. His witness increased in significance after his death. He was interested not only in spirituality in general but also in the possibility of ordinary people being the recipients of extraordinary mystical gifts.

A difficulty Rinus incurred turned out to be a blessing in disguise: he could not meditate discursively. Grace tugged at his heart and drew him to a way of prayer that transcends our imaginative or analytical mind-set and grants us the gift of quiet presence or tranquil union. By the time I entered the novitiate, he had already completed his journey into the mystery of transforming love. Thanks to him, I was as well prepared for the religious life as any young man could be.

Our summers at home in The Hague were among the happiest of my life. We were off for over a month. I spent most of my free time, when I was not with my family, with Rinus and our other friends from the choir. We tried to develop a way of thinking "with our heart" about spiritual transformation. Since I was drawn to the study of literature, I asked Gerard Bol to let me read the papers he wrote for his university courses as well as the books on his reading lists. This habit of reflective presence to the word turned out to be an excellent preparation for my life in the priesthood and the research, study, writing, and teaching that would accompany it.

Notes

1. Father Adrian van Kaam loved the poetry of the Persian master Rumi (d. 1273), who wrote: "Do not fear death, spill your jug into the river. Your attributes will disappear, but the essence moves on." Cited in *A Year with Rumi: Daily Readings*. Compiled by Coleman Barks, et. al. (San Francisco: Harper, 2006), 283.

2. Anton (Antonius Gerardus Maria) Toneman, born in The Hague, was the father of one son and one daughter. He died in the town of his birth on October 10, 1985.

3. Adrianus Jacobus Langelaan (1912–1975), whose place of birth and death was The Hague, had a great devotion to Our Lady. The day he died, August 15, was the feast of the Assumption.

4. Gerard (Gerardus Theodorus Marie) Bol was born in The Hague. Father Adrian van Kaam officiated at his marriage and baptized at least one of his children. He and his wife were faithful Catholics and the parents of two sons and a daughter. Though they separated in 1972, theirs was a cordial parting. Gerard died in Leiden on September 23, 1981.

5. See Marinus Scholtes (1919–1941), *Become Jesus: The Diary of a Soul Touched by God*. Trans. Joop Bekkers, PhD. Edited with an Introduction and Afterword by Adrian van Kaam and Susan Muto. (Pittsburgh, PA: Epiphany Books, 1998.)

3

From Education to Formation

THE SIX-YEAR JUNIOR SEMINARY program I attended in Weert served also as a kind of postulancy for the Spiritans. It was there that Rinus and I did our best to set aside time to talk about and interiorize what we learned in our classes and in our experiences with our lay friends in The Hague. Our discussions centered on a variety of topics, particularly about how to put into practice the teachings of the classical texts we were reading. One of them was by the Cistercian priest, Dom Jean-Baptiste de Chautard. *The Soul of the Apostolate* showed to us that the interior life is the only sure foundation for apostolic service.1 Another book that inspired us was *Yes Father* by Father Richard Graef, CSSp. This German Spiritan outlined in a simple yet profound way how to form our lives around the Gospel principle of the Eternal Son's surrender to the Father's will. This reading etched on our heart the truth that obedience in humility and love is the founding stone of the spiritual life.

Rinus and I added to these selections the writings of Saint Louis-Marie de Montfort on the consecration of our lives as "slaves of Mary."2 We both embraced the devotion of total dedication to our Lady, but in no way did we impose this preference on other members of our class or on the Pioneers of Mary. Every time we came together for an animation session, we encouraged one another to grow in receptive awareness of the Christ-form of our soul. Only then could we respond to his changeless call to become "other Christ's" in our everyday encounters with others in a rapidly changing world. Were the new findings in the human and social sciences to which we were exposed compatible with our belief systems? What falsehoods might erode our faith, dampen our hope, weaken our love? Were our lives in tune with the classical directives and doctrines of the Church or were they contaminated by secularistic propaganda and selfish distortions? Had these alien forces managed to slip past our examination of conscience and become lodged in our heart? How much were we already infected by popular spiritual movements, talks, and publications critical of our Judeo-Christian tradition? Were the ideas and emotions pulsating in our culture consonant or dissonant with the faith formation found in the texts we read and reflected upon?

Especially attractive to Rinus during and after his novitiate was the book *One with Jesus* by Father Paul DeJaegher, SJ In this classic and in the writings of Saint Thérèse of Lisieux to which he introduced me, Rinus discovered the depths of what it meant to become *Alter Christus*. Consoling to him was the fact that Saint Thérèse's "Little Way of Spiritual Childhood" paralleled his own practice of following the hidden life of Jesus of Nazareth.3 These spiritual books, along with the writings of the Venerable Francis Libermann of Saverne, animator and founder of the Spiritans and the servant of abandoned souls, solidified the ground of faith on which we wanted to walk for a lifetime.4

Intimate to our Epiphany circle and life-long friends of ours were Adriaan Langelaan and his wife Marie. Both of them sought a spirituality suitable to their vocation as laity in the world. That this mature married couple trusted us young religious enough to share such longings was quite edifying. Rinus and I assured them that our vocation to the religious life and the priesthood was a grace of God. Since we were all on the same journey to intimacy with the Trinity we had no right to impose our charism on them. The faith and formation traditions to which each of us adhered had to be lived in dialogue with our own God-given calling as unique and communal.

Gerard Bol witnessed to the fact that the general call to ecclesial holiness was not confined to a particular type of spirituality lived exclusively within a religious community. He thanked God that he still profited from the spiritual writings to which he had been introduced during his time in the Jesuits, but he appreciated the distinction we made between a special spirituality associated with a religious order and the foundational spirituality to be lived by all people of faith, especially the laity.

Needless to say, as budding Spiritans, Rinus and I followed to the best of our ability the rules and constitutions of our community. At the same time, we encouraged our lay friends to continue to form their lives of faith in the light of the basic spirituality of the Church articulated in liturgy, word, and sacrament.

Believers like ourselves had to find new ways and means of being formed in Christ and of living the resources of our faith. Only then would it be possible not to become side-tracked by a bewildering variety of forces alien to our distinct calling in Christ. We sought an integral theology of everyday formation that would enable us to address the problems being thrust upon us day after day in the light of the foundational truths of our faith. At that time in Holland there was an inclination to promote the notion that for anything having to do with a deeper walk with the Lord one ought to consult with a member of a religious community.

What sparked the most interesting discussions we had was the question of how we could implement these catechetical teachings amidst the churning waters of a culture in chaos. How could all of the information we had about our faith become the guiding light giving form to our lives? As the dark clouds of war gathered around us, we knew we dared not risk living in a vacuum created by a lack of detailed faith formation. The militaristic fascism that encroached upon our own country placed the self—not God or the Divine Forming Mystery—at the center of life. Selfism, not self-sacrifice or other-centered love, aimed to push aside the kenotic love of Christ. None of us could have imagined in these pre-war years the downward spin into the hell of hatred we would soon have to endure, but for the love of God we wanted to ready ourselves to face the worst.

Most helpful to us at this time was a series of articles published in a highly respected periodical, *The Movement,* founded and edited by Professor Albert Verwey, the man whom Bol's mentor, Pieter Nicolaas van Eyck, was to succeed as chairperson of Leiden's department of language and literature. *The Movement* dominated Dutch literature in the first quarter of the twentieth century. The principles guiding this publication were honored by van Eyck and Bol, both of whom reacted against the dominant literary movement at the turn of the century, which sought, in the spirit of "impressionism," to elevate one's immediate individualistic grasp of reality with little or no respect for tradition. *The Movement*, to the contrary, opposed the excessive bent towards individualism inspired by these subjectivistic ideals. Its guiding principle—that every person is unique and worthy of respect—gave birth to a generation of poets and thinkers who had in common a feeling of discontent with the principles upheld by an increasingly materialistic, mercantile, and mercenary society. Van Eyck, Bol, and other Dutch authors of that period tried to find a solution to the restlessness of soul one feels once transcendent modes of thought and action begin to be eroded. Van Eyck initially sought spiritual meaning in a stoic life style and the discipline of duty. In the end he found his joy in the wisdom of the Judeo-Christian mystics and spiritual masters.

Rinus and I and other like-minded students with whom we associated felt as alarmed as our mentors did by the destructive despiritualization that seemed to be invading our own and other European nations. We, too, wanted to join the struggle for the survival of the human spirit in defiance of the steady growth of rampant individualism with its undercurrent of disrespect for human dignity. The sustenance we received from *The Movement* prepared us to confront and contest the erosion of our faith tradition, soon to be escalated by the power of the Nazi propaganda machine.

Van Eyck's conversion to the study of the classical Christian masters was a turn welcomed by all of us since it pointed to the importance of formative reading. We benefitted from Gerald Bol's conviction that literature should be more than a matter of dissecting words on a printed page and reducing them to one's impressions of them. He appreciated the "divine potency" of poetry, which was for him a point of access to all that was worthwhile in life. As time went on, this dedication to literature and its transcendent orientation became the main focus of the legacy he passed on to me. Our love for the word became a mutual sharing in adoration of the Eternal Word, who became one of us in the wonder of the Incarnation.

Through the influence of van Eyck and Bol, this circle of friends and choir members concentrated on writers of serious spiritual depth and inspired vision. We shared a passion for meditative reading and reflection that became second nature to us. In his own epic poem, *Medusa, A Myth*, published in 1947, van Eyck strove to integrate his life's journey with his love for poetry. This lyrical work, consisting of approximately 5,000 verses, communicates the story of his own spiritual quest. In his creative mind, it becomes a rendition of the life of every artist and, indeed, of every spiritual being. Medusa, the mortal daughter of the gods, knows herself to be one of the "elect" because of her divine genealogy. However, she is contaminated by a "mortal downfall" into lust. It is this sin, coupled with her own pride, that warrants her need for punishment and purification.

Van Eyck saw his own longing for purity of heart further exemplified in the writings of the fourteenth century Dutch-Flemish mystic, poet and prose writer, Hadewijch.5 Given her knowledge of Latin and French, she was most likely a member of a noble family, but more impressive than her sheer language ability was her literary output consisting of forty-five spiritual love-songs, sixteen prose poems, some strictly prose works, accounts of her fourteen visions, and a number of letters.

Her spiritual doctrine reveals a link to the writings of Blessed Jan van Ruysbroeck and perhaps as well to those of Meister Eckhart and Teresa of Avila.6 Thanks to the teachings of van Eyck and Bol, the heritage left by all of these writers came to our attention in our proto-type Epiphany circle. Another book we read line by line was the Dutch spiritual classic, *The Imitation of Christ*, by Thomas á Kempis.7 This book grounded our circle of pioneers in yet another treasure of our faith and formation tradition: the call to true discipleship. So did the works of the movement known as the "modern devotion" (*devotio moderna*) begun in Holland by the *Brothers of the Common Life* to which á Kempis belonged. This legacy imbued in me a great love for literature and the Christian classics. Thanks to it, I felt free to pray that I might become no more and no less than a "little word" in the Eternal Word.

Notes

1. Dom Jean-Baptiste Chautard, *The Soul of the Apostolate* (Trappist, KY: Abbey of Gethsemani, Inc., 1946).

2. de Montfort, St. Louis-Marie Grignion, *True Devotion to Mary*. Trans. Mark L. Jacobson (Aventine Press, 2007).

3. See Thérèse of Lisieux, *Story of a Soul*. Trans. John Clarke (Washington, DC: ICS Publications, 1975).

4. See Adrian van Kaam, *A Light to the Gentiles: The Life Story of the Venerable Francis Liebermann* (Eugene, OR: Wipf and Stock, 2009).

5. Hadewijch, *The Complete Works* in *The Classics of Western Spirituality*. Trans. Mother Columba Hart, O.S.B. (New York: Paulist Press, 1980).

6. A book read and annotated by Father Adrian van Kaam was *Jan van Ruusbroec: Mystical Theologian of the Trinity* by Rik Van Nieuwehhove (Notre Dame: IN: University of Notre Dame Press, 2003). See also *Meister Eckhart: The Essential Sermons, Commentaries, Treatises and Defense*. Trans. Edmond College in the *Classics of Western Spirituality* (New York: Paulist Press, 1981) and Teresa of Avila, *The Collected Works*. Volume 1. Trans. Kieran Kavanaugh and Otilio Rodriguez (Washington, DC: ICS Publications, 1980).

7. *The Imitation of Christ*. Edited by Harold C. Gardiner (Garden City, NY: Image Books, 1955).

4

From Enclosure to Exposure

ONE DRAWBACK THAT BECAME most noticeable to me during the last year of my junior seminary (1938) was that while the world was rapidly coming under fire we had no access to radios or newspapers. It was thought that such distractions were of no use to foreign mission-oriented seminarians whose education was patterned after the style of the classical humanist approach then prevalent in the Dutch gymnasium system. Ours was a kind of culture within the culture, a little state within the state, where we shared only a general desire to avoid war and keep the peace. Many of us, due probably in part to this kind of enclosure, were of a mind that Adolf Hitler only wanted to restore Germany to its former economic prosperity. None of us foresaw the depth of his corruption and lust for total power, to say nothing of his despicable treatment of the Jewish people and his cruel ideology of death. All of us harbored a naive hope for peace; we were loathe to prepare for yet another war. That illusion was dispelled a year later when we novices witnessed firsthand the surge of invaders crossing our borders from the republic of Germany. Instantly, we were thrust face to face with the harshness of reality. Hell broke loose and swept aside like a tidal wave our isolationist tendency.

Those of us like myself who remained in the juniorate for the entire six-year program were eligible, upon discernment of their call, to move ahead to the novitiate. It was designed to be a year of non-academic spiritual and experiential initiation and preparation for the vowed life. At the end of this probationary period, it would be decided if one were eligible to advance to the senior seminary and to bind oneself to the community by making temporary vows, lasting for three years.

My own novitiate experience made a deep impression on me due in great measure to the teaching and witness of our novice master, Father

Henri Strick, CSSp. A man beloved by everyone, he radiated the grace of appreciative abandonment to the mystery. He had the kind of even-mooded temperament that made it possible for him to speak of Christ and the beauty of a bunch of bananas in one breath! Each day in the novitiate was well organized. We rose, cleaned up our room, washed and dressed, went to the chapel for common prayer, meditation, and Mass. Then we had a conference followed by time to record our thoughts about it in our recollection notebooks. When supper time rolled around, we had the cooks to thank for providing nourishing meals despite a growing shortage of food. Our meals were eaten in silence, providing the proper background for readings from a holy book. Whereas others said they could not wait for the novitiate to be over so they could go to the senior seminary at Gemert, I hardly wanted it to end. I loved the silence and the solitude, the calming routines, the morning and evening conferences given by our novice master. I even enjoyed the chores we had to do like repairing the bicycles and tending the garden. Occasionally some novices had to be counseled out of the community, which made the rest of us all the more determined to stay. The singing of the Divine Office reminded me of my days in the choir. We went to bed at a decent hour and the next morning the routine of religious life began anew.

By the end of my novitiate, the war had begun in earnest. Despite this crisis our final hours in Gennep were celebrated with quiet joy. Normally, all family members came to witness the ceremony of the vows and the donning of the cassock, but travel restrictions made a full festivity impossible. The Dutch had all but stopped train traffic due to bombing raids. It was simply too dangerous to risk such transport. Rail workers stood ready to strike in protest and their angry demonstrations frightened ordinary citizens. Our novitiate was located next to the line that connected Holland to Germany. We could see beyond the wall of our garden the invad-

ers crossing over the border despite the dynamite charges planted by the underground under the bridges. Gennep was the first crossing for panzer trucks and tanks. At one point the German troops took over our house and used the church pews wrenched from the chapel for latrines, leaving us to clean up the garden. They raided our wine cellar and took what food we had though we emptied as many bottles and bins as we could.

Fearing reprisal, my novice master gave me his handgun and asked me to bury it in the garden. I hid it so well it was never found again! Somehow we novices took this first wave of occupation in stride, incapable of foreseeing the horror about to descend upon our country when the Nazi occupation was complete. The tears in Father Strick's eyes as he empathized with our plight summarized the poignancy of the novitiate for me. We all went with him to the chapel. Bereft of the presence of family members, we took our vows one by one. After that we had a festive dinner with the rest of the wine meant for Pentecost Sunday and shortly thereafter took our leave.

I and another novice, Adrian Olsthoorn, returned to The Hague by train despite the danger of rail travel. I remember walking with my luggage to the house and being greeted by my parents with tears of joy commingled with expressions of regret because they were unable to come to Gennep. The trip home had been highly emotional for me since we had had no radios or newspapers to read in keeping with the custom to concentrate on the inner life. Now I was among the masses. When the train entered the station of The Hague, I saw a tall SS man reading a newspaper. If eyes could kill they would have killed me dressed as I was in my religious habit. I and my friend Olsthoorn saw Nazis on the street for the first time. It was a chilling experience. The occupation of our country became real for us at that moment.

Following a reunion with my parents and sisters, with neighbors and family members, all of whom congratulated me on completing the novitiate and being accepted into the senior seminary, I went to see my friends from the choir, Bol and Langelaan. We had anticipated a prolonged vacation with a return to our informal literature classes, but that hope was cut short when I got word that I had to leave for Gemert almost immediately. We learned that the Germans had set fire to our "castle," a beautiful old fortress built in the twelfth century and our help was needed there. This news came as a shock to us. The German troops were expected to be far away, not on our doorstep.

A short distance from our castle was the city hall where a Dutch Nazi had declared himself mayor. The superior of our seminary could not hide his fear of what might happen to us. Shortly before I arrived in Gemert, a small troop of Dutch soldiers had quartered themselves overnight in the port house of the castle. By coincidence in that very unit there was a family member of mine, a cousin on my father's side. When the priests and students who were housed in the rear part of the building got up that morning, they saw to their amazement a German soldier scouting the premises. They concluded that he was probably a spy who had come to take stock of these fortress-like quarters. Everyone thought, "There's only one of him. It's probably an accident. He's lost." A Dutch soldier fired a warning shot in the air and the German ducked. Then he saw to his horror that a whole troop of heavily armed German soldiers were behind him!

Immediately everyone on the premises dived down the steps into the basement of the castle. In this large space, surrounded by ancient medieval walls, the huddled group felt much safer. According to what our faculty had heard "on the grapevine," the Dutch troops were not supposed to be near here. Only now our castle visitors had drawn us into this confrontation. The thought was that maybe a whole Dutch army unit would appear to back up the lone soldier who had fired at the Germans, but, to everyone's surprise, the enemy troops were detained for nearly two hours by that troop of perhaps twenty soldiers. They stood their ground in defense of our seminary with what little ammunition they had.

The German troops then made the decision to round up the villagers from Gemert and line them up in front of their soldiers so that these innocents could take our soldiers' bullets! One handicapped man, fondly dubbed the "pope" of Gemert, was shot instantly. The Germans were bent on storming the castle, but before they broke into the chapel, the seminarians consumed the consecrated hosts and received a final blessing in case anyone was shot. They did all that they could to protect this small fighting force, but it was to no avail. The defenders now had no choice but to flee into the fields behind the castle in the hope that they would not be caught. In a flash more enemy troops stormed the castle and set fire to it; they were fully convinced that it housed a Dutch army unit equipped with machine guns and grenades and aided and abetted by us. The soldiers headed for the cellars where the seminarians had hidden. My friend Rinus who was there at the time remembered every detail of what happened, and he was the one who told the story to me. Though older fellows like himself (he was already in first year theology) were separated from the younger men like me, we still managed to exchange the news.

The commanders shouted, "Out! Out! Out! Hands up!" Everyone fled from the basement on to the lawn in front of the castle, trembling before the guns pointing at them and sure they would be shot. The prayers of the community prevailed. Thanks be to God, the officer in charge proved to be a calm person, an Austrian by birth. He asked our provincial superior, who spoke German well, "Tell me, what is the story here?" It took some time to explain, but at last he said, "Sie sind entlassen," "You are free!" One fellow, Groensmit by name, was so nervous he cried out, "Heil Hitler!" We teased him for years about that but at the moment all the Spiritans turned and ran toward the castle because by now it was in flames. As Rinus recalled, they had to draw water from the castle moat by hand since there were no pumps. The fire destroyed some of our living and study quarters, but it did not penetrate the chapel, which to us was a minor miracle.

Trying my best to retain some normalcy, I moved into first year philosophy with a view toward spending the next several years as a senior seminarian. Though I'm moving ahead of my story for a moment, I do not want to forget that it was the custom in the Spiritan congregation to ordain men before they finished their studies. This meant that one year prior to our graduation from the senior seminary we could be ordained. For me that would have been 1945. That first year after ordination was one in which we had to do some ministry in the diocese within neighboring parishes or in the surrounding countryside. There we got the experience we needed before we were given an official first appointment. My goal for the future was like all others to go to the foreign missions, but not only was this plan of mine interrupted by the Hunger Winter; it was also revealed not to be God's will for me. I would not be appointed to Africa or South America but to the position of teaching philosophy in the same seminary in which I myself had finished my studies as first in my class.

I watched with a commingling of pride and regret as almost all members of my class went to places like Angola and the Amazon to endure much suffering and at times veritable martyrdom for the sake of their evangelizing work. I remember in particular Father William Burmanje, a bright young priest, a year ahead of me with whom I shared as a student many reflections and experiences. He went to the Amazon wilderness where I had asked in vain to be sent. On a river tour of his widespread stations, his boat got stuck in the debris strewn in the river. Being near to the shore, he went into the water to try to get the boat afloat. He lost his balance and fell. Schools of voracious piranhas tore at his body. A small piece of the top of his thumb was the only remnant found at the bloody riverside.

My life cannot emulate his or that of the other missioners I knew and loved. The images of confrères who led far more fruitful lives followed by a sometimes early death often haunts me in the light of my own progress as a priest-professor. I am consoled by the conviction that my life's work of research, study, and teaching has always been done for the sake of others, who have assured me of its efficacy in relation to their own formation story.

[Editor's Note: *Condolences sent from around the world on the occasion of Father van Kaam's death offer heartfelt testimony to the truth of this other-oriented commitment of his.*]

Significant in my own intellectual development was my final year in philosophy. I recall that all the lessons were in Latin, which we had to read and articulate with precision. Creative ideas were not encouraged since we were obliged to master the standard texts and no other philosophy books were allowed. A rather tense atmosphere of strict orthodoxy prevailed. We had to study the works of Aquinas and basically memorize their contents to pass our tests. I got good marks but in addition to the time it took to master the required readings I found other books I liked in the library and read them too. We had to take two full years of philosophy. If at the end of that time we succeeded with our oral and written exams, we would be promoted to theology.

In addition to formal study we followed a spiritual routine of prayer, Mass, silence, refectory reading (which I dreaded because I had such a weak voice it evoked loud laughter), meditation, work, and recreation.

I could not help but notice amidst a variety of classes that literature was near the bottom of the list of important subjects. For example, we were forbidden to go to plays. The prevailing mentality seemed to be that priests destined for the foreign missions did not need to waste their time on poetry or fiction. Thanks to the contacts I had during my vacations with friends like Gerard Bol, I managed to keep more balance in my education, including the excellent formation that accompanied it. I also had an extremely lively mind that went beyond the customary ways of thinking. For instance, I began to read some basic books on psychology and educational theory.

At the end of every year, philosophy prizes were given out but mine were mostly in literature and history. I'm happy to say I passed on to theology in 1942 with the intention of finishing in 1946 and being ordained. That did not happen as the continuation of my story will show, due to the year that changed my life, but all I wanted to do for the moment was to concentrate on the study of theology at Gemert.

Despite the mess caused by reconstruction, our life proceeded as normally as possible. For example, my chore was to work in the garden—a task that satisfied my ever-present need for solitude. Though I was not too handy as a gardener, it seemed as if I had a knack to dig out the weeds. I would retire as far as possible into the fields to be alone in

Missiehuis Paters v.d. H. Geest, Gemert   K.L.M. Foto Copyright 22375

thought and prayer. I suppose I needed time to accept the truth that I had been given by God a contemplative spirit that had to be lived in the midst of a highly active community.

One positive result of my poor health occurred when the German troops announced their intention to occupy our quarters. Burdened by yet another bout of severe psoriasis, I was put on display as a health hazard with a disease so contagious the doctors ordered me to be quarantined. The troops took one look at me and backed away. So afraid was the commander that his troops would catch "it" that he informed our superior he would have to find another place.

All the while the war continued to escalate. The media reported, at times clandestinely, the news of deportations and transports to concentration camps. The Nazi who had gotten himself appointed mayor of Gemert tried to cover up the reports appearing in underground publications that were almost too horrific to be believed. The nature of life in the seminary kept us rather isolated from this turmoil and terror. Our task was to concentrate on the study of theology. Our curriculum was rigorously orthodox and carefully planned. We mastered courses in Christology and ecclesiology, in doctrine and dogmatics, in moral and canon law. These requirements gave us a width and breadth of knowledge in informational theology. The truths of faith were the solid rocks on which we had to stand in the swirling sea of sheer evil perpetrated by the war. I was deeply grateful for the complementary formational approach I received in our Epiphany circle and soon enough I would understand why. Some people my age may have found it a waste of time to plunge into these complementary readings, but I saw them as a lifeline. It was this preparation that kept me sane during the horror that was about to descend on my homeland. In the meantime I looked forward to spending some summer vacation time with my friends in The Hague while engaging in the task of collecting money to rebuild Gemert.

5

From Freedom to Captivity

LIFE IS NOT A chain of isolated islands, but a vast continent of interconnected lands leading one to the other, some surrounded by walls of solid rock, others battered by stormy seas. Each opportunity life presents coalesces into an episode in the story of our destiny. It is our choice to view it as a gift of divine generosity or as a curse tempting us to abandon hope for a better tomorrow. In such a landscape, where we remember in faith, imagine in hope, and anticipate in love, glad and sad events pass before our eyes. Considering the peaks and valleys I have personally traversed, I realize the immensity of God's generosity and the providential trials that enabled me to turn zig-zag patterns of dissonance into calls to deeper consonance.

This tension between burden and blessing tightened like a noose around our neck as war descended on the world. Suddenly we could go nowhere without our identification papers. They had to be on our person at all times. The ration cards we were issued never provided enough nourishment. All of us were obliged to scour the farms for food. To find meaning amidst these inhumane conditions, I began to read, under the tutelage of Gerard Bol, a twelfth-century poem on the life of a heroine by the name of Beatrijs whose triumph over tragedy and near despair deepened my receptivity to the consolations hidden in every event of life, however devastating it may be. Since gatherings of no kind were allowed by the occupying forces and since seeking special permission for a group like ours exposed us to suspicion and harassment, Bol suggested that we come together in a bookstore for a "lecture." A daring Christian patriot, whose shop was located opposite Saint Jacob's Church in the historical downtown section of The Hague, opened his doors to us. There our group could mix unobtrusively with the bustling crowds. One by one we would disappear down a stairway in the bookstore. Once there we knew how to get to the entrance of a larger basement space where we could meet without fear of detection. Ours turned out to be an ecumenical faith group guilty, on the one hand, of the crime of civil disobedience to an illegitimate, oppressive regime and serving, on the other hand, a band of lost souls in need of seeing their troubles in the light of the story of Beatrijs from whence we learned a powerful lesson of hope.

Because of its legendary organization and the intertwining of Protestants and Catholics, church membership in the Netherlands on the eve of the war was at its highest statistically. One outcome of ecumenism and the transformation of our country from an absolute monarchy to a democracy with a constitutional government was the shift from uniform state schools into "schools of the parents," be they Islamic, Jewish, Catholic or Protestant. Public schools or so-called neutral schools were also in existence. Both systems received the same amount of money from the state for educational facilities, salaries, and other benefits. All the officials had to supervise were the three R's—reading, writing, and arithmetic. For the rest, students and teachers developed their own programs under reasonable supervision and accountability to the parents.

No wonder the Dutch had a feeling of security when it came to their ecclesial, national, and educational life. We could boast of growing numbers of church goers, strong political parties composed of highly organized and dedicated citizens, a tremendous school system, economic stability, and outspoken trade and workers' unions. How could such a superbly functioning country bear to face its coming downfall? The bigger we were functionally the harder we were about to fall spiritually.

Finally, the turning point from freedom to captivity occurred. Nothing could have scarred the free Dutch nature as badly as the announcement on May 15, 1940, that the Dutch High Command had officially surrendered to the occupying Nazi forces and that Queen Wilhelmina and most of her cabinet had fled to England. All the wind went out of our Dutch sails. Hundreds of German troops marched into the Netherlands, their heels clicking so loudly they seemed to drown the sound of our rapidly beating hearts. Did we have enough inner resources to survive now that our outer freedom had to be forfeited?

Our people were so involved in running their institutions that many had lost contact with the transcendent goodness, truth, and beauty that alone could sustain them. Different churches might have enjoyed a powerful surge in membership, but sheer numbers could not prevent our being hollowed out humanly and spiritually. Too much of life was in danger of collapse to dupe us into believing our careers could save us. We had to step on to the long road of spiritual renewal if we were to survive the war. Only this turn of heart would provide the courage we needed not to be swept up into the Nazi ideology. Its signs of seemingly absolute power were being rubbed in our faces in flags, billboards, and radio announcements, in noisy demonstrations and the wearing of steel grey uniforms.

What would save our sanity? Where would we find the courage to rescue others and not to think only of ourselves? Amidst the loss of autonomy and the indignity we had to endure would the change of heart asked of us by Christ prevail? As persecution, especially of the Jewish people, became not the exception but the rule, we could no longer deny the fact that our faith would again and again be put to the test. Captivity meant that we would have to shift from outer to inner freedom. We had to be ready to engage in missions none of us, clerical or lay, could have anticipated in the peaceful citadels of ecclesial and academic civility we took for granted. For the moment I had no choice but to finish my course of study in theology if I expected to be ordained in 1945. A turning point in my personal history was about to occur that would alter the course of my future once and for all. Instead of finishing my courses I would be catapulted from the ivory tower of the seminary, caught behind enemy lines, and plunged into the infamous Dutch Hunger Winter of 1944–1945.1 Thank God I had already made my perpetual vows. On September 19, 1943, on the feast of St. Januarius, in the chapel of the house at Gemert, in the presence of the community, I prayed:

> Most holy and adorable Trinity, see me here, kneeling down humbly, in front of your divine Majesty, happy to devote myself to you, totally and forever: deign to accept the sacrifice of myself, for all the time it will please you to let me live on earth.
>
> Jesus, my Lord and my God, for Your glory and out of love to you I take these holy obligations upon me. Divine Master, deign to unite my sacrifice with the sacrifice you have made on Calvary and are still making daily on the holy altar.
>
> Mary, my good and dearly beloved Mother, fill my heart with the graces and gifts of the Holy Spirit; make this divine Spirit always be my life, support and strength and help me to be faith-

ful and to observe . . . forever . . . the vows of poverty, chastity, and obedience, in the Congregation of the Holy Spirit and of the Immaculate Heart of Mary, in accordance with its rules and constitutions.

While I would like to erase the pending event of this "winter of my soul" from my memory, I cannot. There seemed to be no end to the persecution and death of our Jewish friends and neighbors, the deportation of Dutch citizens to work camps, and the random executions of anyone who dared to resist the Nazi occupiers of our country.[2] To those of us who ended up being stranded in the West of Holland, it seemed like the end of the world, yet as time went on I often repeated to myself, "You would not have traded this experience for any you have known before or since, would you?"

Notes

1. An excellent account of this wound on the heart of Holland can be found in a book read many times over by Father Adrian titled *The Hunger Winter: Occupied Holland, 1944–45* by Henri van der Zee (London: Jill Norman and Hothouse, Ltd., 1982).

2. See Titia Bozuwa, *In the Shadow of the Cathedral: Growing up in Holland During World War II* (Sanbornville, NH: Triple Tulip Press, 2004).

6

Knowledge from Experience

IN THE SUMMER OF 1944, I myself, along with many other students from towns near The Hague, went home to the West for our yearly summer recess. We could not wait to see family and friends and to continue the collection of funds for the seminary. In that final week of August, it really appeared as if the liberation of the whole of Holland was on the horizon. Hopes for victory and an end to the war ran so high the rector of the seminary did not hesitate to send us on a carefree holiday. I even remember receiving a cheery note telling us to enjoy ourselves and not to return just yet. Suddenly, without warning, all of us were trapped behind enemy lines. While the South where our seminary was, was in fact liberated, the West and North of Holland were still under enemy control since the Allied forces had lost the Battle of Arnhem. We assumed that after the invasion of Normandy in June of that year, that the war would soon be over and that in a brief time these terrors would be behind us. No thought could have been more naive. I longed to return to the safety of Gemert, south of the Rhine and Waal rivers, but instead I had to find an even safer place to live. Staying in The Hague meant that I ran the risk of being rounded up and sent to a work or concentration camp. In short order, I found myself as one among many hungry people in the densely populated western regions of Holland that were in dire straits. No one could live by what was designated for them on their ration cards.[1]

As the winter months approached, food became increasingly scarce because everything had been swept up to supply the enemy lines. The roads from the city to the outlying farms were filled with processions of emaciated men, women, and children willing to barter anything they owned for food. To prevent the people from rising up to resist them, enemy troops surrounded every town and city. A favorite tactic would be to enter a village unannounced and to go from house to house looking for food and fuel. Able-bodied men were flung on trains bound for labor camps in Germany where conditions, though not as gruesome as those in the concentration camps, were still inhumane.

Surrounded by distraught citizens separated from all they held dear, I had to steel myself for whatever God asked of me in the days or months ahead. I could not give in to sentimentality; otherwise I would lose the little energy I had. Gone were the relative protections afforded any seminary student. All of us were thrown together by circumstances beyond our control. It mattered not at all what ideological or religious traditions we represented. Together we suffered the same cruel fate.

To duck the round-ups and to gather food for my family and our neighbors, I, along with other seminarians in the same predicament, went into the countryside, searching out addresses we had been given where we might find help. My first move was to seek refuge with a farm family. This quick decision was exacerbated by the fact that my parents' home in The Hague had become a hideout for a young police officer by the name of Robert who went AWOL from his unit the moment he discovered that they had been commanded to ferret out and capture Jewish citizens marked for deportation to concentration camps. Still wearing his uniform and carrying his weapons, Robert sought refuge in our home, failing to realize that by so doing he had placed us in mortal danger. Were he to be found, it would be the end of us. By now nothing could stop him from joining the resistance, so it was imperative to find another solution for housing him. That's when I agreed to be the person to travel to Nieuwkoop, a small village northeast of The Hague, to prepare hiding places not only for our policeman friend but also for my three sisters and myself.

My parents insisted on remaining at home. They could not believe that human beings were capable of perpetrating the heinous deeds attributed to the Nazi war machine. At one point, while we were hatching our escape plan, we felt our hearts leap into our mouths when several German officers started shouting in the street. They were looking for a man who had run away from the prisoners he was supposed to be guarding. He was purported to have sought refuge in a house not far from ours. The searchers were furious. They saw an elderly gentleman, who knew nothing about what happened, and shouted to him, "Where is that fellow?" The old guy said in all honesty, "I don't know." The solders pelted him with their fists and knocked him unconscious.

I saw what happened from behind a curtain in my room. Before long these oppressors could be at my parents' door. What if they discovered the room where the AWOL police officer was hiding? All of us would be killed, so we had to do whatever was necessary to prevent the Gestapo from discovering through informants that our family home had been used to hide an anti-Nazi special unit officer turned into a cooperator with the underground!

Ironically, my oldest sister, Bep, found herself in a similar predicament. One day a troop of German soldiers, searching for food, came to the front door of the farm house where she had sought refuge. At that very moment she had been enjoying a visit from the same policeman who had to leave my parents' house. Having no time to plan his next move, he jumped over the open half of the farmer's Dutch door and dove into the polder, the wide grassland criss-crossed by ditches to drain the water from wetlands that were lower than the North Sea. He found cover in a small ditch, which was so well hidden that the soldiers, who shouted around him, were unable to find him. Instead they returned to the house and picked up my sister. They took her to headquarters, to a place called "Alphen at the Rhine."

I tore after her in great consternation. By now I had falsified my ID papers, not my name or date of birth, but the fact that I was not a seminarian but a "clergyman." The Gestapo were less likely to pick up the clergy, provided they made no trouble. I presented this documentation to the Kommandant. He saw my name and noticed immediately that it was the same name as that of the girl his men had taken into custody. Yes, she was my sister. "No," they said, "We cannot release her yet, but come back tomorrow when we have completed our investigation."

As soon as I was out the door, I ran away as fast as I could, fully certain I could never return there without arousing suspicion. I found a way to contact members of the Dutch underground in the hope that they might have secret connections in the German army posts. I told them about Bep and assured them that she was totally innocent of hiding anyone. Thanks to their network of supporters, the German police let her go a few days later. I got a call that relayed the message, "Bep is free." Never had I felt so relieved! I was afraid of what could have happened to her, knowing of many similar incidents that propelled people *from* a safe home life, *through* hideous incarceration, *to* an uncertain future only faith in God could enable them to endure.

Restriction of movement, loss of family, property, status, and employment, the constant threat of concentration camps, of famine or violent death were powerful awakening experiences. During the Hunger Winter we had to look into our soul and find ways to relight the flames of our faith in a loving mystery despite the fact that we were falling into a maelstrom of persecution. This was not the time to engage in philosophical or theological speculation. Such discussions might have pervaded the atmosphere of the seminary, but in the fields and hay lofts where I now hid I had to face questions I would continue to ask myself, such as, "Is there any meaning to this gaping wound in the history of humanity that would culminate in the horror of the holocaust?"

Years later I came across a remarkable book by Martin Goldsmith, titled *The Inextinguishable Symphony*.2 It helped me to respond to the questions that tormented me throughout that winter. Goldsmith quotes the Danish composer, Carl Nielsen. He produced his Fourth Symphony at the outbreak of World War I. What he said about this composition serves as a stark reminder that this tragic time devoted to the destruction of human dignity would have the opposite effect: "This," insisted the composer, "is music's own territory. Music is Life, and like Life, inextinguishable." From the day of its premiere in 1916, Carl Nielsen's composition has been known as the "Inextinguishable Symphony."

Let me cite what its Jewish conductor, Rudolf Schwartz, said to the musicians of the Kulturbund Orchestra whose lives for the most part would be lost in the death camps:

> This is music," he said, "that speaks directly to our situation and that of our listeners. All of us—musicians, electricians, tailors, grocers, mothers, and fathers—need to be reminded that life is paramount. Even where it is stamped out, it eventually returns. Where there is life, there is spirit. And where there is spirit, where there is even one human soul, there is music. We are proof of that. We have suffered, yet we have endured. And we have made music.

Schwartz paused, cleared his throat and went on.

> And that is why I have asked you here this afternoon, to play through this symphony with me and to keep it in your hearts until we meet again to perform it for our public in the fall. Some of you, I know, will not be with us then. But wherever you are, a part of you will always be here. And you will have this music, this inextinguishable music, to remind you of us, always.3

Like the Jewish musicians of the Kulturbund, all of us in hiding had to try to hear inwardly the barely audible "music of eternity." Though cruel foes sought every means to silence it, its remembrance still vibrates in our inner imagination.

Being with people on the verge of losing their sanity because any semblance of normalcy had been stripped from them seems to me to be analogous to what these members of the Jewish cultural association were going through. They discovered that the one way to regain their lost wholeness was to simply *be* in the situation where they found themselves and to *do* whatever they could to remain fully human. I, too, learned that the secret of not falling apart, of not losing the sense of life's meaning, was to try to be present to the often unnoticed things and events that flow, like a living symphony, one day after the other. To live these moments as manifestations of a higher meaning, as themes of a concealed symphony always playing in the universe, helps us to refind the "why" of our existence, even if we do not know from day to day the "how" of having to endure our present circumstances.

Just as music orients us to the eternal mystery of sound and silence, so did the wind in the rafters, the rain on the haystacks, the footsteps of farm hands, the voices of children. Relearning the art of being present to simple everyday appearances like a small sparrow, the shape of a buttercup, the weather-beaten faces of old workers, helped us to reclaim our capacity to celebrate life here and now—not to rush ahead to what may happen tomorrow or to retreat to times past that were no longer there.

Amidst the worst winter in memory I met generous field hands willing to share the little they had as well as farmers who hoarded food to sell it at inflated prices. I found myself having to confront the reasons behind any deflation of human dignity. On those long cold nights looking up at the stars, I envisioned, as it were, two centers, guiding our existence. One is our lower ego-self (represented by the greedy farmers); the other is our higher spirit-self (represented by those who could not do enough to help others). Our lower "I" or our "managing me" guides the details of our development for better or worse in dialogue with the circumstances in which we find ourselves. Our functional ego ought not to be seen as an end unto itself but as a servant of our transformative spirit or higher "I." Our spirit-self invites us rise above or "transcend" the best and worst examples of where our fallen condition leads us. Here we discover the deeper meanings of our acts, thoughts, and remembrances, of our motivations, imaginations, desires, and choices.

Neither of these two centers ought to dominate our inner and outer activity; they must be as finely balanced as a set of equal weights. This balance depends on the right interaction between our ego-self (our functional "I") and our spirit-self (our transcendent "I"). Each event we face in daily life offers us an opportunity to bring together in a graceful rhythm the functional and transcendent sides of our being. Rather than one dimension dominating the other, to the detriment of both, these centers perform best in unison like an always unfinished symphony.

With time, patience, and prayer we may return to the original dance of opposites God intended between our ego and our spirit-self. We may awaken from our illusions of power, pleasure, and possession and see the necessity for conversion to a more wholesome functionality in service of an equally necessary way of "transfunctionality"—beyond doing as an end in itself to being and becoming true laborers worthy of gathering the harvest God himself has planted (cf. Luke 10:2) at times in soil as arid as that of the Hunger Winter.

Notes

1. Henri van der Zee documents the horrific levels of starvation the Dutch people had to endure during the Hunger Winter. He notes, for example, that in January of 1945 the caloric intake of the population north of the rivers Rhine and Maas dropped from 1600 to 460 calories a day, "not even a fifth of normal needs" (119). From the first week of September 1944 to the first week of February 1945 in Rotterdam alone a total of 14,000 people suffered from hunger oedema, worsened by skin diseases like scabies, outbreaks of diphtheria and typhoid, plus death by starvation of the aged and infirm. Van der Zee notes that "the hunger was further responsible for the fact that women often stopped menstruating and a great number of men became temporarily impotent" (156). By April 24, 1945, the Dutch government in exile in London received the news from their councillors that the official ration has shrunk from about 400 to only 230 calories a day. The dire prediction was made that there will be no more food in Western Holland. "It is already famine . . . in ten days it will be death." That's when the Dutch received the most marvelous news in months that the "Allies were sending food from the sky" (247). The Hague drop, dubbed Operation Manna, aided people who for seemingly endless days literally had nothing to eat. Gratitude soared along with the feeling thus phrased: "we are fed but still suffer" (253). In total 18,000 Dutch men, women, and children starved to death during the Hunger Winter (304).

2. Father Adrian van Kaam meditated on this book and drew its contents into his Christian response to the Holocaust Remembrance service held at Saint Luke United Methodist Church in Lexington, Kentucky, on May 6, 2000, where he spoke with compassion of the Hunger Winter, of the people hiding with him who came to him for counsel, and of the Jewish friends he helped to hide and save. The inspiration for his life's work received from this experience enabled him to identify with Martin Goldsmith's book, *The Inexistinguishable Symphony: A True Story of Music and Love in Nazi Germany* (New York, NY: John Wiley & Sons, 2000).

3. Ibid., 281–282.

7

A Terrible Toll

HOLLAND IS A COUNTRY of approximately 13,000 square miles. During the Hunger Winter, in the provinces north of the Rhine and Waal Rivers, four and one half million Dutch people had to suffer through one of the worst freezes in their history. Dwindling stockpiles of food, frost and sub-zero temperatures, declining physical resistance and illness claimed victims each day. It was is if we poor souls were forgotten by the rest of the world.

Especially in the densely populated Western zone with its large urban centers like Amsterdam, Rotterdam, and The Hague, the toll was terrible. Citizens ate sugar beets and millions of dried tulip bulbs to still their hunger pangs, though their consumption could be poisonous. Cats, now dubbed "roof rabbits" disappeared since few, if any other, sources of protein could be found. Endless processions of men and women in distress left the familiar streets of their city to seek food in the countryside. Children rummaged through piles of garbage in the hope of finding something edible. Corpses piled up because the ground was too frozen to bury them. Thousands of people died of starvation; countless others had to be hospitalized as food stocks dwindled to almost nothing. According to many post-war observers, the Netherlands suffered perhaps the hardest fate of all the occupied nations during the Second World War.

Once I joined ranks with the suffering, streaming over the frozen, snow covered highways with their meager possessions, desperately seeking any help they could find, there was no returning either in memory or in actuality to my former secure way of life. I witnessed what it was like to be dragged away from the familiar world I knew and to "dive under." Thanks to the selfless efforts of our rescuers, I became a rescuer, too. I led many strangers and friends to a safe place, but many others did not make it. These brave souls became my teachers. They beseeched me to raise their spirits in the face of despair. As much as I valued the academic theology I had embraced as a student, by itself alone it was insufficient to respond to the spiritual needs of dispirited people from all walks of life. Physical survival was our first concern, but spirituality was the glue that kept us from falling apart. For people caught in the extraordinary distress of these traumatic times, routine religiosity fell by the wayside while the test of transcendence came to the fore. Only insight into the meaning of suffering in extreme conditions could counteract the threat of defeat and the agony of depression.

I begged God to let me find the best way to address this morass of despondency. Was it possible to awaken spiritual values that might lessen the terrible toll we were being asked by the mystery to pay? To empathize with all who suffered I knew I had to draw upon childhood experiences that had taught me to respect traditions different from my own. Among the many lessons the Hunger Winter communicated to me, one that stands out was a new understanding of the term "abandoned souls." I realized as a future Spiritan that I could never reduce the meaning of this altruistic ideal only to care for the materially poor; I had to engage as well in missionary dialogue with the spiritually impoverished on every level of society. I felt Christ asking me to empathize with others in their anxiety and distress. What could I do in the present circumstances to relieve the causes of spiritual and social injustice that attack the vulnerable spirit of abandoned souls?

Might the answer to save humanity from this madness reside in the common ways of the world's classical faith traditions that teach us to transform hatred to love, conflict to compassion, depreciation to appreciation? One night as I thrashed around trying to sleep the thought came to me that to carve out new paths to peace was not a matter of inventing a "new age spirituality" to replace the age old traditions to which we adhered. What was needed was to find a way to live the foundations of distinctively human formation undergirded by the ageless spiritual wisdom that inspired them. Every time this revealed body of truth weakens in a culture, the entire culture dissipates with it. To restore the art and discipline of harmonious living would require a return to our own faith and formation traditions and the wisdom they reveal about what it means to be and to act as human beings created in the image of God. The challenge is to discover what we share despite our differences.

Finding what unites us, not focusing on what divides us, would be the first step in the life-long process of forming, reforming, and transforming the deformations that caused the sickness of soul I witnessed daily.

Having come to grips with the fact that my ordination to the priesthood would have to be delayed for as long as God allowed, I felt the peace of surrender combined with the grace of entering upon a path of knowledge through experience that would affect me on all levels of my being. Several early impressions are as vivid today as they were then. The variety of backgrounds of those who went into hiding with me, their everyday differences in language and customs, did not detract from our common experiences of hunger, loss of life as we knew it, and feelings of abandonment of soul. During our exile from our familiar worlds into small farming and fishing villages, we would all have to face the ultimate question of whether life was meaningful or meaningless. Many good people came to me for spiritual guidance and encouragement because, ordained or not, I was a "man of the cloth." The way they expressed their misery varied, depending on who they were: coal miners, farmhands, brick layers, street cleaners, lawyers, soldiers, school teachers, or politicians. Their needs could not be linked exclusively to any one religion. Some shared my Catholic faith, but others belonged to different Christian denominations; still others were Jewish, agnostic, Marxist, or without any affiliation.

In my seminary, students for the priesthood were not permitted to study theology before we had followed an intense two-year program in philosophy. The aim of this pretheological approach was to make us familiar with what people can know about their nature and its distinctiveness by use of human reason. This study proved to be an enormous asset during the Hunger Winter. This anthropological frame of reference made it possible for me to communicate insights into the life of the spirit shared by all people regardless of their faith or formation tradition.

It became clear to me amidst such a diversity of interests and needs that the development of our character and personality never happens in isolation but in interformation with those with whom we rub shoulders under both normal and stressful conditions. I tried to answer the call to assist abandoned souls in all ranges of society, representing many different religious and ideological persuasions. I needed to find a language compatible with their uniqueness that could still express what we had in common. At the same time, this sense of respectful cooperation could not lead to unwise accommodations that would compromise my own or their doctrinal traditions. I soon found out that despite its many benefits a philosophical mindset was not sufficient under such circumstances to create spiritual bonds between people of various backgrounds, who were as unfamiliar with classical schools of philosophy as they were with their more popularized discourses. Questions concerning the meaning of life gave way to practical concerns for survival. Of necessity, I found myself drawing upon findings from the human and social sciences that dealt with loss and grief and the results of abnormal stress. Remote concerns had to be placed on the back burner while we dealt with pressing needs for food, clothing, and shelter.

During the hours we had to spend in black-out periods, I had time to think about the nature of a transcendence crisis. Long talks with a Jewish banker hiding in the same place as I led me to the disclosure of what I would identify in later writings as a "formative action pattern." In his case, he had moved *from* a life of relative luxury to living in a barn. How was he to find his way *through* this radical change? Would the memory of his past life paralyze him to such a degree that he dared not look ahead? Was there a future *to* which he could go as he moved *from* one current life form, *through* this crisis, *to* a new current life form? All we knew at the moment was that we stood on the verge of a gruesome winter that would wrench us *from* any hope of quick liberation, that would take us *through* the ravages caused by occupation, and that would bring us *to* a new time of recovery that for now was only like the dimmest light on an otherwise dark horizon.

8

Longing for Peace Amidst the Chaos of War

DESPITE THE RAVAGES CAUSED by four years of occupation, The Hague still had some of its dignity left. During its heyday this noble city had been the residence of rulers. Reflections of this time of glory could still be seen in the ancient parliament buildings and in the magnificent Peace Palace, which housed the International Court of Justice, the pride of our once peaceful country. The museums and library of the city were famous and rightly so, filled as they were with works by Rembrandt, Vermeer, Van Gogh and many other Dutch masters. I loved my city's old patrician houses, its lovely lanes and parks, its gardens full of flowers. Row after row of dignified dunes crowned with garlands of beach grass protected us from the devastating floods that always threatened our land since it was below sea level. Many a time I would climb up on them to relish the majestic expanse of the roaring sea, at once our friend and our adversary, carrying our ships while nibbling away at our shores.

A man named Arthur Seyss-Inquart was the Nazi state commissioner put in charge of the Netherlands by Adolf Hitler. Having delivered Austria, the country of his birth, into Hitler's hands, this ruthless Reichskommissar had been rewarded with the governorship of Holland. He took up residence in the palaces of The Hague, a pompous gesture that dealt a devastating blow to the city's inhabitants. In a public address that was as chilling as the winter winds we soon would feel, he stated his position in no uncertain terms: "We shall hit the Jews wherever we find them and those who side with them will bear the consequences."[1]

As if nature itself responded to this cold-hearted announcement, the silent dignity of our dunes was now insulted by unsightly German bunkers made of gray concrete. The "Malie Baan," a splendid park in the heart of the city, popular for walks, picnics, sports events, parades, and demonstrations, had been ravaged by dugouts, anti-tank ditches, and endless trenches. A nearby neighborhood had been bombed away due to a costly mistake of the British Air Force, which left most of the town in ruins.

Throughout the city many handsome buildings had been requisitioned by the occupying forces. In an instant, they seemed to lose their charm. The roads leading to them were so fortified that they became constant symbols of our loss of liberty. I walked on them with a heavy heart. The sparse traffic consisted mostly of army cars and trucks. Gasoline had become scarce. "Gas-balloons" of enormous size looked like ghosts on the roofs of dark vehicles. They were the only means left to propel these now awkward looking "stoves on wheels" that made everyone in and around them fearful of an explosion.

The famed shopping lanes, formerly brimming with tourists, were desolate of goods and deserted of visitors. It was as if the entire population were in mourning. The huge windows with no merchandise behind them stared at us like vacant eyes. They looked like the empty faces of victims stunned by an earthquake. Only a bakery here and a butcher shop there were still in business. The liveliness of the Dutch entrepreneurs, who used to run countless, well stocked grocery stores had died too. Spontaneous commerce was replaced by monotonous distributions of the same sparse rations to long rows of people waiting in enforced silence to take their turn.

Not far behind our neighborhood was a dense forest, the "Het Rijswijkse Bosch" or "The Woods of Rijswijk." As a little boy I used to play games there like "Cowboys and Indians," but these woods were off limits now. They hid launching pads for V2 bombs destined for London and other sites in the British Isles.2 We were scared by the threat of counterattacks that would expose all of us to retaliatory bombardments.3 More frightening than that threat was the awareness that these new weapons were still in the experimental stage. Every time they failed to reach their target, more fire power rained upon us and our neighbors, maiming and killing innocent bystanders rather than the enemy forces the bombardiers intended to weaken and destroy.

I shall never forget the fears each night held in store. The sudden drone of a missile fired, the flame in the sky, made us hold our breath. We counted each second that passed. Would this one make it? If the drone shifted to a sizzling sound, we knew it was descending. Where would it empty its deadly load? On others or on us? We prayed with blind faith and trust in the Lord. In the midst of the terror suffocating us, our hearts went out to the countless victims of war in other parts of the world. Would we live to see the time when all people would uphold the dignity of life and the hidden nobility that alone could promulgate a universe of peace? There had to be a way to transcend the rage, greed, and envy that mortally wounded the soul of our already vulnerable planet. The ground of such shared formation should be the affirmation of a higher power that sustains our life on earth. Without abandoning ourselves to belief in an ultimately benevolent mystery, it would be almost impossible to overcome the sense of desolation gripping our country. Its encapsulation by a death-dealing regime, fueled by a dehumanizing, deformative ideology, was like a nightmare without end.

One afternoon my youngest sister, Leonie, came running home from school, sobbing uncontrollably. A plane had passed over and dropped an armed device. Everyone listened, hearts in their mouth. Ominously its sound changed. The teacher shouted, "Quick! Quick! Hide under your desks!" A few minutes later, the bomb exploded not on her school but near a building for homeless boys. Some of them were killed instantly, others badly injured. Leonie and her classmates had to rush home. In her frightened eyes, I read the bewilderment children feel when their reliable world goes completely crazy.

One example of gross behavior that stays in my mind has to do with the scarcity of goods that plagued us during the war. Some shared the few rations they had but many used others' poverty to become rich. Their greed betrayed the self-centeredness at the root of so much evil. The same dynamic of self-preoccupation makes us resist whatever seems to compete with our gain. "We do not need to devise new instruments of war," I said to myself, "but to disclose the selfishness deep within our souls that threatens to tear us apart." Would we choose to heal the rifts that divide us or succumb to the disharmony that destroys what is most noble in our nature? We had to stop focusing on what sets culture against culture, race against race, country against country, tradition against tradition. Without minimizing in any way my commitment to my own faith and formation traditions, I began to seek peace directives that could bridge our divisions and act as divinely inspired conditions to restore hope in an otherwise hopeless situation. Men my age were being rounded up and deported daily to work camps. Hospitals were so filled patients had to be turned away. All of us had lice in our hair because of the scarcity of soap. Civilization as we knew it deteriorated daily, and, as if that were not bad enough, the Nazis threatened to pierce the dikes that protected our lowlands and turn Holland itself into an inland sea.4

Notes

1. Seyss-Inquart knew how to mix "honey with the whip . . . as slippery as an eel, charming and at the same time thick-skinned" (101). Such is Henri van der Zee's description of this inhumane Nazi who ruled the freedom-loving Dutch with an iron fist.

2. One eyewitness, cited by van der Zee, wrote: "Cycling to The Hague I watched the departure of a V2 from the sports field near Rijswijk. I heard an indescribable noise, shrieking and thundering, and saw a long torpedo-shaped monster with a long fiery tail appear." As the rocket took off and disappeared out of sight, the eyewitness wrote, "with trembling knees, I climbed back on to my bike, under the impression that I'd seen the coming of hell" (186).

3. One of these retaliations set an entire neighborhood near The Hague on fire, killing 511 citizens, wounding many more, and destroying 3,250 houses (187). Such were the gruesome sights Father Adrian witnessed daily.

4. Van der Zee reports how the Nazi terror escalated with the threat to destroy the dikes that kept the Lowlands from being swept away by the sea. For example, with the flooding of the Wieringermeerpolder, the Germans succeeded in one stroke in destroying the granary of Western Holland with its 512 farms. They checked the papers of the fleeing inhabitants, looking for members of the underground (Dutch "divers") and shooting 29 of them in transit to the town of Hoorn (227).

9

Mad Tuesday

Though our situation worsened daily, during the summer of 1944 life was still tolerable. Our rations had been reduced to minuscule proportions, but we survived on potatoes, turnips, and other root vegetables. Without much protein, it was impossible to ward off the feeling of a nagging hunger. At my own dining room table, we were able to complement our scarce meals with produce from the black market, transported to The Hague from the fertile "Westland" bordering our city. Diligently as we tried to buoy up our spirits, it was useless to deny the mood of despondency that began to settle over our lives like a fog that does not to want to lift. All at once, on Monday, September 4, 1944, a certain excitement seemed to fill the air. Most of the news we had received during the occupation came from rumor mills since radios had been confiscated. Yet what we heard on that day seemed more reliable than news from media outlets controlled by the enemy. The Allied troops were advancing toward the Dutch borders! A day earlier, Brussels, the capital of Belgium, had been liberated. People felt that at any moment it would be The Hague's turn.

From morning to afternoon rumors of relief continued to spread like wildfire. Our growing elation reached explosive proportions. During the evening meal, we spoke of nothing else. Suddenly a friend of the family rushed through the door. He had hidden a radio in his attic to listen in secret to the BBC and its subdivision Radio Oranje, emanating from the Free Dutch in London. To cut us off from such sources of subversion, the Gestapo ordered that all radios be brought to assigned centers in neighborhoods. Every family that had not delivered a radio became automatically suspect. To be put on a black list meant that your house was in danger of being searched by the secret police. My father had hidden our radio in a garden shed behind our house. He only handed in an ancient scratchy one we were glad to dispose of after polishing it carefully to enhance its appearance. Because my family continued to aid people suspected by the Germans, we did not take a chance anymore to listen to our radio-in-hiding, but our friend, a staunch listener in a closet in his attic, brought the great news.

Professor Pieter Sjoerds Gerbrandy, Prime Minister of the Dutch government-in-exile and the animator of the resistance, addressed us during the newscast. Winston Churchill was fond of this stubborn Dutch peasant who shared his love for large cigars and brandy. He could not resist calling him affectionately in front of others, "My friend, Mr. Cherry Brandy." Gerbrandy prematurely had announced over Radio Oranje: "Now that the Allied troops have crossed the Dutch border their advance is irresistible. I wish to give a warm welcome to our Allies on our native soil . . . the hour of liberation is at hand!"

Our friend told us that on Sunday, September 3, the program schedule of Radio Oranje had been changed. The fourteen and a half minutes allowed to the Dutch by the BBC were filled with the news that our Queen Wilhelmina, in exile in the British Isles, had obtained permission from General Dwight D. Eisenhower that her son-in-law Prince Bernhard, married to her daughter Princess Juliana since 1937, be appointed Commander of the joint Dutch Resistance Movement. From now on it would be called the Binnenlandse Strijdkrachten (BS) or the Forces of the Interior. The Prince himself had spoken on the air, asking the underground to refrain from a general uprising even if liberation seemed to be imminent.

Fifteen minutes before midnight the Dutch section of the BBC brought the exhilarating news that the Southern town of Breda had been taken over by the Allies. A British general said over the radio that the German defenses were crumbling. People living near the Belgian border could see with their own eyes how the disciplined retreat of the German troops from Belgium turned into a stampede of frightened, hunted soldiers, exhausted and dirty, on foot or packed into their trucks. We went to bed that Monday evening with the exalted expectation that the next morning we would be awakened by liberators invading our fair city.

Tuesday, September 5, ("Mad Tuesday") marked a day of shame for the Nazis. Even though these freedom fighters were not there yet, rumors proliferated that Dordrecht had fallen. The Tommies were approaching Rotterdam a short distance from The Hague. People from my city rushed by the thousands, arms full of flowers, to the streets closest to the road from Rotterdam. Leaders of the resistance got ready to take over power. The resistance division in Rotterdam occupied a school. In Axel, German soldiers surrendered to Dutch policemen. Thousands of NSB (National-Socialistische Beweging) fled their houses, leaving everything behind. The mass hysteria they displayed marked the hour of disintegration of this movement. In Naarden, the Nazi mayor gave his gun to his secretary. An underground newspaper in Leiden printed 10,000 "Liberation Specials" all to no avail. The news that British troops had liberated Breda was false. What happened was that a patrol had crossed the border by mistake.

I myself hastened that afternoon to an uncle and aunt who lived on one of the main approaches to our city on the "De Rijswijkse Weg" (the road of Rijswijk). For hours and hours, deep into the night, I watched from their third floor the exiting crowds, waving seas of flags and flowers. I saw another troop of straggling German soldiers fleeing in panic toward the Belgian frontier. Later military carriers with threatening machine guns came from the opposite side. The sharply uniformed gunners stood stiff and tense, their fingers on the trigger, ready to start a blood bath the moment the crowds threatened the movements of either the retreating or the advancing troops. I shall not easily forget the gaping muzzles of the machine guns directed in fast sweeping movements left and right, up and down. At one moment I found myself staring straight into one of them searchingly pointed at my window.

Observing the agitated crowds drunk with longing for a symbol of deliverance made me realize that their behavior was for the most part an expression of a far deeper longing of humanity—the outcry of every human heart for wholeness, peace, and harmony. This everlasting hunger assumed dramatic heights in the wild outpouring of elation of the crowds beneath my window. The invisible human aspiration for freedom became as concentrated as the gases in a volcano about to erupt. In our frenzied expectation to witness the visible liberation of an oppressed city a kind of madness seized us.

Pacing up and down in my uncle's living room, I asked myself how many of us realized that this liberation would only be a starting point on the way to growth from outer oppression to inner freedom? Are not all of us plagued by those wars taking place in the battlefield of our own heart? Do they not tear us apart? Are we not all afflicted by unfaithfulness to our religious and ideological affiliations? Confronted by the worst and the best life had to offer-occupation or liberation-I fell to my knees and prayed for our people. I asked that our hearts be opened to the providential care of a Higher Power, whether we were to be granted freedom again or not.

When nothing happened, when it was clear that these rumors of the war's end were tragically premature, the crowds dispersed and this Mad Tuesday faded into the night. I fell asleep wearily on a couch near the window just in case the liberators would rumble into the city by dawn, but these aspirations proved to be unfounded. For now all that we could hope for was not palpable peace but the "peace of God, which surpasses all understanding" (Philippians 4:7).

10

The Price of Survival

On Wednesday, September 6, 1944, we woke up with heavy hearts. It now seemed as if our liberation would have to be delayed indefinitely. The only oppressors from whom we had been liberated were those hated Dutch collaborators. Now that the Allies were approaching, now that the smell of defeat was in the air, they feared the wrath of ordinary citizens, often called "the good Dutch," and fled in panic, forecasting their own collapse. At a meeting in the Maliebaan, the NSB headquarters in Utrecht, on the evening of September 4, the council discussed with the party leader of the Dutch Nazi movement, Anton Mussert, the possibility of moving the women and children of their members to Germany.

Mussert had sworn, even after D-Day, that he and his cohorts would never give up; they would stand firm to the last man and woman. To prove his point, he had rejected the proposal to develop an evacuation scheme for these dependents. The false news of the fall of Breda terrified both the rank-and-file members and the leaders of the NSB. Among them was Henk Feldmeijer, the absolute boss of the Dutch SS or Schultzstaffel, meaning "Defense Echelon." Mussert, who maintained leadership of the NSB as a whole, was his rival. Feldmeijer called him derisively a "bourgeois." The SS leader announced that he could obtain from the Germans twenty-five trains for women and children. He added maliciously that there was one condition: the men had to remain here and join the Landwacht, the Nazi Home Guard, where they would be under his power. Mussert saw no way out. He assented reluctantly to his opponent's proposal.

The result was chaos. On "Mad Tuesday," the NSB officials themselves led the cowardly retreat. Only Mussert stayed. Mayors of the towns, appointed with the aid of the enemy, were terror-stricken. They fled the city halls they had disgraced with their treacherous betrayal.

Other Dutch Nazi officials deserted their posts too. Many did not even take time to clear their desks. Fanatics had boasted that they would withstand the Allies to the bitter end, but they, too, hurried to the Northeast in disarray. Thanks be to God, once the NSB movement imploded, it never revived again, enabling our beleaguered population to at least gain some relief.

Seyss-Inquart himself, the merciless Reichkommissar, had sent his wife Gertrud home to Austria on September 3. The day after he declared a state of emergency in Holland, he made any flight from Dutch territory that was under threat of the Allied troops a punishable offense. Gertrud Seyss-Inquart left The Hague with five suitcases of loot to settle down in Salzburg. The Dutch people whom her family had ruthlessly robbed and persecuted would never see her likes again. Other German civilians soon followed her example. They took with them all they could collect. There was no room left at the railroad station to store the furniture, office desks, stoves, clothing, shoes, paintings, works of art, and foodstuffs of every sort the looters had stolen and now sought to conserve.

The flight went on for days. The first train stop was at Westerbork, the infamous transition camp near Assen from whose hellish barracks 140,000 Dutch Jews were transported to their extermination in the death camps. When thieving NSB fugitives arrived there, they found several hundred Jews ready to be taken to Germany. These emaciated inmates were ordered at gunpoint to minister to the needs of those who had persecuted them so ruthlessly. Before they traveled on they had to be deloused by the Jewish prisoners they despised.

What was unique in the history of the liberation of Europe was the restraint of the Dutch population during those first days of September. In spite of tension and terrible disappointment, infuriated by the sight of fleeing Germans and hated NSB collaborators, they did not exercise revenge. The Roman Catholic bishops had gained tremendous prestige among the Dutch population because of the defiant public letters they ordered to be read from all pulpits castigating the persecution of the Jews. This show of courage gained them the respect they needed to prevent bloody reprisals. They told an enraged population that "hate and revenge should never be the motive for human action." They stressed the right of asylum in the churches of Holland, and reiterated the urgent request that the faithful abstain from violence against the Nazis. Their words were so well heeded that no Nazi blood was on their hands, not even during the days of madness.

In the meantime, we felt a growing sense of frustration due to the fact that the Allies, under General George Montgomery, had rejected Prince Bernhard's plea to liberate our Western and Northern towns without further delay and to take advantage of the confusion of the Germans. On September 15, Radio Oranje brought us the good news that Maastricht in the South of the country had been liberated. In the meantime many of us began to suspect that we might be destined to remain an isolated German-occupied fortress behind the rivers Rhine, Waal, and Maas until the end of the war.

On Sunday, September 17, 1944, the hope of liberation flared up again. Our fate might be changed within days. Good tidings over Radio Oranje, now broadcasting from Brussels, said that "... great events are at hand ... a great battle is soon to be expected."

Arnhem was one of the towns above the forbidding barricade of the great rivers. It stood on the north bank of the Rhine. Its atmosphere of charm and dignity belied the deadly battles that would soon surround its borders. This Sunday around noon the sky was suddenly reverberating with the thunderous sounds of fleets of war planes. Thousands of soldiers were dropped like gigantic birds by red and green parachutes shimmering in the sun and hovering over the woods around Arnhem. The German radio announced that airborne troops had also landed north of Eindhoven and at Nijmegen. Our hopes soared, only to be shattered again.

On September 10, General Montgomery had convinced General Eisenhower that he should allow the left wing of the British army to take hold of deep-water harbors, such as those at Antwerpen and Rotterdam. Monty also wanted to destroy the bases of Hitler's V1 and V2 weapons since they were raining death and destruction on London. One of these bases was located not far from my family's home. This proximity terrified us. Incidental failures had already caused bombs to fall prematurely in our vicinity. According to the project of attack called Operation Market Garden, the British and American airborne troops had to occupy lands and roads from Eindhoven to Arnhem. This strategy would enable the British Second Army to cross with lightning speed the three formidable barriers-the rivers Maas and Waal and the Rhine.

On the morning of September 17, Queen Wilhelmina and Princess Juliana observed from their garden at Stubbings that "a large American air-fleet, part of which had taken off from the airfield was on its way to our Fatherland with its supplies and paratroops." What she observed and described was but a subdivision of the immense fleet of 3,500 planes and gliders carrying at least 7,000 men.

Such news seemed so promising, yet Operation Market Garden got off on a wrong footing. The narrow corridor from Eindhoven to Arnhem, cluttered with tanks and trucks, became known as Hell's Highway. It took the British four days longer than anticipated to come close to the vicinity of Arnhem. Prince Bernhard had warned Montgomery that his heavy tanks and trucks would get stuck in the soggy soil of Holland if they were to leave the narrow highway. The Field-Marshall did not listen, and the results of this mistake turned out to be devastating.

On top of this quagmire two SS Panzer divisions-not counted on by the Allies-were hidden in the woods near Arnhem. One barred the entrance to the town. Only 600 brave men of the Second Parachute Battalion and other airborne units were to reach the bridge over the Rhine. They and their commander, Lieutenant-Colonel John Frost, held out against superior numbers for four days. Then they had to fall back. On September 25, eight days after the landings, 2,500 men of the First Airborne Division were ferried back to the south bank. Allied troops in the just liberated city of Nijmegen covered their retreat with an umbrella of heavy artillery fire. Seventy-five hundred men could not be rescued. Fifteen hundred of them gave their lives in a poorly planned attempt to liberate us. Due to bad weather, insufficient preparation, inadequate leadership, and plain stubbornness, Monty missed the chance to finish the war quickly and to liberate the Dutch. The Rhine again became an impenetrable wall of water behind which the Nazis could terrorize us as much as they chose to do so.

A long severe winter now lay ahead of us. Famine hung as an ominous threat over our lives. A telegram sent on September 27 to London summarized the situation: "In Amsterdam . . . we still can count on five week's worth of bread, three of potatoes and butter, and for no weeks, meat . . ."

The defeat at Arnhem was an enormous blow to the Dutch people. Our plight became aggravated by a subsequent railway strike. The Dutch government-in-exile had asked for a walk-out of all railroad personnel.

Its request had been communicated at an opportune moment during the BBC newscast of Radio Oranje. First there was the exciting announcement of the landings at Arnhem. Then, immediately after that, we heard the following: "Here is an important message from the Dutch Government. Due to a request from Holland, and after consultation with the Supreme Command . . . the Government is of the opinion that the moment has come to give instructions for a railway strike in order to hinder enemy transport and troop concentrations."

To go on strike was the greatest act of defiance of the Nazis the Dutch had been asked to make since the start of the invasion. The 30,000 employees serving our railway system had to "dive under"—the term for "going into hiding." We were aware of what a disaster this decision would create, especially for city centers in the West like The Hague. God help us if the landings at Arnhem failed to liberate us! Our main means of transport of the food and fuel necessary for survival would be halted. The lines of exchange among resistance groups would be lost and all connections in the country would be broken. On the bright side, these were the same trains that carried forced laborers to work camps and Jewish citizens to certain deaths.

Earlier the managers of our railway system had given covert signals of assent in case of a walk-out. They had decided in advance that the moment the Allies asked them, they would advise their employees to halt all work and to disappear quietly before they were shot or arrested. Supporting their resolve was the fact that transport by railway in July and August had become dangerous. The Allied fighter force incessantly bombed the stations and shot at moving trains everywhere in the country. The request to strike came on September 17. The result was astonishing. Only fifteen hundred to two thousand of the thirty thousand employees refused to risk their income, their safety and that of their families. It was an unheard of, daring challenge to the Wehrmacht.

On September 18, Seyss-Inquart commanded that all newspapers print an editorial warning the strikers about the seriousness of this dangerous game. The editorial stressed that this foolish walk-out would only aggravate the food shortage to which we were relentlessly exposed. As Seyss-Inquart put it: "They suppose very naively that Holland's problems have been solved but, in the interest of us all, we hope they'll wake up and realize that they in fact are doing everything to bring a terrible disaster on themselves, their families, and their compatriots."

A majority of editors refused to print the message. On September 22, Seyss-Inquart sent a follow-up message by telex: "If the railway men do not return to work, a large part of the Dutch population will have to face the threat of starvation." Even then, most newspapers still kept silent. Among them was the *Haagse Courant*, the paper with the largest circulation in The Hague. In revenge its offices were blown up by the Nazis on September 29. The commander of the Wehrmacht asked Berlin for permission to shoot any Dutch person "who was not a terrorist . . . but whose passive resistance endangered fighting troops." The answer was that his troops could shoot Dutch citizens who remained uncooperative unless the German police managed to arrest them in time.

The Germans then began to seize bicycles, cars, machines, and tools from a number of factories and other work places. Worst of all, they carried off the dwindling food supplies held by our wholesalers. "As long as the strike lasts," they told the Dutch authorities, "we will hinder you as much as possible from providing food for the population." None of these tactics worked. Seyss-Inquart decided to evacuate Amsterdam, Rotterdam, and The Hague and then to insulate them totally. They would allow only trains to pass through for transportation of food. In this way they hoped to put before the Dutch the stark choice between death by famine in their isolated towns and villages or ending the walkout. Because of the need for army power elsewhere, this project proved impossible to execute. Instead they forbade all inland shipping of food and fuel. This meant disaster for us. We relied heavily on the transportation of these commodities via our extensive network of railroads, canals, and waterways.

We began to realize that there was no hope for a solution to our plight. The liberation of our country was not going to happen in the near future. The main aim of the war in Europe was a speedy victory over Nazi Germany. Freeing Northwestern Holland, now that the Market Garden operation had failed, had no priority in comparison to this larger, more urgent goal. We feared the worst: we would have to live or die under the occupation forces that aimed to starve us by the end of the war.

The first cries for help got through to London. "Food scarce! Fuel not available! Production of gas will stop between the first and fifteenth of October! Supply of electricity will also stop!" These and similar telegrams were sent to the Dutch government-in-exile through channels opened by the resistance. Their stark content aroused heated discussions in the Cabinet of Dutch ministers in London. They raised the question of whether or not the railway strike should go on now that the battle for Arnhem had failed? On September 30, the Government announced over Radio Oranje: "Military interests demand that the strike continue until the day the enemy leaves the country." An agonizing decision faced us. It meant even more danger for the railway employees and their families, not to speak of the privations imposed on the population as a whole.

The strike went on. The Nazi's fumed, and they took their revenge. Already on September 22, immediately after the strike started, they blew up magnificent buildings in Hilversum. Black soot poured down on the well-kept Dutch gardens in the nearby neighborhoods. In the port of Amsterdam docks were destroyed and ships sunk. Majestic cranes crumbled like cardboard. Warehouses imploded and collapsed. German explosive experts were instructed to destroy the harbor of Rotterdam, the same city whose busy core had been bombed and all but destroyed by the Luftwaffe on May 17, 1940. Soon eight of the twenty-one kilometer-long quays were demolished. Offices, cranes, ships, and warehouses were blown up. The ports of Schiedam and Vlaardingen were ravaged in the same fashion.

Now similar catastrophic happenings seemed to descend upon us with no end in sight. The Germans caught and executed a number of striking railroad workers. In Apeldoorn alone, they shot ten workers who refused to assist them. Then they flooded a large part of the islands of Zeeland and Zuid-Holland. With malice and forethought, the enemy saw to it that the voracious North Sea would swallow a fifth of the choice land that could have been cultivated to provide us with food.

The whole world followed with horror the unfolding drama in the low countries. The *New York Times* devoted its front page to the terror and concluded: "... no country has such claims on Germany after the war as the Dutch." *The Times* of London wrote that the Dutch "have been called on to endure sufferings probably worse than those so far inflicted on any other country in Western Europe." King George attended a church service in the smaller liberated southern part of Holland with its two million inhabitants. On the same day his country men and women in England prayed, in unison with him, for the Dutch residing in Northwest Holland. One clergy person proposed in a letter to *The Times* to replace the traditional sound of Big Ben before the nine o'clock news with prayers for the beleaguered Dutch people.

Amidst these devastating developments, when it seemed as if all normal means of control had slipped out of our hands, I felt in the depths of my heart the anxiety evoked by the occupation and the hope that springs eternal. We were torn between the perils of war and the promises of freedom. How long would we have to wait for liberation? From whence would come our next meal? We had nothing left but our faith in God's mercy.

11

Compassion with Competence

WITH EACH PASSING DAY the strain of this winter of our discontent became more weighty. Every week brought new horrors to our attention. Suddenly I found myself having to confront the stark truth of just how ghastly things could be. One of my friends begged me to come to his home. His mother had fallen ill. The family, whom I knew well, were in a predicament that worsened her pain and fear. They thought I might be able to help them to find a solution to what was bothering them, although for the moment they did not dare to tell me the cause of their trouble. The less said the better, I was told, for everyone's safety.

Intrigued, I went to the house. I remembered it from visits in the past. It was a home with three floors. When I set foot in the Hugo de Groot Street, I recalled that the top floor had been rented to a single man, a lawyer. When I came into the living room and saw a sick mother with the family around her, I was gripped by the bewilderment in their eyes. My friend's sisters whispered fearfully among themselves as if at any moment something strange and frightening might happen. The mother waved me to her bed; her scared eyes pointed to the ceiling. She murmured: "The lawyer has left for a far away trip. We do not know where he is. He gave the key of his rooms to a Jewish couple without telling us. They hide there now. They are on their own without help from the underground. Our neighbors wonder what is going on. The lawyer's things are still delivered here. If these rumors reach the wrong ears, the German secret service will be here in a minute. That will be the end of us. We will be sent off to a concentration camp for not passing on this information. Adriaan, for heaven's sake, what are we to do?" She grabbed my hand: "Please, please, help us. Talk to them."

A host of conflicting feelings rose within me. As long as I stayed in the house, I knew I was trapped with them. If the news of the hiding place leaked out, the dreaded SS could raid us instantly. All of us, myself included, would be loaded in that hateful covered van in which I had seen so many disappear, never to know the light of day again. I felt furious. How could a lawyer of his caliber be so naive? Without any warning, without the backing of any group, he allowed this couple to live upstairs while he himself fled to some undisclosed place in the country.

Looking again at the panic-stricken faces of the family, I felt overwhelmed by their trust. They had put their last hope in me. I could not leave and do nothing. Then it dawned on me that I simply had to go upstairs and talk to the desperate couple huddled there, even if it might mean the end of me. Suddenly it flashed through my mind that the superior of our seminary had warned us that, as inexperienced students, we should not do anything drastic on our own. We were up against a clever, powerful enemy. Yet, what would he do in my place? Even if I went upstairs, what could I tell a man and a woman in fear for their life? The minute I set foot on the stairs, I knew I had no choice but to help them as well as the family downstairs.

The silence around me seemed to thicken. I felt everyone staring at me desperately, as if their entire future hinged on my decision. The sick mother stroked my hand with her restless feverish fingers. The tension became unbearable. I cleared my throat. I heard my thin voice telling them that I would talk to the two hidden above us. Slowly, reluctantly, I went up the stairs, one by one, to meet human beings doomed by a death-dealing regime. The oldest sister of my friend trailed silently behind me. The hunger for justice that welled up inside of me was so strong it almost took my breath away. I even feared they would see me as a fake Christian who did not care either.

Never shall I forget the pale, shaken persons, eyeing me with suspicion. In their fear they clung closer to each other. The woman never stopped wiping the sweat of agony from her emaciated yet lovely face. Her husband, himself shaking from head to toe, put his arm around her shrunken body to protect her. I felt sickened to the core. How could I be the bearer of the bad news that they had to find another place? How many times had this deflation of all hope happened to them? They looked exhausted from their ordeal, trapped like two baby birds with the walls of their cage closing in on them. How hungry they must be! Too little food was left for any of us, but what must it be like for those who had no ration cards?

My heart broke for them, but there was no other way. This hiding place was not safe. How I longed to do nothing more than flee from the grim task awaiting me. Pity overwhelmed me. I sat down and talked with them for over an hour. Their thin plaintive voices pleaded with me to find them a safe haven somewhere. Slowly I convinced them of the truth that their life and that of everyone else in the house could be snuffed out at any moment. This last year of the war our common enemy, enraged by the railroad strike, might not even take the time to transport us to a concentration camp. We could all be shot on the spot. The martyred bodies of many others bloodied the streets of our towns. At the end of our whispered hour together, I gave them my word that I and my friend would get in touch with the underground, who would then find them a safer hiding place than did this reckless lawyer. We parted as friends with a warm embrace and a deep but silent prayer.

On the way home I felt drained and pensive, vaguely aware that I had passed over a threshold into another side of the war. Little did I realize that I would soon find myself swallowed up by it. A few days after this unnerving encounter, the underground connections we reached directed our Jewish friends to a better hideout.

That night, I wrestled with another trait in which we had to be formed if the world were to be a place where justice prevailed. *Competence* meant that it was not enough to be of good will like that lawyer was, to be cheerful of heart, kind and compassionate. That foolish man may have been competent in court, but he was incompetent when it came to a life and death undertaking for which he had not prepared himself properly. To say "God will provide," is true, on the condition that we halt our flights of fancy and do his will with as much skill as possible. God's grace reveals itself in the daily challenges we face; they are meant to bolster our responses with the boldness found in candor and courage combined.

The anguished faces of the Jewish man and woman I helped to safety loom up before me. My memory of them fills me with a sense of mercy for all who suffer maltreatment. Yet compassion without competence will not stop the flow of the blood of the innocent. Only the combination of these two core dispositions, that is to say, *compassion with competence*, endows us with the gift of helping others to find meaning in their suffering. Ours must be a graced and gracious sharing in the mercy of God himself for each person. In the measure of our compassion for others,

God will bestow mercy upon us. In the measure of our competence, God will empower us to do what we can to continue the fight for justice, peace, and mercy.

Infuriated by the injustice done to people because of their race, color, or creed, because of their lack of power or personal possessions, I wrote the word *JUSTICE* down in my notebook in capital letters. It would be a key to the transformation of the terror we had to endure. We must never slacken our intention to serve the cause of justice. Without entering into this battle, humanity will perish due to the misuse of power by evil people. At no time must we give in to the temptation to look the other way or to condone injustice to serve our own concerns. Such cruelty despoils the love Christ asks us to show to anyone who asks us for help. How blessed I felt to have experienced directly the truth that one deed of justice is worth hundreds of empty promises.

12

Splitting of Simplicity

On October 3, 1944, we heard about the fate of Putten, a small village north of the Veluwe. Four Germans had been attacked in an ambush by a group of resistance fighters. The automatic rifle of Keith Banwell, an English sergeant who had joined the Dutch resistance after his escape from the battle lost at Arnhem, stalled at the critical moment that he had to fire. Three Germans escaped. The fourth man, Lieutenant Eggert, was in the custody of the underground.

When General Christiansen, the commander of the Wehrmacht in the Netherlands, received the news from Colonel Fritz Fullriede, the German commander, he exploded furiously: "Burn the place down and line the whole band up against the wall." He told his Chief of Staff, General Heinz Helmuth von Wuhlish, to draft the order: "Shoot the culprits, hand the male population between 17 and 50 over to the SS, evacuate the women and children and burn the village down."

Saturday night and early Sunday morning, German troops secretly surrounded Putten. Entering the village, the SS commanded the women to go into the church and all others to gather in front of the school; they shot seven villagers "in flight," among them a twenty-eight year old girl.

Colonel Fritz Fullriede climbed into the pulpit. He told the women: "Take what you need, gather up your children, and get out of the village at once." All the men were taken captive and put on a train to the transition camp in Amersfoort, Holland. From there they were transported to various annihilation camps in Germany. Out of 589 men, only 45 returned, of whom five died soon after. To cap off their revenge, the soldiers were commanded to set fire to some of the streets in the village. We were horrified by the murder of innocent citizens, who had nothing to do with the resistance. These meek villagers posed no threat to the Nazis. The simplicity by which they lived their lives was split open like a gaping wound. Only a few villagers had tried to escape. Not more than thirteen jumped off the train. Later we learned that some of the men sent to the death camps accepted their cruel fate as proof of their divine predestination. They seemed convinced "because of their sinful lives" that they had received in full the punishment they deserved.

This tragic episode opened my mind to the need to distinguish between the essence of a faith tradition and one or the other formation tradition that tended to highlight parts of its teachings to the exclusion of others. Both the Dutch Reformed and the Catholic faith traditions were designated as mainline churches in Holland. Adherents lived side by side in many regions, towns, and villages. They were employed in commerce and government. They worked as farmers, mill hands, fishermen, and artisans. It took the tragedy of Putten to draw to my attention the fact that the same faith tradition, in this case the Dutch Reformed, might not be lived in the same way in different surroundings. The difference between how the villagers in Putten responded to the enemy and how the family of Corrie ten Boom in Haarlem responded was striking. Believers give form to their faith tradition in ways that differ from region to region, from town to town, from social class to social class in accordance with the shared circumstances of their lives. These practical applications of the faith constitute their formation traditions.

Had the resistance been able to take these traditions into account, they might have seen that not all citizens of our land in every region could be treated alike. Had they been more aware that an homogenizing view of incultration is a fiction, they might not have chosen a region like Putten for their ambush. They would have better understood the formation tradition of this closed off village where simple souls lived devout lives of total submission to their everyday fate as predestined by the Almighty. Colonel Fullriede might have come to the conclusion that something else ought to be done here. Unlike many other Dutch Calvinists, almost everyone in Putten meekly obeyed his orders in spite of the fact that their survival was at stake. With a few admonitions from the local police, young men came obligingly out of their hiding places in the forests bordering the Veluwe. Women walked quietly to the church when they were told to do so.

Nobody is ever directly "inculturated" in a pluralistic tradition. One enters such a culture only by way of assimilation of a limited number of institutionalized or free-floating formation traditions. One becomes acquainted with these traditions through the people in one's vicinity. No child has ever been formed directly by the theological or ideological faith traditions of his or her parents. Initially the only way in which parents practically live and express their faith is through their formation traditions. What is taken in by children, usually without any conscious awareness, happens simply by virtue of their being in an ambience of daily acts of giving and receiving directives about how to eat, dress, think, decide, and act.

How does this difference between the formation traditions lived by adherents of the same faith tradition come about? First of all, a life shared with others, in response to similar practical demands, necessitates ongoing adaptation to our current situation. For example, Islamic people from Indonesia, at that time a colony of the Dutch, who were not living in Holland, could not express their faith tradition as openly in public prayer five times a day as they could in the villages of their birth. They had to select special places of worship without compromising their credal convictions.

Adherents of a specific faith tradition with its corresponding form-traditions do not live by its doctrinal directives alone. While religious or ideological faith traditions remain basic for believers, they add to them the familiar traditions they learned at home as children. At the same time, they are influenced by other traditions, such as the political practices of the party to which they belong. Influential, too, is their social class or position, and their shared professions, let us say, as musicians, artists, writers, teachers, or military personnel. For example, as Catholics in a predominantly Calvinistic country, giving form to our daily life meant taking on some of the styles of our Dutch Reformed neighbors. It was quite acceptable in the Dutch speaking regions of Catholic Belgium to see the pastor of the village in his cassock enjoying a beer at the village café. The same would be unlikely to happen in a café in Northern Holland. His jovial presence might be misunderstood by a population that had absorbed strict Calvinist principles pertaining to how clerics ought to appear in public and the temperance they must observe.

My reflections on the splitting of simplicity in Putten led to the conclusion that people in a pluralistic society develop what I have since identified as a "pyramid of formation traditions," or a "form-tradition pyramid." At the base of this pyramid is the tradition to which one is most deeply and enduringly committed, such as the form of life that unfolds in accordance with one's foundational faith tradition. From the base up, a pyramid becomes smaller and smaller. I pictured on each imaginary level of the narrowing pyramid other traditions that influence the actual form we give to our life and world. Nearer to the base of the pyramid are those that have more influence, for example, the tradition of the social class into which we are born. The less influential traditions I represented by the ascending smaller levels of the pyramid. Toward the top, for example, we see the traditions of certain popular sports or recreational outlets as having less priority in one's life than the familial traditions of being a good provider.

It takes a lifetime to align these form-traditions with the faith tradition at the base of our pyramid. The ideal toward which we strive is to attain harmony among all the traditions in our pyramid. Such consonance enables us to be congenial with who we most deeply are, faithful to what we believe, and reasonably compatible with others in our environs. These reflections on traditional formation and its influence on all people in a pluriform society came too late to help the inhabitants of Putten. The more I mourned for them, the more I saw the need to clarify the power of our faith and formation traditions and the good or ill that rises from them, culminating in the perversion of religion to such a degree that it may indeed become the parent of war.

13

Fighting for Integrity

CONSIDERING WHAT HAD HAPPENED at Putten, the dangers confronting us began to escalate. The occupational forces were on alert to take revenge on citizens due to any actions by the resistance. One day, walking down a side street not far from my parents' home, I felt firsthand the stomach-churning peril to which we were all exposed. Two elderly ladies standing in front of their apartment frantically gestured to me to come into their home. I did not know what was the matter until they pushed me inside and told me how some moments ago German soldiers had been ordered to shoot every tenth man passing in some assigned streets as a retribution for an execution of one of their army officers on an adjacent street. At any moment they were expected to do the same in the lane where I happened to be.

Inside their home, I huddled in silence with several other men whom these brave women had rescued and offered refuge from the treacherous street. Suddenly I realized why the otherwise busy thoroughfare, where I had been walking, was empty of any men. I had been the last and only male walking there, and I was lost in thought. I understood why the ladies had so frantically gestured me indoors with the intention of saving my life.

Some citizens were more in danger than others because of their race, intellectual pursuits, or social standing. They had to hide no matter what. These were the men and women most aided by me and my friends. Often they met with us at secret addresses, taking grave risks to break the loneliness of their hiding places. In the beginning of September, I managed to convene the seminarians in the region for study, reflection, and prayer. Now I was asked to do something similar for our friends in hiding—a task that turned out to be far more challenging than the care of seminarians. For one thing it was extremely dangerous. A raid on the house could mean the end of me and every other person there. Another difficulty with which I had to cope dealt with the variety of backgrounds and traditions, both religious and ideological, of the participants. Each wanted spiritual encouragement and wisdom. All spoke not only Dutch but several different languages. Many admitted their prejudices against traditions other than their own. They might not be openly critical of one another, but these judgmental predilections came through in their manner of looking suspiciously at strangers, withdrawing noticeably, or manifesting stiffness and unease.

In the spirit of the Venerable Francis of Saverne, I tried my best to be open to and respectful of persons not of my own faith and formation tradition. The tolerance he taught was second nature to me as a Spiritan. One letter he wrote on this theme has a special place in my heart:

> Live in peace with the outside world. Be genuine in your dealings with those who have no religion. Have compassion on them and don't be angry with them. Excuse them when they oppose you . . . Be particularly careful to overcome the embarrassment you may feel when you are in the company of people whose habits of thought and judgment are different from yours, who look askance at you, or perhaps despise you . . . Such embarrassment engenders a sort of stiffness, a kind of shyness that gives one the air of being ill-humored and stand-offish . . . That type of attitude makes a very bad impression on them and estranges them from our holy religion . . . In general, you ought to like all people, no matter how they may feel about your religious principles or about you.
>
> If we are able to force consciences to be pure, wills to be good, and minds to be truthful, it is evident that we should do so. Charity would make it our duty. But there is no one in this world who can even slightly force the consciences, wills or minds of his fellow human beings. God didn't want to do it. Why should we?[1]

Such wise counsel helped me to approach all those I met with a warm smile and an attitude of empathy—a trait cherished by Libermann. He told us, his followers:

> . . . to adjust [our] speech and [our] behavior to the emotional make-up and the interest of the people with whom [we] dealt. This emotional make-up and these interests cannot always be known by calculated conclusions, arrived at by reasoning. It takes

a certain tact to do so, and this tact is normally acquired through a general and practical knowledge of the recesses of the human heart, of character differences, and of [special interests]. These things are picked up by observing the people you meet and paying attention to the sentiments and dispositions they display.2

Serving the spiritual needs of manual laborers and professionals, of mill workers and university students of many different persuasions, was a blessed event for me, but one marked inevitably by a clash of traditions. The necessity of cooperation under duress increased my motivation to pursue as much mutual understanding as possible. I soon realized that these dialogues would go nowhere unless I concentrated on language usage, its verbal and non-verbal expressions. This sensitivity became unavoidable. Dialogue among traditions breaks down when we try to impose the language of our own beliefs on adherents of other credal systems.

To make matters worse, the seminary sessions I had improvised came to a sudden halt due to the distressful circumstances in which I and others found ourselves. The resources we once counted on in accordance with the routine rites and customs of religious living had been shattered by the war. Books on which I used to rely now sounded rather remote. It became necessary to guard our hearts daily against the erosion of our confidence in the re-emergence of Christian values in a post-war world. Almost nothing of what we had assumed would happen to us in the course of our studies for ordination had come to pass. We struggled to grow in holiness in and through confrontations with the mystery of iniquity that tore through us at the least provocation. Our faith was tested at every turn in this time of severe turmoil.

Many who came to me were nagged by such unnerving questions as: What kind of God would let such terrible things happen to us? Did we not build in his honor magnificent political, social, educational, and charitable organizations? What will happen to all of these institutions—our state-supported religious schools, our hospitals and free clinics, our radio stations, newspapers, and publishing houses, our youth movements and labor unions? Had we not been acting in ways pleasing to God? Had we not been the envy of many churches around the world? What did we do wrong? Why do we have to endure such suffering? What message may God be sending us through these afflictions? Where was the triumphant "King of the Ages" with the "victory crown" with whom we enthusiastically identified ourselves when we sang rousing songs in meeting halls, stadiums, and sports fields?

The secure spirituality in which most of us had been formed held few answers to the wrenching questions we now faced. We needed quiet time to sort through our confusion, but where was it be found? Not only did we have to cope with an implacable enemy; we also found ourselves squared off against one another in our frantic, often frustrated search for food, fuel, and safe places to hide.

Several seminarians and lay people who opened their hearts to me about problems not meant for other ears confessed to their secret concern that after the war Europe would never be the same again. Their deepest fear was that Christianity itself might fail to survive this severe generational test. Their fears were coupled with the image of a God who, some supposed, appreciated in a special way the meticulously organized Dutch churches. Were they not different, or so they thought, from the less organized efforts of believers in other parts of Europe and the world? The danger of harboring such thoughts was that they could give rise to triumphalistic formation traditions rooted in a kind of magical anticipation of deliverance from all evil on the condition that one managed to attain functional order and perfection in the performance of religious duty and in the orderly establishment of churches and church-related institutions. Undeniably such order has its place, but, in and by itself alone, it is never sufficient to foster in faith, hope, and love, spiritual transformation by grace.

Being functionally imbued with a mythology of measurable success inclines one to believe that good outcomes must be guaranteed by God. How could God not be pleased with one's work for his victorious kingdom? Was it wrong to hope that God's intention would match ours? Was it not best to anticipate the re-emergence of ecclesial power and prestige in the Netherlands? Of a renewal characterized by a return to the womb-to-tomb security reserved for people of impeccable wisdom, taste, and breeding? Once the hell of the Hunger Winter ended, once the Nazi war machine was obliterated, surely this paradise on earth would spring forth once again with more success than ever.

Such naively calculated plans and projects always blind us to the human inclination to place the *self*, not God, at the center of our life and world. The "up" side of these catastrophic happenings was that they initiated a process of demythologizing this triumphalistic vision. My friends and fellow seminarians had no choice but to grow in the spirit of simplicity and total reliance on God in and through the terrors we had to face on a daily basis. We had to admit that Dutch Christians tended to be proud of their down-to-earth common sense, their practical, organizational bent of mind. Helpful as these gifts are, we saw first-hand that they can diminish our humble grasp of the Gospel and lead to sheer forgetfulness of the truth that none of us can know the mind of God.

When functionalism becomes the ultimate and only source of thought and action, the self-reliant spirituality of people caught for a time in catastrophic circumstances may weaken and collapse altogether, leaving them discouraged and depressed. We saw as a side effect of ego-desperation that one could become more gentle towards oneself and others or more mean-spirited. Being threatened by the loss of life could strengthen or weaken our resistance to evil. The sad effects of such weakening could be seen every time greed replaced generosity and neighbors in need were overlooked.

During these long hours of captivity, I prayed that the Spirit would show us how to be and become living icons of Holy Providence in the midst of persecution. Our suffering would only have meaning if we allowed the light of God to illumine our heart with such spiritual messages as: *Return to me, your eternal and true love. Do not forget me for a moment. Can't you see I will never forget you?* Abandonment to the mystery within the bleakness of feeling abandoned by the mystery grants us the grace of inner peace. It awakens us to the truth that mere external organization, represented at its worst by the occupying forces, can never save us. The outer splendor of our belonging no more to a mighty people may have grown dim, but the inner sense of living in the divine light became stronger day by day.

Appreciative abandonment as a lasting disposition of the heart helped me to see the hidden benefits of suffering and the posture of humility that accompanies this pain. In chaotic times like these, our destiny was not to die without hope but to know that our Redeemer lives. This faith conviction does not do away with the reality of sin and evil, but it does lend to this misery an eternal meaning.

The flaw in religious education of many of the Dutch "divers" with whom I now lived seemed to be related to the fact that they had been formed mainly in a literalistic or moralistic understanding of their faith without a complementary initiation into its formative depth and beauty.

They sought information about the faith from scripture and the masters, but they had never been taught to read these texts formatively. The spiritual hunger they now felt easily translated into unrealistic longings for a return to a more blissful time of earthly perfection freed from suffering. Such a mindset contradicted the Christian call to live the cross in our here-and-now situation and to give the highest priority to the needs of our neighbors.

Nazism presented us with another set of challenges. This heinous ideology had not only planted its propaganda in a languishing land; it had also destroyed many channels of influence of the mainline churches. Before the war Christian political parties dominated the chambers of parliament, extending their influence to denominational school systems from kindergarten to the university level. Because of the widespread popularity of religiously based schools, it surprised no one that the number of vocations to the clerical and religious life was at an all-time high. During these five years of Nazi occupation, this secular and ecclesial infrastructure had crumbled. Would it automatically be restored after the liberation? Would the faithful flock to these institutions with the same enthusiasm as before? Would the seminaries, convents, and monasteries overflow with vocations as they did prior to the war?

While we had no way of answering these questions, we felt sure we would witness less denominational strife since, during the war, Christians of many persuasions had been compelled to work together over and beyond their own church-related organizations. Such ecumenicity would be an advantage for post-war Christianity. It would deepen awareness of the unique treasure of each denomination, uphold fidelity to our common ways of faith, and confirm our personal commitment to them.

Such was our hope, even though we sensed that the real threat to Dutch Christianity was not its external but its internal vitality. There was no lack of "head" knowledge, of functional morality, of administrative and political acumen, but were our hearts truly formed in the gracious love and wisdom of the spirit? More than a winter of the body, we feared a winter of the soul. Our faith was at risk of being devastated by the onslaught of secularism, moral relativism, and sheer selfism that like polluted air was being inhaled without our knowing it.

There was no doubt that our parents and grandparents, like the elderly ladies who had rescued me, had been blessed with a deep reservoir of faith. Out of this sturdy conviction grew their willingness to sacrifice time, effort, and money to build the mighty churches that dotted every town and village before the war. Such striking monuments to their faith had stood firm for generations, protecting them in many ways from the perils of modernity. Popularized arts and sciences, promulgated by a veritable whirlpool of ideological persuasions, had not assailed them as they did us. They felt protected in their denominational enclaves, most of which were now being shattered with every bomb that exploded. If we won the war, we might enjoy our freedom once more, but would the beautiful simplicity of the faith of our fathers and mothers still be alive in us? While we might defeat the Nazis from a military point of view, would we ever defeat them ideologically? What would aid our spiritual growth amidst an avalanche of new philosophies like atheistic existentialism that had gained in popularity faster than anyone could have anticipated?

The challenges facing the church in Europe intensified as the days went by, arousing concerns like these that shook us seminarians to the core. Would our philosophical and theological knowledge be enough to protect our vocation or would the whisper of our call be muted by the threats to our spiritual survival that confronted us with such force?

Besides the courses devoted to the training of our rational minds, we had been nourished inwardly by days of recollection, by retreats and inspiring conferences, by uplifting liturgical celebrations, by readings in the refectory, and even by a year long novitiate preceding our seminary study in the sacred sciences. These resources were meant to complement the formation of our philosophical and theological mind, but what would become of us if they did not sufficiently touch our heart? Was the seminary system itself weighted too heavily in the direction of informational theology without the balancing influence of a more formational approach?

What was missing, I mused, might be a truly holistic theory of personality that could integrate in practical ways what we believed and how we lived. Such an approach to faith and everyday formation would sharpen our ability to critique purely secularistic directives bent on ignoring the necessity of grace and eroding our call to transcendent transformation. While drawing upon the formationally relevant insights and findings of the human and social sciences, this approach to formation would not compromise one's adhered to faith tradition nor overlook the indispensable truth that grace works through nature. Experience had taught me that abstract concepts alone could not prevent one's drifting in directions contrary to divine wisdom. I already got the feeling that people who made it through the war might be at the mercy of all kinds of merely humanistic solutions that were neither compatible with nor conducive to the Revelation. I began to wonder amidst the chaos of the Hunger Winter if the Holy Spirit might be calling me to experiment in this crisis situation with the modest beginnings of this missing science of formation, this science of the spirit.

Notes

1. Cited in Adrian van Kaam, *A Light to the Gentiles* (Eugene, OR: Wipf and Stock), 267.

2. Ibid., 268.

14

Prophetic Envisioning

ONE THINKER WHOSE WORK intrigued me from the moment I encountered it was that of the great saint and scholar, Thomas Aquinas. In the thirteenth century, he reached out to intellectuals of his time by devising a pre-theological philosophy that became the handmaiden of his doctrinal theology. In this way he united the two wings of truth: reason and faith. In the light of where my thinking had led me so far, I suddenly understood why Aquinas felt obliged to create, in support of his *Summa Theologica*, a language beyond the biblical and spiritual parlance to which people were accustomed. He needed a metalanguage to integrate the insights of the then-popular teachings of Plato and Aristotle into a synthesis that would be rationally satisfying also to those not graced with faith in the Christian revelation.

The arguments I entered into on this point were admittedly heated at times. People of a more fundamentalistic persuasion wondered why it was necessary to go beyond what one could read in the Bible. Was the only reason Aquinas wrote this way to please intellectuals? Others in our discussion groups, I myself included, defended Aquinas' attempt to develop a universal philosophical language to serve the search for truth. We agreed that faith in the Revelation is a gift of grace not to be compelled by reason alone. Our task was not to proselytize but to create a climate of love in which everyone's spiritual needs would be respected. For the most part, we would have to address these needs by referring to the common language understood by all. Then, to articulate the depth dimension of the beliefs we espoused, together with their formative implications, we had to devise a metalanguage beyond what each of us understood in the context of our own faith grouping.

In the end the method used by Aquinas prevailed, at least in principle. We agreed that adherents of different traditions should try to suspend their particular ways of expression in respect for our ecumenical dialogues—not to belittle for a moment the everyday language used by people in the pew but to open themselves, without undue compromise, to the teachings others espoused.

Having solved this problem, a new debate flared up. At this time in history, philosophical systems were not uppermost in people's thoughts as they were in the thirteenth century when Aquinas wrote. In the forefront of our world was the popularization of various human and social sciences. The philosophical works we studied in the seminary had to be complemented by findings of a more empirical-experiential nature that would aid us in our everyday quest for meaning.

Realizing that a speedy return to the seminary was out of the question, I tried to find a place where we seminarians could read, think, and reflect on these and other matters. To facilitate our need for study and prayer during the daytime, I sought help from the nuns who lived near our parish church. Originally their residence had been a preschool for toddlers. When the state erected a larger building to handle this work, the sisters were granted permission to turn the former school into a convent. I asked them if we could make use of one of the meeting rooms that opened up to the garden. They graciously consented to this request. When the weather was mild enough, we carried the long conference table outside and gathered around it to support one another and to try to find some meaning in the upheaval we had so far undergone. Nature soothed our troubled minds and spirits. We relished the still blooming flowers, budding roses, and lustrous green shrubbery. The chimes of church bells in the tower reminded us of that bygone era when their music rang out across the city. Most of these grand old relics had been dismantled and transported to factories to be melted down and reused for canons and other weapons. Loud speakers now replaced their familiar peals. The empty cavernous holes where they had once displayed their regal beauty stared at us like the soulful eyes of parents whose children were lost.

One of the seminarians expressed his eagerness to pursue the latest thinking in psychology and education. He took the liberty of contacting a teaching brother from the best Catholic high school in town, who was known to be an expert in these fields. He agreed to spend some time with us, since his teaching schedule had been interrupted. My confrère's eagerness for this kind of contact was understandable. Years of studying philosophy and theology within the relative seclusion of the seminary certainly helped us to develop the logical side of our minds but, circumstances being what they were, we knew we had to foster an equally keen appreciation of our own and others' lived experiences and inner feelings.

Our teacher opened up the experiential insights that fascinated eager minds like ours intent on understanding the emotional problems we faced. While I appreciated his reflections on the human condition and his psychological expertise, I saw how easy it was to fall into the trap of humanistic self-development at the expense of divine transformation. The lack of an integrating science of human and Christian formation in our seminary programs made us vulnerable to these new yet still uncritically assimilated ideas. I could literally feel the seductive power sciences like educational psychology exerted on young minds not prepared to critique them by means of a systematic science of spiritual living. Once popularized, these sciences would become part of the atmosphere in which believers of all persuasions would have to recommit themselves to their faith tradition or risk its possible loss.

The excited seminarians sitting around the table with me represented what lay in store for us in the future. No one listening to our teacher could deny the fact that the secular sciences were here to stay. The concern I expressed pertained less to their practical outcomes and more to their unvoiced prescientific suppositions, ranging from biological determinism to mechanistic evolutionism and secularistic self-development, all of which were completely contrary to the Revelation. What would happen to our faith tradition if the population of tomorrow drank in uncritically the often unvoiced presuppositions of these emerging human and social sciences? How many people would they wean away from belief in God before they knew what was happening to them?

Religion was already identified pejoratively as a crutch for those who could not face reality. The theological and philosophical texts that were required reading for us did not seem to address the concrete needs desperate people felt at the moment. I was under no illusion that the language of self-sufficiency could ever be the answer to our deepest questions and concerns. There had to be a way to translate and integrate the useful findings of the human sciences into an approach to spiritual formation that would satisfy the hunger in our hearts. The challenge facing us was to cull from these findings their formationally relevant insights without downgrading in the least our Judeo-Christian teachings and traditions.

Thoughts like these kept my mind in a whirl. I would often lie awake at night, praying that others would be as aware as I was of the secularistic assumptions that were surely going to pervade post-war Europe. I compared them to Trojan horses sneaking into the fortifications of unsuspecting formation traditions and eroding, if not destroying, the faith-filled creeds and doctrines on which we had built our lives in family, church, and society. Surely others besides myself intuited the necessity of developing, as a complement to informational theology, a theology of formation sustained by its own metalanguage and research methodology. I saw no use in settling for a hybrid approach like "theo-psychology" or "psycho-theology" that would most likely water down both disciplines. Nor was it enough to collect unintegrated fragments of useful information that would not take us much beyond the functional level of life. I preferred to seek a more comprehensive framework in which to gather these formationally relevant findings into a holistic theory of personality respectful of our distinctively human orientation to the transcendent.

While most of the time and energy I had at my disposal was devoted to the task of food collection and distribution, I began to write these ideas in my journals. As the pressures associated with the Hunger Winter mounted, more people sought my counsel. Their once reliable religious customs seemed empty of meaning now that the occupation of our country and the deportation of its citizens had  brought them so close to the mystery of iniquity. Famine, violence, and persecution made it necessary for us to find some meaning in life if we were to survive this unprecedented crisis of transcendence.

One night, when sleep evaded me, I lay still and listened to the drone of Allied bombers passing over the roof where my bedroom was. They were on their way back to the British Isles after their raids on German cities and factories. How many would make it to their destination? How many might be shot down before they reached safe harbor? How many German soldiers and citizens were destined also to die this night? "O God, please help us to give form to a new and better world after this war!" Before I fell into an exhausted, restless sleep, I prayed these words at the top of my voice to muffle the sounds that filled me with fear.

15

Grace and Terror

ONE OF THE MOST intimidating organizations of the Nazis—a branch of the German forces given the right and duty to arrest, deport, and execute enemies of Nazi Germany—were the Order Police, nicknamed "The Greens" because of the color of the uniforms they wore. Their very appearance sent tremors of anxiety through everyone. The embodiment of German terror, they executed in cold blood five citizens of Wormerveer, a small town in the West. These victims were chosen at random in retaliation for a policeman who had been killed. This heartless act was followed by three more executions in Rotterdam. A similar atrocity happened near the neighborhood of my parents' home in the suburb of Rijswijk. Twelve people were shot there on October 6, 1944, after the Nazis got upset about a rail sabotage by the Dutch Resistance. When an officer was accidentally electrocuted, "The Greens" killed six more people in Rijswijk on October 12. When some people in Rotterdam tried to pick up Allied pamphlets dropped from planes on our streets, they shot at three of them and killed one. Later that day, four men were slain as retribution for the liberation by a resistance group of forty-eight prisoners from a police station.

On that same day, October 24, 1944, people walking through the Apollolaan in Amsterdam, were forced to witness the execution of twenty-nine citizens while several houses nearby were set on fire. The day after that our citizens were forced to stare at their slain compatriots, who had been flung by the roadside bleeding to death. The smoke of burning buildings choked the air out of our lungs. Such atrocities were committed in revenge for the elimination of Herbert Oelschläger, a successful operator of the German Security Force. This man had lived in Holland before the war. Mastering the Dutch language at that time had made it possible for him to organize an extensive network of people capable of infiltrating our underground cells. His effective operation had led to the arrest of several men and women in the underground, who were either transported to concentration camps or executed instantly. Not to be deterred, the underground decided that he himself had to be eliminated.

By October, The Hague, was in terrible straits. There was no electricity. A large part of the population had been forced into hiding with hardly any food to sustain them. Most stores were shut tight. In the evening we huddled together in unheated houses, our only source of light being a candle or an oil lamp. Seldom did anyone venture outside. Men leaving their houses ran the risk of being caught in one or the other unpredictable German "razzia" or "round-up" that hit one town after the other. Those who were picked up went "missing." Most were transported to labor camps in Germany or to a worse fate. What weighed us down day after day were events like the fact that buses ran for only a few hours a day. Bicycles disappeared. We had no tires and the Germans grabbed all the good bikes, cars, and trucks for their use. Because horses were used again for transport, it was as if we had regressed to an earlier century. The best way to get around was by foot, but most of us had run out of useable shoes since there was no leather to repair them. Old tires were in heavy demand because we found that they could be used to reinforce shoes that were falling apart.

As the former seat of the government and the residence of the Royal Family, The Hague was one of the cities hardest hit. With light and gas depleted, the communal central kitchen had to feed thousands upon thousands of people a day with not much more than watery soup. Over the years, the Nazis had robbed the Dutch of whatever they could use: copper, tin, radios, church bells, bicycles, cars, and, worst of all, our able-bodied men. Now they wanted our blankets and clothes. The Hague was chosen for a trial run. On October 26, yellow posters appeared in the streets, announcing in German and Dutch that every family had to hand in blankets and clothing worth at least 72 guilders, a considerable amount of money at that time. After turning these items over, a certificate of delivery would be given to each family. It could be used as a guarantee against house searches which "The Greens" threatened to inflict on those who had not attained such a document as proof of their cooperation with this order.

At first almost no one complied. Few, if any, showed up at the school that was assigned as a collection center. Infuriated, the Germans sent trucks with loudspeakers through the streets, barking the same demands. They threatened dire reprisals for anyone who refused to submit to the theft of their covers and clothes. This tactic seemed to work. First a small number of people, pale and afraid, hurried to the collection site. Then many followed. Whole neighborhoods submerged any thought of defiance; everyone went in panic to the Van Heutz School, where the enemy waited to collect the spoils. Next day, the resistance retaliated. They copied the certificates the Germans had given us in exchange for these stolen goods and then distributed them for free in the streets. The subsequent confusion forced the Germans to abort their plans.

A few days later they had another idea. This time they wanted to rob the people of all dogs that were large and healthy. People who had such pets were called up for a so-called "inspection" in which big, robust animals were separated from small scrawny ones and summarily confiscated. The little dogs were returned to their owners with an exemption slip. Viewing this scene from a place not far from the "Control Center," I saw the owner of the reject slips offering to lend them to others who had yet to have their dog inspected. Now these poor mutts had to endure a second or third rejection as would-be owners brought them to the inspection site and received an exemption slip. In the meantime they kept their larger pets safely in hiding at home.

Despite the execution of innocent people, despite the collection of clothing and other modes of control, what never let up was the courageous interference of the resistance. They endangered their lives to save others despite the anticipation of gruesome torture had they been caught. For some of these fighters the source of their courage may have been sheer hardiness or blind rage, but I also knew rescuers who were relaxed, rational persons of great sensitivity. They knew normal fear. They were not fools. They felt reluctant to get involved in the fight and had no hate in their heart for the enemy. Yet they grew in heroic love for their fellow citizens, responding in word and deed to the stirring words of Prime Minister Gerbrandy: "In this crusade from oppression to liberation no man should report, no employer cooperate and no civil servant assist. This is the order, this way it has to be, it can be and it shall be."[1]

The fact that many of these brave and loving people did not profess any faith publically helped me to see that we should try to think of grace as a supernatural gift that adapts itself graciously to our natural make-up. These freedom fighters convinced me that our human nature is intrinsically affected by a graced calling that gives us the courage to risk our lives for others. There are countless ways in which people of every persuasion respond to this inherent invitation under the influence of a divine stirring that others may or may not comprehend. From then on I vowed to revere the pace of hidden grace found in the hearts of all who resisted so heroically the evil that had befallen us. Wittingly or unwittingly, they seemed to be sustained by a loving mystery at the center of their endangered lives. This conviction became the cornerstone of my understanding of human nature as *distinctively human* or transcendent through and through.2

Already at that time I felt uncomfortable with any thinking that posits a split between the supernatural and the natural, preferring instead to follow the principle of Thomas Aquinas that grace works through and elevates our nature. In the midst of a humanity struggling for survival and begging for some kind of spiritual sustenance, I had to widen my vision to see traces of grace in all whom I encountered—be it resisted and refused or accepted with joy. I had to approach each person reverently as a child of God graciously beckoned to transcendence from the inception of life to its end.

Notes

1. Cited in *The Hunger Winter* by Henri van der Zee, 121.

2. Validation of this intuition came to light when I read to Father Adrian van Kaam a book by Mark Klempner titled *The Heart Has Reasons: Holocaust Rescuers and their Stories of Courage* (Cleveland, OH: The Pilgrim Press, 2006).

16

Agony of Deportation

THE RAILWAY STRIKE I alluded to previously evoked so much anger among the Nazi troops that their army units descended like voracious locusts on the already sparse resources of unsuspecting towns and villages like that of Venlo where all able-bodied men were ordered to report to the main military post. None of them took such an announcement seriously. When no one showed up, twenty men were caught at random and executed then and there. To prevent the same lack of cooperation in the next town, Zevenaar, the Germans threatened to flatten the whole place if the people failed to obey their orders. Similar raids were executed in Doetinchem, Hengelo, and Enschede. On September 21, the citizens of Kampen chose to resist the Nazi orders, but three men paid for this decision with their lives. To prevent further bloodshed, 6,000 men surrendered on October 7. When the men of Apeldoorn did not report as they were told, the murdered bodies of ten of them were left in the streets as a dire warning to the rest of the population not to disobey. To escape their fate, 11,000 men of the same town surrendered their freedom. Hilversum, with its German-supported Dutch Nazi mayor, sent 3,500 men to their cruel fate after death threats scared the population into submission.

This was only the beginning of a series of atrocious acts. Worse ones were yet to come. Hitler had appointed Joseph Goebbels as the minister in charge of total warfare now that the Allied troops were near. He sent a high Nazi official, Hermann Liese, to Holland to serve as his special envoy. He had to make sure that the male population of our country would be enlisted in this all out war against the Allied invaders. During a planning meeting with Nazi officials in Hilversum, the decision was reached to deport all Dutchmen between the ages of seventeen and fifty to serve in the building of defenses in Germany and at the Allied front in Holland. Others would be slave laborers in arms factories, working under the constant threat of Allied air attacks. Still others would be put to work in devastated German cities, cleaning the rubble left by the bombings.

There were not enough army divisions available in Holland to raid all large towns at the same time. Therefore, the army was ordered to catch and deport the men city by city. The code name for this project was Operation Rosenbranch. On Thursday evening, November 9, the inhabitants of Holland's largest harbor city, Rotterdam, received an unexpected letter notifying all men, between the ages of seventeen and forty, to pack a few necessities and to stand the next morning in front of their houses. They would be picked up by army trucks and taken to work camps. At 4:00 AM the next morning, all roads leading to Rotterdam as well as its bridges were barricaded. Eight thousand heavily armed soldiers, their guns ready to fire, took all weapons away from the Rotterdam police, whom they distrusted. They commanded everyone to stay inside. Finally, the troops marched into the streets, banging on every door. If it was not opened, they invaded the house, searching for unarmed victims.

Gunshots reverberated throughout the following night. When a new day of man-hunting began, the city looked as empty and barren as a cemetery. Fifty thousand Dutchmen surrendered or were caught in their hiding places. At the end of the hunt, on the evening of November 13, the 500,000 inhabitants of Rotterdam had no more than 20,000 men left. They were hiding in closets, under floors, in piles of rubbish, in garden shacks or in their attics behind towers of boxes and discarded furniture. One seminarian told me how his enterprising grandmother had nailed him unceremoniously into a cubby hole under her kitchen floor, keeping him there for three days. The unhappy hermit was only let out in the safely darkened house for a few hours at night.

It was tragic to behold the long, sad columns of the 50,000 captives shuffling forward in the pouring rain in eery silence. No sound was heard except that of the slow stepping of thousands of tired feet. Their captors walked beside them on the pavement, their guns ready to fire. Then, suddenly, out of nowhere, wives and girlfriends appeared, crying, shouting desperate farewells or a defiant "Long Live Orange." A woman in the crowd began to throw apples at them until the German soldiers fired directly at her.

On November 21, The Hague itself was under siege. The rumors of the drama of Rotterdam had been spread as widely as possible since now we ourselves were to be the focus of the raids. As a result, the Germans captured only 13,000 men. I escaped their snare, as did most of my friends, but the ordeal made me aware that we had to seek a safer hiding place in occupied Holland. More raids followed, scarring the country. Warned of the menace hanging over their heads, and supported by members of the resistance movement, many potential deportees were able to "dive under" in time. They were after all seafarers, swimmers, and boaters, who made their living along the North Sea and who were at home in the countless rivers, canals, and ponds criss-crossing our watery land.

During the early years of the war the first people we helped to "dive under" had been our Jewish compatriots and neighbors. The lessons learned from their harrowing experiences were of great help to us now that we ourselves had to try to escape arrest and deportation. The Nazis never did succeed in their grandiose project to deport all able-bodied men from Holland. Only one-fifth of them fell into enemy hands.

Disappointing, especially to the courageous editors of our underground publications, had been the reaction of many men in Rotterdam to the "razzia." A great number of them flocked to the posts for registration in an orderly fashion. They went straight to the collecting points the Germans had erected. I suspected that beyond their understandable fear another motive compelled them to cooperate so submissively. Underneath the correct following of these rules of registration lay the hidden disposition of a false obedience or, more accurately, a blind compliance. The same disposition explained to me the surprising conformity of many practicing Christians to the Nazi regime when it usurped power in Germany and began to persecute their Jewish neighbors. Not many of them were really driven by anti-Semitism. It was the disposition of will-less conformity to laws and directives coming from those in authority that made them a party to this propaganda. After years of being praised for building such a splendidly organized society, the disposition of functioning efficiently began to be dominant. Being a precise functionary, promoted and trusted by those in authority, became the main value to uphold.

Christians in Germany and for that matter in Holland itself were known in Western Europe and esteemed worldwide for their impeccable organizations, their theological systems, their political and economic astuteness, their meticulously arranged mass demonstrations, political party systems and labor unions, their uniform following of any directive given by their leaders. In many instances, creative ideas were replaced by subservient compliance and mindless conformity. Administrative power-brokers seemed in the pretentious mind of many not simply "channels of the Higher Powers" but themselves messengers of the Divine, who lived in a kind of unquestioning idolization of law and order in its own right.

Dutifully bowing to the deleterious directives spawned by functionalism eroded constructive functioning. It distressed me to see that functional productivity, as a servant of the transcendent, was being reduced to mere functionality. As a result, inspiration, reflection, awe, wonder, vision, contemplation, creative love, and imagination—all that makes us distinctively human had to be sacrificed to the idols of dull functionalism lauded by a hyper-organized bureaucracy that tried to force us to forfeit our freedom.

Gray columns of men shuffling towards an unknown tomorrow filed by in the pouring rain. The fact that they had submitted so meekly to the laws of conscription evoked the nightmare scenario of masses who might be enslaved in future years to the "false gods" of consumerism, materialism, careerism, and secularism. These pale substitutes for humane living only spawned more unhappiness. At no time, neither in war nor in peace, could we afford to replace the life of the spirit by projects of self-salvation rooted in functional ambitions devoid of transcendent aspirations.

17

Message of the Sea

On November 8, 1944, Radio Oranje brought the news that Franklin Delano Roosevelt, an American of Dutch ancestry, was re-elected for a fourth term. We were delighted. Just three days before, a Canadian armored division had liberated on the Zeeland Island of Tholen the village of Vossemeer with the famed house from whence Roosevelt's ancestors had set out for the New World around 1650. The conquest of Tholen on November 4, 1944, was part of the eighty-five day bloody Battle of the Scheldt. This inlet on the North Sea is the estuary leading to the port of Antwerp where ships carried supplies necessary for the Allied march to Berlin.

In the light of the loss of 30,000 men in the Scheldt, we lamented the fact that the battle might have been prevented had General Montgomery not made the mistake of not attacking immediately the still occupied port of Antwerp on September 4, when he had liberated that city itself. He waited eighteen days until September 22. This gave the German defenders of the port ample opportunity to take refuge on the Dutch island of Walcheren and other islands on the northern bank of the mouth of the estuary. This error in timing gave the Germans the days they needed to erect forbidding fortifications that would cost the Allies numerous lives. Walcheren was turned into an intimidating fortress, whose German commander announced in one of his orders that holding the Scheldt at any price would determine the outcome of the war.

If the estuary to the port of Antwerp were to be lost, a new chapter in the war would have to be written. Troops, weapons, ammunition, and supplies could stream in freely, enabling the Allies to finish off the remnants of the German armies, to march to Berlin, and to win the war. A message was broadcast, concluding with the stirring words: "The eyes of the German nation are upon you."

Finally, on September 27, General Dwight D. Eisenhower ordered an advance on the Scheldt. The Canadian First Army sustained hair-raising weeks of bloody fighting in water, mud, and torrential rains. Flemish Zeeland and the nearby smaller islands of Dutch Zeeland had been flooded by their defenders. Once the Allied forces had purged them from the enemy, they could plan their attack on the big Dutch island of Walcheren, popularly praised as "The Garden of Zeeland." At first sight it seemed almost impossible to take the place by force. Most of it, like so many Dutch lands, lay far below sea level, protected against inundation by a vast network of dunes and dikes. Stakes had been erected everywhere by the defenders to make it impossible for planes to land or to drop paratroopers. Along the shore twenty-five heavy batteries of artillery, held up in the soggy polders by gun-nests, stood poised to repulse any attack. To breach this forbidding fortress the Allied command decided reluctantly that they would have to bomb the dikes. The sea would inundate the lowlands along with many of the batteries and gun-nests dug within its soil.

On October 2, the population was warned. They fled from the coast to more central sections of the island. The day after the warning 259 Lancaster planes dropped their bombs. They cut an enormous hole in the Westkapelse dike. The sea thundered inland, drowning forty-four of forty-seven men, women, and children who imprudently had sought cover in a mill near the dike itself. They were buried alive under a downpour of stones and beams when a bomb hit their doomed shelter.

After two more air-strikes, most of the island lay under water. British units pushed through the gaping hole in the Westkapelse. Canadians attacked from the east. Hundreds of English soldiers drowned in the fray. The German defenders put up a ferocious fight, convinced that the final outcome of the war was at stake. Several Allied soldiers among the attackers had participated in the invasion of Normandy. They kept repeating over and over again that this battle was far more arduous than what they had experienced in scaling that terrifying coast.

The carnage lasted until November 6. When the day ended, Major-General Daser, the German commander in Middelburg, the capital of Dutch Zeeland, ordered a cease fire. Radio Oranje told us that the general took an aspirin and went to bed. He had hardly fallen asleep when the first British soldiers rolled over inundated fields and roads into Middelburg. They saw the beautiful ancient buildings and towers undermined and devastated by the swirling waters. A force of tidal fury pushed its way twice a day through streets and houses, farms and stables. Ocean waves swirled everywhere. The desolate sight of furniture, tools, and children's toys floating aimlessly on streets that had become polluted estuaries of the North Sea stunned the eye. Water oozed out of the neat Dutch houses, now slimy and muddy. Middelburg's population of 20,000 had doubled because of the refugees from the bombed regions near the coast. Almost all of them braved the waters to welcome the 300 British soldiers who were able to reach the town ahead of the other units.

On November 26, first a Belgian, then a Dutch ship entered the Scheldt. Both were loaded with tons of food for the famined people of this archipelago of Belgium and the Netherlands. On board the Dutch ship was war correspondent John O'Connor. He reported over Radio Oranje his shock at observing the small town of Flushing where no house had gone undamaged. Then he told us how he could not believe his eyes when he beheld what he called a typically unflappable Dutch woman stubbornly riding her bike, the water up to the middle of her wheels, at times swaying dangerously but keeping sternly to the right according to traffic rules. Sitting straight, she rode on, embodying for him the spirit of Zeeland, of its centuries-old fight against the sea symbolized in its motto, *Luctor et Emergo*, "I struggle and rise again."

Zeeland had been liberated, but for us who were oppressed and hungry above the rivers, the end was not in sight. While grateful for the rescue of Zeeland, its story made us realize more than ever our immense vulnerability, living as we did in these lands below the sea, dependent for survival on miles and miles of dunes and dikes. If either our enemies or our liberators would pierce these barriers, few would live to tell the tale. Inundation by the sea would spell disaster for our towns and villages, for the lustrous meadows, source of our dairy culture, for the magnificent yearly display of miles of tulips in blazing colors, whose bulbs many of us were now eating to stave off starvation.

Anxiously I walked along the seashore of my city of birth, as I had done so often in better times. I stared at the vast expanse of unruly waters that one day might drown us. I looked at the endless gray winter sky melting into the sea on the far horizon. I meditated on the waters and on our silent sentinels, those sturdy dunes and dikes that were like age-old friends that had allowed my people to cultivate the soil they had wrested from the sea. "Yes," I said to myself, "I, too, shall struggle and rise again."

The deeper message of the dunes and dikes symbolized for me the graced boundaries of my inmost being, with its limits and blessings. As they protected our lowlands so was the sanctuary of my call sheltered by an eternal mystery embodied in the sacred traditions I had assimilated since infancy. They were the dunes and dikes that shielded me from the raging waters of popular myths of power swirling around me in turbulent seas forgetful of our nothingness before God. These untruths were capable of sneaking into my heart through the estuaries of my outer and inner senses and the tributaries of my excited mind. They could spread like debris the dispositions that deform my imagination, betray my vocation, and inundate the fertile roots of faith that sustain my commitments. Time and again, the mystery of formation inspired me to fill the holes in my dikes, to let grace transform shattered boundaries and etch on my heart the thrilling motto, *Luctor et Emergo*, "I struggle and rise again."

The sea made me think not only of its raging waters as menacing symbols of leveling pulsations that batter our minds and senses but also of the calmness of a mirror in which we can behold the shining sun of God's goodness, truth, and beauty. Just as the flow of the sea fertilizes countless shores, enriching their natural resources, so its ebb cleanses whatever hampers their preservation. I saw in these ancient rhythms an analogy of the grace streaming from the Trinity to enliven our weary hearts and empower us to defend our freedom. The ebbing of grace draws us back into the bosom of the Trinity where, transformed by its boundless flow, we can abandon ourselves in praise and appreciation to God's providential plan for our lives.

The message of the sea expresses the mystery of transforming love and renews in each of us the holy determination, repeated by generations of courageous Dutch men and women, to struggle and rise again. That motto became a cry of hope quelling our despondency and assuring us that these times of tribulation, terrible as they were now, would someday be but a distant memory, teaching us the difference between what ultimately matters and what does not.

18

Everyday Heroism

WHEN CIRCUMSTANCES FORCED ME to leave The Hague for Nieuwkoop, the population was in dire straits. "Hunger-trippers" streamed out of cities to the country on bikes trimmed to the rim or on foot, forming a mass exodus to procure food on the farms.1 Unlike in Amsterdam where there was still some food available from the farms north of the city, unlike in Rotterdam where supplies from the islands in the south could be sent, The Hague could draw upon none of these depots for provisions. Our daily nourishment had diminished by then to less than 900 calories, with no meat or fish. We ate sugar beets and tulip bulbs instead of potatoes. Many in despair began to steal whatever they could find. The city looked empty and dreary. Shops closed their shutters to prevent the smashing of windows. The German forces shot desperate looters without mercy. One of them had to write on a piece of paper, "I am a thief." He had to hold this sign in his hand while they blindfolded him and then murdered him in broad daylight for all to see.

No light, no heat, no gas, no electricity, no means of transport meant that drabness and deadly apathy increased moment by moment. Often at night we were awakened by the heavy boots of soldiers, stamping on the pavement. The eerie sound of the brakes of a military van stopping, then starting, then shrieking to a sudden halt, made us hold our breath. We would hear loud banging on a door, followed by the ominous words, "Aufmachen, Aufmachen," "Open up the door!" When the van departed and the footsteps died away with it, we sighed in relief that we had not been the victims of the raid, only its sad witnesses. After that it was all but impossible to sleep, so overcome were we with compassion for less fortunate neighbors, who had been arrested and led God knows where. The time to penetrate deeper into the countryside had definitely come. Facing the precariousness of life and the loss of certainty and protection,

I prayed for the courage to make the best of these times and for the serenity to accept what none of us, despite our efforts, could change. That being said, I knew as well that acceptance of the will of God did not mean that I should do nothing to improve the situation. I rejected any form of false piety that implied total passivity. In the face of such injustice I was obliged by God to find ways of overcoming it.

For example, I made known my feelings about a Dutch minister-president named Dr. H. Colijn, who in my own and others' opinion grossly mistreated the poor and underprivileged of our country. He was unprepared for occupation and in the beginning did not realize what it meant. The point was, the Germans needed Dutch goods to feed their own war effort like fuel for a merciless machine mowing down everyone in its path. Converting the Dutch to Nationalism Socialism never really happened. The 600,000 young Dutchmen the SS had counted on where nowhere to be found. Infuriated, the Nazis accused the Dutch of succumbing to "Jewish capitalist influences."[2] So strong were my indignant protests against Colin's lack of leadership that some confrères teased me good naturedly by calling me by his name. I believed that social concern was an essential part of Christian spirituality, but this conviction sounded a bit overdone to them. Surrender to the will of God seemed to require docile assent to what those in authority condoned, regardless of the fact that certain decisions and actions were widely believed to be contrary to love of God and neighbor.

A good example of this dilemma concerned the way in which the indigenous people of our Indian archipelago were treated by the Dutch colonials. The more I thought about the injustices reported there, the less possible it was for me to interpret the Christian notions of acceptance, surrender, and abandonment in a totally passive or complacent way. We can only accept an unjust situation as a point of departure—as a challenge posed to us by the Divine—not as the will of God. At such moments sanctification would mean not to escape the invitation embedded in events contrary to the Gospel but to accept them as a call to some degree of reformation.

The practice of social justice, peace, and mercy in Christ's name precludes the selfish intention of serving others only if they agree to support a cause or an ideology we espouse. Living through the Hunger Winter taught me the danger of this assumption. It could tempt us not to risk our lives and forfeit our possessions to help those most in need, particularly our Jewish neighbors. To me, the Christian command to love others as ourselves implied standing with them to oppose persecution by the Nazi regime. What most endangered their survival was our indifference. Justice meant that I must not theorize about sharing the little I or anyone had but doing so daily. Whether or not the indigent of body and soul were open to my personal belief systems and the formation traditions I espoused was not the point. Instead I based my actions on the assumption that all people of good will were in need of finding some kind of spiritual meaning in their lives and that what mattered now was not to engage in further debates but to feed the hungry and clothe the naked.

As a result, I did all I could to help those who had been wrenched from their homes and condemned to face the horrors of forced labor and concentration camps. Never would I want to hear it said of them, "God willed it" or "God intended it." Every fiber of my being rejected this false pietism. The God of life cannot will death or destruction or cruel calamity. God did not, God could not, will the immense evil of the holocaust. It was only the fanatic will of evil men and women that led to this despicable tragedy that paradoxically evoked so many incidences of everyday heroism.3

God does not interfere with the free will of evil people, but once this ill wind is unleashed in any form, God is there with the force of his grace to draw some good from the most wretched of human situations. I believe that one of the best fruits coming from these bad times was a recommitment on the part of many seminarians to become *Alter Christus* in a religious community that served and defended the spiritually and physically poor here in Holland and throughout the world.

Notes

1. See Henri van der Zee, *The Hunger Winter*, 70–76; 105; 154; and 226.

2. Ibid., 100.

3. For example, although the tapping of electricity was a capital offense, liable to the death penalty, four times over, more than 1,200 different underground papers, including Father Adrian van Kaam's own [See Appendix 3], were published and avidly read during the Hunger Winter. Unfortunately, several publishers paid the ultimate price for their bravery: they were arrested and tortured to death. Ibid., 114–115. See also Mark Klempner, *The Heart Has Reasons*, 45–61.

19

Winter of Women

Accompanied by another seminarian, I traveled north to Nieuwkoop where a young priest we had known served as an assistant to the pastor. We were aware of his promise to do what he could to aid resistance groups from his nearby birthplace, Alphen. We had high hopes that he might also be able to help us. Many times in the recent past, we had left the city to beg farmers for food for those in desperate straits. During our trek northward, we joined hordes of hungry people pounding on the doors of farm houses, pleading for something to eat in exchange for their jewelry, clothing, artworks, and furniture. Like a blanket of thick fog, a sense of death and decay had fallen over Western Holland.

The weather that November only added to the gloom felt by exhausted people, lost and alone. Incessant rain soaked their thin wraps and left their already weakened bodies trembling in the damp, cold air. The tall poplars by the wayside offered them little or no protection against raging winds and downpours. Despite suffering from severe famine, they trudged along the open roads of the flat polders unaided by any other means of transportation than their own two feet.

Rickety carriages loaded with what was left of people's possessions were a common sight. They hoped to exchange them for edibles that became scarcer with each passing day. The tired, emaciated women, pushing these battered carts on narrow, unpaved country roads, got stuck in the mud time and again. We did our best to help them move to higher ground, away from the rain-drenched sections of the road. Our hearts were heavy with the knowledge that many of them survived thanks only to the newly established central distribution kitchens. They had to wait in long lines for a small bowl of watery soup made from unpeeled potatoes or for a steamed mash of sugar beets and beet root, of little or no caloric value and without any protein in it. This concoction had to be eaten at once; otherwise it would turn sour.

How could the German soldiers—many of whom had wives and children in their own bomb-ravaged homeland—not feel some empathy with the misery seen everywhere they looked? Many of them seemed despondent and demoralized, even if they themselves had enough to eat. In Amsterdam, the statistics were horrifying: out of 770,000 inhabitants, only 437,000 of them could survive because of the small rations of food offered by the communal kitchens. The average Dutch person that November consumed less than 1300 calories daily.

Making our way to and from Nieuwkoop left us feeling more and more down-hearted. We could not contain our pity for the famined thousands, many in sparse clothing and worn-out shoes, who, like a swarm of hungry locusts covered the country roads and entrances to the farms. Most were on bicycles, barely tottering on worn tires that could no longer be repaired. Driven by hunger, they peddled bravely on with only a rubber or wooden band around their wheels. Others hired pushcarts or used baby carriages or wheelbarrows as a paltry means of transport.

We saw people whose feet were bleeding and crippled from so much walking. Others had no shoes at all. They wrapped their feet in rags. Whatever their condition, no one wanted to give up. All wanted to go on. Neither pain nor sickness nor suffering could prevent them from seeking some food to quell their hunger pains. Soon the amount of calories each person received each day had dropped to an appalling 400. People fell from exhaustion in the streets. Often men, women, and children were so fatigued that they had no strength left to return home. Hiding in barns, they often ended up dying of famine and over-exposure. Old people, who did not have the strength to take part in the search for food, simply went to sleep and died.

What touched us to the core were the heroic efforts and inventiveness on the part of women who fought mightily for the survival of their husbands and children. Many among them also distinguished themselves by their ability to execute dangerous missions for the underground in places where no man dared to go.[1] Before the war began we had been inclined to underestimate the strength, perseverance, and creativity of women. We had taken their gifts for granted. We had not always dealt with them as our equals in dignity; neither had we given them the same chances to develop their particular talents and gifts. I made a mental note while witnessing their bravery that wherever my mission took me, women would command my full respect. The women walking these roads displayed a remarkable capacity for firmness and gentleness. They were not only sensitive but responsible; they were able to stand their ground in all situations with an inventiveness that awes me to this day.

The plight of women who were pregnant moved me most profoundly. All rules of neo-natal care had to be abandoned under the circumstances yet somehow they managed to push on. The cruel reality of famine meant undernourishment for the infants they carried in their wombs. Future generations would feel the effects of the Hunger Winter. These innocents would pay a price for the diminished health of their famished mothers. Children of the war now, they would be the parents and grandparents of the coming Dutch generations and none would go unscarred.

The concerns I felt were well founded. An article I read on "War Babies" verified the untold harm that had been done.2 A professor of physiology at the UCLA School of Medicine, its author, Jared Diamond, investigated the Dutch Hunger Winter in detail. He found that the Nazis had effectively reduced 40,000 pregnant women to starvation. The babies born from these mothers were small in weight and stature. They gave birth—when they themselves became mothers—to normal-sized babies. Paradoxically, it was the women who were themselves normal-size at birth who became mothers of underweight infants. According to the Diamond report, somehow the grandmother's suffering programmed their children *in vitro* so that the grandchildren would be the ones most affected. The indisputable result of this research was that starvation of a pregnant population left its harsh imprint on at least three generations of Dutch citizens.

In total, 10,000 of these women actually starved to death and thousands more suffered from malnutrition, which contributed to their early demise as well. It has also been established from medical records of that time that some women weighed less at the end of their pregnancy than at its inception. In the late 1960's four researchers at the Columbia University School of Public Health—Zena Stein, Mervyn Susser, Gerhart Saenger, and Francis Arolla—all of whom had studied malnutrition in urban ghettos—realized that much might be learned from the now-grown babies of the Dutch Hunger Winter. Both during and immediately following this wretched time, there was a sharp rise in infant mortality in the Netherlands.

My admiration for the brave women I beheld on Holland's war torn roads that infamous winter sealed the promise I made to myself to uphold in some way their story of incomparable courage and perseverance. The men in hiding with me shared this perspective, but others we met still had a hard time thinking of women as equals. They acknowledged their bravery in stressful times like these, but they seemed unable to recognize the wisdom, strength, and originality of women under all circumstances. Then and there I committed myself to develop as an underlying theme of formative spirituality and ministry, *equality in dignity*. As providence decreed, two outstanding women were destined by God to be an integral part of this new venture in thinking, writing, and teaching. One would facilitate its development in Holland, the other in the United States. The former was the initiator of the Dutch Life Schools of Formation for Young Adults, Doctor Maria Schowenaars; the latter was Doctor Susan Muto, my colleague, co-author and teacher in the fields of formation science, anthropology, and theology and co-founder of the Epiphany Association.

Notes

1. Mark Klempner interviewed many of these admirable freedom fighters, including Hetty Voûte and her friend Gisela Söhnlein, both of whom were imprisoned in Ravensbrück for their efforts to help their Jewish neighbors; Heiltje Kooistra, whose house became the scene of much secret activity; Clara Dijkstra, whose frightening encounters with the Nazis never dimmed her devotion to others in need; Janet Wolff, who helped to locate safe addresses for *Onderduikers* and delivered clandestine funds to the families of striking railway workers; and Mieke Vermeer, who dedicated herself to helping Jewish children find temporarily safer identity papers.

2. See Jared Diamond, "War Babies," *Discovery Magazine* (December 1970), 70–75.

20

Miracles of Survival

NIEUWKOOP WAS A SMALL village modeled on many others in the watery world of Western Holland. Its center stretched along the length of one of the thousands of dikes that kept our country from sinking into a swamp. The widespread farms and polders in the lands below the dike glistened in the light of the setting sun.

At the other side of the dike was a canal that at this point widened into a large natural lake used for fishing and boating. Along the length of the top of that dike, a neat row of stucco houses stood like sturdy guardians at the edge of the lake, facing the village street adjacent to the dike itself. In front of them flowed a small stream over which each owner had built a tiny bridge as white as a water lily, clean and picturesque, especially in twilight time. For me, coming as I had from a now ravaged city, this scene was like walking into a fairy tale.

Opposite the rows of houses and bridges, on the crest of the other side of the dike, a church tower pointed to the blue sky. It was one of the many houses of worship standing in the village greeting like sentinels the advent of another evening. That side, too, was ornamented by a long row of houses somewhat simpler in style. Between these rows, extending to the left and the right, was the center of the dike. It was the picturesque main street of the elongated village which was to be our hiding place. Not only were we enchanted by our new surroundings; we were also able to locate the young energetic priest from our community who was in touch with the underground in that region. He was able to lodge each of us with trustworthy citizens. In short order, I had my first encounters with other people fleeing our common enemy. The friendly villagers told us they would try to shelter as many city dwellers in danger as possible. My main duty would be to transport the food that was vital for their survival. It was in this village that I would start my underground journal, *Cor Unum et Anima Una* (See Appendix 3) and produce an ecumenical Christmas play (See Appendix 2). Every performance of *Christmas Night in Ravaged Holland* symbolized the plight of my people and encouraged them not to lose hope. Its imaginative portrayal of the principles by which we were called to live our Judeo-Christian heritage touched many hearts.

The longer I lived in the hay lofts of Nieuwkoop, the more I came to see the difference between *first evangelization* (bringing the Gospel to believers ready to receive it) and *first spiritualization* (helping sincere seekers to find the path to faith deepening and transformation of heart by evoking their awe disposition).

Before the Hunger Winter my formation in religious life occurred within the missionary community of the Spiritans where I and other members of my class were animated for the most part by the notion of *first evangelization*. We wanted to bring the message of the Gospel to those who had not heard it or who were alienated from its truths by the circumstances of their lives. Planting the seed of the word in soil such as this was the typical way we understood evangelization.

In pluritraditional western civilizations like our own that soil had become arid due, among other reasons, to the propagation of numerous formation traditions disconnected from the spiritual heritage we once took for granted. Within as little as the course of one generation, it seemed as if many believers had forgotten the seeds of faith it took our ancestors hundreds of years to cultivate. Non-Christians hiding with me begged for inner animation and answers to their recurrent, soul-searching questions. My Spiritan preparation made me think spontaneously about first evangelization, but I soon discovered how far away from it many were since they had lost not only their worldly goods but their awareness of the Sacred.

People in mission territories at least experienced in a pre-evangelical sense the awe disposition and the hunger for transcendence. The receptivity of their human spirit had not been paralyzed by pretranscendent individualism and the bent toward materialism it spawned. Their spirit had been nourished by the transcendent religious traditions passed on to them by their elders. Their inherent human spirituality had been awakened by a natural openness to the "More Than," kept alive by symbols, images, rituals, and customs.

This pre-Christian spirituality at least offered a point of contact with the Holy. It represented a potency for receptivity to any form of first evangelization. The apostles and the early followers of Jesus Christ enjoyed the same advantage among the Greeks and the Romans. My main concern was that even when the Nazis were defeated unilaterally, their death-dealing ideology, devoid of any sense of the Sacred, might remain in the lands they had ravaged.

What first had to be enkindled in the hearts of people this abandoned in spirit was their longing for the "More Than." No first evangelization in depth would be thinkable in our situation without a *prior* or a simultaneous *spiritualization*. People needed to be awakened by the grace of God to some reason to hope against hope. No merely human outlook on life could explain this need for conversion of heart. We had to begin with their experience of yearning for meaning if we were to fertilize the soil where the seeds of a first evangelization might be able to grow.

In that fateful year that reshaped my life, I had to grapple with more than the worrisome reality of physical hunger. I could not help but notice that my own and others' familiarity with the Gospel and the teachings of the Church, that is to say, our education in the doctrines of the faith, had addressed our need for catechetical information without equal concentration on how these truths could penetrate our hearts and uplift our spirits. Our longing for answers to life and death questions left us in a vacuum characterized by a lack of attention to the transcendent depth and experiential validity of the Gospel message. One fellow sufferer, who shared my faith tradition, confessed to me, "I know from memory the commandments to love God and neighbor, but these moral codes in and by themselves did not prepare me to cope with the horrors of this war. It feels as if I am at risk of losing my faith altogether." I thought to myself, "Here is an exemplary gentleman in need of first spiritualization. He has been, like most of us, informationally evangelized but what he needs—what all of us hunger for—is conversion of heart and a complementary spiritual formation."

An anxious premonition began to assail me. I wondered if Christianity in western Europe could survive in the post-war years or if numerous believers would experience the erosion and eventual depletion of their faith. In spite of all the informational evangelization they had received, would it be enough to awaken renewed zeal and fervor for the Gospel? The fact of famine, the piercing of the dikes that could drown us all, the loss of employment and free movement, of family and familiar surroundings, the threat of concentration camps and deportation threw many otherwise complacent Christians into a state of ego-desperation. The benefit of such crosses was that they brought some souls to a new threshold of receptivity to the transcendent and a first spiritualization of their life. For those among us who were already Christians, I could address this quest for meaning in terms of the renewal of the first evangelization that was ours by virtue of our baptism. What we knew so well through the catechism now began to touch us in a fresh way.

In both instances, among believers and sincere seekers, I felt the blossoming of a more profound life of prayer. In the desert of destruction we had to traverse daily, we sensed a power and a presence mere words could not explain. I personally felt consoled by the famous bookmark prayer of Saint Teresa of Avila, the words of which I felt the Holy Spirit etching on my heart:

> Let nothing disturb you
> let nothing frighten you.
> All things pass away:
> God never changes.
> Patience obtains all things.
> One who has God
> Finds one lacks for nothing.
> God alone suffices.

21

The Cosmic Epiphany

IN A COUNTRY RAVAGED by occupying forces, little of beauty remained. The bitterly cold winter of 1944 forced the Dutch to deface what was left of their once meticulously clean towns. Undernourishment had lowered the immunity of their already emaciated bodies. Exposure to the freezing weather hastened illness and death, especially among the frail and elderly. There was no coal, gas, or electricity. Yet fuel was needed to cook the tulip bulbs, sugar beets and other parcels of food one could acquire at great cost. Men, women, and children of all ages and walks of life crept through the parks and gardens of Nieuwkoop, looking for anything that could provide fuel for the wood-burning stoves they tried to improvise. Many dubbed these burners "miracle stoves" because they consisted of a grid over a small tin can placed in turn in a larger tin that seemed to produce the most heat with the smallest amount of tinder.

Due to the desperate cutting and slashing of trees, a massive deforestation of our country occurred. In as little as one night, rows of stately trees vanished from sight. For generations they had made Dutch streets a pleasure to behold. Smaller parks were cut to the ground. Wooden railings of bridges were torn off. In a few months 22,000 of Amsterdam's 42,000 trees disappeared. Soon the frostbitten, freezing people began to focus on the wooden slats between the tram rails as sources of fuel. Early in the morning or after sunset they would pry them loose to transport them home to heat their stoves.

News came to us that the inhabitants of the Jewish district in Amsterdam had been taken to extermination camps in Germany and Poland. Their houses stood empty and forlorn against the winter sky. They were silent witnesses to the tragic fate of their residents.[1] Condemned to death in the gas chambers, they would never return to these once homey dwellings. The bitter logic of survival compelled those who were left behind to take what they could carry off to burn as a defense against the bone-chilling winter air. Every piece of wood from 1,500 abandoned houses in the Jewish district disappeared as a result of exhausting feats of sawing and hacking. The frames of doors and windows, the beams of floors and ceilings, whole staircases were smashed into kindling. Other homes that stood empty and buildings that would soon collapse were cut into pieces that could be burned. Bombed out neighborhoods, once so bright and attractive, lay devastated, dark, and dreary. Many amateur wreckers were killed or maimed under falling debris. People even began to remove the supporting beams of air-raid shelters, which caved in as quickly as did these empty wrecked houses.

The population of Rotterdam in a frantic search for fuel made another discovery. Most of their town squares were laid on a foundation of slag. Digging into the slag, they realized that pieces of real coal were mixed with it. Many squares of the city soon resembled strip mines.

All of this devastation, combined with the wanton destruction wrought by enemy occupation, spawned a decayed, desolate, filthy environment harboring more serious threats. Rats infested houses. Lice multiplied on weakened bodies of once fastidious people who had no soap left to clean themselves. I often had to beg farming families, who were relatively unaware of the plight in the cities, to let these poor people into their homes. They were horrified by the lice they brought with them.

Having been barricaded by the army with heavy concrete fortifications, many city roads were now impassable, Shelters, barbed wire, and trenches defiled public parks and towns once famous for their cleanliness. Bedraggled children dug through putrid hills of garbage seeking any edible scrap. Canals crossing the towns had become foul-smelling and nauseating with filth of every kind floating and foaming on the surface of their waters. At night the streets were dark as tombs because of the strictly enforced blackout against air raids. Leaving a candle-lit home, blinded by the pitch dark street, one could easily step into a polluted city canal in front of one's house, risking a contagious disease like diphtheria.

One of its early victims was Doctor William Drees, later the Dutch Prime Minister but then a leader in the resistance. At night coming out of a meeting he walked straight into the water. Though saved by a bridge guard, he contracted the disease. Slowly recuperating at home, he used his time to write a plan of restoration of the country after the war. He noted that to envision the future was the only way to transcend the gross reality of the present moment and to find some meaning in it.

On as regular a basis as possible, I rode an old borrowed bicycle back and forth from the farms to the city. I transported whatever food I had collected and distributed it to the most needy. I made every effort to cheer up persecuted acquaintances of mine who were still hiding in this decaying city. I prepared them for their flight into the countryside once I found a safe place for them. Every time I returned sad and fatigued to Nieuwkoop, I experienced a terrifying backlash. Slowly I climbed the ladder to my tiny hayloft in the stable above the cows. I fell exhausted on the old mattress overwhelmed by grief and despondency. Being a poet at heart, the loss of beauty gripped me more than it might have other sufferers. The only way I could process these encounters with "man's inhumanity to man" was to write my wartime poetry [See Appendix 1]. The plight of famined city dwellers filled me with horror. I was powerless to ease their pain. The bleakness of the days spreading before us was like a blanket of fog that would never lift.

The rape of the environment affected my mood in a most disturbing way. How deeply I loved the Creator's first revelation in trees and flowers, sparkling streams and flowing rivers, well-kept houses, neat streets and gardens. I had walked the earth in awe of the mystery of the unfolding cosmos manifested in all of these jewels of nature. For years I had journaled and written poems to celebrate the wonder of it all.

Now the despoilment and desolation struck me with a piercing pain. Welling up from the depths of my being was a new sense of responsibility for nature and the environment. I renewed my humble adoration of the cosmic epiphany as manifesting the Radical Mystery of creation. The face of God seemed veiled from view during these awful days, but, by the dispensation of divine grace, I began to rise above my depression. I told myself to redirect my attention to any fragment of beauty my weary eyes might behold. I must not let my heart be buried by the ruination caused by the war. I had to keep on believing in the promise of a better tomorrow.2

Around that time I scribbled pages of notes about awe for the beauty of the wider world, about ecological concern for our surroundings, about the miracles of human survival. In my ruminations I began to see our life as a formation field (*vorming veld*), which both included and pointed to every manifestation of the cosmic mystery. I began to diagram this field, giving the central place to the Radical Mystery (*radicaal vorming mysterie*) or the Divine Forming and Preforming Mystery, which is the wellspring of our inner, inter-relational, and immediately situated life.

With this new paradigm in mind, I had a better basis for our discussions about circumstances that might be beyond our control but that were still part of our formation field. Young and idealistic as all of us were, we felt we could help humanity leave behind its individualistic bent and give priority instead to our interconnections with one another. Wherever we went, we witnessed how lack of concern for the environment paralyzes awe and wonder. Controlling minds and wills corrupted by the quest for absolute power only value what they can utilize, organize, measure, and quantify for their own purposes. By contrast, the new paradigm of formation I began to devise would be of benefit to everyone. It would assure that every person would be addressed respectfully as a being of unique worth and dignity. I envisioned this dance of interforming harmony as having been ordained by the Most High from all eternity. It was our special prerogative as messengers of the mystery to love humanity and history as sacred gifts, not as objects of ruthless exploitation.

The destruction we lived through was proof enough that the cosmos must no longer be perceived as if it were a machine submissive to human control. Far from being a collection of isolated forms, our world is a magnificent network of relationships. Within this tapestry of interweaving forms, each person, event, and thing in its uniqueness can be seen as related to the transcendent love-will hidden in our soul and holding in being all that is. Despite the seeming triumph of evil trumpeted by the enemy, there was no reason to doubt our human and cosmic significance nor to question our belief in the Spirit's renewal of the face of the earth.

The love we experienced in this village would, for the rest of our lives, inspire us to reach out to the underprivileged, the marginalized, the sick and the poor. Our brothers and sisters are the homeless, the aging, the handicapped, and those suffering from any kind of deprivation. We are bound together by the mystery of transforming love. We are not only in pursuit of sheer survival but also of the purpose for living.

There was no other way for us to remain distinctively human in a world that had been so dehumanized socially and ecologically than by fostering the rebirth of faith, hope, and charity in every soul. The reality of our becoming more interdependent increased with each passing day. Holland might be a small country geographically, but the lessons we learned in this fateful hour had implications for the survival of the world.

Notes

1. Henri van der Zee reports in detail on the atrocities committed against the Jews, 60,000 of whom were sent from Holland to Auschwitz with a survival rate of only 500. During the Hunger Winter itself, many Jewish people were betrayed or starved to death. Of the 25,000 Jews still alive in 1944, more than 15,000 disappeared before the end of the war. By January of 1945, on the orders of Seyss-Inquart, everything was permitted to help the German war effort. The Reichskommissar announced cold-heartedly: "We shall hit the Jews wherever we find them and those who side with them will bear the consequences."

2. Hetty Voûte, whose story is told by Mark Klempner in *The Heart Has Reasons*, shares a poem by Bokaro Overstreet that expressed well how she felt from the earliest days of German occupation of the Netherlands (21):

You say the little efforts I make
will do no good: they never will prevail
to tip the hovering scale
where Justice hangs in balance.

I don't think
I ever thought they would.
But I am prejudiced beyond debate
in favor of my right to choose which side
shall feel the stubborn ounces of my weight.

22

Clandestine Drama of Christmastide in Conquered Holland

As December approached, we did all that we could to guard our hearts from losing hope due to the horrors of the war.1 One service I realized I could render my companions was to devise an entertainment to take their minds off so much misery. I decided to write and produce a play titled "Christmas Night in Ravaged Holland" [See Appendix 2]. On the inside cover page of the Dutch edition, I described it as "*a brief production, depicting the celebration of the birth of Jesus Christ under the oppression of foreign subjugation, for the people of Nieuwkoop, its villagers and farmers.*" I based this drama on what I saw as the starting point of all formation—our actual field of presence and action. I chose to tell the story of the Nativity not as a long-ago happening but as a narrative unfolding in the sociohistorical setting of the people of Nieuwkoop.

In the seven clandestine performances I directed, Mary and Joseph were portrayed as reenacting their search for a place to stay in our village. Like us, they, too, were in need of food and shelter. Mary's part was to recreate that winter night in Bethlehem as if it were today. She lamented the sad times we were living through in the light of her own treatment by foreign hands, saying at the start of the play in one of my working drafts:

> *How well I remember, Joseph, that night in Bethlehem long ago,*
> *so like this winter night of wailing woe*
> *in this watery land as oppressed by a foreign hand*
> *as was Israel in our time,*
> *when waves of kinsfolk streamed*
> *through town and countryside*
> *to obey a count of families commanded far and wide.*

> Here, too, we do not find a hiding place of love and light.
> People wander with wounded feet over snow-filled roads
> and streets to find some food and rest, to be welcome guests,
> to forget their plight this holy night.

Verses spoken alternately by Mary and Joseph express the sacred reciprocity that exists between two people who live in appreciative abandonment to whatever the mystery asks of them. Our need to remain open to the world beyond ourselves cannot be forgotten either. I wanted to signify this point by composing Mary's prayer of praise for universe and humanity and the forming mystery at the center of all that is:

> Adore him, moon in heaven, twinkling stars,
> praise him wide and silent polders,
> exalt him glimmering ditches, gray and mighty water ways.
> Windmills of this windy land bow down
> for the wonder springing up within me.
> Cattle, lowing sadly in stables of lonely farms,
> forlorn in low and frozen lands,
> your power to warm our weary bones
> given to you by the Source of life enthroned in me.

After decrying a farmers' refusal to give them shelter, the wife of the skipper of a barge moored on the lake walks ashore and spots them on the empty road after curfew times when it was forbidden for any non-military person to be out in public. Curious and concerned, this ragged woman looks at them in the light of the ship's lantern she holds in her upraised hand and says:

> Why so late on this dark and empty road on Christmas night, far
> beyond the curfew time set for us in this forsaken land? What do
> you expect? We're pressed under the iron hands of brute assailers?
> Rumors of razzias tonight, yes, yes! Watch out for danger.

Then Joseph takes the lead and confides in the woman that Mary is expecting her first child to which the woman answers with compassion:

> Perhaps I know a place for both of you.
> Homelike it is not, an old, battered boat,
> wet and cold, machine gunned through and through
> from the air a month ago.
> See on the water there, it
> bobs aimlessly moored at the empty shore,
> no door, full of holes, little wood is left,

> *bereft by those who sought fuel for their freezing homes.*
> *Inside you will find some stones to sit on while you wait:*
> *Go fast before it is too late!*

Through these imaginative encounters, I tried to show the Dutch sense of *"onderlinge"* or *"wederzijdse vorming,"* meaning "mutual and reciprocal formation" or "interformation." It can occur whether we know one another as friends and acquaintances or happen to be thrown together unexpectedly as lots of us were in this farming and fishing village. The play stressed this point not only for performance purposes but also because I hoped that after the war this sense of interrelatedness would unlock hardened hearts and help us to foster peace. I tried to portray the centrality of relationships in several symbolic scenes.

After Mary and Joseph board the battered boat, the road leading to it stands empty for a moment. Then four men appear on it, agitated and in a hurry. The first is an Italian, a deserter from his own troops, who offers token assistance to the Dutch resistance. The second is a Scot, who parachuted to safety after his plane was shot down. The third is a Bavarian from Germany, who has also left his fighting unit. The fourth is a Russian, who escaped from a prisoner-of-war camp. They talk clandestinely about the war, the horrors they've seen, their personal pain, and their yearning for a peaceful end to it all. They tell each other in both religious and secular terms what Christmas meant to them at home. The verses featuring their conversations record their growth in mutual trust, which changes their outlook and expands their hope of finding more understanding among themselves and the battling people they represent. Finally, the men ask the Italian, whose faith seems strongest, to offer a prayer all four of them can say:

> *Child of Bethlehem, we welcome you once again on this chilly night,*
> *we four simple men waiting for your light.*
> *Thank you for hiding as a child in a foreign land*
> *where you were banned as we are here,*
> *homesick and in misery as you may understand.*
> *Please make our people friends again*
> *as we are now bonding on this cold and empty road,*
> *no longer carrying alone the load*
> *that burdens our aching hearts.*

> *Take care of our families at home.*
> *They cry this night because they are alone.*
> *Wash away their tears with your little hands.*
> *The wife and kids of Heinrich here, all that was dear,*
> *have been destroyed by fire from the sky.*
> *We cannot know the mystery of the why,*
> *no matter how hard we try,*
> *but please console them in your heaven, dear Child.*

The characters on stage now begin to communicate their awakening to a still deeper region of transcendence. The four men have fallen asleep under a few rough blankets they had in their knapsacks. Suddenly the song of angels fills the air. Alarmed the men wake up. The Russian cries out: "What's happening? A round up?" The Bavarian shouts, "Don't tell me the sky is filled with bombers again?" In hushed tones, an angel appears to them, saying:

> *Be not afraid. I am the angel of gladsome tidings*
> *for people who want peace and harmony*
> *while fighting grimly with an enemy outnumbering them.*
> *Born is the Child that alone can silence*
> *the blasting of your bombs and guns*
> *and dry the blood that drenches the reluctant earth,*
> *the Child who loves all tenderly, especially those*
> *who find no pity for their woes of famine and misery.*
> *The Prince of Peace is born again in a bombed out little boat.*
> *You will find him numbed by cold,*
> *wrapped in pieces of old and scanty cloth.*

The four meet the Child, his mother and Joseph on the old barge. They speak to him, each in their own way, offering him a gift. The Bavarian gives the baby Jesus his dagger; the Italian offers a song which he sings with a Southern flourish; the Russian sacrifices his half-filled Vodka bottle; the Scot plays his flute. At the side of the stage is a set depicting the farm house whose inhabitants refused Mary and Joseph a place to stay. The farmer's wife opens the door, surprised by the light and the singing in the sky. The angel appears with the news.

> *The Child is here again. Tell town and polder land,*
> *bring villagers and farmers round the little Prince of Peace*
> *like a band of harmony begging for release*
> *from blunt indifference for those who suffer.*

Down the darkened aisles of the theater come other players representing the people we all knew—farmers and skippers with their wives, workmen from the mines, an office boy, clerks, merchants and other villagers, among them children. Moving words are spoken between these people and Mary. She tells them how it hurts the Child, who came for all, if they refuse to help those in need.

The play ends with a chorus of voices, expressing with heartfelt sincerity their longing for justice, peace, and mercy:

> *Hear us, Child of Mary, Prince of Peace,*
> *Sufferer of famine along the roads and streets.*
> *You shall no longer remain*
> *a stranger to our heart and land.*
> *Our compassion will welcome the worn out beggar;*
> *we shall revere the starving woman who carries her child;*
> *gentle we shall be with the prisoner who escaped,*
> *the lonely stranger shall share in what is left to us;*
> *those who lost bed or dress shall partake of ours.*
>
> *Hide us, Child, from the fire from the sky.*
> *Let planes and bombs not wreck our homes.*
> *Preserve the domes and spires of our churches.*
> *Spare our brothers and sisters in foreign lands.*
> *Save families from mutilation in the night,*
> *shattering their sleep when evening falls ominously.*
>
> *Let famine not hollow us out and consume our lives.*
> *Let despair not devour our spirit of hope and strength.*
> *Do not allow dikes to collapse, turning this fertile land*
> *into a deadly sea, our lustrous fields into sterile swamps.*
> *Put out the blaze of bitterness engulfing our souls.*
> *Uproot the poison of resentment, the venom of envy,*
> *the mad pain of the small advantage of others over us*
> *in this somber night of dark distress. Let us do with less,*
> *not be callous and merciless, steeped in avarice.*
> *Never allow this people to be splintered by pettiness*
> *into sawdust scattered by the wind.*
> *Instead turn us into a strong, a noble people,*
> *a new nation deeply resolved*
> *to restore to beauty what sadly is defiled*
> *in this hour of bereavement.*

To their pleas, Mary answers:

If people with hand and heart entwined
combine vows and prayers before the Child,
their mind will be less barren, their mood less wild,
their heart more mild.
Carry fruits of compassion to this crucified land;
lend everywhere a helping hand.

Many viewers had tears in their eyes as the curtain closed. Applause had to be subdued so they left the makeshift theater in silence. Our audiences represented many different faith and formation traditions. Even those who had no theological know-how were enthusiastic about the performance. They came from far and wide, under the cover of darkness as word of the play spread. Public performances without miliary authorization were forbidden, but faithful sentinels on the roads stood guard to warn us if any Nazi collaborators were nearing the theater so we could stop the action, disperse the actors, and hide in time.

Shortly after Christmas, a printer in the village, Meister Middlekoop, a devoted member of the Dutch Reformed Church, risked publishing the play. The shortage of paper forced him to use low grade materials. To gain space, he asked me to rewrite the stanzas of my verses as prose texts instead of lining them up in poetic fashion. Prior to its being printed, people secretly spread handwritten or typed copies to whoever wanted them. Thanks be to God, no one involved in this clandestine endeavor was ever caught. During my life I have been blessed with the publication of many books on fine paper with exquisite covers, but to this day I treasure my faded copy of this clandestine Christmas play. I hear in the echo chambers of my memory its perennial plea that we live in a spirit of compassion for vulnerable people everywhere.2

Notes

1. Particularly poignant was Queen Wilhelmina's Christmas broadcast for Radio Oranje to her occupied subjects. As the personification of the enslaved and struggling Netherlands, she understood that "Christmas was a feast of promise" but that this promise could this year point only to the unfathomable and consoling love of Christ for all who suffer as the Dutch did.

2. The Dutch historian, Henri van der Zee, who lived through the Hunger Winter, recalls in his memoirs how short-lived the memory and practice of compassion can be. He notes that the flood of German and Austrian children in 1918 (during the First World War) came to Holland and were grateful for the good food they got there. Then they enjoyed Dutch hospitality and kindness. And yet now, in the Hunger Winter, these same children were helping to starve out and destroy the provinces in which they were once guests.

23

In Hiding, Open to Our Inmost Call

CHRISTMAS, ONE OF THE most anticipated days on the Dutch or any calendar, finally arrived.1 It was quite a challenge to keep a cheery mood. We felt more acutely than ever the lack of traditional goods. The only sweet we could find was a kind of artificial cream called "klop-op" or "beat-up." It was a little piece of foam made from sugar beets. We had to eat it fast without pausing. Otherwise it would melt into a yellow puddle distasteful to behold. How homesick we were for our pre-war coffee, candy, tobacco, and liquor!

Since 1943, the only tobacco obtainable was *Beka*, a product that was so bad it became commonplace to say that it stood for "*Beslist Eerst Klas Afval*" ("Certified First-Class Garbage"). Homemade cigarettes were sold under the name *Consi*. Some claimed that this title for the gruesome weed was an abbreviation of the witty words, "Cigarettes Under National Socialist Influence."

The Dutch Bible Society had for years sold texts of Holy Scripture printed on thin yet strong India paper. The last year of the war their sales soared. Initially, publishers rejoiced about this renewed spirit of Dutch piety. Under the pressure of war and famine, it looked as if countless seekers finally saw the light. To their dismay they discovered that the pages of these bibles were a source of income for people making money on the black market, selling them in batches at inflated prices as "outstanding India cigarette paper." Before the war, other wrappers had cost about eighteen cents for a hundred. Now the price was triple that! As suddenly as these Bibles had rolled off the presses, the Association stopped the sale of their precious product!

Christmas dinner that year was nothing to get excited about either. The ration from December 17 to 23, 1944, was one kilogram of potatoes for the whole week. The same applied to bread and meat, provided these were available, which was often not the case. In the last weeks before Christmas, the overall situation of the war worsened. The Battle of the Bulge was finally won by the Allied forces. For us this victory meant that the end of the war and the liberation of the West and North of Holland would have to be deferred again. The Wehrmacht turned to fighting Allied troops in the Ardennes in Belgium. On December 24, the Nazis gave us their Christmas Eve surprise. More Dutchmen were needed to build up German defenses. Posters signed by their representatives announced this measure in all towns and villages. Men between the ages of 16 and 40 would be conscripted to work for their forces. These same hated posters were swiftly overlaid with warnings from the underground. They asked all Dutchmen to reject this announcement in principle. The posters promised abundant food for the famined families of the men who fell into this trap, but that was a lie.

On Christmas Day of that fateful year, we streamed into our bitterly cold churches, hungry in body and starving in spirit. We joined in the pleas for prayer issued by leaders of the Roman Catholic and Protestant churches. In their sermons they told us the truth about the sufferings of 4.5 million people in the western part of our country, many of whom were perishing this day due to slow and painful starvation. Their reports were published in various letters from the pulpit, followed by a whole series in defense of the Jewish people and other refugees. A German historian would later write that churches in Holland offered the most "pervasive and widely influential opposition to Nazi ideology." From the beginning of the occupation to its end, their representatives stood up courageously for Christianity and for humanity. In revenge, many priests, ministers, religious, and lay Christians were sent to concentration camps, following in the footsteps of the Jewish people they had defended so valiantly.[2]

We felt beaten, bullied, and forgotten. Yet the smaller we shrank bodily, the stronger became our conviction that the flames of war would not destroy our faith. To survive this time of transition and to follow the lead of grace into a new springtime of the spirit after the war, we had to pass through the test of this endless winter. As long as the ground of our lives was watered by the rain of our age-old traditions, we did not need to fear the present conflagration.

The sacred refrains I heard in my heart when the noise of war made outer silence impossible came mainly from the Bible. A favorite of mine from Psalm 46:10 was *Be still and know that I am God.* As I whispered these words, I became quiet enough within to hear the Lord's soft but steady confirmation of my calling. It was as if my human spirit were being sustained and nourished by the Holy Spirit. I cannot explain these moments of profound peace amidst chaos from the viewpoint of analytical reason. They were more like leaps of faith that allowed me to dream about a tomorrow that seemed out of my reach and to make plans for a future still veiled from view. These tidings of the transcendent emanated from a higher plane of reality.

The more I listened to the gentle whispers of the Spirit, the more sure I felt that an invisible mystery of formation guides every phase of our life. My forced confinement in the countryside made it easier for me to still my mind and to allow the wisdom of my inmost call to well up in silence and solitude. A main condition for listening to its message was to diminish my anxious preoccupation with the terrible tragedy that might befall us. I had to rise above the negative voices of doubt and depreciation competing with the divine directives I received so gratuitously.

As long as I tried to follow what I heard inwardly, I detected at times inexplicable feelings of happiness. Amidst the desert of ego-desperation, I would be inundated, beyond any sense of vital gratification or functional satisfaction, with waves of transcendent joy. It was as if I were in the embrace of an all-pervading love that made full stomachs or reports of success of secondary importance. Such experiences come and go capriciously but joy of this kind is a constant companion. It changes our focus from the evil around us to the goodness within us.

Every time I returned to such meditations, a sense of relief swept over me. It did not exclude the admission that I felt terribly fatigued and at times disappointed in myself due to my all too human inclinations to self-pity and impatience. To confess to being a sinner before God heightened my resolve to focus on divine mercy and to show more compassion for those suffering around me. This focus saved me from anxious self-reliance and placed control of my destiny where it belonged—in God's hands.

Notes

1. Clara Dijkstra relates to Mark Klempner in *The Heart Has Reasons* (92–93) her memory of *Sinterklaas* in the Netherlands during this bleakest of times: "... everything is supposed to be fun. But we were all poor, hungry, and unhappy. No one even remembered that it was *Sinterklaas*. An icy wind was blowing, but I went out for a walk. I crossed a field where a freight train had stopped ... what do you think I saw? Apples, potatoes, and onions!" Clara took a chance, stuffed her bag full of produce, and headed home. It was as if she herself had become a reincarnation of old Saint Nicholas! She went from door to door in her neighborhood inviting all the hollow-eyed waifs to her apartment for a *Sinterklaas* party. What little she had was what she chose to share.

2. Among them were Dietrich Bonhoeffer, Maximillian Kolbe, and Edith Stein, to mention only a few of these martyrs. See also Franz Jägerstätter, *Letters and Writings from Prison*. Trans. Robert A. Krieg. Edited by Erna Putz (Maryknoll, NY: Orbis Books, 2009). Having refused conscription in the Nazi Army, this Austrian Catholic farmer and martyr was killed by guillotine at Tegel prison where Bonhoeffer was also held until his execution in 1945.

24

Quest for Wisdom in Wild Times

MOUNTING THREATS FOR THEIR safety forced me to bring my sisters from the city to the country. I had already arranged for the police officer who had deserted his military unit to go into hiding in the farmlands around Alphen Aan De Rijn, a larger town not far from the village of Nieuwkoop. Now I had to see about my parents. It was not easy to move them from The Hague nor to convince them of the danger they faced due to hiding the young man they had befriended, but an incident had shaken my father to the core and made him change his mind. He had gone with this man, who was dressed in his old police uniform and who carried with him his gun and false identification papers, to deliver food to a family some farmers knew. A soldier stopped them to check their papers. My father looked aside at Cor, who put his hand in his pocket, ready to draw his gun and fire if the soldier threatened them. They stood there, realizing in terror how close they were to his old command post. The soldier's comrades in arms would have come to the guard-post with drawn guns, felling both men before they could run for their lives. Thank God, the soldier let them go. This fright convinced my father to give the go-ahead to my plan.

To bring my mother around was much harder. For months she had taken care of the young fighter as if he were her own son. She could not stand to give him over to such a risky future. I felt that I had to be brutally decisive since her own life was at stake. To lessen the danger for both of my parents, I had to put my foot down. I told mother that I would stick to my plan no matter what. It was well before dawn when this "second son" got ready to depart. My mother came downstairs, sobbing softly. The flicker of sputtering candles threw weird shadows on the walls around us. She talked to me with the sad voice of a woman disappointed in her child: "You seem to have all the answers, and we have no say."

In ordinary times I would never have driven my parents to do anything against their will. I felt caught between my duty to defend and protect their lives and my desire to please and honor them. The tough love I had to exercise broke my heart. Walking out of the house with Cor into the dirty snow blowing around the dark and deserted streets, tears filled me eyes. The war not only left our country in splinters; it split every family apart. My feet felt like lead. Slowly I pushed myself out of the house, shaken by having to harden my heart, but I had no choice. I had to find this good fellow another hiding place.

As it turned out, my sense that Cor was a bit trigger happy proved to be true. One day he came to my hayloft flushed with excitement. On a road along the dike where he had been riding his bike, he was halted by a policeman who ordered him to show him his papers. The officer put them in his pocket and moved to arrest Cor, who pulled out his gun, shot the man to death, and then pushed his body into the ditch. The sound of gunfire brought people rushing from their houses so he had to pedal away as fast as he could. In a flash he realized that his papers were still in the coat pocket of the police officer—a dead giveaway! He turned around, shook his gun at the curious on-lookers to drive them away, lifted the corpse, and pocketed his own papers. Then he sped off again.

When he broke this news to me I shook my head in dismay. I respected human life, my own and others, at all cost, but I could not condemn Cor, who had decided to shoot another person in self-defense. Similar incidences affected the decisions and actions of many fighters. Raids on German depots to get food for the famined was a regular occurrence. At times it was necessary for resistance fighters to hold the guards at gunpoint and, if necessary, to kill or be killed. A few days later, in as empathetic a way as possible, I felt obliged to speak with Cor and other resistance fighters and to remind them of their religious upbringing, not to question their choices under the strain of war, but to suggest that what they had learned at home and in school about Christian doctrine ought not to be forgotten—not even in the dangerous situations in which they found themselves. Often they reacted to the heat of the moment without any reflection until after the event. They had to admit that faith, reduced to an abstract list of do's and don't's, was not enough to sustain them in the dire circumstances in which they found themselves. With a flush of embarrassment they admitted that the slogans they read in patriotic books or the songs they heard over the radio were what influenced them the most. They never bothered to discern which of these popular directives upheld and which betrayed their own traditions. They did what they had to do as fighters for a good cause and suppressed their emotions in the process. Our conversations became a time to vent their misgivings and to look at their behavior from a faith perspective.

In challenging Cor to reconsider his actions and not to make snap judgments unless he had to do so under extreme duress, I knew, wild as these times were, that we had to exercise the wisdom of compassion. The distance between love and hate could shrink in a flash without the compass of faith to guide our wayward hearts. It felt good to be able to talk with one another about these matters and their relevance to our quest for peace in a beleaguered country. If we were to hold our heads high above the horizon of the evil inflicted upon us, we had to resist the temptation to succumb to its dehumanizing tactics. It was our duty to fight without losing faith. Lacking that intention, we risked becoming inundated by an ideology contrary to the Gospel that showed little or no respect for life. My greatest fear was that we might defeat the enemy militaristically while underestimating the power of Nazi propaganda that seeped like silent poison into the whole of Europe. To remain naive in this regard would be the worst mistake we could make.

25

One Heart and One Soul

As the Hunger Winter wore on in a relentless manner, over one hundred priests, seminarians, and brothers of my community were cast into a diaspora not of their own choosing in the still occupied provinces of Holland. There had to be a way for us to stay in touch with one another and to do something to bolster our spirits. It was forbidden to start any publication without the explicit authorization of the Nazis, who had suppressed all journals except those spreading their own lies. I decided to take the risk of bypassing this ruling and to begin an underground journal designated as a "bulletin." In it we would ostensibly share only news from the Spiritans and offer each other words of encouragement. In truth, I hoped as editor to address the spiritual needs of readers wherever they were.

My religious community had chosen for its motto the scripture text *Cor Unum et Anima Una*. In the Acts of the Apostles we read that the community of believers were of "one heart and one soul" (Acts 4:32). This was the ideal name for the "bulletin" since its title would already be recognized by my confrères and anyone else this publication might serve. This motto tied in well with my understanding of transcendent formation in which the soul is the form-giving principle of the unique-communal life call meant for us by God from all eternity. We do not know at once where this call will lead us, but in our heart we know we must be faithful to it. Our life takes on new purpose and meaning as we come to experience the directives flowing from our call and begin to walk in its light.

I hoped that the "bulletin" would give my brothers a forum to speak from their hearts about their experiences and the thoughts and feelings thus evoked. How had these disruptive times transformed their sense of mission and ministry? I would encourage them in my editorials [See

Appendix 3] to tell of the generosity extended to them by friends and strangers who shared their torment. I began this project by contacting other seminarians from the same region. The youngest among them were especially eager to deliver every issue. Before I knew it, *Cor Unum et Anima Una* (CUAU) became popular among people who were not seminarians. This success was a mixed blessing since it placed us in even more danger. If the secret police found out about this endeavor, everyone connected with it could be arrested and subsequently "removed."

In my editorials, I stressed the need to uphold human dignity at all costs, an idea considered to be subversive in the climate of the day. My main concern was to raise enough money to cover the expense of printing and distribution. Thanks to the intervention of Holy Providence, it so happened that in the German army itself there were health officers and male ambulance nurses, who had been taught by priests from our congregation's province in Germany. Despite their public positions, they decided secretly to befriend us. They gave up part of their salary to help fund CUAU. It was ironic that the "enemy" without knowing it, contributed to paying for our illegal publication.

The date for the first issue was to be February 2, 1945, the feast of the Presentation of Jesus in the Temple and of our Venerable founder, Francis Libermann. It was around that time, on February 13 to be exact, that the Dutch resistance sent a telegram to London saying: "We shall hold out." After a first stenciled edition of the "bulletin," I turned to our courageous Protestant printer in Nieuwkoop, Mister Middlekoop, who, with two employees, took the risk to print it on a weekly basis. The first edition began with words to this effect:

> *Dear confrères: In our beloved community in Gemert, we had the forum of our student society (SOOS) to share with one another our personal interests and to bring to light our spiritual inspirations. We knew the value of those special occasions during which we could express our common thoughts and feelings. Our student society was a fine setting for continual contact, but all that has been taken away from us. Still the need and the desire for these exchanges, especially over the past few months, has been elevated to a greater intensity than we could ever have envisioned in our quiet, more or less enclosed community life.*

The motto, "one heart and one soul" manifested the hope that we might be able, with God's help, to overcome our differences by coming together in that place of grace where unity can be found amidst diversity and equality in dignity is the rule. Only in the light of these Christian formation ideals may the rivers of blood shed by Jewish people and Muslims, by socialists and humanists, by Protestants and Catholics, by city dwellers and farmers not run in vain. We had no choice but to address each other respectfully from the heart. Over and above the babel of tongues that divided us, we pledged to find a way of communicating that went beyond the limits of one or the other religious or ideological tradition. Had we insulated ourselves in our own parlance only, we could not have moved the heart and soul of people with such different backgrounds. By virtue of the pluritraditional situation in which we found ourselves, we had to craft a language so linked to human experience that all could resonate with it. We could come to appreciate, despite our diversity, how much we had in common. Rather than use words that might pull us apart, we tried to find those that would bring us closer together.

Before saying or writing anything, we first had to learn to listen to one another. True listening gives us a chance to break through our own traditional slant of thought and to respect where others are on their journey. We learned to forestall what came first to our minds and to attend to what those around us had to say. On the tightrope of terror on which we all had to walk, we returned to our own traditions to see what they had to tell us about what was good and harmonious in human nature as graced by God. This practice of *returning* to the sources and *reiterating* (*herhaling*) what they meant encouraged us to defer to what someone else was trying to say. Only after we had listened did we begin to speak. Listening in awe-filled abiding and attention helped us to apprehend, appraise, and affirm the meaning behind once unfamiliar expressions. We were then able to appreciate the experiences of life to which they pointed.

One master of the Christian tradition of great inspiration to me was Saint Gregory of Nyssa. In reflecting on the beatitude, *Blessed are the pure of heart, for they shall see God,* he said that "this saying teaches us that the person who cleanses his heart of every created thing and every evil desire will see the image of the divine nature in the beauty of his own soul." The soul, as seen by Gregory, carries already the beautiful image or form of the divine nature. This transcendent image can only touch the core of our life if we cleanse it of evil desires and deeds. There is a difference, Gregory says, between our soul and our heart. We cannot pretend that we own our soul and all that it holds because it is God's treasure, given to us. The beautiful form of the Divine is already in us by virtue of grace. This image is our founding life form with its mysterious directive to live in the light of our hidden beauty, of our inmost nobility. "Heart" symbolizes the core or center of our life. God's form in our soul touches our heart, provided we drop our attachment to any created thing as ultimate. As Gregory puts it:

> If by a diligent life of virtue you wash away the film of dirt that covers your heart, the divine beauty will shine forth in you. Take a piece of iron as an illustration. Although it might have been black before, once the rust has been scraped off with a whetstone, it will begin to shine brilliantly and to reflect the rays of the sun. So it is with the interior man, which is what the Lord means by the heart. Once a man removes from his soul the coating of filth that has formed on it through sinful neglect, he will regain the likeness to his Archetype, and be good. For what resembles the supreme Good is itself good. If he then looks into himself, he will see the vision he has longed for. This is the blessedness of the pure of heart: in seeing their own purity they see the divine Archetype mirrored in themselves... You will find what you seek within yourself, provided you return to the beauty and grace of that image [or form] which was originally placed in you.

In writing my editorials for CUAU, I strove to translate the wisdom in this and other classical texts, many of which I found in my breviary, into a language that would make sense also to non-Christians. They, too, felt the lack of transcendent transformation in their lives. Their interest in going beyond the dynamics of human development led to my formulation of a theory of personality rooted in this paradigm of the soul-form as the essence of our existence. It is that in us which has been preformed by the Divine Forming Mystery. This founding life form embodies itself in our actual existence through our heart or core form and its matching character. The soul in its forming activity in our spirit, heart, mind, and will invites us to let go of our ultimate attachments to anything pretranscendent. The lasting dispositions of our heart like candor and courage can then reflect the beauty and grace of our soul-form and its expression in our unique-communal life call. In the measure that we give form to the gifts of grace we have received, we become "one heart and one soul" whether God invites us to walk hand in hand on the arid soil of war or the fertile ground of peace.

26

Blessed Calamity

As soon as the first issue of *Cor Unum et Anima Una* was ready, I sent it to every interested reader I could find. I asked them to give me the addresses of other confrères and to duplicate for them the issues they had received. We had no idea how long the war would last or if it would "divide and conquer" more of the Netherlands. Before anything worse happened, I wanted to be sure that as many readers as possible had this first sign of contact in their hands.

Confiscation of the journal by the Nazis or the imprisonment of the editor and printer remained an ever-present threat. To lessen this danger I found some students who were willing to deliver the papers on foot and by bike to central points. There others could distribute them more widely and thereby lessen the risk that they would fall into the wrong hands.

Once I had a real scare. One of our bikers pedaled with a pack of issues toward the territory behind the river Ijssel. Since he had to go to that region anyway to gather food from friendly farmers, I asked him to organize delivery to that part of the country. He stuffed the journals in one of his knapsacks, happy to give others, in his words, "bread for the body and letters for the soul." A few weeks later I got a frantic call from him saying that he had lost that very bag and its contents near the river.

Imagine what might happen if it were picked up by the Nazis! What would become of me and our printer or, for that matter, anyone else associated with CUAU? I was especially concerned for the German members of my congregation. In the spirit of "one heart and one soul," we had contacted them in spite of the war going on between our country and theirs. Though some of them had been conscripted by the occupying forces to perform a variety of works, they were eager to read these publications secretly, even taking the risk to send us support funds from their allowance.

One of them, Father Lud Naarmann, served in a German military hospital in Delft. The other was a German Spiritan, a theology student, working in Laag-Soeren near the border of the occupied territory that had already been liberated by the Allied forces. It was impossible to reach Spiritans there any longer, but I took the chance to send him an issue, assuming that he was not in Allied captivity. The German Security Service could most likely no longer get to him, even if they discovered his name in our paper. My anxiety lessened about the lost delivery when I received a letter from Meintje Swart in Winschoten, a town located at a distance from the river Ijssel.

> The mailman brought me your letter. Hurrah, Brother, and cordial thanks! On it there was no date, but there was a note enclosed with it from a priest assisting in a parish. His name is Kievitsbosch. Somebody had brought him a bag in which he found several copies of *Cor Unum et Anima Una,* some bread, and a few other letters. The assistant gave the bread to the people there and asked a truck driver to take the letters and journals over the Ijssel . . . I must stop now, for this letter will be taken to you by a person on the way to The Hague.

The response to our paper soon proved to be so enthusiastic that we had to alter our original intention and turn it from a monthly into a weekly. News bulletins, articles, and poems came in from all sides of the country, especially from those still in occupied territory. I continued to remind my readers of the need to put our beliefs into practice in everyday life in favorable as well as precarious circumstances. The feedback I received confirmed the importance of this message and began to spawn some exemplary testimony.

I had invited our readers to pass along for publication anything heartening they wanted to say. It came as no surprise to me that only one article on the topic of professional theology was ever sent to me. All other communications touched upon memorable events, times of human loss and spiritual gain. Many writers referred to the thoughts and sayings of Venerable Francis of Saverne, because his life and teaching exemplified the joy of practicing appreciative abandonment to the will of God in the most harrowing of circumstances.

One encouraging yet sad piece of news I received concerned the survival of a classmate and friend of mine, Ben Hendrikx. In the Battle of Arnhem, a direct hit on his family home had forced them to seek shelter with other victims. Shortly thereafter they had to evacuate to the town of Loenen. The bombardment there took the life of Ben's mother and his youngest brother. The memorial I published in our bulletin went something like this:

> We all heard about it . . . the mother and the youngest brother of Ben are no longer with him. Unexpectedly, they have been taken from this earth to God by a sad accident. That is the set phrase for the terrible and cruel events that can plunge every family we know into pain and mourning. It is the fact that hangs over the head of every one of us. Scattered in the chaos of the war, we feel deeply the loss suffered by Ben. His mother and his youngest brother have been taken away from him . . . We appreciate so much more what our mother means to us. Many of us bike and walk endless roads to find food to relieve her worries for her family. We see at close quarters how she neglects herself to do [everything for] her children.

The letter Ben himself wrote was so touching I published it in a later edition of CUAU:

> It does us so much good to hear from and at times to see our brothers! This bulletin gives us an opportunity to talk with and to encourage each other, to help us to carry the cross of our sufferings and to do so in the spirit of *Cor Unum et Anima Una*.
>
> I experienced this oneness when my mother and brother lost their lives. I received letters from everywhere that showed such heartfelt sympathy for our great and heavy loss, a loss God in his infinite love asked of us. Much has happened in these months. We all have to bear our cross. Is it not admirable that God complied with our longing for suffering? In Gemert, in our seminary, we have had so many quiet years. Often we asked ourselves if we religious would come through the war without hurt while countless others brought the greatest sacrifices. At last we have been found worthy to suffer something. There are no limits to our joy. We must not cease to thank God for that. Our joy has no limits when we know that, through our suffering, we cooperate with the liberation of souls. Now we can be real sacrificers.

> Don't we have much to be appreciative about? Are we not carriers of the truth? Don't we have "Good News" for our neighbors? How often do we have the opportunity to tell something good to others? We come into contact with so many people, either when we are on the road to get things needed by them or when we help others who are evacuated. At every moment we can share with them the great happiness that we ourselves received without deserving it.
>
> When we are aware of that, our work-no matter what-is beautiful. Then there is less chance that we become materialistic or, as someone told me, that we "get lost in potato problems" (*veraardappelen*). Above all other things we remain enjoyers of God, from whom we have received a great treasure to make others happy.

Ben, like so many others who entrusted their experiences to *Cor Unum et Anima Una*, confirmed our desire to meet the spiritual needs of all people just as the Protestant heroine, Corrie ten Boom, had done, first in her home in Haarlem and then in the German concentration camp in which she and her sister Betsie were imprisoned. Ben's experience validated in a similar fashion that the spiritual life is far more than an isolated "God and I" relationship cut off from the real world in which we have to live and care for others. Our war experiences forbade us to drift into the safe harbor of self-sufficiency. We had to live our faith, as Ben said, by remaining "enjoyers of God, from whom we have received a great treasure to make others happy."

In the light of these experiences, I thought again of our life as a field of formation, consisting of five intertwining spheres: our ongoing formation by the mystery at the center of our existence (*centrale vorming*); our intraformation (*innerlijke vorming*); our interformation (*wederzijdse vorming*); our situational formation (*situatie vorming*); and our formation in the wider world (*wereld vorming*). Ben's testimony shows that faith in the providential plan of God pervaded the direction his thoughts, feelings, and actions took after the death of his mother and brother. The same depth of faith formed his inner life and shed light on why he felt he had been chosen by God to stay alive. Ben also expressed his appreciation for the way those with whom he shared his plight, especially his confrères in the religious life, helped him to cope with his loss and encouraged him to put this wisdom to the test in his service of others. He does not close his interiority off from the situation in which God asks him to live his priestly vocation. The opposite happens. He sees this outreach as an integral part of his spiritual response. Neither does his spirituality exclude the wider world, for he points to the whole of humanity as the beneficiary of his commitment in and through Christ to care for every soul he meets.

Ben's dark night of faith led him not to despair but to hope. He chose to abandon himself appreciatively to the mystery. He detected little points of light that pierced through the shadows cast by the mourning process. Less complacent than in the old days, dependent on the generosity of others, begging for food and a roof over his head, he found the true meaning of his call to suffer with and for abandoned souls. Before this blessed calamity, Ben, like the rest of us, took the gifts God gave him for granted. Now he found joy and serenity in accepting the Cross as the only trustworthy avenue to spiritual renewal.

27

Terror and Transformation

LETTERS KEPT ARRIVING IN our editorial offices. It was as if every reader wanted to tell us some story of the crosses and resurrections in their lives. One was sent to us by a young Spiritan, ordained a priest for only a year and a half. He had been deported with other Dutchmen to Germany after they were caught in a raid in Helden in the Southern province of Limburg before its liberation by the Allies. He was now separated from his family in the liberated part of Holland. He wrote from Lehrte in Germany to a classmate in the occupied part of our country:

> ... I take care of the Dutch here. Oh, it is sometimes miserable. They don't have anything. And I cannot help them because I don't have anything myself. Do you know any people who have some leftover rags for my dear countrymen? Everything is welcome... The main point is that I am here. What matters is that I do something for them. With God's help I shall be able to do much good.
>
> [Stuck in the occupied West of Holland] you cannot, of course, contact my family [living in the liberated South]. If you can get in touch with them, you would have to do that as soon as possible and ask for clothes and underwear, not for me but for our Dutch people. Here there are also many men from Rotterdam [caught and deported in the great *razzias* there]. Every day I meet Dutch people. They tell me of their worries and miseries. My life becomes busier daily. My pencil does not stand still... Pray for me,

too, but especially for the thousands of evacuated [and deported] Dutch men and women. They need so much spiritual strength, especially those who hope to return to Holland as better persons. The bombardments are terrifying. With God's help I may stay alive. If not, I must adore God's will in offering my life for the lives of our people here.

How deeply does a priest feel the needs of souls. Greet all my classmates for me. I think so often of Gemert [our seminary], of that wonderful time. If you can reach me, write me a letter; it will do me good in my loneliness. What a terrible ordeal our poor country must go through . . . Every kind word, every old rag against the cold, is received here with tears . . . All of society, from the highest to the lowest, are present here. I must speak all languages. I celebrated the night mass at Christmas in barracks in a camp, in which all nationalities of Europe were represented. That was beautiful! Every day brings new experiences . . .

Pray, pray for us, poor plodders. Do you perhaps have some matches left? There are no matches here at all. Prayer books, medals, crosses, if you can get them please send them; they can help immortal souls who don't feel strong enough. I should stop but I cannot because I have so much to say. How I would love to talk with you at least once, to be able to speak with anyone about what is going on inside of me. I don't have that opportunity, I feel all by myself, alone in the great desolation of the German Reich. But for my boys I go through fire; God wills it. If I never see you again, then so long until we meet in eternity. How beautiful is our priestly life when we minister among suffering people. Day and night I heard confessions while we were still on transport from Holland, and I would not have wanted nything else but to be there], not even to return home.

—From Mat, Lehrte, Hanover

P.S. Greetings to all and ask for prayers for me, a poor priest, that I may know God's will and fulfill it. For yourself many greetings from your friend and confrère, Mat.

This letter of Mat's, like so many others, confirmed how impossible it is for anyone to fathom the depths of human suffering, the tortuous struggles one goes through in the quest for meaning in seemingly meaningless situations. Faith alone supplies some light. The wisdom gained by the blood, sweat, and tears of priestly heroes like Mat had to be passed on to future generations. The significance of transformation through affliction is not easy to articulate, but there is no doubt it happens. Mat's testimony proves a point I tried to make as often as possible: in every obstacle there resides a formation opportunity.

In God's loving plan each story told from the heart contains a seed of everlasting wisdom. It benefits not only its victims but all who hear it. Mat's letter encouraged everyone who read it to remember that none of us alone could have hidden so many people, outsmarted the enemy, relieved their hunger, and arranged for their escape. Amidst the spiritually oppressed and depreciated, nothing was more important than to stay the course, to restore through compassion their dignity, and to help them to recover a sense of their self-worth.

The idea of "call appreciation" (*het prijzen van onze levens roeping*) struck me as a way for people to move beyond equating their deepest value with what they do or accomplish. Many avenues to success had failed. What remained was the validity of their transcendent transformation, their true identity in God. Their unique-communal call and the dignity it bestowed upon them were gifts no captor could destroy. Never will I forget the Jewish people whom I had the privilege to serve. They were without property or position, on the verge of being discovered and deported, and yet they praised Yahweh for his fidelity. They revealed their calling as the people of God with a poise and sense of purpose that made our paltry complaints appear shameful.

Mat showed a similar awareness of "call appreciation" and its divine efficacy. He spoke about the threat to his life during a terrifying series of bombardments. Death puts the whole of one's time on earth into perspective. It reveals our commonality as no other experience can. When it knocks on the door, every memory of life passes before us. For what reason are we here? Are we only a speck of dust in endless space? Life must have a more lasting meaning, but what is it? Little by little, slivers of our destiny begin to come together. At first we wonder where they fit in the puzzling reality of our journey. In facing death, Mat had to ponder his life as a vessel of love sculpted by God. It holds the secret of his destiny, though he only catches glimpses of it here and there. In faith, he chose to abandon himself to this unknown calling. He offered his life to help others and only prayed that his death might be beneficial to them. The threat under which he lived kept him conscious of the preciousness of his call. He showed his abandonment to it by giving himself wholly to what the war required of him. Amidst the frightful diaspora of deportees, the light grew dim, but he strove to keep aglow the flame of God's love.

What was anyone to make of the meaning of this confused mass of demoralized exiles taken like slaves from conquered quarters of Europe? The chance that he might be among those bombed and burned out by armadas of Allied and enemy troops was great, but the reality of life's fragility only served to deepen his dedication. Almost daily bombs rained down; streets went up in smoke. He wrote a touching farewell in his letter, just in case his life might be taken. In the meantime he said he would go through fire for his boys, if God so willed. All he wanted was to be faithful to his call.

Another letter of Mat's confirmed the formative pattern I had frequently pondered: the from (*van*), through (*door*), to (*naar*) event no one in dire straits can avoid. Mat had to cope with being wrenched *from* his familiar surroundings in Gemert; with going *through* the hell of the bombardments; and with trying *to* put his own and others' lives together again. Though he would never be the same, these changes would have far reaching consequences. Mat seemed to foresee what might happen in the following reflections on the seriousness of his situation:

> . . . Life is at times so bitter, so hard. Now I know better what that word *sacerdos* [priest] means. Suffering and loneliness have taught me that . . . all come [to a priest] with their problems. Sometimes they ask me brashly: "How long have you been a priest?" "A year and a half." "Oh, then you cannot yet talk to me." This is what some reply when I tell them the truth about their immoral behavior.

> I may sound pessimistic. Yes, that may be because yesterday I escaped death narrowly when a massive bomb fell near me. After escaping the blast I tore loose as the fire brigade does. You get into your civies and there is nobody who recognizes you. You go to the burning houses looking for where your help is most needed . . . you cannot walk here in priest's clothes for they will throw stones at you. When I travel I wear a cap for the Hitler Jugend [Hitler Youth]. Then you can go everywhere. But now traveling has been restricted, and I cannot reach the many people I have to take care of . . . I spent four weeks in a camp. That was a good time. I played bridge with the Poles, drank with Estonians, and smoked cigarettes from Lithuania.

> Confession in such large groups [under these emergency conditions] has been made easy. You take them all together. As a sign of remorse, you ask them to strike their chests, say an act of contrition or beg for God's mercy, and then you give general absolution. Poor priest, I have so little to give to souls who ask so much. May Jesus and Mary bless my wretched efforts.
>
> Often I doubt if I'll see you back here. Sometimes the bombs fall so close by. Please pray for all of us here in Germany.

More and more of my stranded confrères received *Cor Unum et Anima Una*. They shared it with as many people as they could. Some of them were living in the far North of occupied Holland beyond the river Ijssel that ran majestically between the Northern and Western provinces of our land. A number of the readers living there had been born and raised in these parts. Like me they were at their family homes during the summer recess when the Allied armies invaded the South where our seminary was. They echoed in their correspondence the longing for liberation we all felt, but the division of the Netherlands by the German and Allied forces had made it impossible for any of us to return to freedom.

Through our underground paper we heard for the first time the stunning news that many of our fellow students, whom we thought were safe in the South, had been driven by the retreating German army back into the occupied North. They had lived through terrifying battles that left their lives in shambles. The first news of their plight was published in CUAU. It reached us in a letter from Toon Lindeman, who was now in the Dutch city of Leeuwarden. He wrote:

> Until October 25, the situation in our city of Roermond was normal enough. On October 6, we had a few bombs. They destroyed a whole family but everything went on in its old way. On October 28, more bombs fell, killing eleven victims. The heavy bombardments on November 11, however, marked the beginning of our misery: there were thirty-four victims in our wrecked and ruined city! Almost every street was hit by bombs; houses were smashed to pieces. I myself got off unharmed, though I sat in a big house on which a bomb fell. November 16 marked the first army shelling of Roermond. In the midst of the night a constant rain of grenades fell. Because this was the first time we had to go through this [shelling], we did not yet realize the frightening impact of simple grenades. Since November 16, we have had a daily rain of them . . . If a grenade slams through the wall of a house a

whole room is destroyed. No one dared to stay upstairs any longer. The people of Roermond migrated to their cellars. We said Mass for them mostly at night. During the month of December, I said Mass twice a day, in the morning and in the evening. I went mainly to the larger cellars where seventy or eighty people crowded together. In all it seemed like a desperate situation. Yet we held novena after novena that we would not be evacuated. We'd much rather stick it out for a few months than have to leave our city.

At the end of January, we could no longer escape what we dreaded most. The army ordered us to leave. Poor people. Hunger is bad but the forced evacuation of a whole population in the midst of war and freezing weather is worse. Thousands of people, the sick, the invalids, the handicapped, old men and women, small children and infants all had to go, first from Roermond, trudging through the snow for twenty kilometers over the Dutch border to the German town of Brueggen. There we were put on straw in mills and factories waiting for cattle trains to transport us further into Germany. Thousands and thousands of people went without sufficient care. After that came the awful journey in cattle cars deep into bombed out Germany in icy cold temperatures. You ask yourself why, for what?

It took us fifty hours. The biting cold was unbearable. In each car we sat or stood packed together with over sixty people and towers of luggage. Sleeping was impossible. Often the train stood still. Then the bitter cold was at its worst. In the German town of Dorsten we had to wait all day long because it is too dangerous in Germany to travel during the day. Yesterday a train with evacuees arrived here. It had been parked for a long time in Wesel. During its stay it had been shelled and shot up by English warplanes: twenty were dead and sixty wounded.

After seemingly endless days and nights of riding through Germany, they finally found themselves once again in Holland, albeit in the occupied North. He continues:

> Now in Northern Holland I have the care of a small school building turned into an asylum for about seventy people, the most poor materially and spiritually, the outcasts of society.

Let me give you two other news items. Piet van der Ploeg, poor Piet, who was in our seminary in Gemert and so afraid of war planes and bombs, went through a lot in the village of Koningbosch in the South where he was rector of the sisters of Bethany. Koningbosch and its convent are totally destroyed. For months they were kept under fire. The Germans had dug their trenches in their village; the response of the Brits struck home time and time again. Piet himself got a grenade splinter which cut mean, deep wounds in both of his upper legs.

Nico Tekstra has been in prison for a few days. Riding his bike, he carried his camera with him. The Germans accused him of espionage. He did six weeks of hard labor in a work camp.

An article sent by another confrère, Henk van der Putten, had been inspired by the feast day of the innocent children murdered in Bethlehem. He directed his thoughts to all of us who now knew first hand the afflictions of the war. As did many of the other letters and papers we published in CUAU, it showed why our mainly academic theological background had to be complemented by practical ways to keep our faith alive in the midst of these chaotic times. As Henk wrote:

What about your philosophical and theological studies? Do you fall badly behind in your academic life: Would you not want the opportunity for intense study, the quiet search for truth, the taking in of the highly necessary knowledge of divine things? But now, by force of circumstances, you find yourself often occupied with all kinds of practical chores. You have to take care of the material needs of yourself and of the people around you. Gone are the hours that you could study with others in a large hall, reading big books and hurriedly scribbling down your notes.

Academic life! Another kind of life had to come to the fore in these months. You had to engage in an ancient kind of study. You felt invited to a difficult growth in virtue. You were being raised up in the things of the spirit. Whether we like it or not, the words of the saints force themselves upon us: first of all, create a hermitage in your heart and live there together with the Lord.

Within that hermitage you should grow in gentle wisdom and in the sincere striving of your will to give your life the form of the Lord who abides with you. Attentiveness, trying, persevering, starting again—these virtues make us heedful of his word. If the

> Master speaks, everything else should fall silent. There should only be our still and humble receptivity and our doing of his Word in the midst of our daily misery. This is the ground for the most sublime study. It transforms us into truly religious people.
>
> ... Our days are filled with threats and oppressive sufferings. It does not matter, whether we live here or there, if we have been lucky so far or not, if we are poor and dependent on others ... No matter what, the Lord shall come to us as the Sower. He shall sow in us that one Word (from the liturgy of the innocent infants of Bethlehem murdered by Herod's soldiers): *Non loquendo sed moriendo? Not by speaking but by dying* did these children witness for Christ. We meet with injustice, with oppressive small-mindedness and the iniquity in ourselves and others. But we know that Christ will make us understand his own suffering; he will let us share in it. To flow with that grace wisely, we must give ourselves now, with heart and soul, to the study of the only thing necessary.
>
> We should not only mediate, no, we must also die with Christ, with the innocent children of Bethlehem, and transpose our own life, into *non loquendo sed moriendo*. Often these days we must witness to his love *not by preaching but by dying* to many conveniences.
>
> We cannot let this chance for enrichment, this opportunity for dying to a lower life pass by ... We must be raised to a life that, while appreciating academic theology, goes far deeper than a merely scholarly existence.

Henk's testimony, as that of so many others, confirmed my own call to pursue and practice a theology of everyday spiritual formation. I prayed that the Holy Spirit would grant me the stamina to do so. I wanted to put to good use my personal experiences before and during the war and above all to find a way to honor the heroic souls with whom I lived. With God's help, I vowed that the lessons I learned in the Hunger Winter would never be forgotten nor would the lives lost there have been in vain.

[Editor's Note: *Here ends the first part of Father Adrian van Kaam's memoirs. Before starting Part Two, it might be wise to read in the appropriate appendix the collection of his wartime poetry; the full rendition of his*

Christian play; and his editorials in CUAU, *the last of which captures the glorious day when Holland is finally free and he is able to plan his return to the seminary to complete his study and prepare himself for his long-awaited ordination to the priesthood.*]

Part Two

Springtime of My Heart

Foreword

WHEN THE WAR ENDED and Adrian van Kaam was able to return to his seminary in Gemert, he finished his theology courses. Then, on July 21, 1946, he celebrated in unspeakable gratitude to God his ordination to the priesthood. Because of his generally weakened health, the assignment Father van Kaam received from his superiors was not to evangelization in the foreign missions but, as if by providential design, to pursue higher education and the tasks of research, writing, and teaching that would be required of him for the rest of his life. Out of good will, pending permission from his superiors, he had requested to be sent as a missionary either to the Amazon River region in Brazil or to the Spiritan mission in the then Belgian Congo (now Zaire). Shortly after the medical missionary screening board in Rotterdam rejected his request, he became a teacher of philosophical anthropology in Gemert where he dedicated himself to fulfilling the academic and educational traditions of his community.

His assignment to seminary teaching gave him the time and space he needed to lay the groundwork for a new science of formation of the human spirit. An unexpected chance to apply his findings to everyday life situations in a non-seminary setting emerged when he received permission to accept an invitation to teach in the Dutch Life Schools of Formation for Young Adults between the ages of 17 and 25. This unique system of learning had grown out of the pioneering work of Doctor Maria Schouwenaars, a renown school supervisor and educator from Belgium. As a single Catholic laywoman committed to a formative approach to secular and religious education, she served, first in Antwerp and then in Holland, groups of young working women denied the opportunity to study during the Nazi Occupation. The post-war demands placed upon them to rebuild the economy of their homelands meant that Schouwenaars had to take her schools to them, teaching classes in the mills and factories where they worked.

After the war her innovative approach gained increasing recognition in the Netherlands. The directors of the local school in Gemert called to her attention the work of Father van Kaam. After meeting Schouwenaars in person, he agreed to teach the classes in religion. Theirs was a joyous meeting of minds and hearts. The two of them had traveled a similar path rooted in their commitment to transcendent character formation. In accordance with the democratic constitutional government of the Netherlands, each acknowledged religious or humanist group could have their own schools subsidized by the state, including the Catholic based division in Gemert named *Mater Amabilis* after the image of Mary, the *aimable mother*. Besides his original contributions to the curriculum of the Life Schools, Father van Kaam initiated the first parallel program for young men, *Pater Fortis*, which celebrated the ideal of the *courageous father*, modeled on Saint Joseph. If the *Mater Amabilis* schools strove to foster the formation of young women in the light of the gentle sensitivity of the Mother of Jesus, then the *Pater Fortis* schools focused on the firm and responsible commitment to fatherhood best symbolized by Saint Joseph's care for mother and Son.

Both divisions helped married and single people to understand and live their distinctive calls to parenting as well as to spiritual motherhood and fatherhood. The vision that guided Schouwenaars and van Kaam was to form and reform the youth of tomorrow in the Judeo-Christian view of family life and friendship, of love and service, that had been so eroded during the war years. These pioneers had observed first-hand the disintegrating effects on character development of conscience formation cut off from the wisdom and truth found in Holy Scripture and writings of the spiritual masters. They each discovered from experience that any developmental or educational theory bound exclusively to secular humanism was inadequate to address the hunger in their students to live a distinctively human personal and spiritual life. The alternative they chose was to foster an integral approach to Christian formation in the context of van Kaam's depiction of one's whole field of life with the mystery at the center. They saw to it that their curriculum was moral not moralistic; foundational not fundamentalistic; mystical not mystifying; social not fanatically socialistic.

A few years after Father van Kaam had been teaching in the seminary and partnering with Doctor Schouwenaars, another providential happening occurred that changed the course of his life. Monsignor Giovanni Baptista Montini, who had become acquainted with the efforts of the Dutch Life Schools and who was later to become Pope Paul VI, requested under the auspices of the Vatican Secretariat of State that his provincial superior, Father Henri Strick, CSSp, release Father van Kaam from his full-time obligations as a professor in Gemert. Then he could concentrate on expanding his formation anthropology and theology in service of the rapidly expanding life schools but more importantly of Christianity as a whole.

In response to this request, his superior changed his place of residence from the seminary to the Spiritan novitiate in Gennep. While living there he could travel to the nearby University of Nijmegen where he could complete his degree work in the fields of pedagogy (the education and formation of children) and andragogy (the education and formation of adults). He could also devote quality time to writing articles on the theology of human and Christian formation, most of which he published in prestigious Dutch journals. At the same time, Monsignor Montini, who himself served as general chaplain of Catholic students in Italy, communicated through Schouwenaars another thought that would have an impact on Father van Kaam's future. He said he would like to see their entire life school program adapted to a university curriculum perhaps in the form of an independent center at the heart of a Catholic college or as a free-standing institute of service to higher learning in both religious and secular settings.

Another providential thread in this story revealed itself when the then president of Duquesne University, Vernon Gallagher, CSSp, paid a visit to Holland in September of 1951 and opened the door to two Dutch Spiritans, Adrian van Kaam and his colleague in the field of philosophy, Father Bert van Croonenburg, to join his faculty in Pittsburgh. Father van Kaam had to delay his coming for a few years because his provincial superior had already made arrangements with the motherhouse of his international order in Paris for him to do research in their archives for the purpose of writing a biography of their second founder, the Venerable Francis Libermann. This book had to be completed before he could go to the United States. All of these arrangements had to be done with absolute discretion since neither he nor his provincial superior were permitted to divulge the plans Monsignor Montini had in mind.

Finally, in 1954, he left Holland for the United States and took up residence on the Duquesne campus, only to find that his hope of beginning a program in the field of spiritual formation would have to be delayed. Instead his assignment would be to teach in the Department of Psychology, to study for a doctorate in this field, and to initiate a distinctive approach to psychology as a human science. Over the next nine years, his task would be to establish and evolve a necessary complement to the informational, empirical, and statistical approaches to psychology dominant in those days.

In service of this task he studied under and benefitted from the tutelage of people like Professor Calvin Hall, the acknowledged critical historian of personality theory at Case Western Reserve University in Cleveland. That is where he received his PhD upon writing his dissertation on the feeling of really being understood by a person. As part of his uniquely designed curriculum, he went to the University of Chicago to be trained in psychotherapy and counseling by the founder of the client-centered school of therapy, Professor Carl Rogers. He added to these theoretical and practical approaches courses at Chicago's Alfred Adler Institute under Doctor Rudolf Dreikurs. At Brandeis University in Waltham, Massachusetts, he studied under Professor Abraham Maslow, the eminent personality theorist who later invited him to take over his courses when he himself went on sabbatical leave.

In these and other academic centers, Father van Kaam worked with numerous outstanding professors and students in the fields of experimental and existential or humanistic psychology. He soon realized that excellent as these approaches were, he could not accept certain underlying assumptions in them that countered the essence-existence structure in which he rooted his own courses. This existential, not existentialistic, anthropology permeated his teaching and writing. Following nine years in the psychology department (1954–1963) he was able to establish his own independent Institute of Man, later renamed the Institute of

Formative Spirituality, based on the original courses he had developed in the Netherlands.

What happened was that the administration of the University decided that the program Father van Kaam had started in "religion and personality" under the auspices of the psychology department ought to be housed in an independent institute that could sponsor its own master's degree. Having started a new journal titled *Humanitas* and being the editor of numerous other professional publications, Father van Kaam had need by 1966 of an assistant in the editorial field and a co-director of this new venture in higher education. By a series of providential events, that coincided with my own undergraduate work at Duquesne University in journalism and English, I came to campus to see him for what I thought was to be an interview to write a newspaper report on his Institute, only to discover that by his invitation my life was about to undergo a radical change in direction. I would be called from that moment on to leave my place of employment as an editor of the *Jewish Chronicle* in Pittsburgh and to join the Institute not only as a new job opportunity but as a lifelong commitment. Over the next several years, the Institute advanced from the granting of masters' degrees to the launching in 1979 of our own fully accredited doctoral program. All of the core courses we taught on the graduate level—his in pretheological formation science and its complementary formation anthropology and mine in the literature of spirituality—were seen as servant sources of formation theology. These three fields taken together crown our Epiphany Academy in-house and out-reach programs today.

I am eternally grateful to Father van Kaam for advising me to pursue my PhD in English literature with a specialization in the pre- and post-reformation masters of the spiritual life. A distinctive feature of our Institute curriculum became the six-semester cycle of courses I initiated and taught in the classics of our faith and formation tradition. This cycle facilitated in a special way our central commitment to formation theology. I presented this entire cycle in my classes for over twenty years in the Institute and I continue to offer them today as part of the curriculum taught on a post-graduate basis in our co-founded Epiphany Association and its Academy of Formative Spirituality. Under its auspices we honor, in Father van Kaam's memory, the culmination of his efforts for over sixty years to complement informational-formational theology with its formational-informational counterpart. In the second part of these autobiographical memoirs, *Springtime of My Heart*, he continues the story so vividly presented in Part One, *Winter of My Soul*. My hope is that by the end of this book all of us will be better able to understand what God set this humble servant of his apart to do for the Church and the world in the twenty-first century.

Susan Muto, PhD

28

Return to Normalcy

ONCE HOLLAND WAS LIBERATED and I could return to the seminary, my longing for a more normal life began to be fulfilled. Due to the study time I lost during the Hunger Winter, my ordination to the priesthood had to be delayed by one year. It would be almost another year before I received my first official appointment as a priest—not to the mission field but to teach courses at Gemert that would include philosophical anthropology, educational psychology, and the philosophy of science. In fidelity to the Thomistic tradition, I taught philosophy in its pre-theological context as the "handmaiden" of doctrinal theology. I tried to structure my courses in such a way that the students received in a complementary fashion both informational theology about the Revelation and its application to everyday life as formational. The experiential approach I formulated during the Hunger Winter came to fruition in the seminary. As much as I had wanted to be assigned to the missions as most of my classmates were, I was blessed in retrospect by the fact that my health in those days, aggravated by a severe bout of psoriasis, precluded travel to tropical climates. This condition meant that I had to befriend books while my confreres secured the official documents they needed to do first evangelization in foreign lands.

One of the most amusing "side jobs" I had in the community was my appointment in the Fall of 1947 to be our bursar! The irony of my being given this assignment did not go unnoticed as this letter from my good friend Gerard Bol, written on September 21 of that year, reveals:

∼

Dear Adriaan,

If the news told to me by my friend Jan Smith (who visited me last night) is based on reality, then the fact he mentioned is proof that God loves humor: you have been appointed bursar! I see you busy with the grocer's and the butcher's shopping booklets, and with judging if Father X's shirt must be replaced by a new one a month sooner or later. Congratulations! And I mean this—my congratulations, for this work will help to form you into an all-around harmonic man, full of reality. Hence this second note to you within three days: I did not want to lag behind with the well-meant congratulations and . . . mockeries, which no doubt will be directed to you these days . . . Strength, and success with a balanced budget, with your friend's greetings,

Gerard

∼

A parallel appointment as a librarian seemed more appropriate. In Gerard's words, from his October 9, 1947 letter, it was "right up [my] alley!" He did add a word of caution, saying, "For the rest, [I know] you will not let the monastery go bankrupt."

In addition to tackling these unexpected avocations, I had many class preparations to do. This meant that I could not ignore processing the impact ideological systems of belief like Nazism and Marxism had had on my own and others' lives. I had seen at the time how a perverted set of ideas held to be absolute could twist the truth and change one's perspective from a value system that honored the dignity of life to one that proffered a culture of death. I also felt myself drawn to study what makes us distinctively human from a phenomenological perspective. Like the late Pope John Paul II, who lived in the same era as I did, I turned to the works of the German phenomenologist, Max Scheler, to increase my knowledge of the acting person. I tried to make my courses as life-oriented as possible, challenging the seminarians under my care to think with head and heart, that is to say, to bring reason and faith together in their quest for truth. By the same token, I tried as a consecrated religious to listen to God's gracious command to maintain the necessary rhythms of contemplation and action, worship and work, presence to the Blessed

Sacrament and dedicated participation in all my assignments. There was no way I could teach others what I did not live myself.

I discovered both in the classroom and in the confessional that the terrors of life under which most of us had lived in the recent past made us not only philosophically-minded but also in need of processing emotionally the traumatic experiences we had undergone in the war. As a result, I began to present in my courses, talks, and writings a way to analyze formative events that would disclose their transcendent potential, thus enabling us to find meaning in crisis situations.

By God's blessing, I was given the opportunity to test my ideas in a context beyond that of higher academic living. I found out from mutual friends that Doctor Maria Schouwenaars, a well-known Belgian educator, had opened in Gemert a division of her Life Schools of Formation for Young Adults aged 17 to 25. Meeting Doctor Schouwenaars, proved to be a life-changing event for me. I remember the day I went to the clothing factory run by the Roelof family where she held her classes. I knew the family already as benefactors of the seminary. Maria was pleased to see me in person because she had already heard of the courses I had initiated at Gemert from my confrère, Father Bert van Croonenburg. She told me that her purpose was not simply to run a school where girls could learn domestic skills like how to cook nourishing and attractive meals and how to do professional tasks like bookkeeping; her aim was also to teach them about life as spiritually formative. She wanted them to learn the art and discipline of connecting the values they adopted religiously with the reality of the demands they faced as married and single women.

More than a chaplain and a professor who could partner with her, Maria had been seeking the help of someone capable of entering into the life experiences of young women whose worlds of meaning had been shattered by losses too demoralizing to articulate. Almost as soon as we met she invited me to teach religion not in a strictly informational way but in a manner that would help the girls to find the bridge between the beliefs they espoused and the life-oriented courses they had to take.1 Meeting the expectations these young people had of their future offered me a God-given opportunity to develop this integrative curriculum and to offer it in the Fall of 1949 in the Gemert division of the Life Schools.

Teaching in this innovative system enabled me to apply the results of my research in formation anthropology and theology at the seminary to the formation phases associated with one's growth to adulthood. At first my only students were young women, but, with Schouwenaars' permission, I took the step of opening the Gemert division of the schools to a male audience. Addressing both genders was an eye-opening experience and a good testing ground for some of the basic constructs and concepts I had begun to formulate, such as the full field model of formation.

At the center of the curriculum of our divisions, I recommended placing two courses, the first being "formative spirituality" itself taught from a humane (anthropological) as well as from a spiritual (theological) perspective. The second course dealt with one's adhered to faith tradition, which, in most cases, was Christianity. Regular contact with these eager-to-learn young people provided an ideal testing ground for my idea that all of life (inner, situational, relational, and mondial) had to be integrated around the mystery at the center of our field of presence and action. The more familiar our students became with the methods of formative thinking and full field appraisal that I devised, the better they began to understand their own interior life not in isolation from but in relation to their immediate situation, their relationships, and their place and purpose in this world.2 Since most of our faculty and staff members were volunteers pursuing a variety of careers—only a few of them were on salary—the ideas they brought to the Life Schools could be expressed in the most down-to-earth terms possible.

One teacher I remember was a whiz in cosmetics and personal hygiene. Her task was to define what appearing well in public meant for girls pursuing a profession. Why ought they to bother using make up to achieve an amiable, modest yet attractive appearance? Use of my formation field model with the mystery at the center made it possible to explore one's inner motivation for wearing cosmetics; the effects of pleasant dressing on one's situation at work; and the benefit of looking well on one's relationships both in the community and in the wider world. Another teacher was a banker. He helped students to organize their finances as any investment expert would as well as to relate monetary matters to their Christian life within family, church, and society. Other courses dealt with interior decorating; still others with health and health-related issues and with the meaning of human sexuality.

With the help of a medical doctor and a nurse, we were able to link these sociohistorical and vital matters to a holistic theory of personality that included the functional and transcendent dimensions. We always took care to view the foundations of formation theology in the light of an underlying, theistically compatible anthropology. In this way we showed that grace does work through nature. I had the joy of seeing in both the female and male divisions of the schools the fulfillment of the intuition I shared with Schouwenaars that every dimension of our existence provides some opening for growth in spiritual maturity. As Christ-centered persons in the world, we ought to be capable of relating what we believe to everything we do from good grooming to handling family and community finances. Each aspect of our existence—cooking, cleaning, gardening, child rearing, wage earning—had to be integrated with our call to fidelity to the Divine Forming Mystery in whom we live and move and have our being (cf. Acts 17:28).

In the midst of developing these original courses in faith formation, it became clear to both me and Doctor Schouwenaars that we faced formidable foes when it came to integrating everyday life with Christian spirituality. One main challenge centered on the seemingly unstoppable avalanche of popular psychologism permeating, already at that time, writing and teaching having to do with the life of the spirit. Any illusion of our living in a stable Christian climate was rapidly being dispelled by the onslaught of secular humanism promoted by an increasing number of psychologists, sociologists, counselors, clinicians, and social workers. Choosing teachers for our now expanding life schools was not easy. We sought instructors who had some inkling of how to integrate the human and social sciences with a theology of Christian presence in the working places of family and society. We wanted as a group to prevent the reduction of spiritual formation to "pop-psychology." Were such a mentality allowed to seep into our faith-based schools, our mission might be compromised unwittingly by self-fulfillment posing as self-transformation.

As I pondered with my colleagues what course of action to take, I realized that our overall motivation had to shift from a "work and worldly success only" mentality to a commitment to remain faithful to the unique-communal call meant for each person by God. The meaning we attach to one or the other situation may change but "Jesus Christ is the same yesterday and today and forever" (Hebrews 13:8). The foundational courses in formative spirituality taught at the life schools were the glue that held together all other facets of the curriculum.

To resist the temptation to pursue a way of being rooted in an agenda of self-actualization, oblivious of the Sacred, was a struggle not to be taken lightly. Not for a moment could we allow passing or current expressions of cultural "must do's" or "must have's" to erode the ground of faith on which we had to stand.

Typically at their age our students craved to be liked, to be complemented and rewarded for their efforts with acclamations of public popularity. If they did not find within themselves resources of moral strength, they might miss the chance to choose the greatest good of all: fidelity to the life of Christ hidden in their heart. We as teachers and they as students had to counter any one-sided, secularistic perspective that held that life is mainly a matter of willful self-absorption disconnected from the love-will of God. To the contrary, union with God was shown by word and example to be the key to maturation in personal, professional, and spiritual ways.

From our rich treasury of faith traditions, I gathered into a new synthesis general principles of formation that were as theoretically relevant as they were practically applicable to daily life. I began to disclose in my research ever more effective ways of seeing our sociohistorical, vital, and functional make-up in the light of the transcendent. To live other-centered lives of love and service is a work of grace, not the outcome of our own self-centered efforts. An uncritical adoption of insights based mainly on a psychology of individualism always proves to be counterproductive for committed Christians. God calls us to cooperate with grace, not to co-opt its power by means of our own egocentric controls. By the same token, mere information about our faith and formation traditions by itself alone is insufficient to guide our ability to connect what we believe and the way we live. That was why in the Dutch Life Schools we focused on a comprehensive conceptual framework that would enable us to place any partial insight we received from the human and social sciences into an integrated theory respectful of the dynamics of formation, reformation, and transformation in and through the grace of God.

Above all, we found it necessary to reaffirm what was compatible or incompatible with the foundational wisdom and doctrine of the Judeo-Christian tradition to which we were wholeheartedly committed. What had sustained us over these years of turmoil and transition was the guiding power of God's Word, which no ideas of ours could ever penetrate nor any efforts of ours exhaust. Our joy was to preserve and expand "the truth that sets us free" (cf. John 8:32). Our place was to keep aglow the "light that shines in the darkness" since we had seen with our own eyes that "the darkness did not overcome it" (John 1:5).

Notes

1. See Adrian van Kaam, "Mater Amabilis: The Spiritual Backgrounds of Religious Formation in the *Mater Amabilis School* and their Integration into the Structure of this Education." *Epiphany International* 2008, 56–95.

2. For a detailed explanation of this model, see Adrian van Kaam, *Fundamental Formation* in the Formative Spirituality Series, Volume I (Pittsburgh, PA: Epiphany Books, 2002). This book was first published by Crossroad, New York (1989).

29

Long Range Influence of the Dutch Life Schools

ALONG WITH MY OVERSEEING of community finances and my librarianship, a rhythm of religious observation, study, and classroom instruction began to be established in my life. I settled into being a professor of philosophical anthropology at the seminary and a teacher of spiritual formation in the Life Schools. I made sure that in addition to their customary studies in philosophy and theology, my students in both settings were apprised of the latest findings in the human and social sciences. Equipped with this knowledge, they could better distinguish between what was compatible or incompatible with their own faith traditions. They had to make educated and prayerful decisions regarding what to accept in these new ideas and what to reject in fidelity to their own beliefs.

This double teaching assignment gave me the opportunity to test and retest my emerging formational-informational approach to theology and to determine what in the curriculum was or was not conducive to this Christian articulation. The challenge we all faced in these postwar years was to open ourselves to that deep conversion of heart that alone would enable us to give spiritual form to our everyday lives in the working places of family, church, and society. Since the Life Schools promoted a truly holistic approach, we conducted our classes insofar as possible in those places where the students themselves worked. They followed a three-year curriculum of life-related courses offered during release times from their paid positions. Our typical setting was the cafeteria of a local mill or factory for four hours a week. The contrast between the formative atmosphere we created and the inhumane treatment many had endured under the Nazi regime in Belgium and Holland was obvious to everyone.[1]

Now that we were a liberated country, our program was able to operate in a less clandestine manner. I felt free to write about our endeavors in the journals for catechists and other educators in Holland that could now be openly published. As a result, our schools gained in popularity, received legal standing, and benefitted from economic support from the restored Dutch government as well as from leaders of industry and the institutional church. Many supporters expressed their appreciation for all that we did to meet the demands of post-war restoration. It became second nature in my courses in the religion department to stress to the students the need to foster social justice, peace, and mercy among the spiritually and physically poor. Daily we witnessed the plight of people who felt abandoned in body and soul. What could each of us do in our own way to offer them a new lease on life? Especially devastating was the disillusionment experienced when one's excited expectations after the liberation did not match the harsh reality one still had to face. In this climate of discontent, the disposition of appreciative abandonment to the mystery was essential for one's spiritual survival, to say nothing of one's state of mental and emotional health.2

In classroom settings and casual conversations as well as when I did vocational discernment for my own congregation, I could not help but notice how much young adults were swayed by proponents of secular humanism, who preached the "me-centered only" meaning of modern life. Traditional faith convictions seemed to be relegated to an earlier era of history. People of all social classes became vulnerable to any suggestion pertaining to a quick solution to their problems with little or no reflection on the atheistic or agnostic assumptions underlying these quasi-redemptive projects of self-salvation. A balanced anthropology and theology of human and Christian maturation could not be based any longer on the stable values that upheld family systems in the past. The solid faith foundations that sustained our parents had been badly shaken during years of war and occupation. The next generation was already being bombarded by post-war existentialistic, anti-religious ideas that, so to speak, hung in the air throughout western Europe. The country in which we lived boasted of an open door policy to humanistic and socialistic traditions whether or not they dampened the practice of the faith that was an indelible feature of our pre-war upbringing.

My work in the Life Schools taught me that teachers of religion had to start from where the students themselves were—with their needs, their desires, their ideals and problems. Only then might they be able to see how Christ is the answer for them. Let me try to clarify this formational-informational approach with an example.

Working with adolescents convinced me that they need support first of all against their own inner reproaches; they need someone who meets them with understanding and forgiveness; who encourages them in their striving upwards, who accepts their weaknesses without condemning them. Adolescents, especially those who have difficulty in the realm of relationships or who work in anti-Christian surroundings, often feel as if they have been contaminated and affected by evil. There is in them a certain inner dissatisfaction, a vague self-reproach, a feeling of more or less unworthiness. Somewhere inside a strange tug of guilt nags at them. There is a shadow of fear and shame about their life. Unwittingly they think that a "Catholicism of law" may in their case have predominated over a "Catholicism of love." They harbor, after repeated falls into sin, a vague impression that God is now angry with them, that, as a matter of fact, it is strange and improper to talk cordially and confidentially to God, that one cannot look God in the face, that all religious idealism that is preached in church does not at the moment apply to them but only to those who are not living in sin. They feel oppressed by the thought of how really faithful types would look down on them "if only they knew."

It became easier than I thought it would to describe Christ as the answer to this inner feeling of depravity. The renditions of the encounters between Jesus and Mary Magdalene, the Samaritan woman, the woman caught in adultery, the tax collectors and so many others who received his mercy offered ample illustrations for how to approach this aspect of the adolescent's psyche. I found it necessary to arouse, in a natural way, as it were, almost unintentionally, an unconscious identification between these students and the sinners Jesus befriended. Consider, for example, Mary Magdalene. In service of the purpose of psychological identification, I tried in my classes to describe the inner self of this woman, perhaps in the way a novelist or a film scenario might do. In terms of the story of this Jewish woman, I found I could project the half-conscious guilt and inferiority feelings that were alive in my students' psyche but that had been repressed. In short, by the use of expressive questions and responses, I challenged them to compare Mary Magdalene's fate with their situation: how she, being high-spirited, frivolous and haughty, clever at business yet standing alone, inwardly suffers; how she cringes with pain when women of a higher class pass by her condescendingly, when the eyes of the righteous avoid her stiffly; how isolated she must have felt when she was by herself on a lonely evening, reviewing the business of the day but with no one around who really understood her. While identifying themselves with this woman, the students unconsciously identified their own related concerns and the uncertainty they felt about their future. They recognized in compassion how much greater her need to follow Jesus was than their hitherto indifferent or casual approach to discipleship.

Then Magdalene's liberation is suddenly upon her. Perhaps on a nondescript street corner she meets a man who does not despise her. His look, so full of understanding, is unforgettable. Hidden among the crowd, she hears his voice. Hope begins to grow in her heart as she remembers his kindness to her. She starts at that moment to save money for the jar of ointment she will one day use to rub his feet (cf. John 12:1–8). I saw in the students' response how important it was to describe the intensity of Magdalene's feelings when she hears that "the man from Galilee" is in town again. Here the story comes to its climax: think of the excitement she feels as she puts on her shawl, holds the jar of precious oil in her trembling hands, and goes to the house of the rich man Simon. In all of these details her inner experience comes vividly to the fore. Consider the courage with which she pushes her way through the invited guests, avoids their irate looks, and falls down in front of Jesus. Compared to the dignified yet despising people around him and her, he blesses her gesture of hospitality and offers her in return the gift of redemption. From then on, she would be his faithful disciple and the one to whom he would reveal his resurrected glory (cf. John 20:11–18). The identification of the students, first with the boldness of this woman, and now with her liberation from guilt and fear, drew them from the story itself to the point of their personal meeting with Jesus. Magdalene's love for him was like the love they felt at this moment. Slowly but surely, they grew stronger in faith, thanks to this formative retelling of a familiar passage from the Gospel.

Teaching done in this style, with my attention focused on serving the unconscious needs of my students, turned out to be the best way to engage them in the process. The grace-filled results of this approach were noticeable not only in the classroom but also in the confessional. This is one of many examples of how adolescents encountered Christ in the

Life Schools. Dependent on the degree of one's education (elementary or secondary), such an illustrative reading of the story met with continual success. Once the students entered into a relationship with Christ over several lessons, they found him to be the answer to their uncertainty, the deliverance from their fear and guilt, the solution to their problems. He was the one who understood their weaknesses and failures. Renewed interest in his person made it possible for them to describe the sobering yet uplifting message of the Gospel. After explaining Christ's nature as fully human and fully divine and after conveying the *information* that he is High Priest, Prophet and King, I strove to unveil the meaning of the meeting between him and each of them. Until now, in their thoughts and feelings, they had been far away from him. He had been more or less a stranger, but no more.

This split between faith and formation became most noticeable to me when I was asked to serve as a chaplain-counselor in a Dutch detention camp for juvenile delinquents.3 The young men there were living proof of the ultimate failure of aggressive individualism cut off from the other-centered orientation of our faith tradition. These youngsters had the advantage of being entitled to every possible counseling method, but they still chose a life of crime. No one seemed to care for them so why should they care for others in this dog-eat-dog world? We did our best to redirect them away from such crass self-centeredness and toward a more mature, self-giving life, but our success rate was not that high. It was at this time that I began to practice what I would later identify as "transtherapy."4 It allowed those for whom I cared to acknowledge their hidden longing for the "More Than," perverted though it had been by substitutes for the transcendent. For some the waters of selfishness receded, but for others the riptides of thoughtless, immoral choices further dragged them down. I prayed that the Spirit would inspire me and everyone who revealed some desire for self-knowledge in humility and truth to see beyond the superficial luster of materialism, narcissism, and moral relativism that had been the breeding ground of criminal activity.

In my notes, lectures, and published articles, I began in the light of these experiences to examine the dynamics of formation influencing both believers and sincere seekers in a time of transition like our own. Especially from 1949 to 1954, I tried in theory and practice to solidify the empirical-experiential curriculum I devised for the Life Schools.

One way I did so was to recruit experts in the *sociohistorical dimension* to teach courses on how much people are influenced by their ethnic and cultural backgrounds and their initial formation in family life. In regard to the *vital dimension*, the medical doctors and nurses on our staff showed young workers how they could implement the principles they were learning about healthy and responsible hygiene into their home life as single Christians and married people. The *functional dimension* of life expressed itself in such practical matters as how to build a budget and pursue Christian excellence in every circumstance of one's life. We saw functioning well not as an end in itself but as a means to embody Christian virtues like prudence and fortitude. Focusing on the *transcendent dimension* enabled us to stress the importance of letting go of self-preoccupation for the sake of showing genuine care and concern for others. I remember how fascinated the girls were by the thought that there could be a spiritually motivated reason for using "make-up." They ought not to see cosmetics as a source of excessive self-interest but as an expression of how their love for others inspired them to appear in a gracious and pleasant manner. What could they do to enhance their everyday formative interactions with the people they loved?

In all of these ways, the Life Schools put young women and men in touch with their true calling in Christ. Marriage was never praised without giving equal commendation to the single vocation, lived by choice or by circumstance. No matter where our call takes us, the formation mystery speaks to us personally and communally about who we are and what we ought to do.

I recall with great affection how well my mother expressed similar thoughts in a letter I received from her on September 15, 1950, in which she wrote:

> Dear Boy,
>
> I received your letter in Bergen; I was there on retreat. That suited me, and I went at once to the picture of Jesus crucified—that is the picture that strikes me most here, and I have told him all about your great responsibility . . . I lit a candle so that the good Jesus can remember it for a while—and, further, I will . . . keep asking him to go on blessing you for the sake of his precious suffering.
>
> I hope, my boy, that you can keep at a distance in a nice way whatever you should not let get into you. Likewise I do my household

chores trying not to hurt others, and yet I manage to keep away whatever does not belong there. Your father and mother keep praying daily for you, and I always ask your heavenly Mother that you may be and remain her slave. Do you remember that when you were students you and Rinus gave yourselves to her?

I have had wonderful days here, but I am glad to return home, for it is getting a bit intense now. The first day I was dead tired and I could not sleep. Now it goes better, but next year . . . I will go to Noordwijkerhout again (*an institute for retreats in those days*).

I have recommended Bep [his sister] and [her fiancé] to Mary, Mother of Perpetual Help. I do not know how that is going to turn out. They are both dead tired. [He] is seeing a doctor and he has already had two penicillin injections against the pain in his stomach. They are buying things for their household, but I think Bep should be careful about his health. Imagine if it were to become TB. He applied for a job with Hoogenbosch (*a shoe firm with more shops in the country*), but he was not appointed. Say a prayer that a solution will be found. You should never give up. Bep does not mind wherever she may be, even if it is in the smallest village . . . Well, my boy, very many cordial regards from all of us,

Your Mother Anna.

～

Encouraging correspondence like this was never wanting in my life in those days. God had given me an excellent setting in the Life Schools and in the camp for juvenile delinquents to craft and test the truly holistic theory of personality I had begun to initiate during and after the war. The programs I devised helped me and my colleagues and counselees to find the inner healing we needed. These terrible times had nearly destroyed all that we believed in as followers of Christ, but nothing could destroy our commitment to be his faithful ambassadors in the liberated world once more entrusted to our care.

Notes

1. It was interesting to discover in Father Adrian van Kaam's archives the following series of testimonials pertaining to his work in the *Mater Amabilis* and *Pater Fortis* schools. These letters were written to support his appointment approximately five years later as a professor in the Department of Psychology at Duquesne University. They offer a first-hand description of his work in the Dutch Life Schools. The first was written by Doctor Schouwenaars herself; the second by the directress of the girls' section in Gemert; the third by the director of the boy's section also in Gemert; and the fourth by the governmental inspectress of the schools.

I

(Letter Undated)

Ministerie van Openbaar Onderwijs
Schooltoezicht
Hoofdtoezichtsgebied
Antwerpen

I, the undersigned, Miss M. C. Schouwenaars, Governmental Inspectress of Education in Belgium, who designed the pedagogical and psychological outline of the Mater Amabilis Schools (which are very common institutes in Holland for the education of youngsters from seventeen to twenty-five), quite willingly declare that Father Adrianus Leonardus van Kaam, CSSp, has done much pedagogical and psychological work for the above-mentioned schools in many and various ways from September 1949 till August 1953. I like to point out that of all my cooperators he grasped the psychological background and idea best. He did excellent clinical work at the schools at Gemert, Oss, and Boxtel (Holland); he planned the first section of these schools for young men in Holland, and he founded with us the first school for them at Gemert, Holland. This school became a great success. He also did excellent work by publishing a series of articles in *Verbum*, which is the best Dutch review of pedagogical catechesis. Another of his merits were the lectures throughout the country on the subject of education, both for the directors and teachers and for the parents of our pupils. A special appreciation I owe him for the clinical work he did for some years among factory girls during their working hours, viz. the factories of "Organon" and of "Zwanenberg" at Oss, Holland.

M. C. Schouwenaars
Governmental Inspectress of Education in Belgium
Foundress of the Mater Amabilis Schools
14, H. Kruisstraat, Mortsel
Antwerp, Belgium

II

Mater Amabilis School
Gemert, Holland

7 August 1954

The undersigned, Mrs. F. Roelofs-Kalkhoven, Directress of the Girls Section of the Mater Amabilis School in Gemert, Holland is very much satisfied about the educational work done by Father Adrianus Leonardus van Kaam as a spiritual director and teacher from September 1949 till September 1953 among the one hundred fifty girls of our school. I am most thankful for the expert pedagogical and psychological advice he gave regularly both to directors and teachers in view to their important task, and to the students who went to him with their problems.

Directress of the Mater Amabilis School
F. Roelofs-Kalkhoven
Gemert, Holland

III

Mater Amabilis School
Gemert, Holland

7 August 1954

The director of the boys' section of the Mater Amabilis School at Gemert, Holland, Mr. A. W. Roelofs, appreciatively declares that the first section of our school for boys, as planned and outlined by Father Adrianus Leonardus van Kaam, was a great success. He also did excellent practical work as a teacher and spiritual director. After this plan had been put into practice and published by our school, it proved to be successful in other towns and villages in Holland as well.

A. W. Roelofs
Director of the Boys' Section
of the Mater Amabilis School
Gemert, Holland

IV

Inspectrice Nijverheidsonderwijs
E. Lommen
Willem III Laan 13

23 August 1954

Miss E. M. M. Lommen, Governmental Inspectress of Housewifery Schools and Mater Amabilis Schools in Holland, declares that she is extremely happy with the practical teaching and educational work done by Father Adrianus Leonardus van Kaam at several Mater Amabilis Schools.

Governmental Inspectress of Housewifery
Schools and Mater Amabilis Schools

2. See Adrian van Kaam and Susan Muto, *The Power of Appreciation: A New Approach to Personal and Relational Healing* (Pittsburgh, PA: Epiphany Books, 1999).

3. The following two letters written in support of Father Adrian van Kaam's entrance to Duquesne University validate the importance of his work with juvenile delinquents and mental patients. The first is from the principal of "Overberg" and the second is from his friend and colleague, Doctor A. Severijnen.

V

Rijksopvoedingsgesticht
Kamp Overberg
Post Veenendaal

5 August, 1954

The undersigned, M. Kroll, in charge of the Dutch governmental psychological observation center for criminal boys, "Overberg," herewith declares that Father Adrianus L. van Kaam, CSSp, living at "missiehuis Rhenen" worked from August 1953 to August 1954 at "Overberg" in perfect cooperation with the headquarters and the other members of the staff of this institute. He is full of praise for the fine educational and psychological work which was done by Father A. L. van Kaam among the boys of the institute. He highly appreciates the gentle and tactical demeanor of this Roman Catholic priest among the Catholic and non-Catholic governmental officials.

M. Kroll
Principal of Overberg
Department van Justitie

VI

Juize Padua
Boekel (N.Br.)
Psychiatrische Inrichting

6 August 1954

The undersigned, Doctor A. Severijnen, psychiatrist and medical superintendent of the lunatic asylum at Boekel, Holland, declares that Father Adrianus Leonardus van Kaam studied and observed under his personal guidance the various patients at the asylum from May 1948 until August 1949. [In a compassionate manner, edifying to all]

Doctor A. Severijnen

4. See Adrian van Kaam, *Transcendence Therapy* in the Formative Spirituality Series, Volume VII (Pittsburgh, PA: Epiphany Books, 2004). This book was first published by Crossroad, New York (1995).

30

Discovering the Centrality of Formation Theology

OLD FRIENDS LIKE MARINUS Scholtes, Gerard Bol, and Adriaan Langelaan, and new ones like Maria Schouwenaars kept my thinking grounded in the truth that spiritual formation has to be bound to the ordinary world of study, seeking employment, establishing a family, finding a place to live, and all those other myriad details that give meaning to daily life. One letter I treasure in this regard was sent to me by my provincial superior, Father Henri Strick, CSSp, who had been my beloved novice master. In the course of sharing some news about various priests in our province, he told me how fervently he prayed to our founder to help him to bear patiently with the day-after-day demands of community life:

> My dear Father Adrian:
>
> Truly I agree with Father Libermann that heroic patience is needed to achieve something lasting. Patience is necessary, more and more. You would sometimes fret with vexation [over the fact] that they all know [it] better. One literally needs heroic patience to bear, day after day, [with the truth] that everybody meddles with everything, judges everything—and that one must bear responsibility, often without being able to do what one would really like to do. I am fully convinced that monastic life would be impossible if it had to be lived in the merely natural order. If it is already such a mess in the order of grace—with sacraments, prayers, the example and teaching of Christ and the Church, etc.—what would it be like if one did not have these means? I will give you an example: I want to take a measure, appoint somebody or so. Your assistant is against it? What to do? Reluctantly you do as he wants. You make another decision, make another appointment . . . things do not turn out well. There you are . . . you have not wanted things this way. Living together is bad but working

together is a hundred times worse. I am in favor of "dictatorship," not because I feel a need for it (at least not naturally, I think) but because the person responsible can make his decision and if in that case things are not right and he has done wrong they can point to the guilty person—and if things demand this, well all right, they can choose somebody else who can do and does [it] better.

Now it is your turn to smile, but that is not bad. I like to have a good long talk at times . . . Do not tell everybody, that is no use. Please pray for all our cares. Cordial greetings to Father General. God's blessing, all the best. *Totus tui in Spirito Sancto.*

~

Father Strick reminded me to cultivate the virtue of patient presence, especially with people who sorely tested this virtue. I had to resort time and again to moments of stillness to beg Christ for the grace of a calm heart to hear his whispered call to be with him in every situation, however trying it might be. I asked the Lord to reform my impatient ways by drawing me into the peace of intimacy with the Trinity. Despite my brokenness, I believed in his promise to be with me wherever I was on my journey through life. I prayed that he would grant me the humility to see the good will in all people and to trust the place reserved for them in God's providential plan.

Teaching Thomistic philosophy inspired my passion for what, for lack of a better phrase, I described in my classes as "theological holism." By this I understood, on the one hand, that formation theology must always defer to the revealed truth upheld by the authoritative teaching of the church while, on the other hand, attempting to establish its relevance to every decision and action that comprises our life from our first to our last breath. This holistic approach lessens the danger of causing a false dichotomy between what we believe and the way we live. It preserves Aquinas' principle of the substantial unity of grace and nature. Dualistic thinking corrupts formational practices by causing a split between the doctrinal truths we teach and the practical actions we take. Theological holism binds together the informational and formational facets of faith as revealed in scripture and the masters. It protects the interconnections between these distinct yet complementary modes of believing and acting. In short, formation theology wholly respects the doctrines and dogmas that constitute the credal system to which we vow allegiance without underestimating the lifelong challenge of fulfilling the call to be and become faithful servants of the Lord. The biblical verse I reiterated in this regard is one of the most experiential ever written by the Apostle Paul, who confesses a struggle with which all believers can identify: "I do not understand my own actions. For I do not do what I want, but I do the very thing I hate . . . I can will what is right, but I cannot do it. For I do not do the good I want, but the evil I do not want is what I do" (Romans 7:15–19).

To further validate these formational insights and to incorporate them into my teaching, I received permission after my ordination to go to the Hoogveld Institute at the University of Nijmegen where I could specialize in pedagogy and andragogy. Both fields heightened my knowledge of childhood and adulthood in the light of formational and educational theory and practice. I remain deeply indebted to two of my professors there, Stephen Strasser and William Perquin, SJ. Both of them confirmed my commitment to draw forth from empirical-experiential fields like psychology, sociology, and cultural anthropology, insights that are formationally relevant to phasic maturation from infancy onward. Following these admittedly theoretical endeavors, I went on to obtain my degrees in advanced education at the Dutch Study center at Culumborg. There I met another great friend and colleague, Professor William Luijpen, OSA, a renowned phemenologist, whose thinking influenced my own approach to the existing person.

Later, at my invitation, Professors Strasser and Luijpen, as well as Doctor Maria Schouwenaars, came to Duquesne University as visiting scholars. I invited Professor Perquin to come for a lectureship as well but illness prematurely ended his fruitful life.

Around this time, the innovative practices and evident successes of the Dutch Life Schools came to the attention of Monsignor Giovanni Baptista Montini. Through contacts with Doctor Schouwenaars, he expressed the desire that I might be released by my community for full-time work on and further development of these anthropological-theological methods of faith formation. On the basis of his authority within the Vatican, the Papal Nuncio in Holland contacted my provincial superior, Father Henri Strick. He readily consented to this request, but he knew it had to be executed as discretely as possible. So as not to call any undue attention to this somewhat unusual arrangement, he simply put me to work as an assistant to the novice master in the novitiate at Gennep, which was only a short distance from the University of Nijmegen where I was already enrolled.1 This move gave me the time I needed to do further research and writing in the comprehensive field of formative spirituality; it also aroused the hope that perhaps one day I might be able to teach the same at a university or other center of higher Christian learning.2 I could not help but think that because Monsignor Montini himself served as national chaplain of a Catholic student organization, he might have seen first-hand the necessity for this kind of approach to lived formation in the faith.

In a providential manner, beyond any personal planning I could ever have initiated, I met the then President of Duquesne University in Pittsburgh, Father Vernon Gallagher, CSSp. He came to Gennep for a visit and asked if he could talk to me in private. He asked many questions about my current academic endeavors and my recent work in the Life Schools. We enjoyed a good rapport, but it quickly came to my attention that this was more than a social visit. To my immense surprise he invited me and, as I soon discovered, another Holy Ghost Father, Bert van Croonenburg, who had been a chaplain in the girls' division of Schouwenaars' schools, to come to America and join the faculty of Duquesne University. Surely this proposal was God's way of making the vision of Montini a reality. Perhaps after all I could bring this work of integrating faith and formation to the world of higher education. The invitation, sound and acceptable as it was to the Dutch province, could not be put into motion, however, until I fulfilled another obligation to my community. Only then could I make plans to come to the United States.

In the interest of better understanding the educational commitments of our founder, Father Strick had suggested that I had to go to Paris in 1952 to research and write an autobiography of Venerable Francis Libermann, who, as he observed, focused not only on serving in the foreign missions, but also on reforming the seminary and promoting quality education for clergy, religious, and laity. Before continuing the story of how I came to the States and what happened at Duquesne University, I must turn to the time I spent at the motherhouse in Paris. What I learned from Libermann's life solidified my own convictions of the need for a theology of formation to serve already established and new apostolic works in the Church.3

Notes

1. This appointment was greeted by van Kaam's colleague, Bert van Croonenburg, as "bad news" as the following letter attests:

Gemert, June 22, 1951

Dear Adriaan,

Today I received the letter [regarding your appointment] with the bad news . . . [but at least] two years of *Mater Amabilis* work have shown [you] that there is a Providence whose "ups and downs" we cannot always understand. I feel sorry for the work, but it will go on, even in the face of difficulties . . . I feel sorry for you, the more so because you do not know what will be in store for you. Pittsburgh is too good to be true, but, as Mrs. Roelofs [Translator's note: *A well-known family near Gemert in those days*] said: "He is a saintly priest, if they give him other work he will do that well, too." Remain humble. The Roelofs family are sad about it. I went to see them yesterday to ask if they had already heard the news. At once they called Gennep for [confirmation], but the Superior of the place did not know anything yet. It is also sad for Miss Schouwenaars, but she will overcome this with her confidence in God's Providence. Meanwhile, be brave. Don't do anything foolish and try to accept whatever comes, in the way it comes . . . Our Lord will give you a hand. I will also ask him for his help for you . . .
With promise of prayer,
Bertus

2. Another friend of Father van Kaam's Sister Marie Anne, intuited the providential nature of this move in her letter to him:

Keldonk, June 27, 1951

Dear Reverend Father,

These last few days I have been checking the letters thinking, "Will there be any news from Father van Kaam?" The other day Father van Croonenburg asked for special prayers for you. I sensed that a decision would be made about the work you are doing at the moment, and I hoped for a favorable solution. It appears God has other plans about you . . . I read [between the lines] in your short letter and saw there deep suffering [mixed with awe]. I can only imagine what it means for you to say farewell to this apostolate. It is not easy to suddenly see one's whole future at stake . . . [Now we are] forced to have recourse to Christ and to let him act. When I consider your situation, which I still often do, the thought arises in me, "Le disciple n'est pas au-dessus de son Maître" (*The disciple is not above his Master*). Your priestly years have already been rich in experience in this regard. That is why they have been so fruitful. Father, I hope and pray that you will be given the opportunity to do good to many souls, wherever in the world you go. Miss Schouwenaars will regret very much that she has been deprived of what at first she had been granted, but above all she will miss your cooperation in all possible fields. *Le bien ne se fait jamais aisément (The good is never done easily).*

Father, I hope soon to hear about your Superiors' plans for you. Meanwhile we keep praying for all those who, together with you, have been hit by this measure, but of course most for you.

Respectfully and cordially,
Sister Marie-Anne

3. A glance at the biographical/bibliographical review at the end of this book will reveal the width and breadth of Father Adrian van Kaam's critical and creative output in the Netherlands at this juncture of his faith journey. In his contributions to a variety of clinical and education publications, one can find the seeds of his later volumes on the science, anthropology, and theology of formation.

31

Events in Paris

As soon as I began my research on the life of Libermann, I learned what an exciting place the motherhouse of our congregation was now and used to be. I walked the same halls where the learned

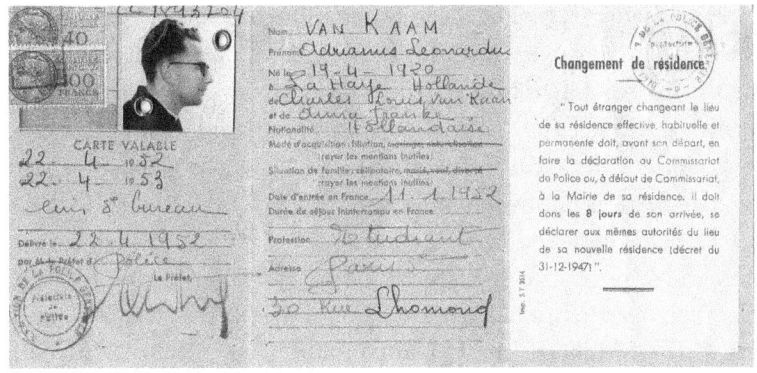

Benedictine, Dom Pitra, who subsequently became a cardinal, had a regular room. So did Abbé Bouix, famous for his studies in Canon Law; Abbé Rohrbacher, another renowned writer of Church history; Abbé Martinel, celebrated for his apologetic and political books; Abbé Gaume, renown for his catechetical works and an epoch-making indictment of contemporary education; and, perhaps, the most illustrious of all, J. P. Migne, who gathered up a veritable army of collaborators and published an ecclesiastical, multi-volume collection of Greek and Latin Patrology, which every priest had to read in the course of his study.

Other eminent persons and learned prelates like Bishop Gousset and Bishop Parisis stayed on the Rue Lhomond where, in the spirit of Francis Libermann, intellectual life flourished in its ancient halls of higher learning. Dom Cabrol described the vibrant atmosphere he encountered at the motherhouse in these words: "Here was a scientific and literary group where everyone spoke freely about things that pertained to the Church, where everyone contributed not only his personal views but the results of his research as well . . . Sometimes a veritable debate took place among the members of this scholarly areopagus."1 In the spirit of discourse that was so important to Libermann, I enjoyed while in Paris the company of a fellow Spiritan, Father Cor Neven. He was studying at the Sorbonne to learn new teaching techniques to apply to his catechetical courses in the Netherlands. He and I, together with another priest-friend from Canada, went almost every Sunday to the Louvre, enjoyed the theater and, needless to say, partook of lots of marvelous French cuisine.

Returning to the history of our congregation, I learned that Father Gaultier, who was Libermann's first assistant, facilitated the rebirth of the Spiritans' academic tradition. He placed himself at the service of learned visitors, supplying them with precious data for their research and letting them have access to the well-stocked library of the motherhouse. He shared with all who came some of his own original approaches and views and saw it to that many of these prestigious professors would be welcome there as permanent guests.

Father Rohrbacher, for example, found the atmosphere on the Rue Lhomond so conducive to research that he asked permission to live and work there for the rest of his life. One of his last wishes was to be buried next to Father Libermann. When another priest, Father Bouix, found himself without a place to live due to a disagreement with his archbishop, Francis offered him hospitality even though he himself could ill afford to incur any displeasure on the part of Church authority. It came as no surprise to Francis when he received a summons to appear at the Archbishop's residence with Father Bouix, who left the following personal account of the audience:

> When he came home, Libermann described the conversation with that quiet serenity which even the most painful events could not affect. The prelate had reproached him with these words: "You are harboring in your seminary priests who are at odds with their bishops. There's Father Rohrbacher, for instance." Then the Venerable Father added for my benefit: "I believe you were uppermost in the Archbishop's thoughts, but no doubt he

didn't dare to name you. Moreover, I can assure you, I didn't say one word about you." Father Libermann then answered regarding Rohrbacher: "I did not know that he was at odds with his bishop, but Your Grace can trust me to set things straight with that prelate." Then I [Bouix] offered to leave the seminary if my presence there would do harm to his congregation, but he told me to remain. That question could be considered later on (N.D. 13, 600 f.).

The more I probed into the life and times of our venerable founder, the more I realized that his contribution to spiritual formation spanned the ages and that it appealed as much to believers in the world as to members of a religious community. Thanks to the graces he received and the depth of his calling, Libermann was inclined to focus on the foundational elements of Christian spirituality and to elaborate upon them in service of his apostolic concerns.

Among his many remarkable contributions to the literature of spirituality, I felt particularly drawn to his identification of two key dispositions of faith formation: firmness and gentleness.2 He understood from experience that our life as called forth by grace follows an upward or transcendent path. Our response to this movement meets with countless resistances, some as huge as the war we had just gone through and some so minute they may go unnoticed. Unappraised, these resistances may disturb our inner consonance, but, in cooperation with grace, we can face and overcome them with courage. The gift of firmness enables us to welcome these resistances not as sources of distress but as invitations to turn whatever is difficult on our faith journey into an opportunity for growth in inner sensitivity and responsible action.

If our life is to continue on its upward path to transcendent maturation, the disposition of firmness has to be complemented by that of gentleness, which prevents us from becoming uncaring or insensitive towards others or ourselves. Lack of gentleness can lead as much to impetuous overexertion as to a destructive style of asceticism. Libermann warned his confrères against both deviations: "This sort of [willful] energy has another defect. It has a penchant for methods and remedies that are radical. Now, radicalism is good and even necessary in the realm of dogma, but it is detestable and destructive of all good when it comes to the administration and supervision of sacred things" (N.D. 12, 319 f.).

Firmness carried to the extreme betrays itself in an inclination to rigidity or inflexibility. It must be balanced by gentleness since these two dispositions of the heart modulate one another. Firmness without gentleness deteriorates into severity; gentleness without firmness becomes an excuse for laziness. The balance of these two virtues proved to be one of the main characteristics of Libermann's personality and a cornerstone of his directive outreach to everyone in need of guidance.

It follows that Libermann did not want the members of his congregation to withhold their gentleness from anyone. He said:

> Live in peace with the outside world. Be genuine in your dealings with poor Frenchmen who have no religion. Pity them but don't be angry with them. Excuse them when they oppose you . . . Be particularly careful to overcome the embarrassment you may feel when you are in the company of men of the world whose habits of thought and judgment are different from yours, who look askance at you, or perhaps despise you . . . Such embarrassment engenders a sort of stiffness, a kind of shyness that gives one the air of being ill-humored and standoffish . . . That type of attitude makes a very bad impression on them and estranges them from our holy religion . . . In general, you ought to like all men, no matter how they may feel about religious principles or about you . . . If we are able to force consciences to be pure, wills to be good, and minds to be truthful, it is evident that we should do so. Charity would make it our duty . . . there is no one in this world who can even slightly force the consciences, wills, or minds of his fellow men. God didn't want to do it. Why should we? (N.D. 9, 248 f.).

When this sense of gentle love begins to pervade our life, it affects for the better anyone we meet and every good work we perform. By attending gently to whomever the Lord entrusts to our care, we grow in reverence and respect. By contrast, losing ease of heart and mind happens all too frequently if plans do not go our way. We feel a coercive need for instant accomplishment instead of flowing gently with the challenges that emerge day by day.

Libermann was a master in this regard. He repeats many times that exalted ideals, endless worries, and violent emotions should not overwhelm us or cause us to rush here and there at a feverish pace. Simply being in touch with what is and with who we most deeply are is enough. He summarizes the process of being true to one's self in one word: "simplicity." In his understanding this character trait has nothing to do with pleasant inclinations, lack of intelligence, or disdain for culture. For Francis simplicity is the virtue that best promotes faithfulness to what is most genuine about us and to what is in accord with God's plan for us.

Working in the archives on Libermann's life made me mindful of so many of the people who had brought me to this point of my faith journey. At home in the Hague, at Weert in the junior seminary, at Gennep in the novitiate, at Gemert in the senior seminary, I learned that life in family and community requires a heart disposed to firmness (perseverance) and gentleness (patience). One of my beloved readings from Holy Scripture was taken from the First Letter of Paul to Timothy (6:11–12): "But as for you, man of God, shun all this; pursue righteousness, godliness, faith, love, endurance, gentleness. Fight the good fight of the faith; take hold of the eternal life, to which you were called and for which you made a good confession in the presence of many witnesses."

Bad spirits, rebellious against one's better judgment, to say nothing of one's rule of life, must be resisted. I myself had to be on guard against depreciative thoughts sparked by grumbling groups as disinclined to be compassionate as they appeared inclined to make fun of anyone who did not fit their model of what religious life ought to be like. I remember being told by someone of note in the junior seminary that I acted in too refined a manner and that I should be a more "regular guy." That meant using "masculine" language, so I mastered expressions like "damn it" and "go to hell," totally shocking my mother when I brought them home with me at vacation time! She exercised great firmness in being sure I wiped them from my vocabulary. I always welcomed any sign of gentility and respect for uniqueness—mine or anyone else's. I disliked the homogenizing mentality as much as Libermann did. I appreciated, for example, the way in which my friend, Father Cor Neven, shared while we were in Paris his love, like mine, for art, literature, and the theater. Knowing that I had been made fun of for my "shaky" voice and realizing that I would have to become a better speaker, he helped me to develop my preaching skills. We would take books of prepared sermons and rehearse with them, one of us "preaching," the other listening. Later, when he, too, had become a professor in the seminary, I recommended him for the editorship of the journal *Verbum* in which I published many articles on formation and education. I will always appreciate his jovial spirit with me and many others who benefitted from his intuitive grasp of their real needs.

Studying Libermann's life in the light of my own experiences of balancing firmness and gentleness in respect for each person's unique-communal call was one of the joys of my life. Libermann's *yes* to God's will drew him into depths of silent wonder where he felt, however unworthily, the embrace of Father, Son, and Holy Spirit. The power of gentle presence opened his soul to the ineffable reality of the faith that moves mountains—be they sources of physical debilitation or spiritual darkness. From these mysterious depths God granted him the wisdom to deal with the ups and down of daily life without showing the least bit of discouragement. His faith in this mystery was firm enough to never waiver, gentle enough never to doubt his oneness with Jesus and the assurance of his redemptive love.

As firm as this convert from Judaism to Catholicism was in matters of faith, he remained remarkably flexible when it come to readying his priests and brothers for the rigor of life in the missions and the reality of social and educational work. Libermann was as gentle in complementing his companions for their accomplishments in the apostolate as he was firm in rebuking them for clinging stubbornly to attitudes inherited from a time that was gone forever. As he wisely observes:

> It has been the misfortune of the clergy in recent times that they hold to ideas out of the past. The world has progressed, the enemy has set up his batteries in line with the situation and the spirit of the age, but we have lagged behind. We must keep abreast of the times. With complete fidelity to the Gospel we must do good and combat evil according to the state and the temper of the period in which we live. We must attack the ramparts of the enemy wherever they happen to be set up and not give him a chance to entrench himself and consolidate his position while we are off seeking for him in places where he is no longer to be found. Clinging to olden times and retaining thought patterns that ruled a previous era will destroy the efficacy of our endeavors and enable the enemy to establish a stronghold in the new order. Let us then frankly and simply embrace the new order and breathe into it the spirit of the Gospel. We will thereby sanctify the world and the world will be on our side (N.D. 10, 151).

Francis then did something to embrace this order that shocked a lot of people. He gathered together those of his confrères who were eligible to vote and marched them down to register. He accepted the right of suffrage for which the people of Paris had paid a bloody price on the barricades. "I understand very well," he said, "that elections are not ecclesiastical affairs, and yet we must keep in mind that we no longer live in the political situation of the past" (N.D. 10, 151).

Because he understood that realistic planning is one of the cornerstones of apostolic success, Francis resolutely opposed impulsive and emotional approaches to missiology. Instead he urged:

> We should avoid forming vague and general ideas of things. If we want to know them precisely, we have to consider them practically... Don't picture things in your imagination. Observe them calmly, consider them practically... insofar as you can. Then, when you have taken every precaution, put all your trust in God alone... We should not go adventuring, banking on the breaks of the game (N.D. 7, 82, 192 f., 287).

Africa was a case in point. Nearly three hundred years earlier, scores of zealous missionaries had left Europe to evangelize thousands of souls and yet by Libermann's time hardly a trace remained of the tremendous work they set out to do. Their fate taught our founder the necessity of good planning if a self-perpetuating church was to be established in various parts of that vast continent. He clearly felt that action without appraisal of the culture and the climate is like a flower severed from its parent stem. Feverish activity followed by the passionate engagement of powerful but erratic forces is no better than whistling in the dark unless it is directed by observant, reflective planners. The best-equipped army is powerless without tactical and intelligent staffs. That is why Libermann almost shouted these words: "For the love of God and the Blessed Virgin, don't be just a missionary. Be a leader as well. Get to know men and things. Look to the future as much as to the present situation."

From the most astute envisioning to the trivialities of life, he kept this same practical outlook. When one of his missionaries, Father Collin, became overwrought because he had to wear long pants instead of the usual knee-length culottes, Francis wrote back: "I don't see any problem here. You say it's not our style, but the Rule doesn't prescribe our [manner] of dress and we cannot adopt any one in particular. In Guinea, for instance, they wear straw hats... Father Tisserant wore long trousers in San Domingo... If God sees fit to enable me to send you the confrèrers

I have in mind, I'll put . . . pants [of the right length] on them" (N.D. 10, 90).

Libermann also warned that oppressors of the underprivileged may only play at being gentle, preferring to keep company with high society and thinking nothing of being ruthless toward those whom they exploit. Their gentleness may be only an imitation of genteel appearances customary in certain circles. Such surface gentility is as useless for growth in the life of the spirit as for success in the apostolate. In no way does such falsehood bring us nearer to the mystery of divine gentleness that indwells our souls. Libermann condemned make-believe or pseudo-gentility that shows no semblance of true reverence for those in need. One must never cover insincerity with a veneer of piety. As he once told a priest:

> If you cringe before the world, if you flatter it, or if you merely ape its manner, you may be sure that your priestly work will be sterile. Don't be afraid of the world. Approach it as one who belongs wholly to God. Face it without fear. Do not stop to consider what people will say or think about you. The world's judgments have little effect on a true priest (L.S., 1, 41).

This respect for individuality, this reluctance to hurt anyone, this disinclination to force people to act contrary to their temperament demanded an astute knowledge of the human psyche and spirit. Libermann had this gift. In his writings he urged his priests and brothers to develop sound psychological insights, complemented by a good dose of empathy:

> They [the (confrères] ought to adjust their speech and their behavior to the emotional make-up and the interests of the people with whom they deal. This emotional make-up and these interests cannot always be known by calculated conclusions, arrived at by reasoning. It takes a certain tact to do so, and this tact is normally acquired through a general and practical knowledge of the recesses of the human heart, of character differences, and of interest specialties. These things are picked up by observing the people you meet and by paying attention to the sentiments and dispositions they display (N.D. 10, 545).

The French word *douceur*, a keynote of both Libermann's life and his counsels, defies precise translation but it connotes creating harmony within the personality; it excludes harshness, tension, compulsion, and rigidity towards oneself and others. It moderates all hysterical agitation, relieves anxiety, and controls aggressiveness and hostility. It is the fruit of quiet self-possession gained through growth in self-understanding through the light of grace. Far from generating a superficial make-believe conviction that all is sweetness and light, it rests firmly on an awareness of our fallen condition.

Once grace frees us from the illusion that obedience means blind compliance to rigid regulations that weaken over time and belie the experience of faith, we can begin, in Libermann's view, to grow resourceful, resilient, and even ingenious in our struggle to witness to God's reign to earth. He was a man of sober realism, who offered no panaceas in this regard: "All the works that have been undertaken and carried through in the Church have had difficulties yet those difficulties did not scare off the apostolic men who initiated the projects, nor did they prevent them from going ahead with constancy as well as courage. It has always been the way of Providence to manifest itself in the midst of obstacles and the happiest results have normally lain beyond the greatest handicaps" (N.D. 8, 91). Libermann never hesitated to advise every member of his congregation "to avoid timidity, excessive precaution, lethargy and other faults that stem from false prudence . . . We must courageously make a decision . . . and then follow through on it energetically" (N.D. 10, 546). He lived by the robust conviction that we ought to welcome resistances as gifts of the Lord, which is to say as occasions for growth in the firmness and gentleness the Holy Spirit waits to grant us. He saw the challenging times in which he lived in sickness and health as stepping stones to a dynamic expression of faith, hope, and love, fervent and daring to the end. As this saintly founder said on his deathbed: "Be fervent . . . always fervent" (N.D. 13, 659).

As my research for *A Light to the Gentiles* came to conclusion, I understood why Libermann placed little or no value on extreme or external mortification. He refused to consider such aberrations as flagellation, penitential chains, hair shirts, sleeping on wooden planks, and fasting on days other than those prescribed by the Church. He mistrusted the unhealthy atmosphere in which these practices are apt to flourish, and he was particularly apprehensive about their effect on young people. He saw that all too often they end in pride and conceit, in nervous tension and a distorted scale of spiritual values. Ready surrender to God's will at all times and under all circumstances provides the only sure path to holiness. As Francis said:

> In order to go to God with your heart, your mind must be undisturbed, indifferent. Keep it quiet. Do things simply, without too much analysis. If you really want to please God and intend to be in full agreement with his will, you can't go wrong. It is important for you not to spend time trying to find out exactly what is agreeable to him or what pleases him most. Act like a child that is fond of its father. It can't analyze or figure out what its father likes most . . . It does the first thing that comes into its head. It gets the idea that Daddy will be pleased and then goes ahead and does it. Why not do the same? Sometimes the child makes a mistake. So will you. But that doesn't matter. God knows you meant well . . . and that pleases him. It's essential for you to develop this unconcerned way of doing things. It will improve you much quicker than any self-conscious striving for perfection (N.D. 4, 105).

In contrast to the wounds inflicted by our exalted and exalting pride form, gentleness tempers the multitude of illusions that distort our feelings and lets us appraise in peace the reasons why we fail or succeed. Gentle presence entails a return to our original call to loving consonance with the mystery from which we emerge and to which we return. Our hearts should not be tightened by pained concern about our progress. Excessive forcefulness has to be softened. To be faithful to our divine destiny, we must elevate our spirits beyond enslavement to popular opinions and the paralyzing need to please people at the price of our integrity. In Libermann's words:

> We must distrust ourselves all the time, distrust everything we do, everything we say and think. We have to be circumspect, and not act with the boldness which manifests itself at times under the guise of genuine abandonment to God, and yet is far from it. Let everything be done in God, gently, unpretentiously. O dear brothers, how perilous is all that haughtiness of mind, that presumption in acting, that determination and violence in the will. You have no idea! (L.S. 1, 503).

Avoiding extremes is an indelible mark of Libermann's teaching. Experience had shown him that anyone who engages in excessive firmness risks taking on a perfectionistic style of life molded by the harsh hammer of inflexible willfulness. Functional minds forgetful of the transcendent may have a tendency to master the mystery for their own purposes. Without a softer touch responsive to grace, projects of self-salvation may erode our growth in wisdom and prudence. Gentleness becomes a facade if it does not flow from our inmost center in Christ, the Good Shepherd. Under the pressure of perverted gentility, we may deny our humility, lose our tranquility, and fail to discover the true meaning of discipleship articulated in the Great Commandment: to love God with our whole being and to love our neighbors as ourselves.

This revelation guided my pen as I marveled at the lessons of Libermann's life and at last completed, with as much firmness and gentleness as possible, the first Dutch edition of my book titled *The Jew of Saverne* (1953). Thanks to the help of my friend, Father Henry Koren, CSSp, the book, later retitled *A Light to the Gentiles*, was published in English in 1959 and has remained in print to this day. In the intervening years both my personal and my professional life were set on a new path. I witnessed my sisters beginning their married lives and raising children of their own. Though saddened by the thought of my immanent departure, my parents were happy that I could fulfill my dreams. I saw them as often as I could while I still lived in Holland and promised to return for home visits, which I did on a regular basis during summer vacations. At last, on the feast of the Assumption, August 15, 1954, I landed on the shores of my new country, determined, as soon as I saw the Statue of Liberty, to perfect my use of the English language, to apply for citizenship, and to become the best servant of God and others I could be.

Notes

1. See Adrian van Kaam, *A Light to the Gentiles: The Life Story of the Venerable Francis Libermann* (Eugene, OR: Wipf and Stock, 2009). All future references are to this edition.

2. See Adrian van Kaam, *Spirituality and the Gentle Life* (Pittsburgh, PA: Epiphany Books, 2005).

32

On to America and University Life

Once I completed the biography of Libermann and oversaw its initial publication, I was told by my superiors that I was free to accept the invitation I had received to continue my ministry at Duquesne University. Word came that I would be joining the faculty in the Fall of 1954, exactly ten years after the Hunger Winter. At the age of 34, I entered upon another divinely directed phase of my life, one replete with new and incredibly challenging disclosures.

Hardly had I caught my breath then I was hurled from a life of quiet study, relative solitude and ecclesiastical work into the midst of a fervent time of Catholic thinking, represented by authors like Jacques Maritan, Max Scheler, and Gabriel Marcel, and into a revolutionary movement in psychology in which I soon found myself becoming a figure of some influence. My seminal works on the nature of personality, on existence, religion, and the human sciences, began to attract scholarly attention. I was sought out by many of the leading figures in what was then seen as a newly emerging, theoretical and practical movement in the field of humanistic psychology. The influence I exerted was no less significant than the inspiration I derived from others' illuminating views, works, and personal friendships.

Due to this interplay, I was able to produce a number of books that bolstered and enriched this approach from its inception. Further thinking and writing enabled me to celebrate these advancements while addressing some of their shortcomings. My contact with many of the brilliant minds affiliated with the inception of the humanistic movement in psychology helped me to shape my own empirical-experiential theory of human and spiritual unfolding. From my pioneering work in the 60's in the area of religion and personality until the publication of my master works in formative spirituality, I continued to develop my own comprehensive model of human nature as distinctively human or transcendent.

As much as I had hoped to continue my research, writing, and teaching in the complementary fields of education and formation, I soon discovered that another task awaited me. My Dutch publications would not be lost in the process of my Americanization, for I was able to translate many of them directly into English and to reformulate others in the light of my pending work in the field of anthropological psychology.1

The opening offered to me by the president of Duquesne University came as a surprise. Instead of continuing where I had left off, I was to replace a Spiritan father, a professor of psychology, who had died unexpectedly. Though my higher degrees were in pedagogy and andragogy and though I thought it might be best, if I had to be assigned anywhere, to teach in the school of education, the President persuaded me, under obedience, to start my university career by shifting to a new specialty. To do so meant that I would have to obtain the appropriate doctoral degree. The conversation ended on the note that perhaps in the future I would be allowed to establish a center of study more directly related to spiritual formation but for the time being that was not to be my first priority.

Knowing that I had already explored the anthropological facets of psychology in the Netherlands with a group of colleagues interested in this approach gave me some consolation. One of them was Father Bert van Croonenburg, who was already teaching in the department of philosophy; others in that Dutch study group included Koos Meekers, a Holy Ghost father and a scripture scholar, who had received his doctorate from the University of Nijmegen, and Professor Severijnen, the psychiatrist, who directed the mental health hospital near Gemert where I had worked for a time while teaching in the Life Schools.

Unlike American schools of education that seemed to place the emphasis on training people in the art and discipline of conducting classes at various levels of matriculation, my study had a different focus. Its emphasis was on the full-field formation of younger and older learners. Although President Gallagher was well aware of my educational background, he decided that I would eventually feel at home in the setting of the psychology department. Since a place had already been opened for me, I accepted his assessment that this "detour" from my work in the Life Schools would offer a step toward rather than one away from the formational vision dear to my heart. I remember his saying to me, "Consider this for now the unique way God is calling you to be a missionary."

The schools to which I would go for advanced study had oriented their psychology and counseling departments more toward humanistic or humane approaches rather than modeling them exclusively on the behavioristic sciences. I was to enroll for degree purposes in the psychology department of Case Western Reserve University in Cleveland, where the renowned personality theorist, Professor Calvin Hall, taught. To complement my interests in areas of theory and practice not presented there, I sought and received permission to take courses for credit at the Alfred Adler Institute where I met Professor Heinz Ansbaucher. Another opportunity presented itself at Brandeis University where Abraham Maslow, with whom I established a personal friendship, shared my interests in the experiential actualization of the human personality. To hone my therapeutic skills I took courses in the counseling division of the University of Chicago. At that time its chairperson was Carl Rogers, whose client-centered approach to psychotherapy I wanted to learn, too. Within three years of having arrived in the United States, I completed my course work and defended my doctoral dissertation for Case Western on

"The Experience of Really Feeling Understood by a Person" in which I pioneered my own humanistic-phenomenological method of analyzing the formative experiences of 365 subjects. The assignment to develop as a new academic offering at our University "psychology as a human science" proved to be less difficult than I had initially expected. I realized that I could translate the main ideas of my Dutch formation anthropology in such a way that they would be acceptable to psychologists in the United States interested in the lived experience of the person. My central concept of what is "formative" could be translated into what is "existential" or empirical-experiential. In this way I would be able to adhere to the classical tradition I taught in my seminary courses on philosophical anthropology that characterized the structure of the distinctively human person as that of *essence* preceding *existence.*

The human essence or the soul-form we most basically are accounts for our uniqueness while reminding us of all that we have in common. Existence or existentiality in this structure refers to the form we give to our successive disclosures of this unique essence and its subsequent "existential" unfolding. The phrase I coined to summarize this description of the holistic development of the human person was "unique-communal."

My use of the word "existential" referred to a theological not merely a psychological tradition. American psychologists, who were not as familiar with this traditional meaning, highlighted the opposite idea that "existence precedes essence," resulting in "existentialism" or "existentialistic" philosophy or psychology. Lost in the process was the link between human existentiality and the essence of humanity. In the interest of accuracy, I designated this approach to the human sciences "existentialistic" to distinguish it from my own "existential" or "formative" way of thinking. I was aware that these existentialistic approaches could be useful to the unfolding of the general field of psychology, provided their proponents remained attentive to the objectively given empirical-experiential facets of human formation. It would be my task to formulate insights that could be integrated into this new field of "psychology as a human science" in fulfillment of the task assigned to me by the university administration.

Let me pause here to say how fortunate I was to be able to cultivate professional relationships as well as warm personal friendships with humanistic psychologists like Abraham Maslow and Carl Rogers and with psychoanalysts like Henry Elkin and Erik Erickson. Studying their innovative approaches led me to the conclusion that no already existing speciality provided a sufficient counter-balance to the pessimistic and behavioral models predominant in the country at that time. To foster as an alternative "psychology as a human science," I had to draw rather extensively upon the work of such continental thinkers as Max Scheler, Viktor Frankl, and William Luipjen. Being fluent in German, French, Dutch, and English, I was able to steep myself in existential-phenomenological literature. I thank my friend, Father Henry Koren, CSSp, PhD, former editor of the Duquesne University Press, for helping me to bring to our campus in the late 50's and 60's many outstanding European authors who met and dialogued with the faculty I had begun to assemble for the department, including, among others, Amadeo Giorgi, Charles Maes, Anthony Barton, and Rolf von Eckertsberg.

At that time in our country, I say "our" country because I had by now become an American citizen, a number of psychologists were already moving toward the formulation of a more humane type of psy-

chology. I concurred with their efforts by drawing upon the findings of "existential philosophy" and its phenomenological analysis of the essence-existence structure of the acting person. My post-war experiences in the Life Schools enabled me to critique the atheistic assumptions of "secularistic existentialism," which were the direct opposite of my own Christian existential understanding. While taking into account the formationally relevant findings of the human and social sciences, including those of all existing schools of psychology, I kept my thinking grounded in the revelation of our being preformed, created, and redeemed by God. This was the firm rock of faith on which I stood. I could still critically appraise and creatively transform the insights I derived from the works of existential thinkers while rejecting what in them was incompatible with my faith perspective.

My version of existential or anthropological psychology, with its underlying stress on the formation of the whole person, was received with enthusiasm by many faculty members and students at Duquesne University and in various institutes of higher learning as well as in a number of clinical settings. I accepted invitations to write several articles in professional, psychological, and educational journals, which were seminal to this challenging endeavor.

In his historical introduction to the place of phenomenology in psychology and psychiatry, Herbert Spielgelberg (Northwestern University Press, 1972) wrote:

> Adrian van Kaam, a native Dutchman, has done a great deal to establish phenomenological psychology, not only at Duquesne University but generally in the American academic world, particularly through his editorial enterprises. However, these by no means exhaust his energies. Trained in Holland, he did his doctoral dissertation at Case Western Reserve University . . . under the partial supervision of Kurt Goldstein, Abraham Maslow, and Carl Rogers. It now figures as the main illustration of applied phenomenology in his book on *Existential Foundations of Psychology* (1966).

This recognition seemed to play a role in attracting a sudden influx of outstanding students to the Department of Psychology. Such increases in our enrollment made the hiring of new faculty members necessary.

While I was gratified by the success of my lectures and publications, I still felt a strong urge to pursue the fulfillment of my original dream to establish a program devoted specifically to the theoretical and practical field of formative spirituality. While that dream had to be placed on hold for a while, I felt understandably gratified by the fruits of my obedience to the assignment to study and teach psychology as a human science. The master's theses being written by our students were recognized to be of such a high quality that the representatives of the Middle States Association declared in 1962 that the program I initiated in 1954 ought to be elevated to a doctoral degree in the field of psychology.2

I found myself immersed in a climate in the 60's that demanded my participation in many conferences and seminars To defend and sustain the type of psychology I had been asked to develop, without losing sight of my first commitment to my own and others' renewal of religious life, it was necessary not only to conduct workshops and seminars but to remain as engaged as possible in the demanding tasks of writing and publication. I tried to stay open to new findings while simultaneously finding a way to critique popular psychologism, cultic and "new age" spirituality with its gnostic and pantheistic undertones; and, above all, aetheistic existentialism and any other "ism" that threatened to erode our distinctively human transcendence dynamic and dignity.3 While participating fully in the direction and growth of the psychology department, I continued on my own time to ponder the connection I had begun to explore in my book between "religion and personality." Patience and perseverance were the virtues for which I most prayed. Where the religious dimension of my work was concerned, I had no choice but to trust in God's perfect timing. While walking with great care the fine line between psychology and religion, I found to my happy surprise that I was invited to speak as a psychologist and a spiritual animator in many schools and retreat centers across the country. My audiences ranged from scholars to movie stars! I was especially touched by the invitation I received from Abraham Maslow to teach his courses at Brandeis University for a whole year when he went on sabbatical.4

These guest professorships and other speaking engagements enriched me professionally and kept me in contact with many friends and colleagues in the field of existential psychology, notably Rollo May and Henry Elkin, who encouraged me to serve as an editor of the *Review of Existential Psychology and Psychiatry*. Having fulfilled my obligations at Brandeis, I returned to full-time teaching at Duquesne, to overseeing our degree programs, and to directing a number of dissertations. Articles based on my presentations had to be readied for publication in breakthrough journals like the *Review* itself and in standard periodicals like the *Journal of Individual Psychology* and the *Harvard Educational Review*.

REV. ADRIAN VAN KAAM, C.S.SP., professor of psychology at Duquesne University will speak on "The Rise of Anthropological Psychology" at the 49th meeting of the Weston Science Coloquium. The meeting will be held at Weston College on Sunday, April 5 at 7 P.M.

Among the many new friends and colleagues I met at home and on the road, one to whom I felt especially indebted was Professor Rudolf Dreikurs, whom I had first encountered at the Alfred Adler Institute. He was a Jewish psychologist from Germany, who published several articles on the place and importance of children in the family system. Another influence I must again acknowledge was that of Erik Erikson, whose works I had studied before I had the privilege of meeting him in person when he came to the University of Pittsburgh as a guest lecturer.

My counseling training under Carl Rogers gave a tremendous boost to my own therapeutic skills, but no relationship was more beneficial to me than the friendship I enjoyed with Abraham Maslow. Conversations with him confirmed my own renaissance outlook on life and deepened my already firm commitment to dialogue with people of many different ideological and cultural backgrounds with the aim of coming to better understand the reasons behind their character formation.

Maslow and I shared the desire to pursue, beyond the typical behavioristic models which were acceptable at that time, a new view of a humanly oriented psychology, which had as its object pole an analysis of the true nature of the person. This research entailed the risk of seeking to integrate into psychology, humanistic, phenomenological, existential, and anthropological thinking. Duquesne was and remained a mecca in those early years for such visionary outlooks, thanks to its outstanding philosophy department where many European scholars and practitioners came as guest lecturers. All of these contacts kept my teaching and practice as life-rooted and life-related as possible. Books like *Religion and Personality* spawned many speaking engagements here and abroad. My audiences were not only secular but religious, especially among congregations of sisters, who asked for my help in integrating pretranscendent psychological insights with their commitment to the transcendent vows of life they, like I, had espoused.

This was the era when many nuns and priests, pressurized perhaps by the popularity of self-discovery and self-actualization, made the choice to leave religious life. Many reasons accounted for such wrenching decisions, but with every leave-taking I realized that I had to work harder to build models of formation that fully respected our human condition as fallen and forgiven, as sinful and redeemed. New insights in fields like psychology, sociology, and cultural anthropology had to be taken into account but not at the risk of eroding our faith and formation traditions.5 One of the premises of formation science is the distinction between people's way of life (their formation tradition) and the creeds they profess (their faith tradition). In many of the cruelest conflicts, participants share a way of life; their appearance, homes, and customs are identical. Yet because some are Hindu, for example, and some Muslim, they despise one another. People are less likely to demonize a religion other than their own when they perceive that, although their beliefs and practices may differ, they share a common universal longing for what I referred to as the "More Than," which all strive to express in their own way. To be moving towards the same end is to be companions on the journey, whether or not we belong to different faith traditions.

I did my best through teaching, writing, and speaking to demonstrate the importance of understanding the differences between the faith tradition and its life-giving foundations and the formation traditions that emerge from it but may be cluttered with bellicose or prejudicial accretions. Ideally, the formation tradition is a lived and authentic expression of the faith tradition, but alas, this is often not the case, thus leading many to the sad conclusion that religion is the parent of war. The alternate view I espoused held that true religion has everything to do with the possibility of world peace. One proof of this assumption is the fact that my students work and teach in the fields I initiated in centers from Australia to North America, from South Korea to Canada, from East and West Africa to Western Europe. Along with the services I would one day be able to offer under the auspices of the Epiphany Association, I lectured in the United States and throughout the world in such places as Australia, Barbados, Canada, Germany, Ghana, Guyana, Holland, Hong Kong, Ireland, Italy, Jamaica, Kenya, New Zealand, Nigeria, South Africa, Taiwan, Tanzania, Thailand, and Trinidad. In 1982, I received the prestigious William C. Bier Award from Division 36 of the American Psychological Association, "Psychologists Interested in Religious Issues."[6]

Well into my 80's, I still conducted seminars, conferences, and outreach programs sponsored by the Epiphany Academy of Formative Spirituality. I co-edited *Epiphany International: The Journal of Formation Science and Formation Theology* and *Epiphany Inspirations.*

Though I have gotten slightly ahead of my story, the accomplishments noted here and those that followed began to accelerate with the founding of my own institute in 1963. This life-changing event was not only a matter of outer adjustments in the administration of the university but of inner realizations I recorded in a number of personal journals.

Notes

1. The following letter from Father W. Bless, the editor of the Dutch scientific journal *Verbum*, reveals the extent of Father Adrian van Kaam's output in Holland. He published in *Verbum* and other periodicals a number of seminal articles on his theory of formation as a complement to his work in the field of religious education.

Katechetisch Centrum Canisianum
Tongersestraat 53
Maastricht, Nederland

1 October, 1954

I, the undersigned, Father W. Bless, PhD, director of the Dutch Center for Religious Education and editor of the Dutch scientific periodical for religious education, *Verbum*, declare that Father A. L. van Kaam, CSSp., has been an excellent psychological contributor to this periodical for the past four years. Especially praiseworthy was a scientific series of seventeen articles, written by Father van Kaam and published in our journal, about the psychology of adolescent girls and the religious education corresponding with their psychological needs and mentality.

Dr. W. Bless, SJ

2. By that time, according to the testimony of Father van Kaam's longstanding colleague and friend, Father David Smith, CSSp, PhD, "hundreds of doctoral graduates and thousands of master's graduates have gone forth to humanize American psychology."

3. In addition to numerous articles written between 1959 and 1966, Father van Kaam published five major, best-selling books, the first of these being the English edition of his biography of Venerable Francis Libermann, *A Light to the Gentiles*, in which he revealed one of the consistent themes of his life's work: that humanity and holiness are wholly compatible. The second book from this period is *Religion and Personality* (1964) which contains this seminal thought: Any spirituality not based on "openness to the voice of God in every changing situation is suspect, for if openness is not present our project of life deteriorates easily into a blueprint or scheme." I concur with the observation of Father David Smith that Father van Kaam harbored a profound antipathy toward every form of rigidity, formalism, and calculation in the religious and spiritual spheres. In 1966, Father van Kaam had a most prolific year, producing three new books: *The Art of Existential Counseling: A New Perspective in Psychotherapy* in which he strove to recover the full humanity of the client in the face of Skinnerian or Freudian reductionism; *Existential Foundations of Psychology* in which he continued to critique behaviorism and psychoanalysis for failing to give due honor to the dignity and freedom of the human being; and *Personality Fulfillment in the Spiritual Life*, which articulated the message by which he lived: "The life of the spirit is a life of presence inspired by the sacredness of people, of things, and of events in their deepest reality."

4. An article that appeared in a Boston, Massachusetts newspaper described the excitement this appointment generated. Its headline read: "Brandeis Priest Pens Jewish Convert Study" and it went on to say:

> Jewish merchants have a reputation for being generous to Catholic priests. Reverend Adrian van Kaam, CSSp, PhD, is especially aware of this. He gets a discount for two reasons: his priesthood and his professorship at Brandeis University, Waltham.
>
> Founded by members of the Jewish faith, Brandeis is officially non-sectarian and has had several priest professors in its short history. Reverend Walter Gouch, a political scientist, and the late Reverend Albert Smijers, a musicologist, were both attached to the university staff in the past.
>
> For the present academic year, Father van Kaam is the only Catholic priest on the faculty. He is a visiting lecturer in psychology, teaching courses in motivation and personality. Father came to Brandeis from Duquesne University in Pittsburgh where he was a psychology professor. At Brandeis he is substituting for the Head of the Department, Doctor A. H. Maslow, who is now on sabbatical leave.
>
> As a member of the Congregation of the Holy Ghost, Father van Kaam has a special interest in Jewish culture. That religious society looks to a convert from Judaism, the Venerable Francis Libermann, CSSp, as the most prominent spiritual leader in its two hundred and fifty-six years of existence . . .
>
> Sometime this Spring (1959), the Duquesne University Press will publish the psychological and biographical study of Venerable Libermann written by Father van Kaam. The volume will be titled, *A Light to the Gentiles*. It is part of a collection of books known as Duquesne's "Spiritan Series," related to the Holy Ghost Fathers.
>
> With the completion of this term, Father will leave Brandeis to aid in the start of a new doctoral program in psychology scheduled to open soon at Duquesne. He regrets having to absent himself from many friends in the Jewish community of Greater Boston.

5. A prophetic word of advice Father van Kaam gave to graduate students in the psychology department two years before his death summarizes the legacy he has left us: "Follow your heart. Be faithful to your unique-communal life calling. Do not let functionalistic pressures of careerism, money-making, or fame and fortune obfuscate your original ideals to make a difference in this world and to make it a better place when you leave it." Then he added: ". . . dream your dreams and with God's help do what you can to shore up your foundations at the highest level of integrity and service to others. Nothing serves humanity so well as the truth. No wonder we read in scripture that it alone can set us free."

6. For further insight into Father Adrian van Kaam's contribution to the field of humanistic psychology, see "Portrait of Adrian van Kaam and Humanistic Psychology," by Susan Muto, PhD, and Frederick Martin, RN, MA, PhD. *Journal of Humanistic Psychology*. Vol 49, July 2009, 355–375.

Intermezzo 1

Fidelity to My Call

∼

[Editor's Note: Before proceeding to Chapter 33 and its description of the founding of the Institute of Formative Spirituality, this Intermezzo reveals the extent of the soul-searching Father van Kaam underwent at this time. *While attempting to put in order several unpublished papers of his as part of the Epiphany Association's archival project, I came across the journals to which he refers and realized that they were of the utmost importance to him. He kept four notebooks covering the years 1962–1964, years that marked the transition from the period of time he had spent in the psychology department to the return he made in 1963—with the establishment of the then Institute of Man—to his first commitment to spiritual formation. In this story line, six months, from June to December of 1962, are revelatory of the inner struggles he experienced. All are rooted in his deep desire to be faithful to his calling as a priest, a writer, and a teacher. Entries from this period form the basis for the following, slightly edited transcriptions that comprise this Intermezzo. For example, I have changed the "thee" and "thy" references to God, to Father, Son and Holy Spirit, to the more familiar words, "you" and "your."*]

June 1, 1962

Dear Lord, the Holy Spirit granted me the insight that my main mortification should be writing or preparation for writing. I can only maintain this constant mortification when I live in an atmosphere of prayer and recollection, open to your presence in me.1

My former motivations for writing were too worldly, too profane, too secular and ambitious. Thank you for intimating to me that I must write in and for you alone. Only that aim will give me the rest, peace, serenity, and detachment I need [to accomplish this task] . . .

You ask me, Holy Spirit, to be faithful to your light. You do not assure me earthly success, appreciation, acknowledgment. I should humbly and serenely suffer the possibility and actuality of ridicule, suspicion, persecution, anger, dislike, unpopularity. I am not better than you, O Master.

Holy Spirit, make my poor heart free from all earthly ambition, all desire for success and recognition. You have destined some, O Lord, to be losers, perhaps because of their own lack of tact, purity of intention, and holiness of life. Make me accept, O Spirit, the prospect of being a loser, of never attaining a position of respect, of remaining humble and hidden for the rest of my life. Your will be done. Do not allow me to put my trust or hope of happiness in any attainment, only in you, in your presence, O Lord, in your love.

Don't allow me to judge or to be angry with those who may condemn or ridicule or wreck my efforts. Let me believe in their basic goodness. Make me aware that they are better than I am—a sinner, who betrayed you . . . dwelling far away from you.

Make me see in humility that I have to follow the light that is granted to me while knowing that I may be mistaken . . . This awareness of my limitations will help me to accept any condemnation out of love for you. If condemnation comes, make it an occasion of my being more deeply united with you, not one of drifting away from you as I did in my proud past.

Lord, take away all my earthly egoistical concern for acceptance and success. Prevent my being upset by threats to my secure scholarly existence or by what others think and say about me. If I sacrifice all of this to you, that peaceful atmosphere, so necessary for the writing task, will no longer be disturbed. Your Holy Spirit will find in me a better tool for the dialogue between the spirit and the world, between the Holy Spirit and the science of human behavior . . .

June 18, 1962

Lord, you ask me to mortify my pushy, impatient behavior. It is this straining, forcing earthly fervor, this impetuosity, this conceited will power which deafens my ears to your silent call, to your beauty, goodness, truth, and illumination.

Holy Spirit, please enlighten me the very moment such pushy impetuosity takes over.

Detach me so much from my task, from my writing and study, my university . . . and [academic] community that I can live with you alone, not disturbed in the core, of my being by failures, pains, and shortcomings that cannot be healed perfectly. They should affect the periphery of my being, not the core which should be as quiet as the eye of a hurricane and hidden in you, O Lord.

Lord, be present when I am on the verge of losing my whole being in the throes of impatient idealizing. Don't leave me alone in tempests of arid activity.

June 19, 1962

Holy Spirit, thanks to your guidance this new notebook of mine starts off in an atmosphere different from the others. I was blinded for years, my Lord, by the wisdom of this world, which is blindness for you. I was seduced by the glittering inventory of "self-actualizing" tricks . . . which removed me more and more from union with you. You were good enough to deliver me to my . . . misery so that I would shamefully and desperately know what I am . . . without you.

This afternoon when temptation struck and when you made me flee like an anxious bird to you, I received your illumination. You made me see that the main sins are pride and conceit, either individual pride or the shared, intersubjective pride of a group, whether religious or scientific, either that of a nation or a country. You made me feel that pride is a movement of isolation. Every moment that I think of myself or of my group in isolation from you, I am proud and conceited . . . thrown back on myself and cut off from the vitalizing nourishment of your presence and your love, from humanity itself . . . from the communion of saints. Why would anyone opt for such horrifying isolation, such terrifying loneliness? It leaves me . . . shaken and alone in a desert without borders.

The next or concomitant temptation, Holy Spirit, is to strive for my own virtuous response, my own clever solution and self-complacent heroism. This "solution" is a temptation worse than the former. When sinning, I will be made aware sooner or later of my sinfulness . . . when I follow the path of successful, self-made virtue, obtained by tricks of self-actualization, no wonder it feels as if you have abandoned me. Thank you, Spirit of my Lord, for not allowing me to succeed. In every temptation, let my soul flee to you. Let me use all natural psychological means complemented by a spirit of prayer [to improve]. Make me experience them as expressions of my prayer to you for help, as tangible, incarnated gestures indicating that your poor creature begs you to fill those empty, idle moments with your grace . . .

Pride carries its own punishment, conceit its own condemnation, self-sufficiency its own unbearable suffering. My Lord, relieve me from my pride, my conceit, my self-centeredness. I know this cancer, deep in me, will be with me, my Lord, until my last breath.

Spirit of my Lord, keep me aware of this isolating force . . . when I . . . attempt to be virtuous without you, who have revealed yourself to me, when I leave no room, no openness, to your presence. Every natural virtue then becomes poison for me, for example, a success in chastity becomes a failure of humility; the clever avoidance of a bad thought or perception becomes a means of proud isolation from your grace; the transcendence of a carnal movement reinforces my betrayal of your presence. I become a lonely, moralistic acrobat, who performs before a mirror in order to admire himself until he is bored to death.

Lord, relieve me from this isolating narcissistic virtuosity, which is *not virtue*. My "virtue" removed me farther from you than my sin. Thank you, Spirit of my Lord, for [releasing] me from [sin] so that I might find my way back to real authentic virtue—a free gift from you alone because . . . it removes me from my ego and makes me share in the goodness of God alone . . . My hope and my prayer is that Christ will transform these psychological means into his virtues and so bind me to the mysterious Godhead, the incomprehensible mystery of the Holy, my Ground, my Source, my Beginning, my only Nourishment, my Sanctity, my Health, my only Joy, my only Beauty. Come, O Jesus, come, take possession of this sinner after destroying mercifully my [pseudo]-virtue.

June 20, 1962

. . . Lord, you made me in such a way that I need a mortifying [covenant] task, which binds my creative will, emotionality, and imagination to you. If I cannot use them constructively, they will destroy me as they almost did. Unbound, they noisily interfere with recollectedness and silence before your face ... my creaturely faculties will seek their own elation, uncontrolled by higher idealistic purposes or by a noble assignment fulfilled in and with and for you. My attempt to be ... satisfied with the little pleasures of everyday life became my downfall. The repressed need for creative exploration, excitement, elation, ecstasy overwhelmed my existence, O Lord. I could have lost my eternity with you.

It took years to grow out of this dangerous state. My silly attempts to do so without you isolated me more from your light, your grace, your serene, healing presence. It is only in the last few months that your saving and redeeming grace has shown me the way out. Lord, be with me. Don't leave me alone ... don't expose me too soon to an emptiness of existence in which my creative powers tend to become means of self-destruction ...

Keep far from me the temptation to escape this cross—my cross—by cowardly refusal to accept my condemnation to a creative mode of being. Don't allow me either to envy or to despise those who are blessed with a seemingly less complex, more carefree, more pedestrian life. Help me to accept to be considered strange, unbalanced ... ambitious ... by those holy persons whose lack of natural creativity makes them genuinely fearful of all out of the ordinary thoughts, feelings, dreams, and related enterprises ... Make me see that ... condemnation to creativity does not mean that I am any better than those who are destined to serve you in ... more or less routine ways.

My holiness and [theirs] is dependent on you alone. You give us the grace to accept and to live a basically compliant or creative endowment [with] their concomitant sufferings, in such a way that it detaches and sanctifies the bearers of these destinies. Creative or compliant orientations of life, even if they attain overwhelmingly natural successes, do not mean anything in the order of your grace ...

Lord, do not allow me to curse the spiritual isolation, loneliness, and unpopularity—the atmosphere of suspicion and distrust—to which creative and renewing existence is exposed from birth till death ...

June 22, 1962

Holy Spirit, thank you for showing me that my main cooperation with you should consist of a continual pacification, an incessant "serenifying" of my existence. I cannot hear you, I cannot contemplate you, I necessarily lose contact with you, if I allow pushing, exciting, strenuous, forcing "will power" [to prevail]. It cuts me off from you, my peace, my hope, my love, my inspiration . . . Teach me to relax completely my mind, my imagination, my body, my eyes, my hands and fingers, my face while performing the tasks you gave me to do.

The work you assigned to me, Eternal Wisdom, is meant also as a mortification of the undisciplined roaming around of my modes of existence in all their dimensions. It is a discipline of direction so that I may not be caught by interests which remove me from you, O Love and Beauty.

The next mortification you ask of me . . . is such a detachment from my task and its results that I am able to maintain a . . . calm and placidity which are unperturbable. Research, writing, and speaking should be done for you alone. It should be a relaxed play before you, a serene liturgy, a slow invisible growth, harmonious and painless as a flower blooming . . . as [Christ] was in Nazareth and in his public life . . .

July 3, 1962

Lack of restraint in memory, imagination, perception, and anticipation is not an isolated phenomenon, my Lord . . . It is an overall deficiency [allowed by you] . . . a loss in the ability to . . . distance myself in union with you . . . in contemplation of your veiled presence in my being . . .

Spirit of my Lord, you made me see also that consistent renunciation is only good, healthy, and holy when it is an expression of your spirit and not of mine.

Renunciation not inspired by you but by a peculiar, self-centered mode of being leads to a . . . stern resolve of mind and heart . . . It ends in dessication of soul, for secular renunciation is a drying agent, negative, conceited, and harsh . . . You teach me, Holy Spirit, that renunciation inspired by you is humble, wise, modest, and serene; it pacifies the soul and fills it with the dark or luminous light of the Divine Presence. A still white or obscurely dark veiled light is growing in the core of [my] existence, a hidden force, a veiled gift that is not me but you, that draws me out of myself into you, but it should always be [the result] of your renunciation and not mine.

There is a sure tell-tale sign that I am blending my willfulness with your inspiration, spoiling it and turning it into poison. The ominous symptom of this moving-away-from-you is the slight formation of strain, stress, and contentious striving, [accompanied by] a certain inner harshness, severity, compulsiveness, and willfulness.

Both the absence of consistent renunciation and the presence of willful detachment lead to my fall. Holy Spirit, teach me the deep strengthening joy and relaxation of authentic, restful renunciation . . . never a rejection of being but a moderation of [my] exhausting clinging to its external manifestations . . . Inauthentic renunciation is nothing but a forceful shift from shared isolation-from-being to a lonely isolation-from-being, from you. Holy Spirit, teach me [the way] of detachment in service of consistent, contemplative encounter, obscure or luminous . . .

Renunciation in service of contemplation will even speed up production, for what slows it down are the many attachments to my isolated ego on all levels of my existence, such as imagination, perception, thought, emotion—the rumor of the inner and outer senses, which keeps out the awareness of your presence and also prevents continuous, deep, relaxing concentration on your work. To fight this inner noise which I myself madly foster . . . is exhausting, energy consuming and draining. It makes many hours behind the desk an ordeal while they should be a delight.

July 5, 1962

[Editor's Note: *In this entry Father Adrian outlines four conditions necessary to practice authentic renunciation.*]

The first and most important condition is the openness of my freedom, of the core of my existence, of my primordial source of self to [the Lord]. Only when my freedom is bathed either in your obscure or luminous presence will [I] be able to resist the humanly irresistible attraction . . . for sensuous delight . . . to the degree that I am already involved in this world pre-reflexively. The second condition is the growing sensitivity for the slightest initial involvement of the body subject, which may then become centered in the self—in the actualization of these . . . sensuous possibilities . . . The third condition is the restructuring of my life world in the light of your grace [versus] . . . the attitude of sensuous selective attention, which differentiates itself in a number of past attitudes or habits . . . The fourth condition is the care for supportive attitudes, such as that of distancing or delaying the actualization of appealing possibilities . . .

July 8, 1962

Holy Spirit . . . make me present to you continuously so that the noise, the mist, the heat of this [sensuous] mode of existence will not deafen my ears and blind my sight of you. Let me hear [you] when the process of fast and subtle rationalizations weakens my resolve and reinforces the mode of existence which threatens to overwhelm [my service to you] . . . Let me see in your light what I am heading toward, for you protect me from self-deceit and illusion. The clearer your light and the more vivid your presence, the more intimate your encounter [with me], the more I will be able to perceive . . . the prison [of self-actualization] as a prison and not as a liberation . . . Lord, align my whole being with your enlightening traces at these moments . . . show me that dying with you is never an ending but a beginning, a resurrection into a new existence . . . 2

July 22, 1962

. . . you tell me, Holy Spirit, that I easily lose my guard at those moments of necessary distraction, relaxation, unwinding, letting go . . . At these unguarded moments, the overwhelming life of the "old me" permeates, as a matter of course, the relaxed imagination, the carefree heart, the controlled avenues of perception and reason.

Yet tell me, Holy Spirit, of the "new man," of [the me] that should always relax, go to sleep, enjoy people, music, paintings, and nature in an attitude of supernatural contemplation rather than that of discursive meditation that requires active, intense application. Contemplation presupposes rest, relaxation, unwinding. Meditation may tire me all the more; contemplation will refresh and renew me. Meditation [requires] thought and feeling about revealed truth; contemplation is a relaxed presence to the Revealer.

Without your gift of contemplation, Blessed Spirit, I will be unable to survive temptation. Give me the grace to take many free moments of this "vacation in the spirit" of contemplation—in places like cars, cottages, boats, on lakes, in recreation rooms, in houses of friends and family, in bed, and on the shore. Make me [always] present to you.

Holy Spirit, you want to keep alive in me the attitude of detachment so that holy spontaneity may replace sudden impulse. This attitude will sustain my ability to overcome moments of crisis [and to let] your grace and light permeate all modes of being. It is useless simply to abandon [every] pleasure! Such mortification becomes a routine, an easy habit, a dead custom, which does not vitalize any longer the ability to distance myself when I am pulled and pushed to indulge in an aroused impulse. What you ask me, my Lord, is to take distance numerous times a day, when I feel a sudden strong impulse to . . . talk or not to talk, to stay or to retire, to choose a special food, to take an extra helping, to look at certain pictures or persons . . . to read a letter. The delay or the postponement of indulgence in these matters is not directed against them—neither against the limited joy which they give me in your light. They may be expressions of your concern for your servant. This postponement is directed against the dominance of impulsivity, which will wreck my union with you, my Lord, which undermines my strength for the decisive moment of crisis, which prevents the coming of the new man in Christ, who can emerge only from the ruins of my impulsiveness.

These are the two main protectors of my union with you: continuous contemplation [plus] continuous refusal to indulge in impulses.3

July 28, 1962

Make me aware that I have not chosen you but you have chosen me, that you have imposed on me in love a priestly mode of being with which the mode of existence developed in forty blind years is completely incompatible. You have posited me as a light for many, my Lord. If I fail, I fail you and the many you've entrusted to my care as a priestly writer, speaker, teacher, and counselor. You have posited me as a branch to bear fruit for many. I failed miserably and I am on the verge [of finishing] this life as a complete and utter fiasco, the greater because of the splendid magnitude of the mission given to me by you. Lord, redirect my life. Holy Spirit, cure my sick and perverse existence. Turn the bad into good by allowing me to reform my life, pen in hand, so that others may profit from my errors. Divine Word, this will be possible only when I keep close to you . . ." 4

September 11, 1962

Holy Spirit of my Lord and of my Church, you made me see today that concern for contemplation, for presence to Christ and the Holy Trinity in peace and serenity should be central. Without this contemplative attitude, I cannot maintain the peace of mind and heart which are so necessary for my writing, teaching, and counseling. Contemplation is the only lasting source of happiness and peace for me.

Holy Spirit, grant me the blessing of contemplation. Let me do all things in such a way that they grow out of the silence of contemplation or lead to [it]. Blessed Spirit, inspire me to ask myself spontaneously in every event: "Does it come forth from contemplation?" I will do all things then in a different way.5

October 2, 1962

My Lord, you reveal to me that I should escape the overwhelming excitement of thought, emotion, fantasy, and creativity, which leads to loss of control, exhaustion, and to the destruction of that discipline, which is a necessary condition for well organized production.

You made me experience again that I cannot escape by "active relaxation," "thought control," or "will power" but only by means of involvement in you and in and through you in the Holy Trinity. The loss of self in distracted moods and situations can be counteracted only through loss [of self] in you, my God, my love, my goodness . . .

November 1, 1962

Lord, make my life a liturgy. Sublimate every one of my movements to a liturgical gesture. Raise every task-fulfillment to a holy service . . . make me perceive and feel the world not merely as a field of tasks and assignments but as a divine invitation, a holy appeal to celebrate and consecrate the world by a participation in your creation [and its unfolding] in the actualization of possibilities given by you, omnipresent Divine Word . . . My beloved and adored Presence, bring me back to you at those moments of being scattered . . . Help me to regain focus many times a day by returning to pure contemplation. Forgive me, my Lord, for leaving you for so long. You taught me again, Divine Presence, that contemplation remains the necessary ground for peace, serenity, and vitality and for the serene and faithful execution of all possible projects of existence . . . this equanimity, my Lord, is what I need most. It is not merely an affect or a feeling, but more like an underlying existential attitude . . . an *evenness* of mind [and will]—calm, composed, and wholesome. Equanimity does not deny or destroy particular moods, feelings, inspirations, and imaginations. [It] is the constant ground against which those particular feelings show themselves as figures without ever becoming ground themselves . . . Equanimity is that quality of the core of my being that is usually not perturbed, shaken, agitated, or excited, even if my body and senses and the surface of my being may be in an uproar.

This equanimity is the necessary and most effective condition for the development of contemplative wisdom, regular working habits, creative productivity, chastity, good human relationships, authority, wholeness, and happiness . . . its absence leads to my disturbed, polymorphous agitation. Equanimity, like every virtue, has its counterfeit . . . [It] is not the absence of feeling but the transcendence of feelings, not cold functional control of emotion and impulse but a mitigating, moderating, mellowing presence in every feeling and impulse. It is not merely a fundamental mood but an all-pervading existential attitude, an underlying tune or melody, which colors all thoughts, feelings, strivings, moods, inclinations, anticipations, bodily movements, language, and encounters. It is the accompaniment of the music of life . . . [It] grants aesthetic harmony, agreeable measure, and poise to the person as a whole. This poise and . . . balance are not the result of tight control but the flowering of a very profound state of being . . . Equanimity is the virtue of the second half of life. It is the hallmark of maturity . . . a gift of grace [that] transcends infinitely natural equanimity . . . [it is] the fruit of detachment from particular individuals and from the cultural and social aspects of every situation . . .

The core of Christ's deepest being was with the Father when driving the merchants from the temple; when suffering agony; when enjoying the wedding at Cana; when betrayed by the Apostle [Judas]; when insulted by Herod and blasphemed by the crowd. The equanimity of his existence is due to the constant presence of his being to the Father, while dealing with other beings.

No task should absorb [one] so deeply that this primordial presence gets lost or obscured. No event should impress [one] so vividly that this presence is dimmed and, if it [is, one] should leave as soon as possible all occupation to recollect [oneself] and to reestablish [oneself] in the primary situation . . .

Blessed Spirit of my Lord . . . you communicate to me that holy equanimity . . . allows room for more holistic moods and feelings in the deepest level of my being: the joyful experience of humble prostration before the omnipresent Divine, the deep experience of growing in rock-like solidity and inner strength in the face of a multitude of pushing and pulling desires, wishes, and ideas . . . a deep feeling of reverence [and] love in the encounter with the Infinite, with Christ . . . The world will reveal itself in a new and mysterious light; it will be a temple, a sanctuary, a sacred space. My dwelling will become a poetic and prayerful dwelling place on the earth. Existence will come into its own . . . into its sacred dimension.6

November 16, 1962

Lord, thank you for your light in which I experience an increase in joy, in strength, and even in physical vigor and calm, especially since I've started to exercise the easeful asceticism of order in all things. This relaxed detachment from particular feelings [and] experiences . . . this quiet concentration on the concrete writing task and especially the effortless vigilance [I try to maintain] against the incipient, preflexive dwelling on potentially sensuous profiles of reality, is quite a revolution, my Lord! It's a conversion from wallowing in the experiential to the reestablishment of relaxed order and discipline . . .

November 25, 1962

Jesus, you accompany me, you sustain me in this attempt to be open to all my daily situations: lectures, counseling, writing, eating, thinking. Be before my eyes, be in my eyes, and let me see every situation as you would see it"7

November 30, 1962

Thank you, Lord, for your grace. A wholly new life opens up with the discipline of the perspectives you inspire in me. I still have a long way to go, but already I feel an increase of joy and inner strength, of order, of purity of mind and emotion, and a decrease in moodiness, disorder . . . exhaustion, tension . . . Lord, be with me on this new road . . . When confusion strikes . . . teach me to transcend [it] immediately by *doing* the reverse of what I am inclined to do, my *delaying* that which animates me until it loses its momentum, by listening to the realistic call for . . . order . . . to balance my inclination to . . . disorder . . .

December 1, 1962

... Lord, I accept my cross. Help me to face it, to keep on struggling.

December 2, 1962

... Blessed spirit of my Lord ... give me a chance to find peace and wholeness before I die, to achieve the aim and end of living ... which is to grow in readiness for eternal contemplation, for never-ending, joyful presence to the whole [and Holy], for an eternal transcendence of perspectivity.

Spirit of my Lord, be present to me at the crucial hours, in the coming months, when the new situation [at Duquesne] will become strong and stable or be jeopardized again.

[Editor's Note: *This diary ends on* December 7, 1962, *with further reflections on the necessity of equanimity, including the place of* "active relaxation" *when worry and tension strikes; of the necessity of doing all things in a different, more serene, less forceful way; of actively detaching oneself from over-concern for the future; and of retiring in the goodness, truth, and beauty of the Lord. Father van Kaam then pens this final prayer: that the Lord will lead him to* "a committed, holistic, ordered, and serene existence lived with equanimity."]

Notes

1. See 150 *Writing Guidelines* by Adrian van Kaam (Pittsburgh, PA: Epiphany Books, 2009).

2. *Throughout the months of July and August, entry after entry reveals the struggle between pre-reflective responses based on past "pushy" stubborn determinations and overly sensitive dispositions and the need to practice true renunciation of willfulness and total surrender to the call to contemplative prayer and less worldly preoccupations. For example, Father van Kaam prays on* July 10, 1962, "Do not allow me any longer to do all the right things for the wrong self-centered and worldly motives, which take me away from you. When writing becomes tiring and cumbersome make me grateful and delighted that I may suffer a little in the performance of your work." He adds: "Names are made and lost, universities have ups and downs. Nobody knows the secret of your history. Only you are immovable, unchangeable, always the same, yesterday and today and forever." *In the same vein, he writes on* July 12, 1962, "My smile, Holy Spirit, should not be a placating or seductive maneuver, which begs for sweet sympathy, soft kindness, and sentimental consideration, but it should be a radiant, vigorous expression of spiritual presence to you." *Then the emphasis on his call to contemplation becomes increasingly central.*

3. *Reflections in this same vein continue through the summer of 1962. Father van Kaam focuses, especially while on vacation, on such formative themes as* "surrender in peace to your mysterious project." *He prays for the* "serene courage and the sublime wisdom to explore without panic all my feelings, thoughts, modes and modalities of existence" (July 24, 1962). *He says that the Lord gives him a vacation in order to recreate him* "for your work" (July 27, 1962). *In that same entry he adds:* "Therefore, I feel free to let my attention wander from my writing to interesting events and views. Vacation is the absence of deadlines, not the withdrawal of orientation, the removal of the duty of production, not a dismissal of the basic course of my existence." *Always, with great candor and courage, he explores the tension he feels between his old and his new current form of life—the movement from a more impulsive to a more contemplative mode of being.*

4. *As the summer progressed, Father van Kaam unraveled more layers of meaning associated with "rehabilitation" or "reformation" of deformed dispositions. For instance, he writes on* August 5, 1962: "Rehabilitation is learning a new way of seeing; it is a patient alteration of perspective, watching from a novel angle. [It] is basically a change in sight, panorama, vista, or scene—not by transforming their given object poles but by modifying my apprehension, appreciation, and comprehension of them." *He says in reply to his own observation:* "This, my Lord, requires a patient labor of re-education and reconditioning of my perverted perception and its reverberation . . . in my feeling, projecting, forecasting modes of being . . ." *This retraining of perception implies several conditions that he lists with terms like* "becoming aware," "becoming alert," "becoming on guard"*—against the tendency to perceive the situation in isolation from* "my belonging to you, from my priesthood, and from my special, responsible mission." *As far as Father van Kaam is concerned,* "The first necessary condition for this regeneration of

lived behavior is a deep and continuous contemplative life with all the detachment and all the exercises which it entails" (August 5, 1962). *Following this is the second condition or* "indispensable prerequisite," *namely,* "the constant application to my assignment as a writer in and with Christ." *Amazingly in this entry, he forecasts his best-selling book of later years,* Religion and Personality, *saying:* "One way of integration of those two necessary prerequisites . . . is to write about religion and psychology in the serene and pure light of your presence. You communicate to me that there is even a combination possible between those two conditions and my daily struggle. I can write in your presence about the psychology of changing a perverted secular existence into a Christ-like existence." *He confirms on* August 7 *that his only salvation is* "continuous contemplation" *and recalls his having pondered long ago entrance to a contemplative order, adding that* "the analytic consideration of my life, its problems and projects, should not supplant contemplative prayer." *He adds,* "I should engage in creative and analytic endeavors only when I am fulfilled by your peaceful, holy presence. I should interrupt my activity when your presence wears off. I should restore it before involving myself again in non-contemplative occupations such as reading, writing, watching television, counseling, conversation, and self-analysis *[as in this journal]*." *He also cautions himself in a lengthy entry on* August 12 *to avoid the non-contemplative tendency to compartmentalize certain feelings like that of guilt and instead to foster* "a fuller, undiminished awareness of disharmony, sinfulness, failure." *To further clarify what he means, he says:* "Compartmentalization allows the awareness of only those failures which cannot be repressed because of their grave and serious nature; it isolates this experience insofar as possible from similar failures in the past and of countless repressed experiences of minor incidents which manifest the same ominous explosive and perilous mode of being . . . the compartmentalizing attitude [is] a means of keeping existence in its control [and it poses] a grave threat to the whole of my existence."]

5. *Themes that recurred in the months of October and November could be summarized in phrases like the* "transcendence of emotional wallowing," *which does not mean the absence of all emotions and their replacement by logical reasoning, cold, distant and conceptualizing. Rather it means* "full presence in which the clear light of reason is predominant and penetrates emotionality, which is balanced by the all pervading light of reason." *He describes* "spontaneity" *as the opposite of impulsiveness. It* "is the outcome of our integrated, elucidated emotionality that immediately responds in the right way." *Then he draws this interesting analogy:* "The good therapist is like a courageous fireman. He enters the burning world of the patient in order to lead him out before he himself is caught by the flame of undisciplined feeling. After extinguishing the fire he investigates with the patient his crumbled house, his one-sided feeling world. They discuss together to rebuild it better with many windows, doors, and emerging exits." *In describing* "relaxed detachment" *on October 25, 1962, he compares it to being free; he says that it leads to an* "invincible calm and strength, like a quiet, massive rock in the ocean or a lighthouse in a harbor. The poplars that bend in the storm do not break. My Lord, when I am not self-directed but directed [by you], I participate in your stability, your strength, your wisdom. I am no longer at the mercy of my *limited situation . . . my sudden emotions and impulses, anxieties, worries, and . . . fears.*" *In this same reflection, Father van Kaam draws upon the inspiration of Father Francis Libermann, who persevered in his mission despite opposition and whose mildness and mercy edified everyone who crossed his path.*

6. *For the rest of the month of November, 1962, Father van Kaam continued to ponder the difference between disorder (inner and outer) and the far deeper order spawned by the disposition of equanimity, further described as* "possessing my soul in peace" (November 4, 1962). *This virtue effects everything from one's eating habits to the smoother organization of one's room or office. All activity has to be freed from* "emotional harshness" *or* "keyed up tension." *For instance, he notes that the inability to go to bed and fall asleep* "is as much an expression of a perturbed, disorganized existence as the inability to resist the urge to sleep, rest, and retirement."

7. *The next day, Father van Kaam summarizes the lessons in living he has learned in all his previous reflections—such lessons as mistaking* impulsiveness *for* spontaneity; *as blending serene activity with* "fits" *of creation; as engaging in regular religious exercises in the interest of growing less compulsive and more free to follow the Lord. He notes on November 27 that feelings of guilt must be* "permeated by the light of redemption, hope, and humility" *lest any* "sordid situation lead to despair." *Rather equanimity, joy, and peace should pervade the heart of the* "believing sinner." *He reminds himself that no* "attachment" *should ever upset or embitter him or make him anxious. Rather all such episodes and the emotions they evoke ought to be accepted in the light of the Lord,* "in humble surrender." *Such relaxed, smiling imperturbability* "will be more convincing than any excitement."

33

Founding of the Institute of Formative Spirituality

BY 1963, THE OPENING for which I had waited and prayed for nine years revealed itself. The possibility of starting an independent institute became a reality when, under the auspices of the Department of Psychology, I began to offer a sequence of courses that were designed to produce enough credits for one to earn a masters' degree in *Religion and Personality*. The idea was to expand this program to include all that adherence to a faith tradition implied, but the question was: could it remain a subdivision of that department?

To answer this question, my proposal had to be examined by representatives of the Middle States Accreditation Association. It received their approval on the condition that this so-called subdivision be designated as a separate institute to be named temporarily the "Institute of Man." I chose this designation because the Dutch word *mens*, means the whole person, male and female, but in English it translates *man*, which to American ears might seem exclusive of women. Since the accreditors investigating the programs had no objection to this title, I decided to let it stand for the time being.

Support for the establishment of the Institute followed forthwith on the part of the administration of the university since no one was in favor of mixing up the objectives of spirituality and psychology. A meeting between me and the then academic vice-president confirmed what Middle States had recommended, namely, that by the start of the academic year I should separate this fledgling program from the psychology department and make it an independent entity under the canopy of the Graduate School of Arts and Sciences. It was impossible for me not to see the hand of Holy Providence in this development. Frankly, I was overjoyed.

While memory cannot contain all that transpired in my life during these exciting days and years of transition I did keep a copy of the following letter written to my mother Anna on January 14, 1966 from my offices in the Institute of Man:

∽

Dear Mother:

My heartfelt congratulations on your birthday! It is wonderful how healthy and strong you and Dad remain. I feel so happy that you are well and enjoying your old age. I will say a special Holy Mass for you and your intentions, hoping and praying that God will keep you both with us for many more years to come.

On my return from my work in Puerto Rico and Miami, I saw all the gifts you sent to me from Holland. Many thanks for the wonderful Saint Nicholas parcel and the two interesting books, which I will read with great pleasure.

I hope you both will be able to go to Austria. What a shame you had to pay postal charges for my letters. I am enclosing some money for all [those extra] expenses. The remainder is for your birthday. I bought a present for you in Puerto Rico, but I am afraid that the firm that mails it and the post offices there will need a lot of time before it is sent. Probably that is the cause of the postal expenses...

It is a pity Bep suffers so much from her [stomach ailment]. I'm glad she has a good lady doctor. Bep, be careful about your precious health. We all love you so much, even more so when you are ill...

Here things are going wonderfully. The Institute of Man that I founded in 1963 becomes known more and more, here and abroad. Now we have modest offices for the Institute, one room of which offers a view on the river on which our University looks down from the hillside.

Bep wrote a cordial letter to me some time ago, saying how good it would be if I could celebrate my birthday in the Netherlands on April 19. That would be really nice, but it is impossible. I've got to finish my lectures in April and I could only come the last week of the month. She asked me if I had a special wish for my birthday. If all of you together would like to give me something you might perhaps select a gift I can put in my office, a little statue or a painting or a wall covering, an artistic carving or a reproduction; in short something aesthetic. It need not be large or expensive.

Dad, you are rewarded for your sensible moderation with many extra years. You would be proud of me: I'm trying to stay as lean and healthy as I can.

Lia, too, many thanks for the cordial communications. Leonie, thanks for your Christmas card. We are all curious about the baby. A good kiss for Mother on her birthday . . . and special regards to my brothers-in-law and the grandchildren.

Adrian

⁓

[Editor's Note: *Despite the joy this letter conveys, Father van Kaam would have to cope with many sad losses over the next several years. The first was the death on July 1, 1971 of one of his best friends and traveling companions, Father Gerard Krapf, a Redemptionist priest. His beloved mother Anna died on September 29, 1972, followed two years later by his father Charles' death on December 24, 1974. Father van Kaam presided at both of his parents' funerals.*]

Since this fledgling graduate level only institute had to survive without the benefit of undergraduate students, I had to be extremely conscious of meeting our budget. One way to do so was to take on as faculty members of the Institute of Man persons who were already employed in related departments like those of philosophy and psychology. For example, my Dutch confrère, Father Bert van Croonenburg, agreed to develop courses for our students that reflected his expertise in ontology and theology as well as his teaching and spiritual direction experiences in the Dutch Life Schools. From the psychology department I turned for help to clinicians like Charles Maes and Carolyn Gratton, who empathized with my formative approach and whose courses embodied experiential facets of the life of the spirit.

The first full-time person I was able to hire was Susan Muto, whose background in journalism and English literature proved to be invaluable. Susan had been recommended to me by the chairman of the journalism department of Duquesne University, who informed me that she had received the Gold Medal in that field upon her graduation in 1964. She had also been the first woman editor of the student newspaper, the Duquesne *Duke*. Her work after graduation on the public relations staff of the United Jewish Federation had led to her present position as an editor of the *Jewish Chronicle* in Pittsburgh. My contact did not know if she would consider leaving this excellent job or not, but he agreed to arrange a meeting between us at my office in the Guidance Building on October 26, 1966, a date neither of us will ever forget because of its life-changing implications.

When I sat down with her and began to tell her my story, Susan assumed she was in my office for an interview for a feature article based on my war experiences. I noticed that she took copious notes and hardly looked up, so rapt was her attention. At the end of the hour, I asked her what her thoughts were about what I had said, and she replied in wonder that this was one of the most fascinating accounts she had ever heard. She could not believe that she was a carefree two-year old in America when I was struggling to find food for my family in Holland. She said how much she would have liked to be a "fly on the wall" when I and Doctor Schouwenaars joined forces to reeducate the youth of our country after the war. She congratulated me on the work I had done in Paris and said she knew of my book on Libermann through her classes at Duquesne a few years earlier. She reminded me that she herself had chosen two of my psychology courses as electives and had been deeply influenced by them. Finally she said how much she loved my vision of the Church after the Second Vatican Council, especially my respect for the lay faithful. Then she promised to do her best to complete a free-lance article on all of the above and to make my story known to a wider audience.

I remember smiling and asking her somewhat naively, "What story do you mean?" She looked at me with a puzzled expression as I shook my head and tried to dispel any journalistic intention. Then I asked her point-blank if she would join me as the assistant director of the Institute and as editor of our journals, *Envoy* and *Humanitas*. She drew in her breath and without a moment's hesitation said "Yes." Once this affirmation was on the table, I am happy to say, she never retracted it, not in all the years I've known her. Then it was my turn to listen to what was behind this unconditional affirmative response.

After filling in further details about her undergraduate work at Duquesne in journalism and English and her present position on the *Chronicle*, she relayed the good news that she was in the process of attaining her master's degree in literature in night school at the University of Pittsburgh. Though she had to return to work that afternoon, with the intention of talking to her publisher about this life-changing transition, she took time to tell me a bit more about her personal life: "I was born on December 11, 1942. I am the oldest of three children. I have two younger brothers, Frank and Victor. Our father, Frank Muto, emigrated to the United States from Calabria, Italy, and eventually, with only a sixth-grade education, began his own contracting company. For a long time before that Dad had the reputation of being the best barber in Pittsburgh. Our mother, Helen Scardamalia, was born here. She finished the equivalency of technical school and devoted herself to a career in retail fashions before she and Dad married in 1941. We lived in Niagara Falls for the first seven years of my life where my father worked during and after the war in the Naval shipyards. After we moved back to Pittsburgh, I attended grades one through eight at my parish school, Saint Catherine of Siena in Beechview. I chose to commute to Catholic high school at Saint Mary of the Mount in Mount Washington where I graduated in 1960 with the highest honors in literature and history. After being accepted at Duquesne University, I took a test that resulted in my being the recipient of a full tuition remission scholarship. As you can tell, I love learning and I can't help but feel that being a part of this Institute will expand my mind and spirit by leaps and bounds."

Then Susan shared how deeply grateful she felt to her maternal grandmother, Elizabeth Scardamalia, for planting in her the seeds of peasant faith that had drawn her to ask God many times what her life call might be. She confessed, rather awesomely, that three weeks to the day of our meeting she had had an experience of great confusion about her direction that had caused her to say to God as a child would: "Unless you show me what you want me to do with my life, I shall be lost." Her spontaneous "yes" to my request seemed to well up from that spring of grace.

Based on what else we shared of our stores, I realized that Susan had been a "book worm" like myself, spending hours each summer in the Bookmobile of the Carnegie Library reading "everything I could lay my hands on!" As much as she loved solitude, she found herself in a people-oriented career, enjoying inordinate success at the age of twenty-three but not really feeling as happy as she had thought she would. She cautioned me that her parents would probably be shocked at this change in her career. The Italian family assumption was that she would work for a while and then marry and raise a family, but she was for the moment happily single and most concerned about what God wanted her to do. With that disclosure, this milestone conversation ended, but not before she asked a favor of me. Would I give her time to oversee publication of an upcoming commemorative issue of the *Chronicle* and to consult with her publisher about what had just transpired? She thanked me for respecting her current obligations and offered to drive me to Oakland where I was due at the Jewish Health center for my regular exercise program. On that brief drive uptown, we chatted as old friends in an atmosphere of cordial affinity that would characterize the lifelong gift of our "partnership in the mystery of redemption."

Later that week I learned that her meeting with the man who was her chief editor and a spiritual leader of the Jewish community sealed the "yes" she had already uttered. After she tearfully told Albert Bloom what had happened, he asked her the only question that mattered: "What is your heart telling you to do?" Her tearful reply was: "To join Father van Kaam." Then he answered her with the words she needed most to hear: "Then go with my blessing!" From that moment until now, Susan's affirmative response has only deepened. She has been a co-laborer of the highest caliber and, both spiritually and professionally, a true soul-friend.

Susan received her master's degree in 1969 and started immediately thereafter to teach seminal courses on the writings of spiritual masters like Thomas à Kempis, John of the Cross, and T. S. Eliot. On the side, as it were, she sat in and annotated every one of my courses and attended as many lectures as she could from visiting professors in the philosophy, theology, and psychology departments. She wanted to supplement her literary education as much as possible with courses in fields like these that complemented all that she learned in my Institute courses on formation science.

By 1972, Susan had attained her PhD in English literature from the University of Pittsburgh with a specialization in post-Reformation spirituality. Drawing upon the work of the French philosopher Paul Ricoeur, whom she met at Duquesne, she wrote her dissertation on "The Symbolism of Evil in Milton's *Paradise Lost*." With a teaching talent that surprised her but not me, she accepted the task of developing from that point on a six-semester cycle of courses in the formative reading of scripture and the masters, a cycle that was destined to be at the heart of our shared form-theological concerns.

In addition to being my most trusted colleague, an inspiring professor, and co-author of over thirty books, Doctor Muto served the Institute from 1966 to 1988, respectively, as its assistant, executive, and full-time director. Along with these administrative positions, she taught her original courses in the literature of spirituality, taking her students on an unprecedented journey through the ancient, medieval, and modern texts of the most renowned spiritual writers of the Christian East and West. Her courses, all of which I personally audited, proved to be a godsend. Not only did she introduce us to the art and discipline of formative reading of scripture and the classics of the Judeo-Christian tradition; she showed us how the light of faith must shine through our everyday experiences regardless of the era in which we live. Susan understood my insistence on the fact that the ecclesial reliability and the long-time survival of our program would depend in great measure on this course sequence; she herself also continued to follow my core courses in the science and anthropology of formation, thoroughly imbibing their content as well as connecting them with the principles of formation theology they were intended to serve.

Her expertise in the world of literature rescued her from any leaning toward the self-actualizing psychologism popular at that time on the American scene. Her goal was to enter into the original inspirations of the spiritual masters, revealing their timely yet timeless insights into faith deepening and daily life. In addition to her own books on such disciplines of faith deepening as reading, meditation, prayer, and contemplation, she co-edited our journals and helped me in the production of all my books, most notably the first seven volumes of my masterwork in the science and anthropology of formation. Four of these books were completed while both of us taught at the Institute. The rest were written and published, as were our four co-authored volumes on formation theology, under the auspices of the Epiphany Association, which we co-founded in 1979. How it came to be and why it represents the crowning phase of our life's work is a story still to be told. In the meantime, our tireless labors to design, develop, and deliver the original work of the Institute resulted during the previous ten years, from 1969 to 1979, in what the Middle States Association identified as a three-year doctoral style master's course, leading to the recommendation that we start in 1979 the world's first PhD program in formative spirituality.

In devising the methodology to guide our doctoral dissertations, we made sure that each topic chosen for research would be rooted in a formative event and expounded upon in universal human, religious, and Christian terms with the application of one's findings to the segment of the population one intended to serve. This truly holistic approach helped one to avoid encapsulation in any already existing theory of personality that focused only on one's sociohistorical, vital, or functional make-up without sufficient reference to our orientation to the transcendent and our centeredness in a mystery both in and beyond us. We also avoided falling into trends of thinking such as "psychologism," "transpersonalism," and "psychotherapism" whose underlying assumptions were incompatible with biblical revelation and the faith traditions flowing from it.

The inspirational courses taught by Doctor Muto succeeded in forestalling a harmful disproportion between pretheological formation science and the foundations of formation theology toward which all of my work was and is aimed. Students without this same background might be tempted to put more emphasis on speculative theology, existential philosophy, or, for that matter, pretheological formation science rather than on formation theology itself. Lacking such a form-theological approach, I feared that the classical solidity and trustworthiness of our own or any other formation program would be in jeopardy. Any course offering that purports to be about faith deepening must not degenerate into an odd blending of eclectic elements catering to popular fads that ignore the rich treasury of formation wisdom. The frustration I felt in this regard concerned the tendency to move from one theory to another without rooting oneself in the legitimate authority of one's faith grouping. One might be in danger of responding to formational issues and concerns in mainly psychological, transpersonal, transcosmic, sociological, or philosophical terms, perhaps coated with a thin veneer of a "self at the center" spirituality. It would be impossible under such conditions to respond to the concern for solid formation voiced by laity, clergy, and religious whose hunger for spiritual deepening cannot be answered by either "pop" spirituality or the invention of strange hybrids like "theopsychology" or "psychotheology" that end up as I had already seen in a watering down of these two independent fields.

The program I started at the Institute with Doctor Muto's dedication and devotion became the seedbed for the evolution of a new human science designed from the beginning to be conducive to and compatible with the Revelation. Already in the Netherlands and now in the United States, I was acutely aware of the need to integrate into this new body of work the formationally relevant findings of the human and social sciences that ought to be taken into account by both believers and sincere seekers in pursuit of truth.

From a human, religious, Christian, and applicative perspective, our students were encouraged to excel in experiential and ecclesial reflection in line with the mind and heart of their respective faith community. Their thematic research had to center around the question of how to integrate what we believe (our faith tradition) and how we live these beliefs in everyday life (our formation tradition); otherwise an influx of new and appealing social and clinical sciences or spiritual movements not rooted solidly in the time-tested wisdom of formation might engulf one like the sudden surge of a riptide in an ocean that looks perfectly calm.

Even while doing the work of the Lord, one can fall away from prayer into a dry well of pure functionalism or careerism. I had fair warning about this danger in my own life. Once, while I facilitated a retreat for professionals in California, some of whom were from the Hollywood community, a woman in the audience came to my door one evening to relate a "message" she had received in a dream that she was instructed to relate to me. I've never forgotten her words: "If you keep making excuses for yourself, you will be be lost." I could not allow the reservoir of my contemplative life to dry up; otherwise all my actions, even on behalf of faith formation, would come to naught. When I related this experience to Susan, she said, "I guess it means that God has snatched you from the clutches of functionalism just in time. It seems as if all of us must return to stillness if we want to live in fidelity to what God asks of us."

It would have been easy to slip into the trap of worldly success and the know-it-all posture of "academic arrogance," especially after we had started a doctoral program in formative spirituality that attracted graduate students from over twenty-six different countries. By that time we had written quite a number of books and had been invited to speak in many national and international settings. As if that were not enough of a sign of our "having made it," both of us had been promoted to full tenured professorships; received honorary degrees respectively from King's College for Susan and from the Franciscan University of Steubenville for me; and been awarded university-wide recognition for excellence in teaching. Ironically at the very time when such accolades seemed to seal our direction in academic life, we were hearing the "cry of the poor" from the pews of churches and the hallways of familial and professional life. It seemed to us as if the hunger for spirituality had reached epidemic proportions and that many of the people in our audiences during weekend seminars and workshops could never afford the time or money to attend our classes at the Institute. What were we to do? The answer would eventually be revealed to us, but for the moment we had a lot of praying and thinking to do.

An example of what we were up against arose when I tried to reinterpret the term "self-actualization." For humanistic thinkers it summarizes what happens when individuals by their own power alone actualize themselves without recognition of a mystery of formation outside of their own controlling ego. Without clarifying this term in the light of transcendent formation, one may be left with the impression that pre-transcendent self-actualization is the ultimate aim of our existence. In truth, the self-in-isolation can never lead to fulfillment.

The spiritual hungers felt by people in the 80's seemed a repeat of what I experienced during the Hunger Winter. People then and now were still bombarding me with questions that went far beyond text book replies. Those with whom I worked long ago in my seminarian days wondered how they were to make sense of the loss of freedom and the trauma of mental and emotional captivity in which they found themselves. Abstract philosophizing fell on deaf ears. They wanted to know the meaning of their here-and-now lives in a situation where familiar supports had been stolen from them? Was trust in some deeper reality the only sensible response? Would they live to see the day when their current state of ego-desperation would be lifted and a new springtime of serenity would come upon them?

The more I listened to story after story of agony and terror, the more I realized that people were not looking for the "why" of their misery but for the "how" that would enable them to carry on despite this temporary loss of meaning. What they sought went beyond the confinement of their present existence at the mercy of enemy occupiers and the handouts of the farmers in whose houses they took refuge. They ached for neither an old nor a new philosophical view of life but for basic spiritual wisdom and a vision of the future that could inspire and empower them to bring form and meaning into the fragments left of their previous lives. Speculative thinking was hardly possible in the face of having to find enough to eat in these life-threatening circumstances.

In this most unlikely of places I found myself concentrating not on the books I had to leave on the seminary shelves but on the practical problems surrounding the transcendent quest for meaning that had a direct bearing on the experiences of formation and deformation all of us one of these days will have to undergo. Two paths of reflection seemed to open before me: one was a general anthropology for all people and the other a specific articulation of these principles for those who were already committed to one or the other adhered to faith and formation tradition. The focus of this research, theory, and practice would be human life itself as receiving and giving form in the light of our distinctively human transcendence dynamic. Its content and language would facilitate our understanding of our formation field as a whole from the perspective of our always changing and deepening transformational experiences.

From the time I returned to the seminary, became an ordained priest, and accepted my teaching assignments, to the years I spent in the psychology department and now in the Institute, I made sure that my classes remained intertwined with the events that comprised the boundary experiences I had undergone during the Hunger Winter. Family members, to say nothing of the clients I would later serve, were reticent to bring to light their fears and losses, but I challenged them to dive into these obstacles and find in them openings to the new depths of understanding intended by God.

This turn to experiential formative thinking was as difficult for me as it was for those I taught. In the midst of a lecture, I would find myself drifting away on the nostalgic wings of remembering my family and what they went through. I wonder even now if they understood where my mission would lead me. Once, with the best of good will, my parents said, perhaps in jest, "We'd be happier if you were not so learned!" I suspect they would have liked me to be a parish priest in a nearby village, but my call would take me farther and farther away from Holland and the cozy togetherness everyone longed for after the war.

For whatever reason I began thinking not only of the heroic efforts of my parents, Anna and Charles, to care for us but of my mother's eldest brother, Ferdinand Franke, or "Uncle Ferry." Though not a practicing Catholic he impressed me with his commitment not to the socialist movement on the rise in the Netherlands at the time of the war but to a humane socialism that, I believe, accounted for how good he was to me and my sisters. The fact that he was not a practicing Catholic made his behavior all the more impressive to me. We lived within walking distance of his home so I was often there, enjoying the pleasant mood that prevailed among him and his wife and their girls.

Uncle Ferry was the soul of goodness. He became involved with helping the poor who suffered so much in a depressive economic climate. He encouraged my love for reading and from the age of three supplied me with fascinating books that always had a moral to offer. As I grew to adulthood, I found him to be a person to whom I could talk about my life, especially the poetic and religious side of it. He was also open to the dangers of socialism, especially the way in which this ideology had seeped into communism in Russia, Nazism in Germany, and fascism in Italy. The Dutch seemed to be drawn to a kind of capitalistic socialism that might be of benefit to the common people, but the shadow side of this approach was that only money mattered. Uncle Ferry and his son, with whom I also became fast friends, shared my concerns about these socio-political developments that led to such disastrous results on the Continent, one of the worst being a general loss of faith in God, and a subsequent reliance on self and the worship of worldly wealth and power. The humane beginnings of socialism with its dedication to helping the poor were a far cry from the illusory promises of capitalistic socialism invading Western Europe.

Floods of formative remembrance like these drew me to deeper reflection on my call, aided by the humble admission that in the world of formation everything matters—what is consonant and consistent with our "yes" to God and what is dissonant and has to be dealt with when life takes an unexpected turn. And so it did in my sixtieth year. Just when it seemed as if my life in 1980 had at last settled into a comfortable routine, the biggest challenge of all was about to explode, literally from within the cavity of my own chest.

[Editor's Note: *Father Adrian van Kaam suffered an acute myocardial infarction on April 28, 1980, less than ten days after his 60th birthday, and approximately one year after the launching of our PhD program in formative spirituality at Duquesne, and eleven months after the co-founding of our independent, non-profit Epiphany Association. Father's condition for the first forty-eight hours was, as his physicians told those of us who had assembled in the waiting room for a prayer vigil, "touch and go." Thanks be to God, it was not his time to go. On the afternoon he felt that terrible pain in his back, he was able to be transported immediately to Mercy Hospital where the actual attack occurred in the emergency room with his physician at his side. His pains were not typical but atypical so his condition*  *had been diagnosed at first as pleurisy rather than angina. When the doctors announced later that day that his condition had improved, we heaved a collective sigh of gratitude and relief. His athletic heart saved him, but for the rest of his life, he would be a heart patient, undergoing not only coronary by-pass surgery a year later but incurring the need after that for a pacemaker since complications from pericarditis had further compromised his already weakened heart, leading to arrhythmias and symptoms of cardiomyopathy.*

Despite this strike against his physical well-being, he chose to make the necessary life style changes to cope with his condition—all of which revealed his fidelity to the key notion of appreciative abandonment to the mystery. As soon as he was out of intensive care, he asked me, with that beam of his always beautiful smile, if I would be willing to take his place as director of the Institute of Formative Spirituality and forthwith to serve as his successor. I answered in the affirmative, saying yes *again with all my heart. His next request was that I bring him a notebook and a pen because he wanted to start a diary about his near-death experience. What follows is another remarkable intermezzo at this juncture of his memoirs. It reveals his complete commitment to find the full meaning of this formative event. After he suffered the heart attack, he knew intuitively how therapeutic it would be to begin this reflection on his own "core form." He had had a number of life-threatening experiences, especially during the Hunger Winter, but this organ in all its frailty now symbolized the crossing point between life and death. In his own words, "The heart is the core out of which Christ forms the soul in a deeper way." What follows are excerpts of the diary he kept from May until September, 1980, when he underwent open heart surgery at the Mayo Clinic. He was so weak from his lengthy hospitalizations that he had to be transferred to Rochester, Minnesota, by a life flight I arranged on his behalf. His left descending artery was ninety-five percent occluded and without this surgery he would not have survived.]*

Intermezzo 2

Blessings of a Coronary

~

May 28, 1980

My heart attack is four weeks behind me. Only now has its truth begun to sink in. I could have lost my life. I may still lose it. Any number of patients like me the world over will die during the first seven or eight months after their first acute attack. Shall I be one of these statistics? After that time has past, will my life still be in danger . . . and even more so if I don't change my way of living? I must live daily with a vulnerability unknown before, with the strange knowledge that I may die at any moment, suddenly, without warning. My own father, Charles, died after a year of recuperation from his attack. He was at a rest home for the elderly called Favente Deo at the Loevensteinlaan in The Hague. This was his wish as it was run by the same Congregation that ran the RK Weeshuis at the Warmoezierstraat where he grew up after his mother died and his father traveled around Holland working for a company that built bridges. Unexpectedly stricken again, he received the Sacrament of the Sick, felt well, asked for a cup of coffee, then lost consciousness, never to regain it. It was the day before Christmas. I was at the other end of the world, lecturing in New Zealand. I had to fight for plane reservations on Christmas Day, not knowing if or when I would arrive in Holland. The detours were horrendous—first from New Zealand to San Francisco. There the English company with whom I had a reservation had canceled its night flight from "the city by the bay" to London. I made an agonizing run from ticket counter to ticket counter, getting to the gate of an Air France jet on the point of departure to Paris. The next day, in Paris, I had to wait until nightfall for the last Air France flight to Amsterdam. There I was driven to the chapel of the senior citizen's home in the Hague to see the body of my dad. Little did I realize then that I, now at age sixty, would suffer the same first attack he had suffered around that age. More strokes and attacks followed until he died from this last one. Will that be my story? Heredity? One thing is sure. Once this condition manifests itself one will never be the same. From now on I must live with death around the corner. I must make my peace with the undeniable reality of dying.

My dear friend of old in Holland, Adriaan Langelaan, also had his first heart attack around the age of sixty. I remember how fast and unexpectedly this Epiphany pioneer passed away when he was only sixty-six years old. His wife Marie handed him a piece of Dutch rusk at the breakfast table. He smiled at her and said, "Thank you." Then there was silence. Marie looked up. He sat there dead. It was suddenly all over. I was in Holland during one of my summer vacations. I preached at his funeral and accompanied the family to the grave. A neighbor at his summer home told me how pleased my friend had been by the book I had sent him a year earlier, *Type A Behavior and Your Heart*. The neighbor remarked that he had read it line by line. I myself read it, too, along with my own book, *Spirituality and the Gentle Life*. Now I had no choice but to "gentle down." Well before this attack, I did my exercises and watched my diet, as much if not more than any of the priests and brothers with whom I lived in community on the university campus. I was known as somewhat of a "health nut" among them. I had given up smoking many years ago. My yearly medical reports were excellent. No wonder that the naive thought crossed my mind at the grave of my friend: "His story will never be mine." The need for time control, time gain and manipulation, the resulting feeling of time urgency are all typical manifestations of the exalting pride-form of life. Basic to it is the impossibility to surrender, to let go, to simply be and let be, to tolerate the limits of finitude.

One tries to be the "god" of one's own time, to rush the pace of one's life achievements, to attain the perfection of the prospect of success our own pride imagines. Anything that stands in the way of that single-minded use of time irritates coronary-prone people like me, elevating our levels of serum cholesterol and affecting our heart.

In this debilitating and, in the long run, fatal state of time control, illusionary ambitions play a major role. They can be integral constituents of a consonant life form; they only become dangers for coronary survivors when they are no longer integrated in the flow of phasic formation that characterizes the unique, divinely given epiphany of our embodied soul.

Ambition is the normal expression of our functional dimension. We should try to function as well as we can, but not better or faster than we are able to. Without harming our health, we are called to give our best within the time limits set for us. We should never stray beyond the boundaries that frame our lives or any of their phases. To battle the borders of our potential to give and receive form by hurry and over exertion is *hubris*, an idle battle with the gods, a desperate struggle to accomplish the impossible, resulting in the constant overloading of a heart that may soon collapse under the burden of our proud but foolish perfectionism.

FIRST REFLECTION

Sheltering My Weakened Heart

The survivor of a coronary must live on with a heart vulnerable and easily upset, a heart that needs peace and moderation. This precious organ must be shielded from the physiological and chemical irritation that wells up like poison gas from aggravation. Not all aggravation can be avoided; anxious concern is bound to arise sometimes due to the sheer fact that we live and work in the world. However, the wise and humble survivor shields his heart from excitement that can either be avoided altogether or mitigated gently.

> *Help me, Lord, to create a shelter for my heart, a shield and a fortress to be found in you alone. Your presence is my hiding place. To abide in you is to build a hermitage inwardly. I must protect my heart from sources of excitement that are still legitimate for my colleagues in the teaching profession—as they once were for me during the fascinating past you granted me. You put me on the right track. You brought the person into my life to whom I could entrust the directorship of the Institute you inspired me to establish. You caution me to avoid excessive concern with campus politics and controversial publications. They may distract my heart too much. You don't want them to affect my peace of mind. Blissful ignorance*

> *may save my life for many years. You want me less involved in fervent discussions or tirades about issues and enterprises. You want me to avoid heated meetings that tire me needlessly. You speak to me in this regard through my physician, who has begun to know me better. You want me to read in rest and relaxation only what is immediately helpful for my work. You seem to ask me to refuse graciously to participate in any board or committee meeting, at least for the time being. You want me to protect, above all else, the hermitage of my heart, especially in conversation.*

Conversation may excite my imagination and endanger the hermitage of my heart more than anything else. Though I cannot always escape such exchanges, I can avoid controversial topics and, if possible, turn the talk in another direction. If others heatedly pursue the latest "hot" topic, I must tell myself: "Turn off your inner heart; close the windows of your soul. Graciously, with a pleasant smile on your face, disappear in your silent shelter. Be content with God alone. Try your best not to hurt the feelings of others whose healthy heart enables them to share in the commotion of the world as you used to do in the past."

Enjoying as they do their own strength of heart, they may be unable to understand that the limited energy and life time left to me must be cautiously reserved in reverence for the tasks God still wants me to do: "Save yourself for his service while sparing their feelings. Remember that shuttered window panels can still be pleasing to the eye. If necessary, write a note to those in charge, explaining that your doctor asks you to abstain from these sessions because of your heart condition."

In conversation, seek for the humorous pleasant side of a topic. Avoid what is ponderous, argumentative, or controversial. Cultivate the art of telling a little story. Have ready to hand light, humorous anecdotes that leave your heart unburdened while recreating your mind in a playful way. Look at television but not at controversial programs and discussions. Turn the dial to entertaining shows and plays instead.

9:10 PM, Saturday, June 21, 1980 at the Motherhouse of the Sisters of the Divine Redeemer in Elizabeth, Pennsylvania

[Editor's Note: *Father van Kaam went to this retreat-like setting at the invitation of the Sisters to recuperate away from the commotion of campus life.*]

Intermezzo 2: Blessings of a Coronary

Surviving after a coronary is an art and a discipline illumined by grace. Living with the fact that one is a heart patient can be a burden or a blessing. Like any event in our life, it is potentially formative or deformative. The choice is ours to make. God intends every event that happens to be for the best, especially in regard to those crucial transitions with which he graces us for the sake of drawing forth aspects of his divine form in our inmost being that would not be disclosed otherwise. A coronary is one such blessed event, one of great magnitude; it invites us to detach ourselves from a past form of life and to flow gently with grace into a new, more contemplative mode of being.

> *Thank you, Lord, for the blessing of this coronary. It is your tender knock on the door of my life: a sweet announcement of the life to come; of the joy and beauty of leaving this sinful earth; of the delight of death and dying; of the splendor of eternity; of the meeting with you face to face. From now on this happiness may come to me at any moment, suddenly at night, during my sleep, walking in a street, teaching a class, or taking a bite of food. At any moment the great deliverance may be mine. In one blessed second it may all be over. Thank you, Lord. Thank you for this invitation to make myself ready for this lovely liberation. What better way to be prepared than to blossom in your presence! Give me the grace to pray always and everywhere. Let every experience turn into a mode of presence to you, especially in those danger zones of aggravation.*

A heart patient in his sixtieth year of life would be wise to build an inner hermitage, a dwelling place of silent contemplation. The gentle hermit's existence will keep him ready for your lovely coming, silently and swiftly as a thief in the night. It will also help him to conserve his remaining energy so that he can give to his life, to his work, to his world the final form you want him to bestow on them. *Before you softly blow out the last flickering light of my burnt-up candle, sustain my efforts to serve you fully.*

The coronary patient is not allowed to lose that last reservoir of energy in useless emotional, mental, or physical struggles, in hurry, heavy-mindedness, irritation, or negative anticipation. It is surely not pleasing you, my Lord, if this inner dialogue is due to people, events, and things, to community, family, and world affairs, that no longer nourish the small task you ask your hermit to complete gently and quietly before his joyous departure. This lack of detachment would mar your servant's readiness for your coming; it would stain the purity of his love and diminish the compassion and surrender you want him to display in all ways. Worse still, it would disperse and deplete his life in useless passions. He would be unable to finish the final assignments you impose on him at the end of his short and perilous pilgrimage through this valley of sin, suffering, illusion, and tears.

I shall be glad to leave and yet I should be faithful to my last task and to my loving friends as long as you want me to do so. *Non recuso laborem.* With your grace I shall bear the cross of this life as long as you desire, Lord Jesus. You are displeased if I do or omit anything to shorten it. Enlighten me so that I may not do so unconsciously. The time of liberation is up to you alone.

I now feel fatigue coming over me. I am tempted to look at some papers I just received. Yet any sign of fatigue is for a heart patient your invitation to rest, to detach himself from what he likes to do. You want him to surrender to the weakness you allow in his life. *Yes, Lord, I surrender.* I shall forego this life-endangering pleasure and excitement, this preconscious intensity. Please, accompany me in my sleep. Are you going to call me this night? I would love to see you face to Face. But I feel sorry for those who may suffer because of my leaving and sorry for a work still unfinished. May your will be done. Good night, my Lord. Have mercy on my soul. Above all, teach me to be less intense in my thinking, planning, reading, speaking, imagining, writing, and correcting, to be less impatient and more relaxed. What I need is the grace of holy apathy.

3:40 P.M., Sunday, June 22, 1980. Elizabeth, Pennsylvania

This morning I read in the Divine Office for the 12th Sunday in Ordinary Time the psalm prayer after Psalm 24, that says: "Watch over your people as the treasure of your heart and guide their steps along safe paths that they may see your face" (1124).

The heart of the coronary patient can bear only a little pressure. Excessive bouts of it stem from the pride-form of life. Anything that makes us feel as if we have to watch anxiously all we see around us tends to cause constant, or at least periodic, tension. The heart of the anxious watcher is an organ under pressure. He is literally sick at heart. A coronary prone person has to forget the words, "I," "me," "mine," and "myself." Such terms may be justifiable in some cases, but the deformative pulsation of our culture has linked them to the anxious pride-form of our life. They evoke almost automatically feelings of threat, defensiveness, control, manipulative anticipation, and isolated lonely responsibility.

Remove these words from your vocabulary until they have lost their self-centered, pressurizing quality, endangering your vulnerable heart. Substitute for them words like: "it" watches, "it" controls, "it" concerns, "it" acts, "it" heals, "it" protects, "it" purifies, "it" allows opposition and exclusion to form me, "it" defends, "it" shapes, and so on. It is much wiser to say "the mystery of eternal formation" in and around, over and above me, forms, acts, controls, purifies, concerns, heals, directs, and makes me be. Then cares and woes will not threaten, divide, hurry up, and aggravate your heart.

The devout sense of awe for the mystery makes your heart beat quietly along with the Divine Heart of the universe. You begin "wholeheartedly" to feel at one with all people and with their shared limitations—at one with all of nature and everyone around you. In forming love you are watched as the treasure of that Divine Heart that also beats in you. Your controlling, always threatened and threatening pride-form begins to recede. Your tense, vulnerable, fearful, easily aggravated heart begins to experience less pressure, less heaviness, less seriousness. You become lighthearted. Your heart beats rhythmically with the joyful, gentle heartbeat of Christ in you. With him you begin to look at all that is as an epiphany of the treasure of your heart. You start to appreciate with Jesus your, that is to say, "our" opponents, "our" detractors. We in "our" heart pray for them lightheartedly without hostility or intensity, anxiety or anger whenever these passions arise or persist.

Never deny or exclude such feelings. Always face them prayerfully in deference to the merciful heart of Jesus. Share in his watching over your opponents in gentle love and compassion. They, too, belong to the treasury of "our" shared heart. Share Jesus' heartfelt prayer that their steps-no matter how destructive or sinful—may be guided ultimately along safe paths. Hiding your anxious little heart in the heart of Jesus, desire for all of them the only thing that ultimately matters: "That they may see his Face."

> *The blessing of a coronary is your invitation, Lord, to ready me through a quiet life of prayerful presence for the grace of seeing your Face. Thank you, thank you, for your invitation. You want me to cooperate with your wish that this heart of mine will still beat quietly and rhythmically for some time to come. Your will be*

done. The best cooperation is to let my heart sink away in your heart, the immense, never threatened Divine Heart of the universe that treasures gently and joyously all that is, that wants only, as the psalmist says, "to guide all my steps along paths that safely lead to the seeing of your Face." Move our hearts in such a way that we see your blessed countenance in every human face and form, in the unfolding story of every life, in every star, every blade of grass, every bird, butterfly and budding tree, until we are led to see you face to Face, form to Form. Lord, deliver me from my intensity and grant me holy apathy.

Monday, June 23, 1980

The recurrent chest and back pain, the dizziness I felt this morning, in spite of calming meditation, seem to indicate that I must also apply the technique I tried this afternoon: a "meaningless sound" that seems to quiet the heart completely, followed by a concentration on one word inwardly to reach a level of equanimity. Religious meditation and contemplation, while necessary for calm and quiet surrender, may prevent a silencing of the heart, especially if we remain too much in our head as I am prone to do.

In service of the Lord's "survival-will" for me, I must now and in the future initiate a discipline at least twice for twenty minutes a day of "meaningless sound" or equanimity exercises. I must be faithful to this practice, no matter the circumstances. Such exercises should not replace other kinds of contemplation and meditation, except when heart trouble necessitates that replacement temporarily or when I have to overcome my inclination to intensity. At this period of recovery I should train myself in as much "meaningless sound" and its calming effects as possible.

Looking back at my life, this practice seems more crucial than exercise or diet, though neither should be neglected. Such inner relaxed simplification of mind seems a normal means to regain the "heavenly homecoming" I need to prevent strain of life, heart pressure, and other disturbances. Also, it offers the only means available to me to ward off the spontaneous intensity of my mind and spirit that inclines me to outrun my body and my remaining vital resources. *Help me, Lord Jesus, in this way of gentle mortification of my "spiritedness" and of my disposition to intensity in all things.*

9:04 A.M. Tuesday, June 24, 1980, Elizabeth, Pennsylvania

My "meaningless sound" exercise was helpful during the night to diminish chest and back pain. Only in the morning did it return. I felt sorry, my loving Lord, that "meaningless sound" did not make me more explicitly one with you. I felt this morning that my mistake had been in trying too hard to meditate last week on a selected text of the Liturgy of the Hours. I should instead rest in a contemplative word of presence. Such a word will do the same and perhaps more for my troubled heart and my lack of apathy than "meaningless sound."

The best remembrance of the past is my "one word" or "wordless" presence during concelebration of Holy Mass here with Father R. I should have maintained that atmosphere all day long. Maybe you did not want me to do so during prior times of my life because of the activity and productivity you wanted from me. But a coronary is an invitation to a more contemplative life style. From now on you may want a more prayerful way of presence for me, one that permeates the whole day. I must say to myself, "Don't worry about slowness in looking around, in moving and in writing, or about less productivity." God forgives you because you are blessed with a heart ailment. Be all day long like you were in those concelebrated masses, especially during your work of writing and reading. If you lose this equanimity, stop what you are doing until his grace allows this presence to return, and the heavenly homecoming to happen again. This presence should be nourished by meditation, but at this moment of slow recuperation, it, too, may be too much.

Thursday, June 26, 1980

The heart patient endangers his heart most by aggravation. It delays his recuperation; it takes him away from the peace of contemplation. The sick or wounded heart may only begin to thrive again in the mellow climate of prayerful presence. To return to this basic equanimity is the condition for rest, relaxation, and healing, for overcoming my intensity.

It is impossible for coronary victims to change overnight their often excitable, inflammable, intense temperaments. They should beseech the Lord in all simplicity to grant them the grace of humility, to acknowledge that they cannot cope with certain issues that have rightly or wrongly become "red flags" for them, that their only hope of survival is to escape altogether or to try humbly to dodge these issues. Then they should ask the Holy Spirit to help them to develop effective techniques to do so at least for the time being. *What you now want for me, Lord, is only to recuperate, to survive, to stay alive so that I may serve your kingdom again with some effectiveness and far more inwardness.*

What are the red flag issues that could end my life? What techniques can I develop now to prevent them? Later, if I survive this ailment allowed by you, I may learn, with the help of your grace, how not to avoid such issues anymore but to meet them serenely. At this moment, Lord, keep me humble enough not to run ahead of the grace granted to me. Let the pride-form of my life not tempt me to strive for the perfection of coping directly with upsetting issues that cannot be handled by me.

One potential "killer issue" concerns the battle in my community and in parts of your church to promote certain kinds of apostolates as the exclusive ones for all. I have been aroused to anger more than once by any kind of exclusivism; rightly or wrongly I have always fought against it. Yet today I have to witness in certain circumstances the seeming victory of exclusivism. Make me see, dear Lord, that at this moment of my life you want me to be simply a wounded solider removed from the battlefield. What counts now is survival, recuperation, restoration, and inward transformation, not angry campaigns to promote one or the other cause. Help me to stay away from the battlefield and to prevent aggravation, for, endlessly repeated, it might kill me now or in the years to come.

A Possible Escape Strategy

1. When, in thought, memory, or imagination, a "killer issue" emerges inwardly, flee to the Lord. Ask him to take this turmoil away. Relativize it by saying, "This, too, will pass." "What will it mean a century from now?" "Of what significance is it in the light of eternity?" Pray wholeheartedly for your adversaries. Leave them in the hands of the Lord. Try with his grace to empty your mind, to return to simple, relaxed prayerful presence. Above all, empty your mind!

2. Avoid speaking on subjects that are "killers" for coronary patients. Never bring them up; never be defensive or aggressive about them. Become a master in the detection of your inner urge to return to them again and again. Beseech the Lord and his

Holy Mother to help you to mortify this urge. What is the use of it anyway? It can only destroy your already weakened heart. You will not win the battle; you will only delay your recuperation, your healing, happiness, serenity, and inner wholeness, your harmony.

3. Avoid all literature on "killer issues." It is dynamite for you at this moment of vulnerability; it is poison for your heart. Make it second nature to pass up all articles, letters, community communications, and meetings that threaten your heart. Make health-related excuses. Acquire doctor's affidavits, if necessary, for your doctor has impressed on you the necessity of this avoidance if you are to survive.

4. If others bring "killer issues" up, be gracious and kind, but with God's assistance close your inner ears to them. Enter into his rest. Let them go in one ear and out the other. Don't comment on them or continue to dwell on them. If possible be smilingly and gently humorous about them in as untouched and untouchable a way as possible. Pretend you don't know about them. Accept them silently as another piece among countless pieces of "interesting information." Be inwardly lost in the Lord's presence. If possible, try to steer the conversation as soon as possible in another direction. Become a master in humorous small talk. Be pleasantly and humorously evasive about issues that paralyze your presence to the Divine Presence. This strategy may save your life by sparing your heart.

Lord, help your wounded soldier in the "intensive care" period of his life to escape all such issues in these and similar ways. Be my refuge, my shield, my rock. You seem to say to me that these triggers should become in your light non-issues: "My dear crippled soldier, seek only the Kingdom of God within and around you, and all else will be given to you, first of all a healing heart, rhythmic, restful and light."

I made another useful discovery today, my Lord. Wearing health sandals or using a cane forces me to walk slowly. Slowing down all of my movements is another mortification you want for me at this moment of reformation by your grace alone.

Friday, June 27, 1980

As dangerous for the heart of the coronary patient [as a bad diet] are disturbing topics of contention; they are as aggravating as the lethal enthusiasms he allows to engulf his mind, imagination, and memory. Yesterday night after a phone conversation the situation looked so good for our Institute that I could not go to sleep from sheer enthusiasm.1 This kind of exalting exuberance [as distinct from a normal happy response] never emerges from the Christ-form of the soul but always from the pride-form. It represents the strong deformative surge of [a prideful "my achievement" mentality]. It is deformative insofar as it takes one away from the mystery, from the Divine Presence, from one's eternal home. It exalts in success beyond the finiteness of any project and lifts it out of the totality of the providential flow of formation. For the heart patient such exuberance is especially deformative insofar as it threatens one's quiet harmonious heartbeat and therewith one's survival.

The coronary prone person must develop serene equanimity, smiling indifference, and relaxed apathy in the face of success and failure, praise and blame, assent and dissent, acceptance and rejection. Only such constant equanimity and holy apathy may save his life. Such a disposition of the heart is only possible on the basis of a continual presence to the Lord, nourished by prayer, spiritual reading and meditation, and by countless prolonged pauses during the day, especially in the midst of one's work.

Here again avoidance, prevention, and escape techniques are necessary if blessed results are to be forthcoming:

1. Develop among your formative dispositions an early warning system. It should signal you the moment feelings of elation and exaltation begin to surge. They do not emanate from Christ's presence in your life. They stem from a self-enhancing delight in what *I* or *we* so marvelously do in isolation from the Divine Forming Mystery. They lead to the enhancement of *me*, of *us*, of *our* task; they create illusions. They make the heart beat in vain. I cannot hear any longer the forming voice of the mystery nor flow with it in forgetfulness of my self-centered dreams.

2. Resist the temptation to let your memory, imagination, and anticipation run away with exalting thoughts, images, and feelings that build an exciting empire of illusions. Relativize yet

enjoy any good news, any success, any result, as only a passing symbolic pointer to the eschaton, to that seeing face to Face that may happen to the coronary prone person at any moment of the day or night. Praise good news joyfully as only a passing expression of the lasting goodness of God.

3. Transmute the feeling of exaltation into one of gratefulness, of thanks for this passing expression of the forming power and love of God in the enormity of universe and history.

4. Express to the Eternal Beloved that only his forming love counts. Ask him to detach your heart from this exalted pleasure, to rescue it from its isolated, imprisoned excitement before it collapses because of an illusion.

A heart puffed up with pride is tense; a heart united with Christ is gentle. Never feel anxiously that I *have* to do something; always respond playfully that I *may* do something in and with the Lord. The first feeling strains the heart; the second mellows and widens it.

Any exalting and exalted movement of the pride-form constricts the heart by its isolating, grasping nature, dangerously narrowing one's arteries. Disruption of the spontaneous formative flow of the peaceful heart by exaltation may stop it altogether, particularly if it is already diseased and weakened. Any outgoing, gentle Christ-like movement widens the heart in a joyful rhythmic way that benefits one's arteries even if they are diseased and somewhat clogged. Neither let the movements of the heart be halted abruptly by a too willful or too meticulously managing, functional, forcing mind. The enlightened, pacified heart, not the isolated mind, should be life's gentle guide.

Evening of the Same Day, June 27, 1980

A text for the prayer of heartfelt presence is: "Your heart in mine, my heart in yours."

Another deformative disposition, one especially life-endangering for coronary prone people, is impatience and its resulting irritation. Impatience, as the word suggests, lacks the disposition that helps us to "pati," to tolerate, to bear with, to accept gently, to endure joyously the limitations God's eternal forming love allows in people, events, and things, in the situations of our own life with all their ups and downs. Impatience implies not only a lack of gentle tolerance, but also its replacement by the deformative disposition of active or aggressive impatience, characterized by a "pushy" urge to break through divinely allowed limitations willfully, forcefully, and irritably.

This strong force of aggressive impatience mobilizes all of life angrily and instantly for the sole purpose of breaking through the divine limit of time and energy, of human imperfection and weakness God places upon us. It invades and engulfs the core form of our life or our symbolic heart, which reverberates by putting pressure on our physical heart. Such repeated pressure may spell early death for the coronary prone person.

Aggressive, instantly mobilizing impatience is rooted in the prideform. The sin of pride becomes in this case literally a "deadly" sin, for it can lead to the early physical death of heart patients. They may always be fighting time, trying to accomplish more and more in less and less time. They cannot hide their irritation when others act, think, move or speak more slowly than they used to do. They may even despise the slower ones instead of admiring their possibly cleaner arteries! They are always in a hurry. Being always on the go is one characteristic of the aggressively impatient life form.

Now I feel like praying:

> *I have tried, my Lord, for years to change this predisposition of impatience. You know my struggle. Partly you have graced me with success. My many diaries and my book,* Spirituality and the Gentle Life, *are witnesses to my struggle. Yet it was not enough. You want me in a more radical way to become aware of my all-pervading aggressive impatience and its instant surgings. You want me to uproot it totally. Perhaps you want me to let others profit from my transforming experience. Only your grace can do it, Lord. And your grace came to me in a special way in the blessing of a coronary. Thank you, dear Lord, for your radical approach to my final formation before I may see you face to Face. What you did was once and for all to slap the death penalty on the continuation of my instant impatience. You placed me on death row, but my execution may be delayed if I consent to let myself be transformed into a person meek and humble of heart with a core form that conforms to that lovely, gentle heart of yours.*

You want me to apprehend and appraise first of all the numerous, small, irritable moments of instant impatience that link my days together—impatience with myself, with lack of time and energy, with the limits and the slowness of others, with imperfect solutions to pending situations. This instant, impulsive, almost instinctive mobilization of my whole being around the "time-energy-achievement" mentality has to be broken. Teach me to relativize that pushing-against-the-pace-of-grace momentum and to recognize the importance of managing time gently and firmly. Cure my impatience, Lord Jesus. Remind me that nothing on earth—no family, no community, no place of work-is perfect. Demobilize my excitable life and lift such foolish fight or flight pressures from my ailing heart. Make me aware of the simple joys of dwelling daily, amused and playful, in your house of creation. Let me be humorous about countless unavoidable imperfections. Impatient people cannot truly see, hear, love, play, enjoy the moment, be humorous and relaxed. They are plagued by the "hurry sickness."

Grant me especially the gift of the repeated pause, the silent interlude. Only prolonged pauses of transcendent presence at the slightest sign of fatigue or boredom can save the life of your servant. If I keep filling the pauses up, I shall soon die and still be far from ready to see you face to Face.

> *Teach me the art of pausing, Lord Jesus, of often doing nothing. Liberate my heart from its torture chamber of self-imposed deadlines that otherwise will soon bring death to me. Transform my deadline existence into a lifeline. Let me be like a flower before your lovely face, a playful, dancing candle flame, a joyful child, not an anxious performer. Let me never push farther than grace and nature allow me to go. I am the wounded soldier whom you retired from the battlefields on Monday, April 28, 1980. Reconcile me with the imperfections of my own life and that of all people, events, and things. Rescue me from "hurry sickness" and the dream of perfection.*

I hear you whisper: "Don't ever push yourself again, my dear crippled soldier. For you the battle is over." Others in turn still have to learn the hard lesson of a fallen earth and a fallen humanity. Nothing but nothing here can be changed lastingly and perfectly. Only symbolic pointers are periodically allowed. All other striving is an illusion that exhausts and kills the human heart. Some like me are not killed immediately. They receive another, perhaps a last chance to be cured from the great illusion before they enter purgatory for a final purification.

Tuesday, July 1, 1980

I am not saying my Office forcefully or willfully. I am meditating on any part of the day's readings that touch me and healingly affect my heart condition. I have the book with me at all times. I open it when I wake up in the morning or afternoon. I carry it with me as a treasure trove of wisdom for living. *When a word or sentence opens me to your saving, forming presence, I close the book and let your word take over, stilling me inwardly.*

Wednesday, July 2, 1980

Readings from the Office, Week I of Ordinary Time, Psalm 18:2-3: "The Lord has saved me; he wanted me for his own . . . He brought me forth into freedom, he saved me because he loved me" (746). Later I paraphrased this message in two shorter sentences:

"BRING ME FORTH INTO FREEDOM."

"SAVE ME BECAUSE YOU LOVE ME."

Save this heart patient from what? From the impatient, go-at-it attitude that endangers this vulnerable organ. This killer attitude may be different in other patients, and more than one killer attitude may endanger the life of the same patient. Such attitudes are also a hindrance on the way to loving union with God alone.

One attitude that is potentially lethal for some is that of over-enthusiasm, expressed in ardor, fervor, zeal, heartiness, ebullience, verve, and furor. *Scribendi, furor loquendi*. This means raving, cheering, and being wild about things; it connotes worry, involvement, engagement, straining, undue concern, launching or plunging into one's projects or undertakings, embarking furiously on one's task. One tends to overdo everything from devotion to dedication and decisiveness.

At first glance all of these dispositions seem to be potentially formative. Yet they deform the heart patient because of their intensity. For example, yesterday I had a fine enthusiastic day with my visitors, discussing new plans and projects. That evening and all night—once I awakened—I felt the same discomfort in my chest and back that I suffered one afternoon in that hotel in Chicago two days before my heart attack. In the morning I could only slightly diminish it by taking some medication. Finally I tried later in the morning, in bed, meditative reading of the Office until I found the texts mentioned above. That helped slightly. Only while shaving, showering, dressing, and going to breakfast was I able to pray to the Lord to bring me into freedom and to save me because he loves me. Then I was able to see how my discomfort of heart was linked with enthusiasm, involvement, anxiousness, and so on, with good, even excellent, but in the end only earthly ideas and ideals. Relief of discomfort only became possible by taking the absolute opposite inner stance of indifference, translated into tepidity, disinterestedness, unconcern, nonchalance, apathy, carefree inattentiveness, and detachment; it might even mean being lackadaisical, unmindful, unthinking, casual, unalarmed, and unperturbed and behaving with a certain lassitude and sluggishness, a certain listlessness, inertia, and humorousness about everything.

At first all of these dispositions seem to be potentially deformative. Moreover, they may seem unnatural and forced for the kind of heart patient who is by nature enthusiastic and warmhearted. How indeed can such a patient live a somewhat normal and effective life when cultivating "holy indifference"? How can he work at anything with this all pervading, slightly humorous casualness, this laid-backness and smiling apathy? The answer is: the enthusiastic type of heart patient should cultivate a certain equanimity in the face of exciting ideals and ideas, including creative books, plans, projects, and people, none of whom ought to be seen as ends in themselves. By the same token, success, failure, praise, blame, recognition, and rejection should leave him in equanimity. At all times he should direct his heart toward God alone, in prayerful presence, while cultivating as continuously and as deliberately as possible the disposition of smiling, liberating equanimity in regard even to his fondest hopes.

Only insofar as he sees the Face of the Beloved in all these ways will he be able to work at them in smiling detachment and, in the process, perhaps save his life.

Friday, July 4, 1980

This morning I felt chest pain and dizziness; I was afraid to bother the good sisters by passing out. I could not eat. I was unable to do anything. It was probably due to emotional upset about meeting with Father X whose foundational life form is radiant and lovable like all Christ-forms but whose current life form was for a long time harmful to my growth in you, my Lord.

> *My powerlessness makes me feel as if you are speaking directly to me: My dear son and beloved friend, three times I tried to wean you away from your merely human enthusiasms, willful projects and strivings, first by gracing you with a detached retina. It forced you twice to take eight months of rest in the same place of recollection I prepared here for you in eternal love. These periods were not sufficient because of your lack of cooperation with my grace. You drifted off again into the impatient, willful life of plans and projects, of gaining time and succeeding. Yes, you meant what you did for me, but in the meantime you left me alone as the lonely guest of your dissipated heart and soul. I want so much to save you from yourself. Life is short. Past the age of sixty, not too much will be left to you . . .* 2

∾

> *Your last chance, my son, may be this blessing of a coronary. This recent grace is far greater and can be more effective than that of a detached retina. Every time you dissipate your energy too eagerly you will be reminded of your drifting away from my presence by chest pain, fatigue or dizziness. These blessings will help you to detach yourself from countless things you might have otherwise never let go: rich foods, drinks, and desserts; exciting travels and speaking engagements; the pride of looking physically youthful; the unquestioned certitude of another day being granted to you; anxious involvement in causes that excite you but detract from the one cause I finally entrusted to you: detachment from fast production, acclaim and glory; detachment from impulsive, inner and outer movement; detachment from your hurry-sickness.*

> *All such detachments may facilitate your openness to my presence in your soul. That will set the stage for a deep and continual union between you and me. Please, my son, don't let me down this time. Sell all you have to gain the priceless pearl of my presence. Sell your useless and anxious anticipations of your earthly future, your memories of past injury and injustice, your sinfulness and weakness. You worry about things in your community you cannot change anyway. Remember that reverence and respect for the unique-communal call of the person should be the center of any community life. Forget about what irritates you. Don't worry about*

the future. Leave the projects to which I inspire you in my hands. Simply serve them in a relaxed and gentle way, sublimely indifferent to success or failure. The inspirations I have planted in the soul of every person cannot be imitated by anyone else. They are simply there. Your primary concern should be preparation for transforming union with me in anything you think, feel, imagine, say, or do. Seek first this kingdom of union within me and all the rest will be given to you.

My dear crippled soldier, be less eager to recuperate fully and more eager to find me in the midst of the sufferings, disappointments, and rejections with which I still intend to bless you. I already blessed you abundantly with these gifts during your life, but you did not profit from them as you should. You were more intent on escaping them than on using them for our union, which was their only meaning. You made useless what I meant to be useful for our oneness in love. Please don't do it again. I know you would have been glad to die when I allowed the blessing of this coronary to descend upon you. However, was not part of that longing stimulated by your desire to escape the cross of a sometimes lonely, sometimes misunderstood life?

I granted you the gift of radiant joy after receiving the Sacrament of the Sick. I let you also sense, to your disappointment, that life was not yet over for you. Not that you did not suffer enough, but you did not suffer in the right way. You suffered in the way of escape, with some fear and anger, not in the way of joyful, gentle union. Therefore, I asked you to live and suffer a little longer, only now in the way which pleases me immensely and purifies your sinful, self-centered life radically. I want you to find me finally. I want to be your life and your love, your center, your only concern. If you don't listen, my dear, you will soon be broken by the tensions that plague those who live outside my calming and absorbing presence. You will soon die unpurified and not united with me. You will be dreadfully sorry for the chances you missed when I blessed you with your coronary. The more you use this grace to become at one with me, the more I will be inclined to prolong your life because your growing union with me is so pleasing to my own wounded heart. To prolong your life then becomes truly useful after it has been useless and sinful for so long. My poor crippled soldier, I may make you truly useful then for those you may still reach. Because more useful to them than any word you write or say is my presence radiating forth from your stilled and gentle heart, weaned away by the suffering of your coronary from its wild and willful strivings. My stilling presence will speak more volumes than all the writings and teachings that once filled your often anxious days.

Sunday, July 6, 1980

Yes, my dear crippled soldier, I want your heart to be purified from all anger, frustration, and disappointment. The crucial question is: Did you use suffering to deepen the only thing that matters in time and eternity—our union, our oneness? Did you grow in relaxed compassion and surrender, in inner imperturbability, in gentle, passive strength, and prayerful presence, in supernatural motivation, flowing from the Christ-form of your soul as my suffering servant? Do you try to reform your memory, imagination, and anticipation in this same spirit? To heal your broken heart by gratitude for sharing in my suffering? For recognizing and regaining these lost chances?

You bring me into freedom. Thank you, Lord, for bringing my heart into freedom from the great illusion that is the pride-form of life and world-the illusion that popularity, acceptance, and success can ever satisfy the longing heart. The illusion that going places can ever substitute for going through all accolades, travels, gains, and disappointments to the one place that really matters, to the only one I should desire: home to the mystery of your loving, forming presence in which I live and move and have my being (cf. Acts. 17:28).

You save me because you love me. Thank you, Lord, for the great gift of constant disillusionment about mundane projects and their acceptance or rejection, about always receiving one's due in justice, about worldly recognition. There can be no greater manifestation of your saving love than destroying my prideful sense of self-sufficiency. The life of self-centeredness is an illusion. So, too, are health, strength, beauty, and elegance. As perceived, treasured, and fostered by the pride-form, they, too, are illusions.

Save me, Lord, from the empty myths by which we all live. Make me experience inner conversion from the life of illusion with its tenseness and heartbreak. Convert me to the life of truth with its holy indifference and equanimity, its peace, good humor, and lightheartedness.

Thank you, Lord, for granting me the beautiful blessing of a coronary. What a chance it gives me to be converted from the shadows that veil what truly matters in life. Thank you for this period of grace before the moment of transition, of final delivery, from the illusions of life, world, humanity, and nature, from the illusions under which the fall of humanity condemned us to live. Illusionary life will sooner or later be met with disillusion. Disillusion leads to heartbreak. How lucky I am to have experienced a coronary from which I survived. It offers me a last chance to be freed from the illusion of the pride-form, freed for you alone.

How many committee meetings, conventions, talks, books, lectures, discussions, travels, dinners, and clever encounters are futile exercises in illusion? Most projects, plans, and self-help efforts are occasions to "spin our wheels." Most socializing fits into the same illusory category as do so many political and social actions and movements. Grant me the freedom of smiling at them and my own efforts in gentle humor and compassion, content only to do what I can. Because I myself have been there and I am still there so often, I recognize with a big laugh a tragicomedy when I see it-a farce played out by naive, well meaning clowns of the illusionary life. I was and still am one of those countless clowns that make up the world of exaltation, of pride and control. Let me no longer lose my life in illusion. *Save me, dear Lord, because you love me. Bring me into freedom.*3

Monday, July 7, 1980

Since he clings to me in love, I will free him; protect him for he knows my name. When he calls I shall answer: "I am with you." I will save him in distress and give him glory (Psalm 91).

It is as if you say to me:

Be grateful and delighted when human acclaim is withheld from you during your lifetime. All such acclaim carries with it the danger of temptation and isolation-the temptation of being sucked back into that mundane prideful atmosphere that, like polluted smog, smothers the soul, perverts appraisal, and sickens memory, imagination, and anticipation with illusion and exaltation. Human acclaim can be a source of unhappiness, suffering, and depression. It can lead to a life of adulation by the idle-hearted. The hunger for acclaim evokes inner affliction; it may generate a boring and depleting aversion from the daily task I gave you to do.

All such modes of earthly attention could cause you to bend back on yourself and away from me. You could become self-centered, achievement-oriented, and cut off from me as the only true center of you life, glory, and joy. This isolation is a source of dissatisfaction. I formed in you a thirst for my glory that is infinite. You confuse it with your own glory. You begin to outdo yourself to gain more acknowledgment. Each taste of earthly success leaves you more dissatisfied and depression-prone. Disappointment, critique, insult, and humiliation wound you deeply because they threaten the very base of your life of illusion. The hurt pride-form strikes back by over-achievement, and over-adaptation, by strenuous attempts to please, to gain acceptance by authority, to be exalted in one's community instead of being content to be with me alone.

My dear crippled soldier, it is no coincidence that most original people in family life, church, and society suffer misunderstanding. It is my gift to them, my protection of their possibility for real joy! How I protected my good friend, Søren Kierkegaard, against acclaim and acceptance in his lifetime. It was the best sign of my love for him. I shall do the same for you, to keep you happy and unencumbered during your brief pilgrimage on earth, to maintain your heart in the pure joy of humility and simplicity. Don't fight it, my wounded and vulnerable friend. It can only break your heart and kill you prematurely, which is to say, before you have matured to a life-form that will glorify me in time and eternity.

Tuesday, July 8, 1980

"FREE ME FROM MY BONDAGE LORD."

"Bring me home rejoicing."

A heart ailment is a precious means to grow in the awareness of bondage—the bondage to what people who seem important to our perception may do or say. We are tethered then to our need to make an impression on, let us say, fellow clergy or religious, physicians, administrators or other scholars. This bondage to their words, their ideas, their looks is the result of our own pride-form. We let certain colleagues, community members, students, or the "public" take center stage in our concerns.

We have to be liberated inwardly from this slavery; we need the grace to pray unceasingly not to get so lost in the land of pride that we exile ourselves from the land of likeness to Christ. We must come home to Jesus and stay with him until he brings us to heaven. A taste of that paradise on earth is granted to us in the calming, refreshing presence of the Divine Forming Mystery deep in our hearts. *I am in the mystery, and the mystery is in me.*

> Lord, you alone can bring me home rejoicing. Every time this feeling of sacred certitude wanes, give me the grace to restore it. Let me pause from all I am thinking, feeling, and doing to enjoy this glimpse of my eternal homecoming, this inner restoration in the sweetness of your nourishing presence.

Wednesday, July 9, 1980

I'm reading a fascinating book by Martha Weinman Lear, *Heart Sounds*, but I was advised not to keep reading it before bedtime. Nevertheless I did so. The advice was right. I needed to take a sleeping pill.

> Lord, save me from myself, from my eagerness and curiosity, from my absorption in things at the wrong time and in the wrong way. Make me spend the time before going to bed in contemplation and in meditative, prayerful reading.

The maintenance of transcendent indifference, together with the virtues of holy apathy, humorous equanimity, and at-homeness with the Inner Presence, is easily lost while reading secular literature. Yet I enjoy the truth and wisdom I find there. Alas, my vital absorption in the world of the author may take me away from the world of my Lord.

> Help me, Jesus, to keep restoring contact with the mystery of your inmost divine formation, which is for us humans always a mystery of appealing invitation. It is soft, subtle, and unobtrusive, yet for these very reasons, it is easily overwhelmed by other noises.

Reading in the light of the Inner Presence is an exercise in the integration of our everyday formation with our experience of intimacy with the Divine that should be what motivates us in all that we read. The alliance of human nature and divine grace should never be interrupted. At no time should we be doing "something else." There is nothing else. The mystery of Trinitarian formation encompasses all that is, was, and will be. We are never on our own. It is only due to the sinful illusion of autonomy that we have torn ourselves away from God and allowed ourselves to push beyond the pace of grace. What follows—isolation, exalted feelings, excitement, and anger when I do not get my way—eat like acid at my heart. Impotent rage, outside the Inner Presence, is always deformative and destructive. It puts more pressure on the heart than anything else. With this rage the weakened heart may not regain its former strength; freed from it, a climate of partial recovery may be created by the Lord, a climate of presence to the Presence that stills the whirling waters of anger, self-pity, and depression. "We triumph over all these things through him who loved us" (Romans 8:37).

> *Rescue me, Lord, from any inclination to try to triumph over these obstacles by myself alone instead of flowing gently with your Presence. Save me from thinking that the answer to peace lies in doubtful, slavish fear of the Divine. Make me deeply aware that I am already breathing, moving, living, and thinking in the pristine air of your forming love. It is the force that carries and surrounds me. Thanks to your calming, ever beating presence in my heart and in the whole of my being, I may be able to triumph over my rage and aggravation, my idle absorption and lostness in the problems of this life. Without your help there can be no exit from this prison of deformation and depletion.*

Thursday, July 10, 1980

"The Lord has saved me; he wanted me for his own" (Second Antiphon to Psalm 18 in the Liturgy of the Hours, 746).

You saved me from my heart attack because you wanted me for your own. You allowed my coronary, for you wanted me for your own. You inspired me to overcome my instant surgings of impatience so that I may not die but live as your own, for you Lord are the innermost-often refused and forgotten-form of my being. You compel me daily to mortify my sensuality in food, drink, exuberant action, and sensuous excitement so that my wounded heart may survive and be the calm center of a life lived for you alone, a life owned and formed by you, Father, Son, and Holy Spirit.

You make necessary for my survival countless pauses during the day to save me from absorption in plans and projects, in exaltation and aggravation, in writing, reading, and speaking; from furiousness, hurry-sickness, and the surging of instantaneous impatience. All these movements of the pride-form take me away from you. Thank you for saving me in principle by the blessing of a coronary. Thank you for the necessary changes in my life form and life style that bring me nearer to you and make me your own just as you want me to be my own, my most Beloved Lord. Thank you for preventing me from falling back into habits of daily infidelity as often happened before my heart attack. Let me say always: *The Lord is saving me. He wants me for his own.*

Rejoice, my heart, when they persecute, vilify, and malign you and your work. It is the Lord. He is saving you from pride, exaltation, and self-importance. He wants you for his own. Transform all your remembrances of the past, your imaginations and anticipations of possible hurt, rejection, and persecution by the grace of appraisal. Then nobody will be able to break your heart again. Everything evokes gentle gratefulness to the Lord. He wants you for his own. He saves you. His forming mystery is always a saving mystery from the all-pervading pride-form of our life since the Fall.

Take on a "so what else is new?" attitude. What is new in some unjust remark? Don't you know by now that this prideful world is always unjust and narrow-minded. It is as illusory as a soap bubble or a bad dream that cannot last. Christ only *is*; he only *saves*. He wants you to be his own in the real world that is all his own.

Every time you experience the slightest hurrying or forcing tendency, in eating, opening bottles, raising windows, in writing, reading or speaking on the phone, ask yourself before God:

"What barrier am I trying to break?"

"Why am I trying to break it?"

Accept the limits of time, which is to say, accept the limits of life the Lord allows you in his wisdom and love. Embrace the limits of respect and appreciation the Lord allows in your life because of your weakness and vulnerability. To hurry or to exert yourself tensely in order to be approved of by others is an impatient breaking of the limits of appraisal allowed to this finite earthly person you are during your brief passage through time.

The aim of life is not approval of others but union with our Divine Source. Our pauses between actions are infinitely more important than our actions themselves. To destroy these pauses to please others is to displease God. To be disliked and depreciated is a gift more precious than silver and gold. Joyfully and gratefully accept dying to the pride-form and rising in the form of Jesus. You have been abundantly blessed with this special gift, but all too often you did not flow with these formative blessings. You withstood them; you tried to evade them and became at times like a little mouse. Your fear of this abundant blessing made your heart overly sensitive, vulnerable, and, because of your genetic inheritance, coronary prone.

Ask yourself: How many times did I look up from my writing and reading to pause and enjoy the Divine Forming Presence and thereby to relieve the unknown subtle pressure on my vulnerable heart? How often did I move out of my stream of thought, feeling, and imagination by means of this saving pause so as to regain holy presence to my Savior? How many times did I allow myself to become aware of the fine details of the Father's creation, quietly, in unhurried aesthetic contemplation? Do I really see, hear, touch, taste, feel, and sense your love, O Lord? Or do I live and move outside the Father's creation in the world of illusion created by my own power? I know in all honesty that I will fall countless times into the old people-pleasing, hurrying, achieving form of life. The question is: Am I anxious or upset when I become aware of my failure or do I say with a smile of self-forgiveness, "So what else is new?" and begin again gently to do what I can while gaining in humility.

I hear nervous sounds and steps and movements outside my door. I feel inwardly a slight wave of impatience and irritation. This over-sensitivity is due perhaps to the unconscious setting up of certain living conditions that I believe to be necessary for my well-being. This trait lowers my heart's tolerance of life's limits. Sooner or later I will have to go back into the pre-coronary world I left to recuperate. It will be more necessary than ever to learn to live serenely within its and my own limits.

Jesus, help me to make my vulnerable heart invulnerable to these deformations.

Written while walking outside and sitting on my "cane-chair (stool)" overlooking a field

I suddenly felt the urge to begin working again on the glossary.

[Editor's Note: *Father van Kaam wrote a lengthy series of definitions pertinent to formation science that were published in our former journal,* Studies in Formative Spirituality, *the contents of which are now available on a CD-rom from the Epiphany Academy.*]

I took this as a good sign of recuperation. Yet, watch it! Watch the feeling of "plunging in," the exalting fantasy of "how great it is," the slow birth of grim determination disguising itself as virtue.

A better way is to say: "Yes, I must do something in life." "How nice it is to have a glossary to play with." "Lucky you, the thing you enjoy playing with happens to be of some use to others." "How kind of my Lord to allow me to make my living by playing with words." "How safe a way it is to maintain my presence to the Presence, provided I remember that this writing is play." No forcing, no deadline, no exalted fantasy of "grave responsibility," of carrying the future on my shoulders, and other such pride-form nonsense. The reality is that my past, present, and future belong to God!

Never hurry. Remember that life is a process of always arriving. Everyday is unfinished. Every work, every writing, every reading is always still to be done. Live joyfully in this inescapable finitude because it points to your infinite homeland in the indwelling presence of God. Finitude brings you home to him. O blessed coronary, ladened with exquisite graces and inspirations for a sinful, wretched life like mine!

Friday, July 11, 1980

> *My God, my Creator, how wonderfully you've formed me. You transformed dust into your form and image and gave me a share in your own nature—your Trinitarian formation mystery. Even more wonderfully, when we, in Adam, became unfaithful you granted us a second transformation in Christ, your Son. I pray in him: where sin abounds in me, let your grace of transformation abound much more (cf. Romans 6:1–14).*

Difficulty in going to sleep. Aftermath of disturbing telephone calls concerning community newsletter announcements. Besieged by aggravation, temptations to self-pity, disturbing memories, anxiety evoking anticipations and imaginations about the future. Negative, disruptive expectations if this or that were to happen.

Jesus seems to admonish me gently and sadly, saying:

> *Why do you leave me alone, exposing your vulnerable heart to unnecessary tension and pressure, resuming these life-endangering attitudes? I want to fill your heart with my presence and my peace. O man of little faith, do you not understand even now that all this has to happen so that you, in and with me, may enter into my*

> *glory? Have I not said: Seek first the kingdom of God within you and all the rest will be given to you? (cf. Matthew 6:33). Do not be concerned about tomorrow; each day brings enough concerns of its own. Do not ask what shall we eat or what shall we drink? Only the pagans ask that but trust in your Father in heaven. See the birds of the sky, no one falls from the roof without your Father's knowledge. The hairs of your head are counted, every one of them. See the lilies of the field they neither toil nor spin, yet they are clothed in finery, even though they are to be thrown in the fire tomorrow. How much more care has our heavenly Father for you* (cf. Matthew 6:25–32).

Thank you, Lord for this precious reminder. Let me first of all care about the kingdom of heaven within me, my presence to your Divine Presence. Then the solutions and the right words will be given to me at the right time. "Do not be concerned when they bring you before judges and synagogues. The Holy Spirit will tell you what to say and teach you everything" (cf. John 14:26). Only I must pray, pray, and pray some more. I must live in prayer and contemplation of the kingdom of heaven. Then all will be well, and all manner of things will be well.4

Again it is as if the Lord is saying to me:

> *I have given each Christian a task in my church that not all may understand and that some may even condemn. I will not make all faithful Christians happy, accepted, or popular in this life. And this is for their good. It will keep them humble, surrendered to me alone, aware that they are not doing anything but that I am doing everything that is needed through them. Your weakened heart will only be able to take abuse in a light-hearted way if it is totally at one with my heart, absorbed in the mystery of the Trinity. The more Christians live in the Inner Presence, the more they will be at ease in the midst of seeming defeat, gossip, slander, and rejection; the more they will love their detractors as beloved instruments of their formation and pray for my forgiveness of them as I did from the Cross, saying: Father, forgive them because they know not what they do (cf. Luke 23:34). The more my disciples live prayerfully in my presence, the more my Spirit will speak suitable words through them and fill them with the right attitudes and feelings—with those that do least harm to them and the souls of their opponents whom I love dearly with an infinite love.*
>
> *Only my presence can inspire them to deeds and expressions that foster the work I want to establish through them in my church. Their own anxious musings, fearful anticipations, defensive plots,*

and excited imaginations can only harm and delay this work of mine. My disciples should live in faith alone. Every moment they leave my presence, they become spiritually impotent, easy victims of demonic forces, of their own anger, defensiveness, impatience, and aggravation and, hence, more than ever, coronary prone people.

Remember the rest period you had in Puerto Rico? Even that did not prevent your serious heart attack. Remember your endless walks around the gardens there at night trying to figure out your past, your future, your life call. If you would only have surrendered to me in utter faith and simplicity, only cared about trusting abandonment to my forming presence in all things, then you would have been more truly rested. Perhaps then you may have been granted by me the attitude that could have diminished the seriousness of the attack you suffered.

Be aware that lots of suffering, misunderstanding, and vilification await faithful Christians. Your heart can only bear with this cross if you live in prayerful presence to my forming presence. Think about that, my dear crippled soldier. When the next bit of bad news comes your way, say simply: 'It is the Lord,' and praise my name. Hide in my presence as under a tent, and then go on smiling as if nothing has happened.

Sunday, July 13, 1980

The asceticism of the coronary prone person can be summarized in one phrase: *Surrender to the loving, forming will of God.* Adore, praise, and love his holy will in the unclarity and the confusion he allows in your mind and heart regarding the future. Welcome his precious will for you in the pain in your chest, in the wave of fatigue that puts you down unexpectedly, in the new current situation that awaits you. Greet his formative will in the possible lack of understanding you feel by others now and in the future. For instance, accept that others may not comprehend why, long after your recuperation from your first attack, you may still have to slow down and refuse many invitations.

7:55 AM, Monday, July 13, 1980

A reading from the *Treatise on the Mysteries* by Saint Ambrose, Bishop, in the Divine Office: "The Spirit . . . breathes into you peace of soul, tranquility of mind" [488].] That breathing of peace by the Spirit is always going on in my soul. So is his steady breathing of tranquility in my mind.

Lack of peace of soul and tranquility of mind in the coronary prone person is not due to negligence by the always peace-breathing Spirit. His peace-breathing is always there, but it is threatened by the breath of pride that feeds upon exalted illusions, willful distortions, spastic excitements, unfounded fears, foolish expectations, and the resulting "lows" of disillusions, depressions, frustrations, and depreciations.

The tranquil heart is the good fruit of the Spirit. The agitated heart is the bad fruit of pride. When excitement for holy projects enters spirit, heart, mind, and will, I must distrust it. It is not of the Spirit. Appraise it gently before God. Weigh carefully any sign of your all too human enthusiasms. Seek for their hidden source: "I have to do it." "It will be great." "How fantastic it will look." "If only this plan would succeed, I would have it made." "You must get it over with as fast as possible; you must throw yourself into it totally." Such is the language of illusion, of self-sufficiency, of pride, of manipulation, of making myself the center of achievement, and of absolutizing some merely human project. I cannot hear any longer the soft, subtle breathing of the peace of the Spirit in my soul. His tranquility is no longer in my heart. It is suppressed by the pride-filled noises of my fallen life.

Always be convinced that when peace of soul and tranquility of mind does not pervade your whole being like a sweet aroma fills a rose garden in early spring, something is wrong. You are not on the right path. You have lost touch with the Spirit. Once again your physical heart is in danger of the reverberations flowing in waves from your symbolic heart. These express either the felt fragmentation or the felt harmony of your life's ongoing formation. Remember to seek first the kingdom within your peace-filled heart and tranquil mind, and all the rest will be given to you.

The moment a wave of impudent enthusiasm, irritation, or sheer impatience due to the pressure of "getting at a task or project" emerges, distrust it. *Pause and appraise it. Check its origins.* Because I am leaving the Spirit's land of peace and tranquility, I am at risk of losing God's way for me in the land of pride and exile that endangers my heart.

Many coronary prone persons are addicted to a typical manifestation of the exalting pride-form of life, namely, an inability to surrender; to tolerate the limits of finitude, to simply be and let be, to "let go" smilingly in holy apathy, and to practice the wisdom of "tomorrow is another day." The pride-form suggests to us, ever so slyly, that we have to be the managers of our own time limits, the absolute control centers of our universe. It stimulates us to hurry up, "to do more and to do it better" for what we delude ourselves into thinking is God's project or the Spirit's inspiration.

Anything that is experienced, rightly or wrongly, as standing in the way irritates such coronary-prone patients thoroughly. Irritation and aggravation corrode and weaken both their symbolic and their organic heart. Irritation is repeatedly evoked by people, events, and things that seem to slow down or interfere with one's frantic, single-minded utilization of time. This exhausting chain of excitements and aggravations is ultimately devastating; it elevates serum cholesterol and affects the heart dangerously. It is a seemingly innocent, yet factually debilitating, often fatal game of time control, of gaining a few seconds, of "getting things over and done with."

Projects and ambitions accomplished within our unique limits of grace and nature are beautiful and integral constituents of the wholesome unfolding of a consonant form of life in Jesus. They become danger zones for coronary survival when they no longer move smoothly with the harmonious flow of the gentle, graced unfolding of our divine life call.

Ambition in and by itself is a neutral disposition; it is neither good nor bad, morally speaking. Its goodness is determined by its orientation and by the wisdom and style of its implementation. Ambition is the normal expression of the functional dimension of our human life form. We should want to function as well as we can, but not faster, better or more than we ought to do without harming our hearts.

> *Lord, you invite us to give our best within the time limits set for us by your forming love. You want us to live in congeniality with our limits, not to exalt ourselves beyond the boundaries of your forming love. Your mystery of formation confirms our life in all of its formation phases.*

To battle the borders of our unique potential by hurry and overexertion occasions an idle, exhausting struggle with illusions. We enter into a desperate daily battle to accomplish the impossible. Such exalted attempts to expand our life's capacity lead to constant overloading of the heart that sooner or later may collapse under the burden of a secretly proud and foolish perfectionism.

Thursday, July 24, 1980

Visit with my internist on July 17. Excellent progress: weight down to 155 ½ from 164; cholesterol count down to 190 from 240. Treadmill test on July 19. Cardiologist rates it excellent. (Twelve minutes with three elevations.) Finally, heart pressure no higher than 110 and pulse rate normal. No chest pain. According to cardiologist this was due to my commitment to exercise before the attack.

Today the danger of inner aggravation recurred after reading a letter that contained some bad news.

Don't allow this aggravation to get to you. It might kill you. Stay factually and especially emotionally out of it. Rejoice in the will of the Lord! Please, cooperate with the Lord. Accept from his hand that it is your fate to follow a lonely path. Identify with the suffering and joyful courage of the Lord. Love all people dearly. Appreciate serenely that God calls them to follow a different way-good for them but not for you. Accept as your fate that you have to march to the tune of a different drummer. Please, for the love of God, don't disturb them in their calling. Don't try by word or thought to change anything in their journey. Simply forget about it and listen to what the Lord wants for you. What he asks of you mainly is to survive, to become strong and healthy enough to execute his projects in the midst of possible gossip, rejection, ridicule, or opposition. Ask him for the courage to cooperate with the graces of serenity, loving kindness, and equanimity despite all that may happen to you. Without these virtues your heart cannot survive.

Here are some other survival tips: Never hurry in anything. Let my examples be others who are temperamentally my opposites. Change the habits that drive me on to do more and more things in less and less time or to fight inwardly changes in the community and the world that are beyond anyone's control. Grant me the wisdom of inner and outer withdrawal from situations that harass me and that I cannot affect anyway. Teach me to withdraw graciously so as not to hurt the feelings of others or to evoke gossip, resistance, condemnation, and suspicion. Help me to utilize wisely and diplomatically the advice and support of my internist and my closest colleague in this regard.

> *Help me, Holy Spirit, to see in the detachment and withdrawal you forced upon me by my heart disease, a positive pointing to what I can do well without danger. Let me exercise these dispositions many times a day. Help me to avoid pacing or timing or glancing at my watch. Give me the grace, the courage, the patience to establish new habits that supersede and replace my old ones. Otherwise I will remain in constant danger of another fatal attack.*

Pinpoint any emergence of the sense of time urgency, of the free floating aggravation-inclination, of my concern for what I may sound like or look like to others, of my excessive anticipation of the future. See how these obstacles to grace are above all rooted in the pride-form of life. Practice prayers of heart-felt petition for the people who evoke such aggravation; forgive them and learn to appreciate their good points. Ask the Lord to be liberated from time urgency the moment it comes up, from the "get at it" attitude the second it manifests itself again, from exalted enthusiasm when it emerges about the good things of life. Live the contemplative way instead. With God's grace, I can alter my behavior patterns drastically. They are not due solely to genetic predispositions.

> *Lord, help me to wrench myself loose from habits I have learned to view as virtues. Please liberate me.*

Friday, July 25, 1980

> *Thank you, Lord, for helping me to discover the following sources of heart stress and distress.*

Yesterday night I felt over-fatigued. The cause was not my writing and thinking in and by itself. It was the intensity with which I think and write: putting the spirit ahead of my body and especially of my heart. It was the refusal to acknowledge in my inner style of writing and thinking the reality that you created me as an incarnated spirit. It shall be a long time before I overcome these lifelong intensity dispositions, triggered noticeably during my thinking and writing process. They can kill me now. And it seems that you want me to live and work for your glory. Help me to honor your holy wish for my survival and effectiveness by dying in Christ to this intensity, to this rushed style of working that is so deformative. Remind me, Jesus, that this exalted pushing has roots in the pride-form that are not likely to be uprooted overnight. Disclose to me effective ways of reforming such inwardly destructive thoughts and dispositions. Allow me in your mercy to keep in mind the following A, B, C's . . . :

A.

1. As soon as you make me aware that this intensity is coming to the fore, give me the power to mortify it by pausing to walk prayerfully around my room and to calm down in presence to you.
2. Remind me, loving Christ-form of my soul, to have my tapes of flowing, soothing music with me and to play them during such pauses while exercising without strain.
3. Let me print my words as a means of slowing down the excited unreadable writing, which is a sure symptom of inner exaltation.
4. Remind me to have at hand a meaningful text of the Holy Office and to look at it repeatedly to bring myself into your enduring presence.
5. Help me during times of thinking and writing to check any muscle tension developing in my hands, legs, jaws, eyes, back or neck. Then let me try, with the help of your grace, to relax this tension right away.

One consolation and powerful motivation to exercise myself in this asceticism of the gentle life style is the fact that I am discovering more and more that all I have to do in service of survival, in spite of my heart disease, is the same anyone would have to do to practice the disposition of receptivity to the grace of God. The holy work of formation in the image of Christ goes on ceaselessly. Help me to turn my creative thinking and writing into an enduring exercise in purifying formation, illuminating reformation, and unifying transformation.

B.

Another source of tension you've disclosed to me is that of the deforming disposition to aggravation. This morning it happened during a brief conversation with someone here at the Motherhouse.

1. Help me to pinpoint the emergence of such aggravation and its cause.
2. Teach me to "enjoy" injustice, misunderstanding, and persecution as a sharing in your holy passion.
3. Grant me the grace of humble acknowledgment that my life has been more sinful, hypocritical, egoistic, and self-indulgent than that of my opponents and detractors. You loved me and saved me because you wanted me as your own. Should I not share your joyous and serene compassion with them? Should I not be glad to be punished for my offense against your love by their opposition?
4. Help me to pray for them, seeing them in your light and your love.

C.

A third source of tension is my lack of patience with slow story tellers.
1. Make me retire in inner contemplation when this aggravation emerges.
2. Help me to use this time for active relaxation and gentling down.
3. Once calm has returned, let your love in me shine forth in kind and relaxed attention.

Sunday, July 27, 1980

Yesterday and again this morning, I felt the same constriction in my chest and back as on that Friday in Chicago before the Monday of the heart attack; I felt the same at lunch and at the end of the student party in the library. Don't deny what you felt, what your body told you. Don't give in to the temptation of denial! *My loving Lord, grant me the grace to face with courage the setbacks you allow in my sinful life. Spirit of Jesus, make me read in these bodily signals the hidden messages of your love.*

What is the cause of this relapse? What is its divinely inspired formative meaning? It is not physical exertion. I do fine in my long and often repeated walks. Neither is the cause meditative spiritual reading, these days of the *Confessions of Saint Augustine* and other parts of the Divine Office. I do only as much or as little as I can, since these activities sustain my presence to you. To live in this ambience of adoration seems to be "the" healing atmosphere for my heart. It gives me a deep sense of peace and joy.

Things began to go wrong. I believe, for the following reasons:

1. I accommodated my inclination, both during and after the reading of Augustine, to keep on walking instead of sitting on a bench in quiet contemplation under the evergreens surrounding the cemetery.

2. I did not stop because I fell back on my worst habit. Preconsciously I began to push myself towards a self-imposed deadline for finishing a manuscript of mine.

3. In the early afternoon my writing enthusiasm took over. I pushed myself to get more done in less time so as to gain time. I became especially enthusiastic to finish what I started when one of our staff members called to say she would be here tomorrow. I wanted to give her as many pages for typing as I could so as to conclude the manuscript. Against all advice to the contrary, I allowed the pressure of getting the *Envoy* article ready to get to me. Following an enthusiastic call from one of our students about his hope of seeing more glossary segments in *Studies*, I felt pressured to think about getting that work done, too. Then I finished the manuscript for the *Envoy* article as quickly as I could.5

4. Because I still felt well, I did not realize that, while writing, an inner pushing attitude began to take over. Contemplative pauses were neglected.

5. Later in the afternoon, the weather became quite humid. While such conditions do not bother others, they seem to affect me negatively. I should have put on the air conditioning, but I just kept on writing and organizing my material.

6. I enjoyed a sense of achievement, but I lost your presence. I postponed my rest. When I finally got to bed, exhausted in the muggy room, I could not sleep. Some relief came from a return to an admittedly imperfect contemplative presence, broken up by distracting thoughts. Some of the aggravation was due to how little I accomplished in three quarters of an hour of writing, compared with past production.

7. At supper, I ate too much. I sat in front of the television set, watching a first and then a second newscast. After that I saw a show I enjoyed. I turned on the air conditioning. I felt good again, and I began writing for twenty-five minutes. Now the same symptoms return. I stop writing. I lie down on the couch. I am tired, so fatigued that I say Mass with limited attention. I take a short walk outside. It does not help much to relieve chest heaviness. I return to my room at 9:15 PM. I cannot resist finishing the book, *Heart Sounds*. I am in bed by 11:45 PM. I have trouble falling asleep. Aggravating dreams wake me up. I rise at 6:45 AM in spite of nitroglycerin ointment to alleviate chest and back pains as in Chicago that fateful Monday morning. I attempt a contemplative stance. It is difficult since I neglected for so many hours to find the way back into that peace Christ promises. I take a Valium and a nitroglycerin tablet. Neither offer me much help.6

Thank you, Lord, for these undeniable messages. Another attack may be in the offing. In a short while, I may be again on the verge of death. You seem to tell me in either case that contemplative presence to you is the only type of presence that counts. If I get sick again, it is the best, perhaps the only, inner condition to support physical healing. It fostered recuperation after my first attack. Should I be called by your love to die soon, this presence is the best means to support the purification and detachment of my life here as a preparation for my life hereafter. It represents an earthly beginning of purgatory. If I am called by your forming love to live on and serve your kingdom a little longer, then this presence is the only means to detach myself from my sinful, self-centered work and achievement-oriented life. I must become centered in your loving presence. You alone can give a quality of serenity, stillness, depth, and detachment to my life that was badly missing. You may use this new life to illumine others with your light, your love, your presence. I experienced already that I was a holier and wiser guide for the nun who came to ask me for some advice.

Thank you, Lord, for continuing the blessing of a coronary in my life. Every time I lose detachment and leave your presence, you call me back by overwhelming fatigue, by chest and back constriction, by the threat of a new attack. You teach me when and where detachment is most needed.

It is not physical exercise that bothers me. Remember how successful I was during the treadmill test! It is this all too human thinking and writing enthusiasm, generated by the controlling, achieving, exalting pride-form that takes me away from you. Only now, you no longer let me get away with it.

Thank you for this painful redirection of my self-directed life of production. And yet you seem to want me to live on and to write and think in service of your kingdom about topics no one else appears to be able to articulate as well at this moment. It seems that you want to teach me by trial and error how to do this task in total detachment and relaxation, always within your presence. I never, never could have learned this lesson without the blessing of a coronary.

> *Thank you, Dear Master, close to what may be the end of my life, for taking over the reformative direction of my deformative style of being in and at the world.*

As always, after journaling about my thoughts and feelings I felt much better. I am more relaxed and detached again from my thinking and writing projects. I am back in your presence. While shaving, showering, and eating breakfast, every time my thinking threatened to return to exclusive and exalted preoccupation with manuscripts and other types of ministry, it was as if I heard you say to me: *"Don't leave me. Don't leave me alone. Stay with me. Abide with me."* You made me see that thinking and writing in service of your plans for my life are necessary, but far more important is growing in your presence. Only out of that kind of dwelling can I facilitate your formative presence to others.

Wednesday, July 30, 1980

Was my chest constriction yesterday morning somehow related to unconscious inner pressure due to preparing written material for typing when the secretary comes to collect it? This fatigue and tightness remained with me during her visit and afterwards when I looked over some other papers. After talking to my most understanding colleague, these symptoms lessened.

As usual, meditative walking presents no problem. In the evening, I watched two enjoyable television programs. I felt excellent after one hour of walking in the cemetery under the pine trees, simply enjoying your presence and celebrating your first revelation in creation. The 9:00 PM program was relaxing, the 10:00 PM program rather gripping. Scenes in it affected me, probably unconsciously, but I did not realize it at the time. I lost contact with your presence. Afterwards I felt heavy chest constrictions. This morning I woke up from my dreams with the same feelings. After one hour I found these calming words: "*You alone.*" After much inward repetition, the tightness subsided.

It becomes clear, my Lord, that my failing health was not due exclusively to lack of exercise nor to diet or weight gain nor to cholesterol levels. These were all within average limits before you blessed me with a coronary. Now they are even better: my weight is down from 164 to 154 ½, my cholesterol from 240 to190. The treadmill test surprised my doctor, again twelve minutes with only two elevations. God willing, no more serious heart problems will appear in the near future. I was also able to keep calm in your presence during the treadmill test. Therefore, it seems as if:

A.

You want to remind me that only by maintaining presence to your presence at all times, during any occupation or conversation and in the processes of thinking, writing, walking, exercising, teaching, and speaking, may I delay my next heart attack and be available for a longer time to do your work here on earth.

B.

Gentle, relaxing presence to your forming, loving, saving presence, should be my first, my only, and central concern at all moments of the day. The second I lose "it," I should stop everything else, at least inwardly, until I regain contact with you. Exercises that facilitate this life lived in the soft radiance of your love seem to include the following:

1. Inwardly repeating a prayerful text.
2. Speaking with you and listening to you in the way of *He and I,* the book by Gabrielle Bossis that I love so much. You teach me through this book how to remain with you in countless little ways: by talking to you as a trusting child would; by offering simple prayers of petition; by seeing you in nature, in other people, and in lovely things. Thank you for sending this book my

way. Make me faithful to the message you communicate on its pages. Let me read a few passages several times a day.

3. Reading the Holy Office slowly and meditatively, pausing as long as possible with any text through which you touch me.

4. Slowly reading and meditating on the writings of the spiritual masters.

5. Resuming visits to the Blessed Sacrament.

6. Most important, not giving up my work of thinking and writing for your kingdom but learning from you, Jesus, to do it in a different way. It seems that you want me to adopt this new style of prayerful, gentle presence to the task here and now, without delay.

C.

The only way to learn and to practice this new approach seems to be:

1. Preparation before the writing task by recollection, by hiding in your presence.

2. During the task itself, by having a text conducive to the "prayer of presence" before me.

3. Staying gently alert to any sign of my usual unconscious pressure of hurrying, forcing, or exalting—all symptoms of the pride-form in me, which is my greatest enemy.

4. When you bless me with the slightest awareness of such pressures, please give me the grace to hear your voice in the holy reminders that register in my heart.

5. In response to this warning and inviting voice of yours, let me pause immediately, Lord Jesus. Let me interrupt, out of love for you, anything I am thinking, writing, or doing. Let me die to it at that very moment. Let me abide with you alone or through any of the other means you've disclosed to me so generously. Let me remain with you until gentle union is restored. Only then let me return to these tasks for your kingdom.

6. Grant me the wisdom and the courage to reiterate these pauses of healing presence as many times as my deeply rooted habits of

unconscious hurrying, forcing, and exalting demand it. I already know, Lord, that this promise will have to be repeated countless times a day, even within the same hour of thinking or writing.

7. Remind me, Jesus, that even if these exercises would not delay the next and perhaps final coronary, they would at least liberate me for the beauty of the life of purgatory and prepare me for the last great moment of deliverance. Use them to purify me and to make up for my poor, sinful, unpriestly life before the blessing of my coronary.

8. You sent also my way, along with other books on heart disease, *Type A Behavior and Your Heart,* perhaps because temperamental traits have been my main problem. Thank you for reminding me to keep reading passages from it, translating them into your language of loving formation, reformation, and transformation.

9. Another means you have taught me is to print my words instead of writing them in my old way. If the printing takes a bad turn, let me see it as a symptom of the loss of gentle abiding, of quiet detachment from the task, followed by exhausting exaltation that alienates me from you. Help me to pause and return after that awareness to clear and relaxed printing once again.

10. Another means of holy healing of my achievement-oriented pressured life is rereading meditatively passages from this journal itself. It is also a good idea to live all movements—eating, drinking, walking, speaking—as holy rites in a liturgy of love and adoration.

I see now, Lord Jesus, that you don't ask me to imitate the more or less apathetic life style of certain people whose enviable mode of being may have kept their arteries clean. You want me to love and embrace the nature you gave me. You want me to be apathetic toward worldly achievement and acclaim, not by destroying my sensitive nature but by directing it to your love alone.

Remind me to admire the calm demeanor of more relaxed temperaments but to come to this reformation along the different path you trace for me in gentle love.

Thank you again for the blessing of this coronary, for the warning pains that occur when I leave you and the peace of your calming presence. I cannot think of any more effective gift you could have granted me in your infinite love. Without this exquisite sign of your forming presence I would never have entered this way of holy and freeing detachment. To tell the truth, I would soon have left it. Without this undeserved grace, how would I have been able to purify my sinful life? How would I have learned to ready myself for the beautiful life of purgatory? Thank you, Lord, for this [life-changing] favor.

10:15 AM, Thursday, July 31, 1980

My caring Lord, it is as if you are saying to me:

> To love me in your life is to love my forming mystery in the lives of others. You had learned a lot, my son, before I granted you the blessing of a coronary, but you had not learned enough. The aggravation disposition is still in you. I granted you a soul-friend beyond compare. Through this friendship the overwhelming power of your aggravation disposition has been diminished but not eradicated. Your basic, all pervasive inclination to aggravation with people I love infinitely is still smoldering in you. I allowed your physical heart to become so sensitive to your symbolic heart—so moved by it—that even slight experiences of anger, hostility, impatience, and disaffection touch it and unsettle it. Mine is a warning voice of love.
>
> If you allow these experiences to become enduring, they may end your life before the time I need you for service of my kingdom. Aggravations that others can allow themselves without danger for their lives are not allowed for you. The blessing of your coronary will oblige you to grow daily in compassionate love for others, to share in my forming love for all of them. I don't ask you at this moment to focus on manifestations of love. You do rather well with that, but to cultivate feelings, thoughts, and attitudes of genuine care and concern. If your interiority is at disparity with your forced outward manifestations, you are in double jeopardy. The stress on your heart is heavier than ever.

Thursday, August 7, 1980

I pray that I may bless the lives of my students, confrères, and colleagues as they are and not focus on burdening them or myself with wishful thinking about what I did or failed to do.

> *Help me Lord, to see my and their missteps in the perspective of the long road we still have to travel in the company of one another. Grant me the grace to be as patient with their slow pace of progress as you were patient with mine.*
>
> *Give me the wisdom to know when to smile gently when mistakes happen and when to show firmness when a better response is required.*
>
> *Help me to hear the anguish in others' hearts through the din of their angry words or across the gulf of their brooding silence. Having heard [these voiced and unvoiced concerns] grant me the ability to bridge the gap between us with understanding. I pray that I may raise my voice more in joy at what others are than in vexation at what they are not, so that each day they may grow in sureness of themselves.*
>
> *Help me to regard them with genuine affection in the hope that they will feel the same for others. Then give me the strength, Lord, to encourage them to move with fortitude on the way you've chosen for them.*

Yesterday, I enjoyed a fine visit with friends. I felt excellent. Then tonight, suddenly, after my evening walk, overwhelming fatigue set in, together with chest constrictions and one short moment of stabbing pain in the back. The constriction continued. I went to bed around 10:00 PM and still it persisted. I took medication for sleep; nitroglycerin was no help. Though I slept well, I awakened with remnants of heaviness in my chest.

> *Stay with me, Lord, for it is evening. Make my life a song of surrender, a prayerful preparation for the beautiful life of purgatory awaiting me. Don't allow me to do more than I can bear without fatigue, urgency, exaltation or aggravation. Make me stop and forget all about it the moment I lose your presence. Such a loss would mean that I have been absorbed in my own story to the point of losing you. And, if you are lost, everything is lost.*
>
> *It is infinitely better to abide with you with an unfinished manuscript, an unsolved problem, an imperfect life than to finish these assignments and try to heal these wounds without you, as if this were possible! The moment this process begins to haunt me, to hurry me, to excite me, to take over my heart and mind, my memory, imagination, and anticipation I am a lost person. It is infinitely better to be a stranger in time than a loser in eternity. The*

> only thing that counts is presence to you. Only secondarily comes the healing of a life insofar as purification can penetrate its depth softly without leaving your Spirit. Pneumatic appraisal should be predominant, but it can only prevail if you preserve in me the gift of relaxing receptivity to your presence. Psychological analysis can only profit the soul as long as it breathes in the breath of God. Let your light shine forth as the first and ultimate fruit of my prayerful reflections.

The inner work of reformation is always unfinished. It will be so until the day we die. Only purgatory or the miracle of divine mercy can complete the work of purification at the moment of final transition. We should delight in the "unfinished symphony" God allows in our life. We should never push beyond the limits set by you as to what we can accomplish, thanks only to the grace of your presence.

Blessed be these heart pains and bouts of fatigue. They are faithful messengers of the Lord. They tell me that I have left him alone. Of what use is my "solving, worrying, and improving urgency"? You are never in a hurry, Eternal Forming Love. I always am. Please slow me down. Let me utilize to the utmost the grace of the coronary you gave me. You already allowed me to experience how exquisite this means of inner detachment is: slight chest constriction signals the emergent activation of such deformative dispositions as over-concern, pushiness, drivenness, unchecked idealism, and planning in a willful way.

Holy Father, you say to me:

> *My son, these deformations are initiated by your pride-form; they influence your physical heart negatively, releasing certain chemicals in your bloodstream that affect your arteries adversely for many hours. Practice instead holy apathy. It helps to prevent this wear and tear on your vulnerable heart. At the same time, this divine equanimity liberates the Christ-form of your soul. This participation in the life of my Son, this intimacy, unites you with the family of the Trinity that is yours through adoption.*

Sunday, August 24, 1980

Lord, you allowed me a few days of extreme fatigue, chest discomfort, and those brief moments of stabbing pain in the back. *Your will be done.* Still you seem to want me to live and to serve your reign on earth. Help me to cooperate with your healing of my heart, your restoration of some of my energy and creative productivity for your house, the peace-filled home of your faithful, the resting place of all people of good will. I can only flow with your grace of healing restoration if I mellow my intensity of thought and feeling.

Lord, liberate me and all those you have blessed with coronary disease from a certain excess of typical Dutch dutifulness, seriousness, and inner pompousness, of Germanic intensity, willfulness, romantic exaltation, and adolescent heroism. Mix the good side of these dispositions with the gifts you granted to other nationalities like Italian playfulness and affection; English apathy, wit, and understatement; Irish charm, joy, and easy-goingness.

Teach me how to think, write, move, and speak playfully and humorously. Let everything become a dance, a melody, a pleasant play before your lovely face. Only then may my heart be healed, my life prolonged.

An hour long talk by a certain guest appearing last night on public television seemed to exemplify the warm, playful qualities you granted an Italian like him so abundantly. Thank you for making me tune in to this program by pure coincidence. But, then, there are no coincidences, only providences!

Wednesday, September 4, 1980

"I call to you all day long, have mercy on me, O Lord. You are good and forgiving, full of love for all who call to you" (Psalm 86:3–5).

How in need I am of your mercy, Lord, for I have left you and lost you for a long time. I have squandered the exquisite graces you've given me since the blessing of my coronary. I have been unfaithful to the formative directives you granted me in regard to keeping in touch with your loving, saving presence. This intimate in-touchness should always come first in my life. Not my secular readings, not television, not my writing or my health or the excitement I feel about new medical procedures and examinations.

Seek first the kingdom of God and all the rest will be given to you. If I really put first your "presence to me" and "my presence to you," all the rest will be given to me from the simple enjoyment of watching good television programs and reading newspapers to writing books and articles without losing contact with you. Help me to engage in the joy of translating all I experience in the light of its transcendent meaning.

Quiet inspired reflection and cooperation that do not carry me away and exhaust me are wonderful gifts. My health will be protected by the calming gentleness of your generosity. It will prepare me for successful open heart surgery, which has now been advised by my doctors. It will help me to see you in my medical examinations and in the fascinating procedures you initiated in their creative minds. Your presence will fill me with a grace every Epiphany member should radiate into the world and into any apostolate he or she undertakes anywhere on earth.

> Help me to call again to you all day long. Have mercy on me, O Lord, no matter the frequency of my forgetfulness. Deepen my faith that you are good and forgiving, full of love for this poor priest to whom you granted this unexpected grace.

Thank you for the confession I made today and for the offering of such a prayerful Holy Mass. Thank you for the gift of inspiring spiritual talks with my soul-friend and for the tape recordings of her classes on the spiritual masters. Thank you for lifting me up like a vulnerable little bird tired from flying over the heavily traveled highways of this world. You passed by; you saw me in infinite love today; you bowed down; you put me tenderly upon your finger; then you blew me into the fresh air of your divine presence, far away from the crushing, burning, speeding freeway.

Lord, keep me in this atmosphere of your love. Help me to fulfill the necessary conditions for living in your presence, such as always having a holy text at hand. It has been a week since you granted me new insights into my life, and so much has happened. You brought me, by the persistent efforts of my doctors and the perseverance of my soul-friend, to the Mayo Clinic. You showed me the professional dedication of the fine Christians there, reminding me of what you want to do through your Epiphany Association. How providential was its co-founding by us last year! You sent me to an excellent doctor and, through him, opened up a whole new perspective on your loving formation of my life.

For more than twenty-five years you allowed two of my arteries to become almost fatally occluded. But it seems as if you did not want me to die. You inspired me to discipline my body by ever-improving dietary restrictions, by physical exercises, and by gentling down my inner willfulness and its neuroformational muscular expressions. You took me two times for almost eight months out of active life for total rest because of a detached retina. Twice, with the help and hospitality of a few congregations of nuns in the area, you added eight weeks' rest for a misdiagnosis, once of an ulcer, then of a "simple" fainting spell. All these events you allowed in your mercy to keep me alive while masking my real illness. You kept me working for your kingdom without any doctor suspecting the time bomb ticking away in my chest. You made me strengthen my body and all its organs. You helped me to fortify the good part of my heart like the heart of an athlete so that successful surgery would be possible once the time bomb had exploded!

You allowed it to explode at the right time, when your work would be established in its fundamental form, when I needed to return to you as a lost lamb, living for so long outside the shepherd's caring presence. After the attack you did not allow my doctors to detect how bad it really was so that I would have time for a retreat with you—time to return to prayer, recollection, and renewal of my errant, sinful yet mysteriously graced and guided life.

You made me, along with my dedicated colleague, who accompanied me here, meet the doctors at the Mayo Clinic, who discovered that two arteries, the crucial left descending and another one, are more than ninety percent occluded. The verdict is "bypass surgery" or else.

Thanks to your loving and mysterious care during all these dangerous preceding years, you made me build up myself in such a way that the surgery will probably be successful, give me a new lease on life, and the strength to finish what you want me to do for your house, the house of God. But you do not want me to escape the forming meaning of these blessed events. I must become a contemplative soul. Have mercy on me, O Lord. I am so weak, so vulnerable, so dispersed. I am likely to betray you and your project for my errant life again and again if you do not save me *all day long*.

[Editor's Note: *Father Adrian van Kaam's life was saved physically by his bypass surgery at the Mayo Clinic. His recuperation went relatively smoothly though he had a severe bout of pericarditis that further weakened his heart and resulted in "atrial flutter." He had his first pacemaker inserted in 1999 and a second, more sophisticated model in 2002, this time with a ventricular defibrillator. He never had to have a repeat bypass because of obeying dietary restrictions and following the graced advice he recorded in his journal. His health had by 2005 been compromised by several falls and many complicated vascular problems, but his practice of the gentle life style remained until the end as rich and full as he had hoped it would be when he kept this touching and truly candid diary on the blessing of a coronary.]*

Notes

1. Father van Kaam refers here to facts already noted but worth repeating. In 1979 we received permission from the Middle States Accreditation Association to raise our designated "doctoral style master's theses" to an official PhD level, creating the first such degree in existence in this new field. That same year (in May of 1979), we had also incorporated our fledgling Epiphany Association to handle the ministry work we did in adult faith formation on the weekends. This conversation probably refers to news about the initial success of the doctoral program, which had begun to attract students from around the world. Little could we have known that ten years later the University would begin the process of phasing out the Institute and that we would both be beholden to the plan of Holy Providence to continue this work under the auspices of the Epiphany Association. These events made Father van Kaam's response to this "phone conversation" all the more touching and, indeed, prophetic.

2. And yet, thanks be to God, on April 19, 2006, Father van Kaam enjoyed his 86th birthday celebration at the Epiphany Academy of Formative Spirituality. In July of the previous year he suffered a debilitating fall that fractured his left arm and severely damaged his radial nerve. Neuropathy and other neuro-muscular complications rendered him incapable of walking without help and by 2007 he was fully wheelchair bound. Due to further physical and cognitive weakening, he needed the skilled care provided by the Little Sisters of the Poor on Pittsburgh's North Side where he lived from August 2005 until his death on November 17, 2007. To the end, he offered to everyone an outstanding witness of patient endurance or, as he put it, a "crucifying epiphany." He practiced until his last breath, the "ministry of the smile."

3. It was at this time that both of us read, reread, and discussed line by line *The Collected Works of Saint John of the Cross*, focusing frequently on the great paradox he proclaims: that the only key to liberation is renunciation, above all, of our own willfulness in fidelity to our unique-communal life call.

4. This favorite saying of Father van Kaam's comes from the writings of Julian of Norwich, a 14th century English mystic.

5. These were the two journals we co-edited and published at that time under the auspices of the Institute of Formative Spirituality.

6. All of these symptoms would necessitate in a few month's time open heart surgery for a severely occluded left descending artery and another less occluded but still dangerous blockage in need of repair.

34

Fruits of Formative Thinking

THE LIFE REVIEW OCCASIONED by my heart attack and subsequent periods of recuperation seemed not to disappear but to intensify when I returned to a more or less regular schedule. I had to live with the knowledge that from henceforth I would be a heart patient. I would have to ponder the meaning of my setbacks and healings. With the grace of God, I would have to grow in awe-filled abiding and humility. Day by day I would have to sort the wheat from the chaff of my journey so far.

From the time of the Hunger Winter to the founding of the Institute and the co-founding of the Epiphany Association, I had committed myself to the integration of our humanity and our spirituality. The need I saw to reestablish the complementary relationship between informational and formational theology was so integral to my life call that I had striven over a lifetime to be faithful to it. I can trace this two-pronged interest in theoretical and practical thinking to the gifts I inherited in great measure from my parents. From my father Charles I received the inkling to think problems through until a solution could be found. From my mother Anna I learned to put into practice what I believed and to do so with perseverance and patience: "Lace-making takes a long time," she used to say, "but with each stitch, perfectly executed, a work of beauty results."

Despite these early counsels, I had often pursued other paths. Now, as a heart patient, I had no choice but to correct habits of functionalism into which I had fallen and the stresses and pressures they produced. Even on vacation I brought my projects with me, but that sense of urgency had to change. Retaining the aesthetic component of my call—that innate orientation to beauty evoked in me by my mother and confirmed by my soul-friend—was an acceptable disposition, but there were less ordered pockets of dissonance I knew needed to be reformed. My so-called cultural and ethnic, Dutch determined "DNA" had to be softened and reprocessed in the light of my deeper call to a transcendent-functional versus a functional-transcendent life of presence and action. I had to accept the fact that my outlook might not be understood by certain peers in the always changing context of my academic and community life. There was nothing new or unusual about that. My health problems had taught me not to fight feelings of misunderstanding. I realized upon reflection that they could be traced as far back as my elementary school days. Other kids made fun of the refined way my mother dressed me. I had to learn to laugh about these episodes of rejection and simply accept the fact that I was a different person.

My closest colleague, Doctor Susan Muto, identified with this "difference factor" and confessed that she, too, had felt it most of her life. I could picture her, as she said, living in the Bookmobile during her adolescent years when her peers bragged about hating to read. We came to the conclusion that we were the problem, not other people. It was such a grace to find not only a spiritual friendship more blessed than either of us felt we deserved but to be led to a widening circle of wonderful friends, especially in the Epiphany Association. How fortunate I was, to have a person like Susan ready to assume so many familiar and new tasks without missing a beat.

Soon after my heart attack, she took over all the administrative demands of the Institute from attending graduate school meetings to designing curriculum materials to promoting programs and fostering student recruitment. She gave me all the help personally and professionally I could possibly have needed while continuing the voluminous reading necessary for teaching her courses in the literature of spirituality. She also accompanied me and other faculty members on speaking engagements locally, nationally, and internationally. She edited our journals, *Envoy* and *Studies in Formative Spirituality*, and, thanks to her journalistic skills, brought them to new levels of inspirational and scholarly recognition. I never ceased to admire her intellectual acumen and her commitment to pursue Christian excellence on all levels of life. In ways too numerous to count she was responsible for the success we enjoyed academically and in our outreach programs.

Being an excellent writer herself, she helped me to perfect the research methodology on the basis of which our students composed their dissertations in formative spirituality. Due to her love for the ancient, medieval, and modern Christian classics, we were able to lay the groundwork for the four volumes in formation theology that represent the crowning phase of our co-authored work. I benefitted in particular from her companion texts to *The Collected Works of Saint John of the Cross,* which shed much needed light on my own dark nights of sense and spirit.

The disposition of detachment so central in Saint John's writings became symbolized for us in the nomadic nature of the way in which we were moved from place to place on campus. It is a story in itself of endings and new beginnings. When Susan joined me in 1966 our quarters in the Guidance Building were about the size of the average living room. There we published our journals, wrote student recruitment brochures and program outlines, interviewed future attendees, held meetings, drew up budgets, arranged out-of-town engagements, and did whatever else was necessary to start a new venture on campus. Then, without much warning, we were told by the administration to vacate those quarters and to move into one of the old brownstone houses at 1147 Bluff Street where we could have—what for us at that time seemed like a mansion— the first and second floors. With Sister Margaret Gall, SDR, as our secretary, we each had an office and even an extra desk for visitors. Almost overnight, with the help of her family, Susan transformed the space we occupied into a carpeted and curtained home that, in the words of those who came to see us, had about it an atmosphere of tranquility and true hospitality.

Suddenly, once again, we were told around the start of the academic year 1974 that all the Bluff Street offices were to be torn down to make way for a needed parking lot and space for a sports field. Happily for us we were ordered to go to the third floor of the administration building where, after a painstaking move, we once again had a set of reasonable rooms to house our work. By that time we had many students from a variety of faith groupings in the three year master's program, which also attracted leaders in the field of faith formation from over twenty-six different countries like Australia, Africa, India, and South Korea.

Approximately a year later disaster struck again. On July 11, 1975, a massive lightning bolt hit the roof of the administration building and it caught on fire. I happened to be in Holland for my home visit,. At the time Susan lived in an apartment on Mount Washington from the window of which she could see our building. She witnessed the lightning strike, called 911, and rushed to campus. Everyone prayed that the flames would be contained before they engulfed the whole building. Susan begged God not to let them penetrate the third floor where our own offices were. Above them were mainly storage areas so the danger of total conflagration was eminent. Happily for us the fire was put out, but practically everything housed in our offices, including precious archival materials, incurred extensive water and smoke damage. What were we to do now? The students would return in early September. Where would they go for classes and where would we do our work?

The then administrative staff, due no doubt to their being overwhelmed by the disaster, was able to offer us at most a few rooms in a dormitory. With much patience and perseverance, Doctor Muto knew there had to be a better solution. She told me later that she received the inspiration to present our plight to the then Dean of the School of Education and a dear friend of ours, Doctor Helen Kleyle. She had two large classrooms on the fourth floor of Canevin Hall that she said we could use as our new and much needed quarters. Movers would have to climb four flights of stairs, but the space was ours. Susan accepted this cordial invitation and over the next several weeks managed to find the help she needed—even from the basketball team—to transport our possessions step by step. She appealed to the maintenance department and other staff members and volunteers to help with all the cleaning water and smoke damage required and had our new quarters ready for occupation by the time the students arrived. There were no words I could find upon my return to Pittsburgh to thank her and our secretary Jean Feid, for all they had done to ensure the continuity of the Institute. The place had been transformed. We had a lovely set of offices with several book cases dividing one from the other and, at the same time, providing ample shelf space for our growing collection of texts and journals.

We thought that was the last move we would have to make, but our hopes in that regard proved to be naive. Once insurance money paid for an elevator in Canevin Hall, other departments claimed our fourth floor space as theirs. All that was left for us by 1983 was the now-vacated Law Library on the ninth floor of Rockwell Hall. This cavernous space, filled with empty bookcases and covered by layers of dust and debris, was a veritable mess to transform, but that's what happened once again thanks to Susan's tireless efforts and decorative skills, inherited, I believe, from her contractor father and my good friend, Frank Muto, and from her energetic and artistically talented mother, Helen. With little or no money in our budget for remodeling, but with the help, as usual, of family members and friends of Susan's and the maintenance and janitorial staff, often working after hours and gratis on our behalf, we moved into these new quarters complete with carpeting donated by the Epiphany Association, with curtains on every window and with artwork in every room. We stayed there until that space, too, was redistributed and the Institute became part of a graduate level only phase-out mandated by the university ten years later. Thankfully, the mystery had already begun to take our ministry in another direction, for God never closes one door (our program officially ended with the granting of the last degrees in 1993) without opening another.

Already in 1979, when it appeared as if we were at the height of our academic success and before I could ascertain the full extent of my failing health, I felt deeply moved, indeed stirred from within, to co-found, with Doctor Muto's full cooperation and the creative input of several close friends in the legal (civil and canon law), corporate, and medical professions a totally independent, non-profit organization. It would eventually be named the Epiphany Association after the pioneering group I helped to form and facilitate originally in the Netherlands. In our many travels and week-end seminars, we had witnessed the emergence of a growing crisis among the laity. The hunger for spiritual deepening, often unaddressed in denominational settings, was obvious to the discerning eye. No matter their good will, people had great difficulty, amidst the distractions of modern life, to implement what they believed in the demanding details of their daily interactions in the working places of family, church, and society.

My work with the Dutch Life Schools, combined with the invaluable knowledge of formation imparted by my war experiences, made me feel at home in the new times we were entering after the Second Vatican Council. The Epiphany Association was incorporated on May 4, 1979 as a non-profit organization in the Commonwealth of Pennsylvania under the jurisdiction of the United States Conference of Catholic Bishops. As its co-founders, we took to heart this awakening interest in spiritual renewal with its emphasis on the universal call to holiness and on transforming the world into the House of God. To meet the needs of the average laity by asking them to take courses on a university campus was simply not feasible. In the spirit of the Pioneers of Mary, the prototype of

Epiphany, we saw our independent, non-profit association as a haven for like-minded ecumenically sensitive believers, who would benefit from the ministry we strove to provide through our formational writings and teachings. Once Epiphany became its own entity, we tried to fulfill this task mostly during our free time in evenings and on weekends since we were still teaching full time at the university.

Several quite extraordinary and truly providential events occurred from 1980 to 1983. The most amazing was our meeting with the man who would become our major benefactor and friend, George Armstrong Kelly, IV, a professor of political philosophy and religion at Johns Hopkins University. Through a series of God-guided encounters, our work was brought to the attention of Doctor Kelly. Shortly after we met him through arrangements made by mutual friends, we were pleased to honor his request to read our books and to review some of the theses we directed at Duquesne. By virtue of an almost instant bonding among the three of us, our contacts and conversations intensified. We shared, along with many of the same formational ideals, feelings of genuine friendship.

One does not use the word "miracle" lightly, but we felt it to be the only operable term to apply to the moment when this committed Episcopalian gentleman announced at dinner with us in Pittsburgh on an evening in December of 1981 his intention to donate to our fledgling organization the beautiful Italian Renaissance mansion and most of its antique contents bequeathed to him by his aunt, Eleanor Park Kelly, an elder of the First Presbyterian Church in Shadyside. Unbeknown to us Miss Kelly had conveyed to George as her dying wish: "Whatever you do, use my house for a Christian purpose." Doctor Kelly said he was looking for us as much as we were looking for him! Included, along with his gift of the house and its furnishings, were endowment funds to sustain our work; these were later embellished by bequests in his last will and testament. He himself paid for the legal costs of the transfer and even agreed to buy his own house back from us if after five full years our mission there failed and we needed the funds to restart it elsewhere. We only knew this remarkable human being for five years, from 1982 until his untimely death in 1987, but without him, as I hope to show in the next chapter of my memoirs, the Epiphany Association would never have survived.

Following the Kelly Estate bequest presented to us in 1988, the Board of Directors of the Epiphany Association asked Doctor Muto to consider taking another life-changing step. Would she be willing to serve as Epiphany's first full-time executive director? To honor this request meant that she would have to resign her tenured professorship at Duquesne. With prayer and guidance, she came to this decision and by July started a new full-time ministry. Her courageous consent to leave the university meant that she was free to move our research, writing, and publication efforts to the Kelly House while continuing to serve our Institute students on an adjunct basis. Both of us smiled at the fact that we had to undertake yet another relocation, only this one was under the auspices of the Epiphany Association. It is worth mentioning that from 1982 to 1987 Doctor Muto "in her spare time" agreed to serve as principal writer for the committee of Bishops working at the national level on a pastoral letter on women's concerns for church and society. She wrote four drafts of this pastoral, the first being "Partners in the Mystery of Redemption," and continued her dedication to this project until the Bishops approved with unanimous agreement the twenty-five action items the committee members recommended. By her own admission she had asked God many times over these years, "What next would you have me do?" Now she had the answer. Her goal was to settle with a new staff at the Kelly House and carry forward into the twenty-first century the mission and ministry of the Epiphany Association. At first we had to believe—after so many years and five major moves—that the Institute might be able to continue under new leadership at the Rockwell Hall location. That hope was not to be realized. Due to the economic straits in which the university found itself, the phase-out process of the Institute, which had begun in 1989, resulted, as I previously mentioned, in its closure, approximately thirty years after its inception.

Experience confirmed that the work we were meant by Holy Providence to do, would best be facilitated in an independent setting like that which the Association was able to provide. Having reached my seventieth year of age I had already submitted to the graduate school my request for retirement. That being granted, I was then able with the permission of the Dutch Province, to honor Epiphany's request to serve as its first chaplain-in-residence and senior researcher. In 1990, I relocated to the private quarters at the Kelly House remodeled for me by Doctor

Muto and her family, appropriately enough, in the old servant's quarters on the second floor!

Once I moved to the Kelly house, I was able to continue my work on the remaining volumes of my Formative Spirituality series. I could do so on a full-time basis with the steady editorial assistance of Doctor Muto and our secretarial staff. I must admit that health problems were always a part of these painful transitions. Still, amidst these new demands, I knew I could rely on excellent medical care from friends like Doctor David Natali, MD, who became the president of our Board of Directors.

Signs of God's faithfulness to Susan and me too numerous to count enabled us to move forward with courage and conviction. What had happened to us individually and together was not a destiny of our own making but the plan of God for us. For believers like ourselves and Doctor Kelly, it was clear that Christ, "... [gives] a new form to this lowly body of ours and [remakes] it according to the pattern of his glorified Body, by his power to subject everything to himself" (Philippians 3:21). Since it is the Holy Spirit, who nurtures Christ's image within us, "Let us not grow weary of doing good; if we do not relax our efforts, in due time we shall reap our harvest" (Galatians 6:9). Christ, the ineffable mystery at the heart of our formation field, guided our appraisals in the direction of the Father's will and its embodiment in our service to the Church. Through the power of his Spirit, he took us on a journey modulated by the many mountains and valleys he asked us to traverse. He deepened our awareness of our unique-communal calling and allowed us see every event of closed doors and opened windows in the light of his passion, death and resurrection.

Until the closure of the Institute, we did our best to offer adjunct courses for clergy, religious, and laity enrolled there as well as to direct the dissertations we had started. In the meantime we had to develop our outreach and in-house programs at the Kelly House. The inspiration that guided us was not to promote adherence to one or the other special school of spirituality but to teach in a comprehensive manner the applicative facets of formation theology in service of all the faithful who sought our help and expertise. Our goal was not to write an occasional book here or there but to build a body of work compatible with Christian doctrine and tradition and beneficial to our everyday ecumenical and transecumenical commitments and concerns. This ecclesial-experiential approach sheds light on each phase of our human and Christian maturation. Beyond the domain of quantitative analysis, it invites us to look for practical ways by which to implement the life directives we have received from our faith into our day by day unfolding as disciples of Christ; it teaches us how to avoid theological controversy by focusing mainly on the common "river" of spiritual formation in which we together must swim. The effectiveness of our faith can only be tested by its fruits in every phase of life from initial formation in childhood to our dying day. In due time the transcendent aspirations embedded in our consciousness may become more fully known to us. We see, at first dimly and then more clearly, the movements of divine grace that have enabled us to soar beyond the tribulations we have had to endure to the truths they teach us.

I know from experience that a certain puritanical strain in the Dutch Reformed tradition led in some of its adherents to an over-reaction against art and beauty due to the fear of idolizing an "image" of God rather than adoring the Divine to whom it was meant to point. This fear generated a deformative tendency to associate almost any symbol or image with the danger of idolization. Dissonant conclusions of this sort must be worked through alone or with others. Otherwise we risk losing our joy and despoiling the openness to transformation our growth in becoming more like Jesus requires. If there is one lesson writing these memoirs had taught me, it is that we ought never to forfeit the freedom and flexibility promised to us as the children of God.

35

Remembering a Blessed Benefactor

Thanks to the generosity of our dear friend, Doctor George Armstrong Kelly, IV, we were able to make a smooth transition from university life to the Epiphany Association and its central dedication to adult faith formation. George had the means to put the proper financial foundations under this ideal and he did so unsparingly.

His is a story worth telling in these memoirs of mine. We met George through an introduction organized at the Kelly House by a trustee from the bank that managed the family fortune. Initially we knew as little about this excellent scholar and gentleman as he knew about us. Soon we learned that his Aunt Eleanor had raised him from the time of his early infancy, since his parents had been killed in an automobile accident when he was a toddler. I felt a special affinity with George in this regard since both of my parents had been orphans. I can only imagine his loneliness. Once he shared with me and Susan the touching tale of himself as a little boy huddled at the bottom of his mother's closet so that he could inhale the scent of her clothes. When he told us that story, it triggered in me a similar memory of an evening when my mother had to leave me alone in the house because my father, who worked at night, had forgotten certain papers he needed at home and my mother had to deliver them to him. To console me she said that I was not to leave my chair and never to go to the door, no matter who knocked. The terror in my little face brought tears to her eyes, but she had to depart. As a "consolation prize," she gave me a chocolate bunny to keep me company. I grasped that bunny so tightly it melted all over me. The door closed behind her and for the first time in my life I was completely alone. The house was empty and I felt anxious. I tried to get some solace from the bunny, but all it did was melt into a mushy puddle of chocolate in my lap. When mother returned she laughed until she cried because I looked like a little brown bunny! I thank God she came home. George's mother did not.

Before we met our new friend and moved our operations to the Kelly House, we had to conduct our Epiphany sessions in the homes of some of our associates and benefactors and in the parish church of Father Thaddeus "Ted" Maida, the pastor of Saint Teresa of Avila in Perrysville. His brother and our friend, Father Adam Maida, who became the Cardinal Archbishop of Detroit, was then a canon and civil lawyer in the Diocese of Pittsburgh. It was he who assisted us with our 1979 application for tax-exempt status.

Father Ted's parish church was in a suburb of Pittsburgh. To bring Epiphany closer to the city, two associates of ours, Doctor and Mrs. John McCarthy, opened their home in Fox Chapel for our reading, study, and discussion sessions—many of which were centered on what it meant to be made in the form and likeness of God (*Imago Dei*) and to transform the world into the house of God (*Domus Dei*). We enjoyed this family's hospitality for almost two years, but it soon became clear to us, as the number of our participants grew, that we ought not to impose on these good friends indefinitely. We had to start looking for a roof over our heads, for a place of our own, that we could designate as the headquarters of the Epiphany Association.

Mary Henry, the wife of our then Board president, John Henry, asked us to at least drive past the Kelly House on Beechwood Boulevard because its owner had recently passed away and left the home to her nephew and an acquaintance of a neighbor of hers, a realtor, suggested that we see it. One look at this elegant mansion told us that it would be impossible for us to think about "purchasing" such a magnificent domain, especially with a balance in our treasury of approximately $450! Still we prayed that if the Lord willed for the "impossible" to happen, it would become possible. We simply asked for some sign that the mystery wanted our work to continue. Not long thereafter we were informed that the current owner of the house wanted to meet us as much as we hoped to meet him. Little could we have known that it was George's intention to take his Aunt's wish to use the house for a Christian purpose to heart. In the wisdom of Holy Providence what began as a casual, get-acquainted luncheon ended with the launching of a new work in the Church. A letter dated January 31, 2008 from the Bishop of Pittsburgh confirms the facticity of what at that time we could only have held as the fondest of hopes.

Diocese of Pittsburgh
111 Boulevard of the Allies, Pittsburgh, PA 15222-1618
Phone: 412-456-3010 • Fax: 412-456-3185
E-mail: daz@diopitt.org • Website: www.diopitt.org

Office of the Bishop

January 31, 2008

Dear Sisters and Brothers:

We live in an exciting time, one in which many are rediscovering their need for God. The spotlight is once again focused as it should be on the importance of the place of the Spirit in our everyday lives.

The Diocese of Pittsburgh is proud to be the diocese in which Epiphany Association is headquartered. Its founders, the late Reverend Adrian van Kaam, CSSp and Dr. Susan A. Muto, have been part of the local Church of Pittsburgh for over 40 years. Their years of work through Duquesne University's former Institute of Formative Spirituality, through the founding of Epiphany Association in 1979, to the recent opening of the beautiful Epiphany Academy of Formative Spirituality have touched thousands of students and persons of all faiths, inviting them to grow in the spiritual life.

Through the voluminous writings of Dr. Muto and Father van Kaam, and through her ongoing teaching and speaking engagements, Dr. Muto carries on the work of sharing the inspiring insights of Formative Spirituality. Her work challenges everyone to live God's love in the everyday experience of work and play, in the workplace and at home. The work of Epiphany Association is known and respected throughout the world.

It is my pleasure to provide this letter of support and endorsement for Epiphany Association, and it is my real joy that it continues to be a part of the Diocese of Pittsburgh for years to come.

Grateful for our belief that "Nothing is Impossible with God," I am

Your brother in Christ,

+ David A. Zubik

Most Reverend David A. Zubik
Bishop of Pittsburgh

DAZ:lw

Doctor Kelly's scholarly credentials, including the many years he had studied abroad, offered him and us a once-in-a-lifetime meeting of minds and hearts. His own home was in Manhattan where he lived with his wife Joanne, who was a curator at the Metropolitan Museum of Art; he also kept a small apartment in Baltimore near the university campus. George, besides being a highly respected scholar in his own right, was a deeply believing and practicing Episcopalian. Almost from the first moment we met him, we knew that a lasting friendship in the Lord was being formed among us.

George expressed genuine admiration for the aims of Epiphany, for its stress on our radiating the light of the Lord in everyday life. He reviewed with delight books and dissertations we gave him on formative spirituality, expressing particular interest in the methodology of formation science and its link to formation theology. He chuckled when he told us that he had advised a group of his graduate students at Johns Hopkins to go and do the same! These intellectual exchanges, rooted in our shared commitment to the Gospel, sealed the bonds that had grown so naturally between us and him. Still we were understandably taken aback when George told us that he had reached the decision to deed the Kelly House to the Epiphany Association, along with the majority of its valuable Victorian contents and lovely antiques. By offering us this unprecedented gift, that would insure Epiphany's future, George became for us the embodiment of humility and divine generosity.

Our last visit with him took place in Baltimore in the middle of winter, a few months before his sudden death of a massive heart attack while having supper with his son in New York. We knew we were in the presence of a man of faith whose inspiration we shall never forget and to whom we shall be forever indebted. He cautioned us, after he had given us all the treasures in Kelly House, that we ourselves had to stay detached from them, even to the point of our being willing to sell them if necessary to insure the future of the work he had so generously supported. The one condition George encouraged us to honor was not to forfeit the freedom Epiphany needed to operate ecumenically by binding ourselves to any one academic institution or religious community. As an ecumenical lay association we needed to foster as integral to our vision the service of people in the world belonging to a variety of faith groupings in their familial and professional settings. All were welcome at Epiphany because of its rootedness in a foundational approach to formative spirituality.

Sadly, George did not live to see the fruits of his bequest. Would to God he could have witnessed the ultimate legacy of the Kelly House in the laying of the cornerstone at the Epiphany Academy on September 11, 2001. For the years we knew him, we honored his request that we give him no public thank you. He only asked us that should he die unexpectedly we say a few words to uplift and comfort others. In death as in life he was a man of unshakable faith whose wealth never stood in the way of his placing before all else the classic Christian virtues of humility, detachment, and charity. In the letters George wrote to us, he shared a side of himself few others may have seen, among them his love for the Lord and his sense of discipleship, even in the darkest hour. The letters we received from him contained, of course, bits of news and items of business, but what edified us were not only his wise worldly insights but also his transworldly inspirations.

Of all the letters he sent to me, I treasure in particular the one dated December 3, 1982, written five years before his death. In it he comments on the Christian understanding of loss and of the wrenching detachments he himself had to face at an early age:

> Indeed any reading of death for us mortals must be vague, forlorn, and triumphant at the same time if the life has been an honorable one. I had the strange experience of losing both my parents while still a baby. Consequently, I never knew them at all, except by report. Sometimes I bitterly resented that awful state of non-knowledge, while still realizing that I probably had been spared a graver blow. And, at more perverse moments, which I am reluctant to mention, I think that I even begrudged my parents for having deprived me of a deep and healthy sadness. But, in the end, all I know about these things is that life on earth, even for a little while, can be extremely precious to so many and that it is God's will that things happen as they do. We can suffer from but cannot question his supreme wisdom, and we can believe that this end is a beginning, not only for the departed, but for us as well.

There is no doubt in my mind that George would have enjoyed hearing about our first major Epiphany outreach program, which began the year he died and ended in 1989. It was then that we, in our "free time," worked under contract with the Chaplain Corps of the United States Navy, serving its twelve hundred members, representing eighty-six different faith groupings, through the four-day professional development training program we designed, developed, and delivered titled "Spiritual Formation and Pastoral Care." What a joy it was for me to discover that the seeds of formation science I had developed in the Netherlands bore fruit in contemporary military life. The chaplains were so impressed with and so helped by our work that they afforded Doctor Muto and me the recognition of being named honorary chaplains of the United States

Navy. To this day many look to the Epiphany Association to provide the substantial resources needed to foster ongoing spiritual and pastoral care for themselves and the military and civilian population they serve.

With the ending of the Institute phase of our work at Duquesne, we sensed that the Holy Spirit was drawing us once more to expand our Epiphany vision. The decision on the part of the University to phase out our graduate institute was at first a source of disbelief, but the more we thought and prayed about this happening in a spirit of appreciative abandonment to the mystery, the more we realized that without some pain there can be no gain. Having been freed from the limitations found in any academic setting, we were free to prepare and put into practice a worldwide mission aimed at post-graduate certification in the field of formative spirituality.

As much as we loved the Kelly house, we knew that the day would come when the Board had to make the decision to place it on the market and to use the revenue generated by its sale and the auctioning of its contents to fund the building of a more efficient, yet still beautiful center to house the work of Epiphany in a less tightly zoned neighborhood. If we stayed where we were, we would not be able to meet the educational and formational obligations we felt bound by God to fulfill.

We found the perfect setting for our future Epiphany Academy of Formative Spirituality on Crane Avenue in the South Hills section of the city. We purchased our "field of dreams" from the Diocese of Pittsburgh with the proceeds from the auction of the contents of Kelly House. Several benefactors, starting with our Board members themselves, donated the funds we needed to launch the Academy. Providence again guided our future by enabling us to find interim hospitality with the Franciscan Community and parish of Saint Pamphilus adjacent to the acreage we purchased from the diocese. We moved from a twenty-five room Victorian mansion to the basement of a rectory, but our work went on from day to day without missing a beat, thanks to our flexible and efficient staff. I returned to Trinity Hall for a while but, when we found a house for sale at 947 Tropical Avenue, across from the parish offices, we purchased it, and began yet another extensive remodeling project. "Epiphany House," as we called it, became our temporary headquarters. Once again, the Association offered me, as their chaplain, private rooms on the third floor of this residence where I could continue the writing I had begun with my co-author of the volumes that would eventually comprise our Formation Theology series. One splendid experience in the midst of these events occurred in the summer of 1996. The president of our Board, Doctor David Natali, accompanied Susan and me for a trip to the Netherlands to attend on July 21, the jubilee celebration of my fifty years in the priesthood. We were joined on this joyful day by my immediate family, by members of the Dutch Province, and by other relatives and friends. The entire experience touched me more than I can say; it restored my vision of what the Lord might ask of me in the years to come.1

Having found the right family to purchase the Kelly House and having the property on Crane Avenue now in our possession, we were able on October 26, 2000 to break ground for our new Epiphany Academy. The weather that day was more beautiful than any of us could have hoped: the sky was azure blue with a few white clouds drifting by. Sunshine warmed the faces and shoulders of our guests, who listened with rapt attention as Doctor Natali thanked everyone associated with this new beginning and then went on to say:

> We are building this Academy based on a dream initiated long ago by Father Adrian van Kaam. We are united here today in the atmosphere of an interior miracle of the mind and the soul, which can be stimulated by exterior events like this, but which we humans must complete from the inside. The result we see before us is the birth of a new idea in a new place, representing a spiritual contact reaching across an ocean and many decades: the dedication of one man is now realized by many . . . God is in this place.

Doctor Muto went on to read two texts, the first from Psalm 127:1, "Unless the Lord build the house, they labor in vain who build . . ." and the second from 1 Corinthians 3:9: "For we are God's servants, working together; you are God's field. God's building." Then it was my turn to read from the Gospel ". . . when the flood came, the river burst against that house but could not shake it because it had been well built" (Luke 6:48). In my brief homily I said, "Today my heart is especially full because I see this groundbreaking as the harvesting of a seed planted over sixty years ago in my home country, the Netherlands." As I spoke, I thought in silence that the needs the Church had to address in those days shadowed by war had not diminished at all. Now, as in that perilous age, we had to deepen our faith to such a degree that the treasury of truth embodied in scripture and the masters would embed itself in our hearts through grace and help us to bring peace to this troubled world. "May this building be and become a place of grace wherein the Lord dwells—a tent to hold his treasure and share it with every seeking soul."

One more miracle we will always remember is that the cornerstone of the Academy was laid on the morning of September 11, 2001 at 7:30 AM. Two hours later, in Manhattan, the Twin Towers of the World Trade Center would implode due to a terrorist attack and life as we had known it would never be the same. A few months later, on November 16, 2001, the Academy was dedicated as an "epiphany of the Lord" by the Most Reverend David Zubik, then auxiliary Bishop of the Diocese of Pittsburgh, who chose as his reading the Gospel according to Matthew 5:1–2; 13–16:

> Jesus went up the mountain, and after he had sat down, his disciples came to him. He began to teach them, saying: "You are the salt of the earth. But if salt loses its taste, with what can it be seasoned? It is no longer good for anything but to be thrown out and trampled underfoot. You are the light of the world. A city set on a mountain cannot be hidden. Nor did they light a lamp and then put it under a bushel basket; it is set on a lampstand, where it gives light to all in the house. Just so, your light must shine before others, that they may see your good deeds and glorify your heavenly Father."

In his response to these inspiring words, the Bishop reminded us that to be formed in the faith and to persevere in its teachings, we must remember that we have been made to know, love, and serve God in this world. To be salt and light is, in metaphorical terms, the aim and the purpose of the Epiphany Association, its members, students, benefac and friends. In his final blessing, the Bishop gave us a message and a goal we shall never forget, saying to each guest in attendance:

> May the all-knowing God, who is Lord
> show us his ways;
> may Christ, eternal Wisdom,
> teach us the words of truth;
> may the Holy Spirit, the blessed light,
> always enlighten our minds,
> so that we may learn what is true and good and beautiful
> and in our actions embody what we have learned
> in prayer and contemplation.

How providential it was that the new programs we had started at the Kelly house, most notably our Epiphany Certification Program (ECP) for advanced study in formative spirituality, grew slowly but surely. By 1998 we not only honored our first graduating class but also opened our first fully operable joint venture with the Saint Vincent Seton Cove Spirituality Center in Indianapolis, headed at that time by our Board member and friend, Sister Sharon Richardt, DC, PhD. Complimenting this theoretical and practical series of courses was the retreat component of our five-day Epiphany Lay Formation Academy (ELFA) and many other local and national offerings open to associates and other students pursuing ministerial excellence in the service of their respective faith groupings.[2]

The highlight of the year 2002 occurred on June 29, when we held our first mass at the Epiphany Chapel of the Trinity. I greeted everyone by saying:

> On behalf of the Epiphany Association, its Board of Directors, faculty, and staff, I am pleased and privileged to welcome to the Epiphany Association our beloved Bishop Donald Wuerl and everyone gathered here today for this long awaited Eucharistic liturgy and chapel blessing. In many ways it marks the culmination of a lifetime of dedication to the work of spiritual formation begun during the earliest era of the Church and transmitted to us in the Apostolic Tradition. On this memorable day, when we celebrate the feast of Saints Peter and Paul, we can raise our voices in prayer and praise to thank God for all the blessings he has bestowed upon our Epiphany Association, not the least of which is this beautiful new Academy and all of the people who will benefit from its courses now and in the years to come. I am particularly grateful that God has allowed me to live to see this day and I beg you to join me in praying that it will commemorate a new beginning in our pledge to serve the Church and all its members with dedication, academic excellence, and, above all, sacrifice and prayer. Thank you again, dear Bishop, for gracing us with your presence as we continue to celebrate this wonderful liturgy together.

I then invited Doctor Muto to make the following remarks:

> It is my joy and delight as Dean of the Epiphany Academy and executive director of our Association to thank everyone who graciously contributed to this ceremony, starting, of course, with the Bishop, his masters of ceremony, our music ministers, altar servers, Board and staff members, all of whom worked so diligently to make this day as profound and beautiful as it is. One glance around this Epiphany Chapel of the Trinity—from the exterior gardens to the interior design, especially the Crucifix and the carving of Our Lady, and we find ample reason to rejoice as one body in the one Lord. There is no end to our reasons for giving thanks, but we owe a special debt of gratitude to our benefactors and to our Epiphany students and associates in the United States and abroad, who are here with us in spirit. Once again we offer our heartfelt thanks to everyone here and to all those who have helped us over the years to make the dream of this facility a reality no one who knows our story could have imagined. To God be the glory, Amen.

All of these events—to say nothing of the splendid Academy that houses them—point in my mind to God's plan for the future of Epiphany. The only reasonable response is to remain faithful to his will and to go forward in a spirit of unfailing hope and selfless love toward that "unknown land" where Providence leads us. In so many ways my whole life has been one of opening new doors each time old ones close No wonder I identify with the oft quoted words of Dag Hammarskjöld in his diary, *Markings*, "For all that has been, thanks . . . to all that shall be, yes."

Notes

1. Thanks be to God, Father van Kaam lived to celebrate his sixtieth year in the priesthood on July 21, 2006 in more humble but still happy circumstances at the Little Sisters of the Poor.

2. Father Adrian was surely with us in spirit when I and our newly appointed chaplain, Father Ralph Tajak, OSB, launched the Epiphany Certification Program at All Hallows College in Dublin, Ireland in July of 2009.

36

Fulfillment of Our Epiphany Mission

Though the Institute phase of our work ended in 1994, after thirty grace-filled years, with nearly 800 graduates the world over, there was no reason to doubt that we were on the verge of entering a new springtime of this epiphanic mission for humanity. We oversaw as best as we could the final days of the Institute's existence on Duquesne's campus, working with new administrators and helping several doctoral candidates complete their work with as much fidelity to the original project as possible.

Understandably, in this time of transition from the operations of the Institute to those of the Epiphany Association and its dedication to post-graduate research, writing, and teaching, it was necessary for both me and Doctor Muto, along with advisory members of our Board, to spend many hours in confidential talks, reflections, and prayers to maintain our peaceful spirit and to reclaim the traditions of excellence that had guided us so far. I penned page after page in my journals on the necessity of faithfulness to God's call wherever it leads us, on the danger of becoming mini-obsessed with our own plans and projects, and on the need to widen our vision of what in any tradition is and remains not passing but lasting.

We had already seen to it that the founding documents of the Epiphany Association would accommodate our main aim of research, publication, and dissemination of the current and future writings pertinent to the formational-informational project I had begun in the Netherlands. Thanks to the support I received from the Association and its executive director, I was able to complete all seven volumes in my formative spirituality series, and, with her co-authorship, the four volumes that comprise our *Summa Forma Theologica*. Doctor Muto also complied with my request that in some way she continue the cycle of courses she had taught in the Institute on the integration of formation science and theology at the center of which are Holy Scripture and the classics of our Judeo-Christian tradition. These courses of hers were subsequently incorporated into recurrent Epiphany sessions on meditating with the masters. Once again they are an integral part of the post-graduate preparation we offer adult learners from many walks of life who want to pursue study in the field of human and Christian formation. Both at the Academy in Pittsburgh and at the Saint Vincent Seton Cove Spirituality Center in Indianapolis, we invite our students to bring to the table vivid descriptions of their formative events and to reflect on them in the light of the science, anthropology, and theology of formation. We teach them to absorb the teachings of the classical masters in an inspiring yet precise manner that opens them to the art and discipline of integrating what they read with the way they live.

The six courses that comprise the Epiphany Certification Program (ECP) are both theoretical and practical, steeping our students in the dynamics of transcendence therapy and the modes of spiritual direction and training they need to help others grow in the life of the spirit in their religious houses, retreat centers, and schools of formation. We serve believers and sincere seekers in many different settings without compromise of anyone's adhered to faith tradition. All of us benefit from an atmosphere of integrated wisdom and humble fidelity to what we believe and how we live. Most impressive to me are the prayer services with which we begin and end each ECP session. We pray in many voices, representing a variety of backgrounds and traditions and yet it is as if we praise, thank, and petition God in one voice, ending with a resounding *Amen*. Every exchange between faculty and students reveals how much good God can draw from any crisis situation. We reflect together on the ways in which grace prevents the downward spin to deformative depreciation, giving us the vision and strength we need to turn every obstacle into a formation opportunity.

Over the course of my life, I have watched spirituality and spiritual formation attain a credibility I did not enjoy as a pioneer in these fields. Now our graduates, both from the Duquesne program and from Epiphany, serve the people of God throughout the world. Thanks to the basic two-fold integrational approach (informational and formational) which is at the core of my life's work, the fruits of this endeavor continue to contribute to the renewal of spiritual formation in the churches, schools, seminaries, and institutes of higher learning where our graduates and their students prepare to meet the ecclesial-experiential challenges of living their faith in the third millennia of Christianity.

An example of God's leading occurred when a psychiatrist from Moscow and an Orthodox Christian, Doctor Sergey Belorusoff came to Epiphany (when we were still located at the Kelly House) to study our work with the intention of translating key books of ours for his colleagues and students, who, since the fall of the Berlin Wall, enjoyed a more open climate of learning. Sergey entered a year-long training program to learn formation science in general and to specialize in transcendence therapy. Under the auspices of the Epiphany Association, we entered into another joint venture with the Institute of Ministries of the Diocese of Pittsburgh, developing a series of courses on growing in, with, and through Christ and delivering them to over two hundred lay ministers appointed to leadership roles in the Church. By 2006, our students reminded me and Susan that between us we had come to the centenary of our partnership. To commemorate this event our colleagues in Indianapolis presented us with a bound copy of tributes from many of the students we had served first at Duquesne University and then at the Academy. One of these testimonials came from Doctor Malcolm Herring, MD who had completed the Epiphany Certification Program in Indianapolis. Of this experience he says:

> There were many moments of sudden and surprising insight, but there is one component . . . that stands out . . . against a background of the great reflective processes that Father van Kaam and Doctor Muto provided. It stands out not only against but because of that background . . . and because of the [way] the other participants responded to the teaching and spiritual direction of these two giants.
>
> The most transformative part for me began with one of the readings by Corrie Ten Boom. Many will recall how she and her sister were sent to the Nazi concentration camp. One of them managed to sneak a Bible past the guards when they were processed into the camp. Within moments of lying down on her bed she was bitten by fleas, then hit her head on the bunkbed. With all that had happened, she was in despair immediately. Her sister Betsie recalled a Bible verse that they had recently read together, namely Philippians 4:6–7. Sister Betsie insisted that the two of them give thanks to God for everything around them. Corrie balked when

> Betsie insisted that they give thanks even for the fleas. Months later, Betsie reported to Corrie that the reason the guards never visited their barracks and never interrupted their Bible studies was because of the fleas.
>
> This story was like a catalyst, energizing and giving context to Father van Kaam's and Doctor Muto's teachings on the dispositions of awe and appreciation. In the course of this time of study, I began to internalize the meaning of Romans 8:28 that all things work together for the good. Stated in a short sentence, it seems like nothing but when my life perspective changed, the world changed with it and, when your world changes, it is huge.
>
> I thank God for Father van Kaam and Doctor Muto. They have many spiritual sons and daughters. What a legacy!

Such a tribute explains in humility why I can say with no regrets that the years following the closing of the Institute have been among the most graced-filled and fulfilling ones of my life, revitalizing the hope I felt after the War when I taught at our senior seminary and in the Dutch Life Schools for Young Adults. What concerned me at that time still concerns me today, namely, the need for a systematic integration of our credal systems with our everyday spiritual formation in the world. Never again must we ignore the immense hunger felt by everyone for the abundant life Christ promised us (cf. John 10:10) as our most lasting legacy.

I have lived long enough to know that we do not know what awaits us. All we can do day by day is to live in faith and to open ourselves to the purification (*the crucifying epiphany*) that readies us for paradise (*the resurrection epiphany*). As long as we listen to the shy whispers of the Holy Spirit in our heart and continue to say *yes* to them in the always changing climates that characterize our life, all will be well. When the time comes for us to say with Jesus, "It is finished," we will pass over to eternity with the peace he gives. For now our duty is simply to carry on in fidelity to our unique-communal call and the divine destiny that is ours from the beginning of our life to its benign end.

[Editor's Note: *After the sale of the Epiphany House on Tropical Avenue, Father van Kaam resided temporarily at Trinity Hall. Unfortunately, by the summer of 2005, his mobility had deteriorated to such a degree that it was necessary for him to be transferred to the assisted living center of the Holy Ghost Fathers, Libermann Hall, in Bethel Park, Pennsylvania. He resided there until the further deterioration of his health, complicated by a fall that resulted in a severely broken left arm, mandated his transfer, on the advice of his medical doctors, to the skilled care facility administered by the Little Sisters of the Poor. There he lived for two years in serene acceptance of his "crucifying epiphany" until his death on November 17, 2007.]*

Afterword

by
Susan Muto

AND SO ENDS THE autobiographical memoirs of Father Adrian van Kaam presented in this posthumous publication. In memory of him, I would like to highlight some of the factors I believe contributed to his initiation of formation science and anthropology as servant sources of formation theology. The first would be the influence made on him by the infamous Dutch Hunger Winter of 1944–1945. This time of physical and spiritual deprivation, of executions and deportations, was as horrible for him to behold as it was impossible to forget. In this crucible his heart was cleansed of the illusion of independent self-actualization. Reaffirmed was his belief in an ultimately benevolent mystery beckoning us to live in fidelity to our calling in Christ to love and serve all people as children of God.

His discussions with the people hiding with him made him aware that the best way to combat despair was to return to the truth he had learned in the seminary: that our essence precedes our existence and that no matter what happens to us we can refind our center by returning to our "founding life form in the mystery." We can listen to the invitations, challenges, and appeals emanating from our core form or heart and cultivate the lasting dispositions that match our character to the Christ-form of our soul.

After his ordination in 1946, Father van Kaam's mission extended beyond teaching seminary classes to a ministry to young adults in search of life's meaning after losses that defy description. While he watched his classmates going off to the four corners of the world, blessed with appointments to the foreign missions he had so ardently desired to serve, he accepted that it was his destiny to stay on the homefront. As a professor of philosophy in Gemert and as a founding figure in the Dutch Life Schools, he was able to expand the original intuitions he had during the Hunger Winter to focus on in-depth faith formation. An added advantage of these assignments was that they challenged him to study human life in its physical, emotional, intellectual, and spiritual wholeness. His experiences had taught him, as no textbook could, how crucial it was to help people not belonging to his faith tradition to maintain their hope when faced with the temptation to despair. He did so by relying upon the general wisdom of spiritual living to which people under stress were most receptive. He had no choice but to offer those entrusted to his care a way of reclaiming their innate potency for transcendence, which, in accordance with God's grace, might allow them to hear anew or for the first time the message of the Gospel.

Fortunately for him, he found an opportunity to test his ideas not only with seminarians but also with young women and men seeking to integrate their religious ideals with their everyday surroundings in family, community, and professional life. As his expertise in these matters increased, Father van Kaam was invited to share his findings not only with the staff of the Life Schools but also with other audiences of educators and social scientists whose lives had been changed forever by the upheaval of the war and its aftermath.

While completing his teaching commitments in the Life Schools and before obtaining his degrees in pedagogy and andragogy, Father van Kaam's former novice master and now provincial superior, Father Henri Strick, CSSp, thought of a project that would be of great worth to him personally and to the community. It was to explore his interests in formation theology by going to their Motherhouse in Paris to research and write a biography of one of the beloved founders of the Spiritans, the Venerable Francis Libermann. His holiness despite the severe epileptic attacks he had to endure periodically had always been inspiring to Father van Kaam. To understand how Francis could make such progress in the life of the Spirit, his biographer had to read through voluminous archival materials, concentrating especially on the hundreds of letters Libermann had written to clergy, religious, and laity in the world. His courage, his gentle life style, and his determination in response to divine grace to overcome great physical and emotional obstacles to following his call made Libermann an excellent spiritual director. His innate sensitivity to anyone in trouble made his correspondence a treasury of wisdom and truth that Father van Kaam brought to a new audience of readers.

The year he spent in Paris gave him a chance to master the French language, to read widely in French literature, to attend classical dramas, to visit many museums, and to converse with other visitors and students in the community about his work. In addition to writing the life of Libermann, he enhanced his knowledge of the essential structures on which he would base the principles and dynamics of his own holistic theory of personality. He had the chance to test his ideas when he returned from Paris to the Netherlands. While perfecting his biography, he continued his research in the fields of child and adult formation at the Dutch Study Center in Culemborg, Holland. Shortly thereafter, he became a spiritual formation counselor at the Dutch Governmental Observation Center for Juvenile Delinquents. The work of counseling young people accused of various crimes and misdemeanors intrigued him. It gave him the chance as a skilled educator to consult with other counselors and psychotherapists about his formational approach. These dialogues added to his insight into the problems of deformation and their impact on one's initial formation in childhood and adolescence.

Complementing this effort was the writing he did to help other professionals working with Dutch children growing up in deprived circumstances and vulnerable to sources of malformation in a consumer society. He focused on the fact that a depreciative family atmosphere coincides with the passing on of deformative traditions disrespectful of a person's dignity. Such an atmosphere puts children at risk of living in situations so devoid of love that the "oughts" of religion make little or no inroads into their personality.

Upon his return from Paris to the Netherlands, he was at Gennep serving as the assistant novice master when he met the then president of Duquesne University and received the invitation to join the faculty there. The year 1954 was a milestone in his life. Though he had expected to be assigned at Duquesne to teach courses in education and spiritual formation, he found himself appointed instead to initiate the unique perspective of "psychology as a human science." It set the direction for his pursuit of a doctoral degree and for the new graduate program he started at Duquesne. The general inclination at that time was to restrict the meaning of psychology to a science and theory that would match in its methods of research and its conclusions other mainly positivistic or purely empirical sciences about human life. Such approaches contributed many necessary and fruitful responses to the question of humanity's emergence and development in accordance with the validated findings of the "sciences of measurement." Father van Kaam conceded that no truly integrational psychology could bypass these behavioral models, but that they needed to be complemented by another vision oriented around the "sciences of meaning" like philosophy and cultural anthropology. It was his contention that we have to give humane form to our existence as a whole—not only in the light of statistical analysis but also by paying attention to the ways in which humans receive and give meaningful form to their lived experiences. In other words, the positivistic approaches to psychology then in vogue ought not to override the concern for what he referred to as a "distinctively human approach," meaning one that acknowledged the transcendent dimension of life and therewith the relative freedom of the human person.

At that time in the United States two circles of humanistic thinkers had developed a credible way to understand the person as free and insightful. The first circle consisted of existential psychologists and psychiatrists, who gathered around leaders in the field like Viktor Frankl, Erik Erickson, and Rollo May. The second circle consisted of several thinkers represented by colleagues Father van Kaam also knew in person like Gordon Allport, Carl Rogers, Kurt Goldstein, Andreas Angyal, Rudolf Dreikurs, Heinz Ansbacher, and, most notably, Abraham Maslow. Having been assigned to establish at Duquesne one of the first academic programs in psychology as a human science, he was obliged to follow important developments in their thinking while proceeding with his own formal study at Case Western Reserve University in Cleveland, culminating in his highly respected dissertation titled *The Feeling of Really Being Understood by a Person*.

Since humanistic and existential psychology had already received recognition in the United States, his initiation of this original approach was greeted with such profound interest that he was able to attract the faculty members and students he needed for the program's future growth and success. He himself accepted the invitation to be on the editorial board of the *Journal of Individual Psychology*, edited by Hans and Rowena Ansbacher. To engage in ongoing creative and critical dialogue with the existential psychological movement in America, he attended for some time the monthly meetings in New York City of the Association of

Existential Psychology and Psychiatry, organized and chaired by Rollo May. Doctor May asked if he would join the editorial board of the *Review* published by the same association. Before long, he was asked to become the editor of this journal. Similar contacts occurred between him and Abraham Maslow whose place he took at Brandeis University when his friend went on sabbatical leave.

These first hand encounters undoubtedly provided him with solid information about new developments in the field of psychology. However, on the basis of his formational studies in Europe and America, he saw that many psychological schools, even those interested in an existential and humanistic approach, tended to ignore the impact of religious, ideological, or syncretic formation traditions. These had an effect on the psychology of people as well as on the academic and practical conclusions of experts in the field, who were not always aware of how their formulations were influenced by their own, often unexamined, formation traditions.

In response to the neglect he saw in this regard, Father van Kaam developed his original method of elucidating formation dynamics by remaining receptive to the findings of other types of psychology as well as to those of other sciences and formation traditions. In addition, he evolved a comprehensive vision of how psychology ought to be studied and taught, one that would be in tune with the sciences of the spirit or the sciences of meaning and not only with those of measurement.

Though he acknowledged that the emphasis on measurement still dominates our world, he maintained his conviction that it will always be tempered by the love for meaning that he tried to instill in the minds of his students in the Department of Psychology, then in the Institute of Formative Spirituality, and now in the Epiphany Academy. He brought clarity to the question of where the dynamics of psychology leave off and the dynamics of a holistic spirituality, with its emphasis on the transcendent, begin. To be faithful to his original work in the field of formation, Father van Kaam knew it would be necessary to separate these endeavors from the environs of psychology and to initiate an entirely new science of formation. Too much emphasis on the *self* at the center of our life rather than the *mystery* was for him a formula for loneliness and a profound sense of loss leading not to happiness but to hopelessness.

The years from 1954 to 1963 marked the end of one more phase in his history and the beginning of another. In 1963, he founded at

Duquesne the then Institute of Man, which would in due course become the Institute of Formative Spirituality. It represented to Father van Kaam the fulfillment of the mandate to devote himself for the rest of his life to the work of in-depth, always ongoing spiritual formation. It was a great joy to him when he was able to leave the Department of Psychology in the hands of the colleagues trained by him and move on to research, teaching, and writing in his field of choice. In the meantime, he had become an American citizen and was already at work researching what would be the main writing task of his academic life, his multi-volume series on the science, anthropology, and theology of formation. I joined him in 1966, serving as the Institute's assistant director and co-editor of our journals and in due course, from 1980 to 1988 as its director. My appointment to the position was necessary since Father van Kaam almost lost his life due to a serious heart attack, followed by by-pass surgery at the Mayo Clinic and a long period of recuperation. He not only survived this trauma but benefitted from it as an invitation to change his life style and to focus once again on the key theme of his life: appreciative abandonment to the mystery.

My specialty became the Christian articulation of formation science in dialogue with scripture and the literature of spirituality, both classical and contemporary. We both authored and co-authored a number of books on practical spiritual formation to sustain the independent work of our Institute, until that phase of thinking and practice came to an end in the academic year 1993–1994 when our program at Duquesne came to a close. By that time this entire body of work had been subsumed under the auspices of our co-founded Epiphany Association, incorporated as a non-profit entity in 1979. Thanks to this organization and its many benefactors, starting with our friend and colleague, Doctor George Armstrong Kelly, IV, we were able to devote our time and energy to the crowning phase of our combined endeavor represented by the four-volume series and the auxiliary texts that comprise our *Summa Forma Theologica*.

In ways beyond our imagining, Holy Providence has seen to it that the work begun by Father van Kaam in the Netherlands continues to unfold to this day at the Epiphany Academy of Formative Spirituality. History seems to confirm the fact that this mission in its entirety was not destined to be confined to one county or community or campus only but required the facilitation of an independent center to enable us to serve the formation needs of people in ecclesial, familial, and social life wherever they appear. As many of our students have told us neither their clinical training nor their theological expertise alone answered the call they felt in their heart for a deeper understanding of the life of the spirit. We are humbled by the genuine transformations we witness in their classroom experiences and in their daily ministry.

Father van Kaam, in attempting to sum up his life's work, often cited the famous words of Blessed Mother Teresa of Calcutta, that the disease of the West is not poverty but loneliness of soul. Alienated from the mystery at the center of our field of presence and action, he lamented that many of us lead, as Henry David Thoreau once said, "lives of quiet desperation." The rise of drug addiction; the astronomical number of people suffering from depression; the high rate of illicit sexuality, amorality, violence, and rage; the specter of terroristic threats and infidelity to basic truths—all point to the sad reality that our world as a whole is in a spiritual crisis, characterized by a dislocation from what ultimately matters—fidelity to our deepest call by God and a humble bowing to the mystery that is greater than we are.

Father van Kaam has always thought of psychology not as a replacement for spirituality but as a kind of "John the Baptist" preparing the way of the Lord, helping us to see and cope with individual and cultural obstacles that create pitfalls in the path of grace. As long as we never get the idea that we can do it alone, that we need God's help every step of the way, then the work we do as researchers, educators, and clinicians will continue to be blessed.

In the end all of us who read these memoirs are indebted to Father van Kaam for encouraging us to stand on the solid foundations of our faith and formation traditions. As he did daily, so must we pray for the grace to maintain the highest level of integrity in our personal lives and in our modes of service to others. Nothing benefits humanity so well as the truth that makes us free (cf. John 8:32), a truth in whose light Father Adrian van Kaam humbly walked in life until he entered in serene surrender his heavenly home.

Appendix 1

Poetry of the Winter of My Soul

by
Adrian van Kaam

YOUR GLEAMING BLADE

Life is not a chain
of lonely atolls on the wane
in seas that eat away
their stony shores.
Life is not a string
of unconnected chores.

Life from start to end
is a continent
of many shapes,
fertilized by drapes
of blessings raining
from the sky,
announcing a why
that links the bends
of events
in space and time
like chime after chime
of a clock in the hall
ticking against an empty wall,
winter and spring, summer and fall.

You link events harmoniously
as notes in a sacred symphony,
episodes in a ministry
to be rendered to humanity
despite the tyranny of self deception,
the anxious questions
about human fate.
Your gleaming blade
cleaves trails of light
in the wilderness
of an awful night
of fading hope and might.

Show us, O Lord, the secret
harmony of this limping history.
Earthy life is like
a passing word
a tumbling fly,
a shuttle in the sky,
a voyage 'round a stormy cape.
Events are but blossoms
of a tender stem
nourished by a child in Bethlehem,
weaving blessed destiny,
lifting us to eternity.

PLEA FOR PEACE

Lead us kindly, gentle light,
beyond touchdowns of tornadoes,
blunt events pouring down on shaky heads.
Trees and rooftops falling, falling
on winding ways of human calling,
drowning us in despair.
Keep us aware
of the spearpoint of affliction
pointing us beyond attrition
to a mystery

embracing every fallen tree
that frames the road
that leads us to your mystery.

Swarms of armored locusts
descend on worn out people.
Famine, frost, and fever
cannot freeze their believing hearts.
Deceptive slogans shall not
kill the spirit
hiding in their tattered frames.
Ploughed by pains,
waiting in winter's cold
to sprout again,
golden seeds of greatness
give way to the peace of spring,
returning soothingly
to our barren land.

RISING TREE OF NOBILITY

Bombs are raining from the sky.
Children, do not cry,
do not delay in idle play,
hurry, hurry in dismay,
escape the disarray,
flee from fiery death.
Do not sink in mute despair,
evade the tide of mindless hate,
wait for seeds of consonance
blooming into a dance
of ventures for an arid race
thirsty for a wave of grace.
See the rising tree of nobility
planted by a mystery
in the depths of you and me,
its blossoms like open places
for friends and family, loving and wise,

yielding keys to a paradise
of inner peace, a release
from disarray,
despair, and dark hostility.

FREEDOM OF HEART

Frenzied crowds in stony streets
Craving signs of liberation,
Echoing walls repeat, repeat
Cries of wild elation.

Banners, flags, and flowers
Wave as windswept reeds.
Scouts climb trees like towers,
Silent wards of frantic streets.

At last, a new beginning!
Yet soon elation wanes
In the silent trimming
Of idle refrains.

Spurious dreams
Of opulent desires
And luxuriant means
Sink into nothingness.

Freedom of heart starts
With detachment from addictions
As we depart
From present afflictions.

Bodily freedom alone
Cannot end our encapsulation
As long as minds of steel and stone
Defy graced inspiration.

LONELY MELODY

Wounds of war and occupation,
scars of liberation,
valleys of darkness in hearts frozen
like glaciers of ice.

Strident minds shall not be illumined
By swift bouts of reflection.
There are no answers to our questions,
no key to each enigma
that comes our way,
no easy clue to each dilemma
posed to people on their journey.

Listening to the murmur
of the fountain in the garden
quiets our restless minds.
The fall of water sings of life:
a mystery to be lived
not a problem to be solved,
a bearing with ambiguity,
abandonment to what is beyond
the complexity
that assails the agitated mind.

Unwind, unwind…
abandonment is in the end
the panacea for agitation.
Far away in a lonely tree
a bird repeats its melody.

SHATTERED HOPES

People stare and cry:
Fleets of airplanes in the sky!
Above, around the town
thousands of warriors tumble down
as debris swept out with a mighty broom.

Like autumn leaves they fall and fall
to their impending doom.
Parachutes blossom, open wide
like flowers in the light
of a late autumn sun,
bright tulip fields
in festive disarray.
The fighters find their way
in forests 'round the river side,
but the river seems so wide, so wide.
Six hundred strong and lonely men
on a stony span in Arnhem.
They fight in vain, they die in pain, withdraw again.
There is no end to our woes.
Shattered dreams and idle hopes
burn holes in our heart
when fighting men depart, depart.

LORD OF THIS PIECE OF GROUND

Deary soot rains down
on a despairing town
torn by gaping holes,
bleeding bowls
of blown out ports, ripped up quays,
collapsing streets and waterways
drowning docks and sinking ships,
crumbling cranes, their lonely tips
peeking through their watery graves.
Dark and dreary caves
filled with rusty steel, broken stones,
remaining bones, forlorn, alone.
A home of turbulent strife
has lost the sound of life.
The raging sea
begins to swallow cruelly
a low defenseless land

laid open by the hand
of troops that abound
as lords of this piece of ground
we stole from the sea.
Don't give them the key!
If they ruin the dunes, pierce every dike
your mighty sea will strike ferociously.
Your people will no longer be,
swallowed up by raging sea.

SAINT THOMAS AQUINAS, HERO OF A TONGUE

Thomas, hero of a tongue,
abhorrent to complacent types
but food for reflective minds
drowning in seas of confusion,
illusions shouted by sophists
running wild along crowded shores.

I marvel at your bravery:
your standing up against the slavery
of those enchained to old, tired words
that could not strike a chord
in wavering hearts.

New times create new question marks,
new insights dawn every day.
Like you, we are again at sea,
tossed by waves of empty words, vague psychologisms,
sleek and clever gnosticism.

We try to build a language
that could enlighten fellow believers
in their bewilderment,
that could make sense to desperate souls
dwelling behind the forbidding walls
of enclosed and narrow minds.

Great saint, grant us the inner radiance
that made you a lighthouse for travelers lost at sea.
Make us resist the ridicule
of those encapsulated in common connotations.
Make us reach out like you to all
who need another tongue, a synthesis
to help them appraise
right and wrong
in the Babylon of empty rhetoric
swirling around us everywhere.

BATTLING PERVERSITY

The strain of pain
of people dying in many places,
the tortured faces
of ghastly holocaust,
the flood of tears and sighs
the crying out for "why's" of this insanity!
Why don't we strive for a humanity
hungry for the sway of justice everywhere
beyond the pious dreams of people
who tell us sanctimoniously:
"The Lord will care," and thus
absolve us from our battle
for the rights of all.
We must not be pious plodders
crouching behind a veil
of rigid religiosity,
instead of battling the perversity
of murder, famine, misery.

ODE TO PUTTEN

Hidden hamlet of simple believers,
tucked away from the rumble of a ravaged city,
the thunder of the battlefields.

SS men shout commands
that desecrate your clean and quiet streets.
Frightened mothers leave their tidy homes.
Silently they shuffle with anxious children
into the unknown horizon of a dying land.
Men in the hundreds
are sealed off in cattle trains,
never to be seen again.
Flames devour the empty houses
where the pretty lace of well-kept curtains
turns into dark and dirty shrouds of mourning.

My heart breaks, my eyes fill with tears,
My mouth feels hot and dry.
I swear to revenge these innocents.
I shall make their blood blossom
into a new way of thought
that may sow seeds of consonance
in the killing fields of humanity.

ANONYMOUS GRACE

Praise to Thee, Eternal Love,
for gracing wounded nature
with a brightness that illumines
each precious life unwittingly.

Luminosity seems shrouded
by a haze of sadness,
the voice of grace subdued
by forgetfulness of generations.
Yet your grace always moves silently,
inspiring us mysteriously.

Praise for the heroism
You install in the sacred will
of women and men who
do not know your name
yet who are slain for truth,

blood oozing wildly
from their broken bodies.

Rise incense of praise
of the anonymous grace
calling them lovingly
to their tragic destiny
in these turbulent times.

RIPPLING SEA OF MISERY

Rains drop down on wounded towns,
covered by mourning shrouds of freedom lost.
Street by street the somber sound
of shuffling feet of tired women and men,
funeral files between the graves
of homes shuttered and destroyed.

On the highway out of town they melt together
into a river of soundless movement,
not knowing where they will be led,
or if they will arrive alive or dead.

Soldiers step erect and proud
as a mighty forest, their cruel guns poised to strike.
Mothers wail, their shrieks resound
against a dark sky unrelieved by light.

Fathers, though wet with rain, look with dry eyes.
They stare in despair
on the thousand backs ahead of them,
a rippling sea of misery.
Their mind is lame, their spirit deflated
by this savage game of banishment
from their beloved nests.

SYMPHONY OF DUNE AND SEA

Battle of the Scheldt
Where death was dealt
To thirty thousand fearless men
Drowning in unwieldy waters
Dark with blood of ghastly wounds
Pierced by cries of people doomed,
Buried in the catacombs
Of deep and unforgiving tides.
Sturdy dikes, bit by ire
Raining from a gray and silent sky,
Wounded, they can no longer try
To shield the lowlands from these stormy tides.

Furious waves wildly rage,
Erase, deface the marvelous maze
Of windmills, fields, and ways,
Houses, buildings, tumble down,
Browning the splendid crown
Of Zeeland wrested from the sea.
Wait! She will strain
To rise again,
Weaning herself from ashes of defeat.

I love you wounded dunes and dikes,
Withstanding countless strikes
Of angry waves against the stubborn people
Rescuing lowlands from a roaring sea.
You symbolize for me
The sentinels that shield my soul
From deepest pain and woe,
From being drowned by leveling waves
Silencing the call the Everlasting gave
To the lowlands of my failing life.

O mystery of mighty sea,
Enigma of iniquity,
Symbol of fertility
When no longer wild, but mild,

You are a symphony of ebb and flow,
Mirror of a sea of grace,
Flooding in mysterious ways
Defeated hearts unceasingly
Until they beat alone for Thee,
Ebbing and flowing into the bosom
Of a loving mystery.

I CANNOT SLEEP, I WEEP

Drenched in sweat
I awake trembling with fear,
a bird quivering in agony
as when animals paw their flimsy cage.
The hollow sound of heavy boots,
iron nails pounding loud and grim
the stones around my silent house,
echoing in empty streets
where only soldiers can camp at night.
The screeching of the brakes:
Is this the fatal hour, Lord?
The boots pass by,
the heartless banging on doors of other cages,
"Aufmachen, Aufmachen," "Open the door!"
Screams tear the night apart.
People are thrown on the floor
I cannot sleep, I weep
for the bodies of neighbors, friends
gassed and burned to nothingness
in the gaping ovens of a prison camp,
the smell of searing flesh infecting the heavens
with the foul stench of a slaughter house.

DREAD BLANKET OF DESPAIR

Frozen flocks of famined people,
Hungering swarms of locusts coming

Down on muddy roads,
Besieging farms,
Pounding doors, begging food
Pleading for their ebbing life.

Dread blanket of despair
Covering the countryside
In biting winter air,
Merciless the wind, the rain
Mute the grey expanse of endless sky.

Emaciated women move silently,
Battered barques in the steady stream
Of masses of the doomed.
In their hungry wombs entombed
The undernourished lives
Of coming generations,
Their eyes too dry to cry,
Their minds too numbed to ask the why
Of strangulation of emergent life.

OUR HIGHEST LONGING

Play anew the Gospel music
for those who did not hear
its holy chimes with inner ear.

Our highest longing has become
a broken organ long neglected,
filled with dust, out of tune,
our spirit in its doom
is like sonar that has been muffled
by deep sea charges crudely dropped
from surface vessels manned by dealers of death.

Our hearts are robbed
from sacred dreams
like treasures of ancient pyramids
looted by vandals.

Sound the morning trumpet
for those who are asleep so long,
rise and clean the rusted radar of the soul,
restore splendor and passion of spirit
buried like icons
under layers of paint
splattered against desecrated walls.

Deep down we are endowed
with a dynamism of ascension.
Let the death of millions
not be in vain, O Lord.
When we hear your Gospel word
let the spirit ascend
out of the ashes of the martyrs
lost in the marches
of those dreadful days.

RISING AND FALLING FORMS

Houses musty and forlorn
in a gray and listless sky,
mutely mourning infants born
to choke on clouds of cyanide
unleashed by murderous hand
in a strange and foreign land,
their bodies burning in the ovens,
the wood of their abandoned homes
burned to keep alive those left behind:
symbol of undying love
for their city and its freezing people.

Abandoned dwellings
hacked to pieces
in chilling winter air
to help survivors bear
with bitter cold at home

that like a freezing dome
threatens famined life.

Starving town, vile and filthy,
crown of neatness falling down
putrid hills of stinking rubbish
Where hungry children dig for food,
Near fetid canals, in pitch dark streets
under far away offended stars.

Let not my heart be buried
by the devastation of the present.
Shelter me in the gracious dream
of greater days to come.
Make me strive unceasingly
for a new vision of your cosmic
lace of interweaving forms,
calling all of us
to grow in consonance
amidst the awesome dance
of atoms unseen by human eyes,
of rising seas and falling stars,
oblivious to the wear and tear
on every life, everywhere.

CHIMES OF WISDOM

In wild and trying times,
sweet chimes of wisdom
disappear in roaring winds
of war and pride
raging far and wide
in lands and camps
held fast by bloody hands.

People sink in shifting sands
of sickening prohibitions
that tear their heart

away from the tender light
embracing them in better times.

Violent wishes for revenge
poison human minds.
No bench of justice,
no thoughtful jury,
can calm the fury
of famined people.

Mystery of loving light
transforming enraged humanity,
heal the fierce divisions
tearing us to pieces.
Let anger wane,
teach us again
to meet each other
in your holy name.

TENDER MELODY

Small and sober hayloft
above rows of cows below,
I hear them eat and stir beneath.
I pray, I write, I read, I think,
homesick for the tidy ways
when our simple days
as in a lovely dream
flowed peacefully together,
a babbling stream
in a sunlit countryside.

Scattered far and wide
in a diaspora we did not choose,
we feel ourselves let loose
in strange dark woods
of famine, fire, distorted truths.

O turn on in me the tender melody,
the music of my soul,
softly calling me to my destiny
in space and time,
I should not whine.

Relieve my anxious core,
make my heart an open door
to the soft white light
shining bright in the diamond
you buried in my soul.
Let this inner light give form to thought
flowing from a heart bought
by your precious blood,
mingling with the red river
oozing from the wounds of millions,
torn to pieces by tanks, bullets, bombs,
worn out by famine, gassed and doomed.

When others tread on our dignity,
reveal to us our deepest nobility.
Take away the alien brand
of hate that silences
the harp within our heart,
no longer echoing
the music of your call.

Wash away with your wounded hand
the film of dirt that smudges
the mirror of our deepest core,
no longer reflecting your pristine,
precious gift to our soul:
the founding form of our life,
its guiding light, its restless longing
for intimacy with you alone.

LOVE'S DIVINE EMBRACE

Amidst the calamity,
of famine, war, depravity,
save us from the blinding drive
to run our life,
to call the shots,
to keep a string on everything.
Allow to enter into this night
shafts of light
piercing through this canopy of iniquity.
When we expect
to be fed by bread,
we are thrust instead
into a desert of ignorance,
blinded to the meaning of divine providence
announced in unforeseeable events.
Where is the end?
Teach us abandonment:
to dance in darkness,
make music under a pitch black sky,
surrender to not sensing why,
living on the dole
in a night of lost control.
Parched is the flowery tree
of pious feeling, lovely consolation;
left is only the oblation
of idle thought and deed,
weeds that defeat the seed
of inspiration.
Filled to the brim
with spite and sin
everything seems dull and dim
until abandonment
resurrects the event
of love's merciful intent.

YOUR REDEEMING CALL

Save us, sailors on this sinking ship.
Share our anguished trip
on this passing planet,
tiny kayak in the immensity of space,
carrying a contentious race,
resisting every trace
of your redeeming grace.
Flames leap from wall to wall,
yet none can erase
the memory of your eternal call.
Times are mean and tough.
Bombs are raining from the sky,
wailing sirens racing by
screaming people, living torches
falling from their porches,
running wild through lit-up streets
crumpling like burning sheets
of used up paper.
Blackened, butchered bodies
that breathe no longer
force us to believe that your love is stronger
than the madness of this race.
Restore a saner pace.
Turn every sorrow
into a seed of hope for tomorrow
that we may ask of those
who paid the price,
if there is loss enough
to make us wise?

MADONNA OF ROERMOND

Madonna of Roermond,
recall the beautiful bond
between this town and you.
Lovely lady, dressed in white and blue,

behold this wrecked and ruined house,
smashed to pieces,
slammed and pierced
by whistling grenades
that fiercely set
our streets ablaze.

Bombs create craters
of blood and tears.
Amidst the rubble
survivors stumble
to avoid collapsing walls.
Dazed they look around
for cellars underground,
for children, husbands, wives
desperate to save their lives.

Thousands are driven out of town,
old and young, weak and strong,
children crying, "What is wrong?",
As they trudge through frosty snow,
bitten by the icy blow
of cutting winter wind.
Packed behind the bars
of German cattle cars,
they begin a perilous journey
through bombed out foreign lands,
people banned from your beloved city.
Madonna, show your pity!

Under a grey and somber sky
we wonder why
your town suffered so much
from the onrush of a war
that cut every citizen to the core.

The Virgin whispers:
Create a hermitage in your heart.
Make it the temple of a faith
that makes you wait

for a promised time:
My Son shall rise and shine,
radiant and straight
before the eyes of your enlightened faith.

Trust me, the Virgin whispers.
When there is a lump
in your throat and your mind is numb,
when your eyes are blind,
when your heart limps behind,
when you stand before a wall
not seeing light at all,
when you cannot pray or speak,
when you are at the peak
of what you can bear,
then you are at the border
of the paradise of faith.

No longer fearful, tight,
you witness for the light
not by crying aloud
in the market place
but by dying in a blaze
of love and glory to any trace
of paralyzing worry
or loss of peace
in keeping with the pace of grace.

Appendix 2

Christmas Night in Ravaged Holland

An Underground Play
by
Adrian Van Kaam

Written and Performed in December, 1944

The curtain opens; the stage is dimly lit. Mary and Joseph stand still and tired on a long road. Behind the scene, someone reads aloud with a quiet, restrained, yet expressive voice the nativity narrative, Luke 2:1–20, after which Mary and Joseph trudge on wearily.

JOSEPH

Alas, your weak body is shivering again . . . How exhausting it is for you to do nothing but walk along foggy polders in the chilly evening . . . Only the moon shining in the heavens still gives her white light . . . How fatiguing this sodden ground . . . especially now, since the child is going to arrive soon.

MARY

Joseph, I am thinking a lot about that distant night in Bethlehem because this night resembles it so touchingly, like no other in many years.
This, too, is a region occupied by soldiers, just as that was a small, poor country, closely guarded by the Romans.

It was impossible back then to find a roof to cover us, since a flood of people traveled through all the villages because of the census. And now we are still unable to find a safe place since so many are leaving these villages again because of fire or hunger or threats to their freedom.

JOSEPH

And now I'm almost beginning to despair again of being able to shelter you for the great moment.

MARY

Oh, Joseph, can't we even find a hayloft for our Child?

JOSEPH

I'm sorry I can't shelter you from such pain, with that divine burden under your tender heart . . . You are like a fine and pure tabernacle . . . And, alas . . . the raw night frost will nip at you callously . . . You are still so slight and girlishly delicate.

MARY

Don't worry about me, Joseph. I don't care about my own sorrow or distress. Let us think of him instead, this small, dear bringer of peace to the poor world, who again will neither be received anywhere nor thankfully and joyously met . . . Still, how willingly tonight would I tuck his trembling, handsome little body into the whiteness of sheets and the warmth of wool . . . It is such a terrible thought for a mother to do without soft bedding and clothing for her shivering newborn child. What is there for her to say when she knows that this little Boy is God himself?

Joseph
To be permitted to be his foster father and not to be able to care for him sufficiently is the sharpest blow I could endure.

He lifts up his head and hands, grasping his traveling staff.

"God, You were absurdly good to this simple carpenter from a forgotten village . . ."

He lets his head and hands fall again and speaks.

"How would the farmers be able to suspect that this bungling person who patches their stalls and barns would soon . . . (*he looks at his work-roughened hands*) be allowed to feed and handle God himself, the Lord of the universe, with his rough, weather-beaten fingers . . . That this should be allowed to happen to me, an ordinary villager . . . You have chosen the wrong person, because, see, I can't even find a safe shelter for you."

Mary
God willed and ordered it to be thus. To him be thanks and honor, even if his everlasting good will prepares hardship and the bitterness of poverty for us and his own Son.

You have spoken truly, Joseph. He has been absurdly good to us . . . It is your joy, Lord, to make the small and trifling incomprehensibly great . . . I, who travel the roads as a poor woman, one of the many in this ravaged land, who are hungry and ask for food, who are tired and beg for shelter, who want to escape the cutting, freezing wind in order to warm themselves by a fire.

"Oh, God, how is it possible that I am permitted to be the mother of him who created all fires and shelters and food, who can plunge all of this into nothingness with a single press of his finger?"

Joseph
"Oh, God, I thank you for the royal greatness granted to this Woman, most neglected of all."

Joseph withdraws a bit from Mary and remains standing inconspicuously to one side of the stage, as if seeking shelter. Mary stands in the center of the stage, retired within herself. In silent ecstasy, she concentrates on the Holy One within her; her entire being, all her movements, are directed inward; her arms are peacefully crossed over her bosom, her head a bit inclined.

MARY

"My God, I am dizzy; I know and feel that you live and move in me . . ."

Emerging for a moment from this ecstasy and slightly turning her head in Joseph's direction, she then sinks back once again into her all-absorbing contemplation.

MARY

Joseph, the moment cannot be far off . . . the Eternal himself is sacredly and miraculously present once again.

Suddenly raising herself in jubilation from her silent ecstasy, and with a wide and beautiful movement of her head, she stretches her arms toward the heavens.

"Worship and praise him still, moons in the heavens, bright stars . . ."

With a gentle, all-encompassing gesture, she spreads her arms around her surroundings, around all that her rapturous gaze beholds.

"Glorify him, then, silent, wide polders; worship him, gleaming ditches and gray puddles, windmills of this land."

She is intensely reverent, bowing with a soft inclination of her head.

"Kneel down before your Creator, lowing cattle of the stalls. The One who gave you movement is here.

With a slow crossing of her arms over her bosom, she sinks once again into the same heartfelt retiring posture as before.

"Oh God, your mother feels overwhelmed by dizzying love because of your miraculous rustling life under her heart!"

JOSEPH

Here is one last farm; I'll try one more time . . .

He knocks on the upper door and calls out.

FARMER'S WIFE
Who's this so late at night? Can't they ever leave us in peace? People coming and going all day long. We really can't call this a life any more. Do they think we can simply hand everything we own over to them? There's an end to all good things, even to generosity.

JOSEPH
We're only asking for some shelter. Isn't that possible, just this once?

FARMER'S WIFE

She stands there with her hands planted solidly on her hips.

You refugees, we've already put up lots of you. This isn't a boarding-house; we can't keep on accommodating people.

JOSEPH
Maybe just for one night?

The robust figure of the farmer appears at the opening of the dark door.

FARMER
Who are these people? Man, can't you stay in the city? You didn't need us before the war, did you, and do you think we need you now? . . . (*To his wife*) Why are you stupid enough to open the door to all these people? Leave it closed from now on; then we won't be bothered from morning to night.

JOSEPH
Good evening, folks.

FARMER AND WIFE
So long, we're really sorry, but we can't help you.

JOSEPH
(*Going over to Mary slowly, he says:*) There we are . . . (*pointing to the empty road, crestfallen*) on the street (*unnerved by the darkness above and looking around them*). It's night . . . (*very expressive*) and the child is going to come soon . . . (*He is at a loss about what to do*). Where should I turn? What should I do?

MARY
Trust in him . . . God will provide . . . Soon, when our Child is here and together we're gazing happily at his little face (*Both gaze with large, shining eyes at the imaginary vision that Mary's words call forth. A happy smile comes over Joseph's tired face*) and feeling the soft curves of his body and limbs in our poor hands . . . then, dear Joseph, we'll forget about our distress; then there'll be warmth in the sharpest cold and light in the thickest darkness. My longing for him is beginning to grow strong . . . "Come, my God, my Child, my Baby Boy, come . . ."

SKIPPER'S WIFE
> *She comes walking up with a ship's lantern. Unexpectedly meeting Mary and Joseph she shines the light on them; examining them, she holds the lantern high.*

Hey, who's there so late in the street, on Christmas night yet . . . Hey folks, it's long past eight o'clock. Aren't you afraid of being caught? (*In a confidential tone*) Between us, we've heard again that we can expect a round-up here. So be doubly careful and on your guard.

JOSEPH
Dear lady, look here. She is expecting a baby and we have no shelter for the night. I'm at my wit's end!

SKIPPER'S WIFE
I might know something for you both, but I wouldn't call it pretty. It's a houseboat that we riddled with bullets a month ago; now it's almost nothing but holes. (*She points to it.*) There it lies, idle and useless at the water's edge . . . full of holes with little wood left, but, hey, it has no lack of fresh air and a fine view! Come along. I have to get going to my own place soon because I don't want to be picked up or shot on the street. Good evening, folks, and lots of courage to you.

JOSEPH
Good evening, dear lady.

> *Joseph looks sorrowfully and waveringly from the houseboat to Mary and from Mary to the houseboat.*

MARY

She offers a delicate, soft, encouraging squeeze of her hand on Joseph's arm.

Come, Joseph, keep courage. Let there be no more searching or dawdling. Let's content ourselves with this vessel and move in. It will be just as poor and beautiful as that first night in the stall of Bethlehem.

JOSEPH

Be careful, Mary, walk quietly beside me. Poor Joseph wants to be a humble, caring servant of you and the Child who is so near.

They enter the houseboat slowly. Behind the scene a choir sings a quiet, seasonal hymn. When it concludes, the scene changes. Four men run up the polder road in a hunted manner.

ITALIAN

What icy weather! It makes me miss my warm, Italian countryside. How much longer do I have to sit hidden in these gray polders without mountains, trees or forests, with the fear of dying today or being hung tomorrow. I can already see myself swinging like a bag of licorice in a store window . . . a round-up on Christmas night of all nights . . . and the four of us sit here daydreaming and just hoping we'll save our skins. Isn't that right, old Scot?

SCOTSMAN

Yes. And, by the way, did I tell you I rather like Italian licorice.

BAVARIAN

Christmas, *Welhnachten*, that is in the *Helmat so schön*!

RUSSIAN

Everything is always so wonderfully *schön* in Bavaria; I can spin a yarn about it. I was there, but my heart was in Russia; I was a prisoner of war for six months before I escaped. And you, a runaway soldier, you and your *schönlgheid*. Will you please shut up about it?

SCOTSMAN

Come on, can't you keep quiet on Christmas night? That kid can't do anything about it; he isn't here just for fun. And since when is everything *schönlgheid* with us? Man, I didn't find much *schönlgheid* when I let my bombs rain on Berlin and now that I've been rained down here in my parachute and sucked up by this soaking wet, muddy little country with all the time to sulk about it in some farmer's attic, now it's even less *schön*. How about you?

BAVARIAN
Yeah, I know, our people are too proud, too *stolz*; I was *stolz* too! But because we were *stolz*, the Boss upstairs handed us over to the misery of this war to cut us down to size. Honestly guys, I've always fought against the others for my belief and my honor; they punished me and thrashed me. I'm not broken but my *stolz*, my pride, has been broken. I hope that in you guys at least this haughty pride that sees every German as a scoundrel, as someone to be hated completely, and that sees a kind of unassailable saint in every member of your own people, has also been broken.

RUSSIAN
One year ago, I would have shot your head off. But since we've been hanging around together in the wettest corner of the world, on the farms of this swamp, we've discovered that we're all human--real humans with a heart. Even that dour Scot has a heart.

SCOTSMAN
I've heard that, too, but don't tell anyone.

ITALIAN
And if they catch us and wring our necks or if a bomb falls on the four of us, and everything inside is in order, then all of us will arrive in the same heaven, Bavarian or Scot.

BAVARIAN
Welhnachten, Christmas, since you other guys are thinking about it too?

RUSSIAN
Christmas in the Red Army, lots of women and vodka! But when I saw the preparations for Christmas on the farm, and the building of the creche, then I remembered hearing the story of the Christ Child from my parents. It was . . . beautiful, too beautiful to be true!

SCOTSMAN
Christmas in the Royal Air force, at the aviators' club, lots of punch, nothing but punch and plum pudding and then whiskey and more whiskey! But that ultimately doesn't satisfy anyone. There must be something else behind it, something no one talks about but everyone silently suspects, like the farmers here, so devout with their cribs and statues and their children singing sweet songs.

ITALIAN
Oh, if only I were home. We also celebrated the Baby Jesus, the Santa Bambino in his little crib . . . if only I could go home . . . Bavarian, are you also eaten up by homesickness?

BAVARIAN
Shut up, man . . . I . . . oh . . . I don't have a home any more (*he sobs*). It's all gone, all destroyed, even my four blond children . . . my young wife, all torn to shreds, *Krieg* is *krieg*. (*He sobs and sobs.*)

SCOTSMAN
Brother, how grief has crushed you. I'm just a stiff, cold Briton, but let me be a mother to you for a moment. We lonely fellows have to miss so much tenderness in this damp, gray land, so strange and chilly. Here, let me dry away your tears with my handkerchief, poor brother . . . how should I comfort you? Maybe those of us who are homeless and lonely can still take some comfort in that wonderful story about the Child.

RUSSIAN
Does that Child care about people in hiding? Italian, you come from a religious country, so they say. It's true that when life is nice and sunny, you are also pretty good at forgetting your religiousness. But all things considered, you know a whole lot more about those old stories than we do in our red Bolshevik tents.

ITALIAN
You wonder if the Christ Child cares about those in hiding? Man, the Christ Child, along with his father and mother, are the patrons of people in hiding!

RUSSIAN
So, what are you telling me?

ITALIAN
Naturally, those three all went into hiding, didn't they?

SCOTSMAN
Tell me about that. Was it as rotten for him as for us?

ITALIAN
I think it was. The occupying power of Palestine was after his life and Herod let all the innocent children be killed in order to catch them after all. But he hid with his family in Egypt, among foreigners who wanted nothing to do with Jews. You see, he is God and high above us. He is infinite, but still he wanted to suffer everything with us, even to go into hiding.

SCOTSMAN
That's beautiful. We have our leading men and the authorities who assure us nicely, with even prettier speeches, how they empathize with our suffering. But we know better, right boys? They can't sympathize and be compassionate . . . they've never experienced it themselves, have they? But an authority, a leader who himself went into hiding in impoverished and alienating circumstances so that he could sympathize with us, that would be unheard of! . . . Would this eternal God have done that for me, for you and for each one of us? It's strange, but here on Christmas night in the cold, on a polder road, you have deeper thoughts than before, when you were sitting in a night club in your leather easy chair, drinking magnificent punch!

RUSSIAN
Christmas is also a feast day of peace, if I'm not mistaken. What an idea, the four of us sitting here talking serenely about the Christ Child. And we understand and like one another while a bit further up the road guys like us are shooting each other to pieces. Meanwhile the four of us talk in peace.

ITALIAN
That's because our good will is so genuine. Heinrich has the good will to stop being *stolz* and proud, and our Scot has shown the good will to stop being haunted by his rain of bombs on Berlin, and Turgenev no longer wants to shoot everyone who made faces at him at Stalingrad. The Christ Child has brought peace on earth to people of good will. The

angels sang that to the shepherds in the fields. And I once heard a virtuous old woman in Turin say that it sometimes happens that someone of genuine good will gets to see the Christ Child on Christmas night.

Bavarian
Who knows, maybe it could happen to us tonight. Besides that, we poor devils don't have anything to celebrate Christmas with. Before, we possessed so many things that we forgot to think about him. Now we don't have anything . . . maybe he won't forget us.

Russian
Let's celebrate Christmas in our own way. I brought along a bottle of vodka, the only one I was able to smuggle during my captivity in Stalingrad. I've only drunk a little of it; you can all have a sip, but not too much of one, because I want to save some for darker days. And after we've done that, Antonio has to say a prayer aloud in all our names to the Child of this night. Antonio can do it best; a rough Russian like me isn't the man to do it. You must tell him how great we think it is that he was also willing to go into hiding, that we're all of good will, and that we hope he won't forget us tonight.

Bavarian
That's a marvelous plan.

Scotsman
Bring out your vodka. And after that gargle we'll pray and throw the horse cloth around us and sleep well through the rest of Christmas night.

Russian
Hello, here it is. *(He pushes the bottle into the Bavarian's hands.)* You first, Heinrich. You can take a bigger drink than the other guests because your whole darned estate went to pieces.

Bavarian
Danken schön, Turgenev, you are truly a good man.

The Bavarian drinks calmly and passes the flask to the Scotsman.

Scotsman
Hey, that does a man good.

The Scotsman brings the bottle to his lips with tremendous speed and at first seems to make no move to relinquish it. The Russian grabs hold of the bottle.

RUSSIAN
Hey, Papa, how about showing some of the thrift your Scottish race is so famous for.

ITALIAN
Now it's my turn: cheers, comrades.

RUSSIAN
So, now I'll take a little and then it'll disappear, my most precious treasure, in the inside of my jacket for another day.

BAVARIAN
Now it's time for your prayer, Antonio.

ITALIAN
Everybody kneel, guys, and when I'm finished say "Amen."

They all kneel facing the audience. The Russian first goes down on one knee; then he bends the other stiffly and with difficulty.

RUSSIAN
Hey, I haven't done that in a long time; it's quite a job.

ITALIAN
"Christ Child, who is coming to earth again tonight, here are four fellows of good will. We've really gone astray at times, but we've never meant any wrong. You are heartily thanked that you had to go into hiding just like us. You will also understand our misery better than anyone. Please see to it that our peoples become friends again soon, just as we are here at the moment. Say, take care of our wives and children at home. If they are crying tonight because of us, dry their tears with your little hands. Oh, yeah, and see to it that Heinrich's wife and blond children, are happy up there with you." That's it, guys.

ALL
Amen.

Bavarian
That's good.

Scotsman
And now, let's get under the horse cloth.

Russian
Yeah, let's do it.

Italian
Brrr . . . how chilly and cold it is.

Scotsman
I wish that I could crawl into a burning gas well.

Bavarian
Sweet dreams. The cold may be strong but sleep is stronger.

> *The men lie under the covers, sleeping next to one another. The choir behind the scene begins to sing. An angel appears, surrounded by bright light. The men awaken, surprised and frightened. When the speaking begins, the choir hums the melody quietly.*

Russian
What is it, a round-up?

Bavarian
Airplanes in the sky?

Angel
"Glory to God in the highest and peace on earth to people of good will. Men, be not afraid, I bring you good news that shall be for all the people who fight grimly and camp out and have forgotten how to smile at one another."

"The Child is born once more, who brings peace to those of good will."

"The Child is here, who alone has the power to silence the absurd noise of your weapons on earth, and to stop your blood that spills over the entire globe."

"The Child who loves all heartily, but especially those who are inconsolable and who possess no more safety, is among you."

"He is born, here close by on the water. You will find him inside, poor and numb with cold, swaddled in some old towels. "

The choir begins to sing once more and sings or repeats the end of its song.

BAVARIAN
Come, let us go worship him there.

RUSSIAN
But, guys, am I dreaming or am I awake?

SCOTSMAN
That prayer, made in all our names, appears to have been heard . . . miraculous!

ITALIAN
Now you can tell that Child yourselves what hinders or oppresses you. Let's go.

The men approach the houseboat. Joseph opens the door from the inside and, seeing them, says to Mary:

JOSEPH
Mary, the first worshipers are approaching, just like before, when the nameless shepherds were permitted to be the first to adore the nameless Child, who was born in a stable along an unknown road.

Before the boat, under the light of a ship's lantern, is a smaller chest with straw and the Child is in it. Mary is seated on one side, Joseph is kneeling on the other. The men kneel, turned diagonally toward the Child and diagonally toward the audience. On one side, are the Russian and the Scotsman; on the other side, the Bavarian and the Italian. The choir sings a Christmas song. Afterwards, the Bavarian moves, stands up, and kneels before the Child on one knee.

BAVARIAN
Little Child, please forgive the pride of my people. Restore those of us who have wandered from the upright path. You want me to offer you the most cherished thing that is still left to me.

(*He unbuckles his dagger and puts it down by the crib.*) Look at my humble surrender of this pitiful weapon of revolt. (*He returns to his place, kneeling beside the Italian, who is visibly moved; he stands up and says to the Child:)*

Italian

Little Child, let me sing a song from my Italian land in honor of your beautiful, saintly Mother.

He sings with southern bravura an Italian song about Mary, after which he kneels again. The Russian, who has been kneeling on one knee beside the Child the entire time, remains in that posture while he says:

Russian

Holy Child of Christmas, I am only a rough Russian. But I feel myself becoming so strangely warm inside. I wanted to give You the dearest thing that I still carry.

He takes the bottle of vodka out of his pocket and puts it by the little chest. The Scotsman stands up immediately and, remaining in his place, brings out his flute and says:

Scotsman

Let me express my feelings for you in music from the Scottish countryside. And, please, teach me to be compassionate in victory to those who are all too cunning, not to be too greedy in profit nor cruelly selfish toward the small and defenseless, be they friend or foe.

He plays a Scottish air on his flute. Then the farm door opens where Mary and Joseph had just now been turned away. The farmer's wife comes out, looking surprised.

Farmer's Wife

What's happening? All that light and all this excitement. *(The angel appears.)*

Angel

"The Christ Child has been born here. Go to village and polder, farmer and citizen, calling them all together unto the Child who brings peace and who wishes to unite all people."

The farmer comes out of the house. The skipper and his wife appear from behind the scene on the other side. The farmer and his wife, the skipper and his wife, kneel on the stage, each at the side of one corner,

Christmas Night in Ravaged Holland

turned diagonally toward the Child. Another pair of farmers and their wives, fishermen, laborers, and an office worker, merchants and other villagers, come forward from the auditorium, as well as several children, all of whom kneel in the same posture and direction described above on a lower podium placed in front of the stage. The text that follows may be said by all of them together or alternately by individuals or small groups, as the script indicates. However, the closing prayer is to be said by everyone together.

PEOPLE
We have heard that the Christ Child has been born here. We are so thankful for his arrival in our region we want to worship him now and show him our reverence and love.

MARY
Come closer then. Here is the Child who will bring peace to all of you if you are of good will. Accept my Child, for he is gentle and good and full of tender compassion.

PEOPLE
Mother, we love your Child tenderly and wish to look after him with all our heart.

MARY
Of, if only that were true! Alas, there are those who have repudiated him and who have injured his tender heart. I must admonish them sadly: My Child was naked in the wind and rain and you did not clothe Him. My Child trembled with hunger and you did not feed Him. My Child was shelterless and numb with cold and you refused to let him come under your roof. My Child was sorrowful and you caused him even more sorrow through your hardness and impatience.

PEOPLE
When were there those among us who did not warm your shivering Child, who did not share their food with you and your little one who cried from hunger? Who did not give your homeless Child their home happily, who cruelly repudiated a Child who wept in the night? Has he already been among us? For we have never seen him before in our homes or farms, neither on our roads or fields.

MARY

Do you not know that he has said: "All that you do in my Name unto the least of these, you have done to me. Whoever gives a glass of water in my name will not go without his or her reward." Whoever gives a bed to a homeless person puts this Divine Child quietly and tenderly to bed, too. Whoever graciously offers a tired, wandering person his warm hearth and table does it unto him.

Whoever breaks a morsel of bread for a refugee strengthens him on a long winter's journey. There have also been those who uncharitably refused him the gift of bread, the goodness of a drink; they cast the Child, who brought peace to the world, out into the cold once more. Alas, the noise of war may permanently cover this sorrowful earth until they, too, are of good will.

For I am the mother of all people because each person is of my blood; each cost me a tear and a pain that is impossible to silence. My heart ardently wishes all nations prosperity and joy and a restful course of life. Wish the same to one another. Grant peace to one another if you dare.

PEOPLE

But, Mother, if the day arrives that we, too, are unable to give any more, if our storehouse is a dark, gaping hole and we see nothing but the bottom of our milk pails, if the burghers among us only retained that which was necessary for themselves, Mother, what then may be given?

MARY

You may at least break the bread of amiability for all and pour out the restorative drink of a good word. If your storehouses are empty and all your beds are slept on, you are still able to offer numerous helpless ones who ask of you the favor of a gracious gesture, a welcome word, a joyful smile. Then peace will live in your heart and in your house and this peace will reconcile all peoples. Promise this to my Child tonight: ask him simply what you desire and then depart quietly, assured of his blessing.

PEOPLE

Hear our promise, then: Child of Mary, Divine Child, the toiler along the roads will no longer remain a stranger to us. We will at least offer the weary inquirer the smile in our eyes. We will respect the poor woman and be loving to the prisoner who was set free. The ragged will share our possessions and the hidden ones who have no bed, our linen. Protect us from the fire from the sky; may the flame not harm our homes. Spare our brothers abroad from unexpected mutilation in the morning and from pitiable destruction in the evening. Do not let hunger run us ragged and consume us nor despair tear open our hearts. Do not allow our dikes to give way so that our land becomes a dead sea, our ground a fruitless morass . . .

MARY
Ask not only for your temporarily visible ground, but consider as well how the dike of a sense of honor and conscience has burst for many, and how passions, vices and lusts have inundated their hearts until they have become a morass full of fetidness. Is the inundation of your heart not more atrocious than that of your country? Is the barrenness of your soul not more pathetic than that of your fields?

PEOPLE
Deliver our people from the impure lust that saps and undermines us. Extinguish in us the fire of bitterness and hate that devours inner gentleness. Take away from us the poison and venom of envy, our heart-shriveling sorrow at the well being of another and his or her small advantage over us in this day of need. Do not let us grow mercilessly hard in rigid cupidity. Never allow altercation and small-mindedness to splinter this people into weak sawdust scattered by a light wind. Make us a strong, pure and noble people, a new people with a new passion and a new will that seeks diligently to rebuild what sadly went to pieces in this time of fiercest want.

MARY
If all individuals and peoples offer these prayers with intertwined hands to the Child, and if they reflect devoutly on this deed, then good will and peace will become for you an unassailable reality.

> *Each one grasps the hand of the person kneeling next to him, and everyone holds their intertwined hands above their heads while humming a Christmas refrain quietly and motionlessly. Behind the scene, children's voices sing a soft and appropriate song of peace, and all depart with a reverential nod to the holy family. The stage then goes dark.*

Appendix 3

Editorials by Adrian van Kaam
in
Cor Unum et Anima Una

Introductory Note
by
Joop Bekkers, PhD, Translator

Cor Unum et Anima *Una* (henceforth referred to as CUAU) was a bulletin published in the Netherlands in 1945, from February until July, with Adrian van Kaam, CSSp, as its editor.

At the time Adrian was still a theology student. He had finished his second year of study at Gemert. Besides their regular studies the students there—at least those who liked to do so—held meetings where they discussed all kinds of subjects in the "*SOOS*" (their club), with members and a yearly elected chairman like Adrian himself. Somewhere, in between the lines in CUAU, it appears as if he held this position in 1944 and possibly still in 1945. CUAU started on February 2 of that year, but the idea had arisen previously perhaps as early as January 24 (See the tenth issue).

As was the case with most unofficial publications, this bulletin appeared without permission of the German-controlled authorities and was, therefore, illegal, implying heavy punishment or even the death penalty for whoever was connected with it. Unlike other illegal pamphlets, the idea of this bulletin was not to arouse sabotage or resistance but to keep in contact with all the scattered members of the Congregation of the Holy Ghost (whether priest or student or lay-brother), to exchange personal news, to keep courage in extremely hard circumstances, and to appeal to one another for mutual help, also materially—with requests expressly printed in issues four to ten. One statement emphatically declared that the bulletin was not a public newspaper (as referred to in the laws governing official printed matter) but merely a correspondence facilitating contact among members of a recognized religious community. Any publication contrary to this intention was against its will and outside its responsibility. Allow me to further describe the situation in Holland when the first issue of CUAU was issued on February 2, 1945.

After the Allied Forces had landed in France in June of 1944 and broken through the German lines in August, they liberated the North of France at high speed. They took Paris on August 25. Within a fortnight they also liberated most of Belgium and Luxemburg (Brussels and Antwerp were taken on September 3 and 4) and reached the Dutch Southern borders. At the time, as recounted in the memoirs, the students at Gemert were on holidays with their relatives all over the country, and the novitiate at Gennep had just started a new year. It seemed as if the liberation of the Netherlands would only be a matter of some weeks in coming. However, after the English airborne forces were defeated at Arnhem (they had landed there to secure the bridges across the main rivers, necessary for successful military operations) Dutch expectations were cruelly dashed. Most of the Southern part of the country was liberated in October and November, after much hard fighting, including three locations of the Holy Ghost Fathers: Weert, Gemert, and Baarle-Nassau, but the East, the North, and the West remained under German control. The wide rivers of the Rhine delta and the river Meuse (in Dutch: Maas) became the front-line which could hardly be crossed. (By the way, Druten was liberated in September as it lies South on the main branch of the Rhine, but it was in the frontline for six months and damaged by artillery fire.)

Gennep remained in German hands; it lay in the frontline for some six months and was heavily damaged. There the members of the Congregation, with many thousands of citizens of the whole region, were forced to evacuate—mainly on foot—and were scattered in the North and East, around the towns of Enschede, Leeuwarden, and Groningen. As there were no longer any trains running, the food situation in the West with its many large cities became desperate. There was little and later on hardly any food; the situation in the other, more agricultural parts, was better. There were no buses running either. People from the West had to walk or go by bike for a hundred miles or more to the countryside, to the East and North, to try and buy food from the farmers. The Germans also wanted to force all men between the ages of 16 and 40 to go to Germany to work for them. That is why so many men, including Adrian van Kaam, had to hide in the countryside. The Germans had regular round-ups to catch any remaining men. On top of this, the winter months of December and especially January were extremely cold, with temperatures of about minus 15–20 Fahrenheit. Thousands of people died of exhaustion that winter. Such was the situation when Adrian, from his hiding place, tried to establish contact with his confrères.

With two or three confrères he had been lucky enough to find shelter at a farm in the small village of Nieuwkoop, about twenty-five miles Northeast of The Hague, in an agricultural district among many lakes. Occasionally he managed to go to his family in The Hague and bring them some food. His two youngest sisters also came to live at Nieuwkoop; the eldest, Bep, had to work, but when she got diphtheria she also came to the village, as she had more chances to recover there.

Adrian got the idea to start CUAU, and he was able to do so with the help of his nearby confrères. First they tried to locate one another. The mayor of Nieuwkoop allowed him to use the mimeograph at the village hall; and later a printer in the village, a Protestant layman, helped them as well at the risk of his life. The mail service still worked somehow, although with much delay. CUAU soon enjoyed unexpected success: there were responses from his confrères scattered all over the country, telling about their experiences during that year. Other members sent in spiritual articles. It appeared that in some places there were more confrères hiding together; they even held meetings and recollection days. Father Henri Strick, CSSp, Adrian's beloved novice master, who had arrived at Enschede, saw to it that a small group there could continue to study philosophy and theology; another group in Amsterdam got lessons from professors of the diocesan major seminary. The confrères helped one another also in medical matters: Adrian and two confrères managed to get a sick confrère to Nieuwkoop where he had more chance to recover.

CUAU was also read by members of other religious orders and congregations. They liked it so much that some of them were inspired by this example to set up a bulletin of their own. One striking instance deserves mention here: a German Spiritan, Father Naarmann, was the one who helped them! Many German priests among the Holy Ghost Fathers were forced into military service; they often had to do hospital work. Father Naarmann, a professor at the German senior seminary, had to serve in this capacity in the Netherlands, first in Utrecht and later in Delft. He somehow got to see a copy of CUAU, liked it, and helped to distribute it. Close to the end of the war he himself became ill while at Delft. Now it was the turn of a Dutch Holy Ghost priest, Father De Knegt, to see him, a gesture much appreciated also by the other German soldiers at the place, who were very kind to him. (In this connection it is true that many German troops at the time were fanatic Nazis; but there were also Germans who hated the war as much as we did, and on the whole behaved decently to us.)

Another item of interest is this: the citizens who were evacuated from this region were mostly Catholics, who came into predominantly Protestant areas. There they were received most charitably. Some priests were even offered a room by Protestant ministers and told that they could use their church and help the few Catholic priests in those regions.

The winter passed and turned to spring. In their final offensive Canadian troops, starting from Nijmegen in February, took Gennep, which is located about twelve miles from Nijmegen, within a few days. The novitiate was heavily destroyed. On March 24 the Allies crossed the Rhine in Germany. Within a week they crossed in turn the German-Dutch border. The liberation of the Netherlands did not take place from the South, as we had expected, but from the East! On April 1 the Canadians took Enschede, the main Eastern town in our country. Within a fortnight, the Northern and Eastern parts were liberated by Canadians and Poles; the West had to wait for a later date. On the night of May 4, the remaining Germans in the Netherlands gave up and signed the surrender documents at Wageningen two days later. Then, on May 8, the Canadians entered Amsterdam and The Hague; at Amsterdam one Holy Ghost confrère, Joop Hogema, was wounded that day, but fortunately not severely. While Canadians entered the town from one end, and many enthusiastic people waited at the main square for them, some Nazi fanatics hiding in a nearby attic started shooting at the crowd, killing and wounding some people.

A graphic description of what the war years meant, as well as the relief felt by the Dutch at the liberation on that day, can be read in Adrian's editorial in the eleventh issue of CUAU of May 5. On that day we rejoiced at the thought of "public publication in a free country."

Within a fortnight Adrian managed to go to his family in The Hague; his home address now became the editor's address of CUAU. Although the whole country was free now, people were not allowed to travel from North to South or vice versa because of the danger of epidemics; it would take another two or three months before free traffic throughout the country was possible again. So CUAU continued for some time. The confrères had a final meeting at Nieuwkoop and celebrated Pentecost, their feastday there! Mail contact with Gemert was restored, and from Gemert food parcels were sent to their confrères in the West and North. In the last issue their then Superior, Father Strick, as well as their Provincial Superior, Father Lambert Vogel, wrote of their deep appreciation of CUAU.

As regards the contents and style of Adrian's editorials and other articles, I would say that apart from practical arrangements about making up and despatching editions of CUAU, they give news about his confrères and his deep concerns for them. Above all, they contain his spiritual views on the situation, seriously composed but at times also penned with some irony and humor. His style was a surprise to me. I remember his letters as being always clear and direct, but here it is as if the situation required more caution. He used longer sentences, often containing new words, suggesting that he was perhaps grappling with ways to capture his innovative views on spiritual, if not literary, formation. In some sense we meet here a student of his own daring and often inspired ideas.

[Translator's Note: *In the following translations of Adrian van Kaam's editorials, I have added some notes in italics by way of explanation.*]

TO THE WORLD PRESS

The Dutch people have been struggling in occupied territory for nearly five years. Hundreds and thousands of men have fallen; tens of thousands have been put into concentration camps. Many more have lost all their belongings. The railway men have been on strike for almost six months, both for the Allies and for ourselves.

Our cities have been destroyed, but we will rebuild them. Our factories have been demolished, but we will restore and improve them. Our land has been flooded, but we will reclaim it again.

The Germans think they can force us by starving us, but we think of the sufferings other nations have borne.

However, now they have got the idea of the fatal blow to our people, by deporting nine tenths of our men. Our country is densely populated; we have neither large forests nor other regions wherein to hide. Yet hundreds of thousands have gone into hiding. We steal ration cards and forge them; we loot population registers, etc.

If we had arms we would die like men instead of being led to the slaughter like sheep. We resist to the utmost, for the enemy wants to drag away all men (all in all still one and a half million) who will then be doomed to die because they will be without sufficient clothing and medical care while they will be subject to numerous infectious diseases.

We do not ask for pity. But now that an old civilized nation is menaced with extinction, we only want all fighting nations to raise their voices so that their cries may be heard by some Germans who will be able to stop these measures—with a view to the bill that will be settled.

Long live freedom! We will hold out!

—An Editorial Written and Published in Nieuwkoop, 1945

ISSUE 1 - FEBRUARY 2, 1945

Dear Confrères:

In our dear community at Gemert we had our "SOOS." We could tell each other about our interests, express our devotions, and, on some special days, generously manifest our thoughts and feelings. This SOOS was really a good opportunity for continuous mutual contact.

That opportunity has gone today. Especially during these last months, the need and the desire for contact has increased, more so than had ever been possible within [the context] of our quiet community life.

The month of Saint Willibrord and the Christmas month have passed without our noticing anything of our celebrating together, which had become such a simple and beautiful custom at Gemert. Now February is upon us—and its second day marks the commemoration of our Venerable Father Francis of Saverne. He now becomes so dear and eloquent to us with his quiet and pure love of suffering—now that we, his scattered sons in these parts of the country, have become snowed under, as it were, by the sufferings of war. We cannot commemorate his holy death in that fine and tasteful way we used to do so, but should we not at least try to imitate our SOOS a bit and come together on this feast through these simple sheets of paper?

Adrian van Kaam, Editor

ISSUE 2 — FEBRUARY 1945

(Day Undisclosed)

Dear Confrères:

After our first improvised meeting-on-paper, it is again possible to send this second issue to more than ninety confrères in occupied territory. We have gotten an article by the "globe trotter," G. van der Zalm; a description of the events in and about our novitiate by H. Mijnders; and a chat by Father F. van der Poel that may give us a new idea about how to keep junior seminarians busy . . .

As regards sending articles and letters, if possible, please do not do so by mail but try to find someone who comes in this direction, for instance, to Amsterdam or Utrecht. In this case address it to an Amsterdam or Utrecht confrère (e.g., Frater G. Nagel, Haarlemmerdijk 196, Amsterdam, or Frater B. Hendrikx, c/o Elemans Family, Frans Halsstraat 2 bis, Utrecht). We will see to it that a boatman, lorry driver or cyclist takes it to Nieuwkoop.

To the deceased members of our confrères (the mother and youngest brother of Frater B. Hendrikx) commemorated in our former issue, we have to add the father of Fater Q. Houdijk. Of course, the feelings of sympathy expressed in that issue are meant also for him. He, too, as well as his family can count on our Holy Masses and prayers.

Please direct everything regarding CUAU to:

Holy Ghost Fathers

c/o A 227

Nieuwkoop (Z.H.)

ISSUE 3 — MARCH 1, 1945

Dear Confrères:

Originally CUAU was meant to be a SOOS meeting on paper, with its traditional opening, outlined and under careful supervision of a chairman. Now, in an almost unnoticed way, it is developing into a means of speaking to and communicating with the many Spiritans scattered over this still occupied territory. This aim becomes clear, for example, in the cordial and much appreciated letters from our older fathers and younger priests. One of them asked for copies for brother-novices; another asked the same for the eldest junior seminarians; and others again promised to write articles.

Of course, editing an ever more widely conceived bulletin, which was not meant by me originally to be like this, is no longer a matter of competence of a chairman of the Gemert fraters' SOOS. However, as the only Father here, Father Pouw, has neither the time nor the opportunity to take this task upon himself. He is busy in his ministry. Until now, there is no father to be found with the opportunity to arrange for a printer. Father Pouw, who is now our Superior, according to Constitution 240, has thought that, in spite of its extension beyond the SOOS, this work should continue under the original editor. To carry it on to the best of my ability, I must be free, when selecting articles, to refuse, shorten, or delay them to a following issue, even articles by our fathers or other priests. I am convinced, under the present circumstances, that they will understand these [editorial decisions], even if, with their certainly more mature insight, they would think differently. Meanwhile, every good advice and direction will be most welcomed by me and will be put into practice, if possible.

Frater H. van de Bijllaardt will go on assisting me diligently with the more technical work like re-typing articles and arranging despatches, administrative and other financial matters. I am also thankful for the spontaneous interest and encouragement I have received in many letters and even personal visits. I must say that all confrères are most thankful to those who sent in articles and news. After all, this contact alone is what makes this Spiritan effort go on!

Do not let it end after the first enthusiasm wanes! Whoever once sent something, ought to repeat this offering, at least a second time. Whoever has not yet tried to write for our scattered Spiritan community should make a serious attempt to do so. Please do not send letters to various addresses but send everything to:

Holy Ghost Fathers
c/o Post Office
Nieuwkoop (Z.H.)

Don't forget to write on the envelope *Cor Unum et Anima Una*. Father Pouw has rooms there and, as local Superior, he has the right to receive and pass on correspondence.

The last meeting of our SOOS at Gemert was held on an unforgettable "Immaculate Heart of Mary" night, under whose invocation, also during this last year, our meetings were always opened and closed. May this bulletin, too, on a wider basis, be under the tender protection of this Mother's heart as is, of course, our beloved Congregation, its members and all its beautiful and difficult works. Then she will make possible and find for us fraternal consolation in our loneliness. [She will intercede on our behalf] for an unlooked-for exhortation to persevere in religious life and for a joyful growth toward realizing our profound motto, "Cor Unum et Anima Una," to be one of heart and one of spirit, especially in our external separation.

Adrian van Kaam, Editor

ISSUE 4 — MARCH 15, 1945

[This issue gives the names and addresses of the confrères insofar as they are known.]

Dear Confrères:

[It's like] a social activity when a new issue of CUAU leaves our rotating press—a [simple] social activity, somewhere in the wide polder, above a warm stable in the small attic room, full of photos of Gemert's faraway country lanes. Those precious and sometimes delightful letters from confrères, eagerly received in the morning from Father Pouw and as eagerly read, are taken more seriously. The news found in them, contains bits that are annotated and ready for printing; other items are labelled as more fit for a future issue. While the editor of this work feels many regrets about the suffering unwittingly inflicted on others because of his illegible handwriting . . . it suddenly happens quite often that a frater from another place comes rushing in with a load of news . . . Gerard van der Zalm, clownishly fat in an oilskin coat, with a hat that still shows signs of his falling into one of Holland's numerous polder ditches . . . Gerard de Winter, in a priest's jacket, carrying a bicycle pump, a flat tube, and a sacristan's salary . . . Frater N. van Veen from Rotterdam, looking skinny in odd parts of a clergyman's suit, pieces of which he had to borrow here and there . . . Likewise [we receive] many other lively letters. Last, but not least, our host farmer's wife, who feels almost as if she is a member of the Congregation, beams confidentially around the corner, asking, "How long will you be busy with that fathers' newspaper?"

Such social activity continues as we make materials ready for the press, at the office in the home of the village clerk. Fortunately, our Remington typewriter is patient and quite solid. Its restless torturer assures us excitedly that he thinks this hammering on it is much nicer than the philosophy studies he did a while ago! You can see from his face that he means it. Now and then we are interrupted by a helpful villager who comes to tell us that a "rambler" has been seen who might now transport our "parish-priest's newspaper" or who tells us that tonight a transport will go across the Ijssel river. [*This river, being in occupied territory, was difficult to pass over since there were often round-ups at the few bridges left intact.*]

Social activity like this goes on also with our good printer. Dressed in a yellow jacket, he calculates the size of the paper and the number of lines per page, explaining what a hard and slow work it is to print in unheated rooms.

Then, at last, CUAU appears. It is far from perfect and certainly has many defects, but it does not seem to be a miscarriage to us. Everybody has the right to give positive criticism, both as regards the form and contents of the articles. Such a fraternal discussion is thankfully put into print.

In many and various ways these fresh copies are now sent around, some arriving with more, others with less, success. Mostly we follow the line of least resistance, which is certainly not that of the official postmen.

And then, dear confrères, the continuation of this history is up to you. The first and most necessary event will be your speedy contribution. It will be in turn the indispensable beginning of another such "social activity" in which a new CUAU will make contact with all of us.

Adrian van Kaam, Editor

ISSUE 5 — MARCH 21, 1945

Dear Confrères:

Looking through our correspondence files I notice among all of you a similar enthusiasm for this bulletin, which serves as a way of connecting our scattered community. Both at the end of these letters and at the conclusion of many talks, most noticeably in the last few sentences, different distinctions will be made, suggesting subtly that we try to keep our articles at a scholarly level. To the contrary, others suggest that we not make it scholarly as such but [do our best] to keep it in the style of a more casual, recreative exchange. Still others think that there should be room in CUAU for serious articles together with those that are cheerfully student-like. Another statement assures us that more should be done to promote aesthetic and emotional expressions, while still others tell us that our people—having now been toughened in the practice of life—can only be reached in a matter-of-fact way and that, above all, we should avoid anything artistic!

At the base of these different critiques and expressions of gratitude—shared by all with conviction and the best of intentions, there may be a certain one-sidedness, even a narrow-mindedness, that might surprise us.

To be sure, we all carry with us a certain nature, talent, and level of maturity with its consequent unique atmosphere of values and concerns.

We are all inclined to make this character of ours, this particular ability and interest, an infallible standard of what should be worthwhile and useful for the whole community. The cheerful simple man tends to consider more complicated, somewhat lonely and studious persons as dull nothings from whom little use or pleasure is to be expected. The latter types feel compelled in turn to degrade these eloquent, social-minded persons as merely useless drivellers. Thoroughly matter-of-fact natures silently judge in their hearts, if not outwardly, artists to be irresponsible idiots who abuse paper that could be better used to roll cigarettes. Artistic persons, by contrast, sense in themselves an impulse to qualify chilly practical types as unimportant since they dislike a warm, emotive life.

And yet, when we consider the matter quite objectively and without prejudice from daily experience, from either an historical or a social point of view, and when we take into account the philosophy of human and Christian community structuring, we soon recognize that all good talents and natures have their value. We might have to do without the perfect understanding of and the right empathy for a special nature, but we must never be without appreciation and respect for how God has allowed this person to grow in this way. The latter might be helpful to his community in this one manner and no other. It would be as possible to produce an article about the helpfulness of the encouraging sociable talker or solidly practical person as it would be to write about the helpfulness of the more solitary bookworm or artistic type. [Translator's Note: *This point reminds me of a sermon Father Adrian van Kaam gave in 1951 concerning the theme that from eternity God has a plan for every single person.*]

It might be ideal for one individual to possess all of these functions, but in reality this is fiction. Our tolerance and our appreciation have to remain attuned to real people. Unconsciously and proudly making one's own taste and talent absolute only serves to create division within a community, weakening its total achievement and making it one-sided.

A narrow-minded community unfairly destroys the happiness of life and the helpfulness of all those members who, according to its standard, would not be able to promote its advantage.

Mutual appreciation and stimulation nurtures talents that are contrary to ours and moves every individual to optimal achievement in his own way, so that the whole community strives most effectively and many-sidedly after its purpose, thanks to the various gifts and the best [output] of many individuals.

Our correspondents and informants prove their rich versatility by the diversity of unique forms, which they suggest as standards of achievement for CUAU. If I were to comply with only one of these suggestions, our bulletin would at that moment no longer be a community bulletin. It would become an outreach to scholars or talkers, to artists or practical people, to mature or immature readers. Just as in society there are magazines for the arts and sciences, for the trades, for youth and adults, [so ours would become a specialized journal].

The truth is that our bulletin intends primary contact of all with all. This is achieved or at least approached only in the measure that all [interest groups and individuals] feel free to write according to their own different natures and unique characters. In that case one piece may sound a bit immature and shallow, another too superficial, still another overly scholarly, but we will find ourselves as we are in reality. In this way a sound exchange of thought is not excluded [but included]. Exactly this exchange, done in a fraternal tone, can promote each other's growth in the life of the spirit fruitfully and in an enlightened way. A tactful reply of one person or a possibly bold or immature assertion by another will be accepted by the latter as a precious spiritual gift from brother to brother.

In this way we will find one another in our various natures still coming together with one heart and one spirit—still striving after the high purpose of the Spiritan community. One heart and one spirit—in that same high-minded consciousness—we belong to an heroic community. In the midst of times and nations, full of purposelessness and unquiet irresoluteness, [we stand together]. Already hundreds have fallen silently at the fronts of God's kingdom while we go on as a community that without reservation exerts itself for the irresistible expansion of the world church. Ours is a community that will soon throw itself, doggedly and certain of victory, into Christianizing a continent (Africa) that will probably be *the* continent of the future.

May the Holy Virgin, our Mother, whose vocation we remember on March 25, give all of us a heart full of loving appreciation for one another's unique gifts. Her own Immaculate Mother's Heart appreciates and loves the good expressions and acts of her children, from the most elevated to the simplest.

Adrian van Kaam, Editor

[Translator's Note: *In this issue one father who was there gave an extensive description of the heavy bombing of The Hague on March 3, 1945 by the English Air Force; they mistook military objectives and bombed residential areas. Hundreds of citizens were killed. These mistakes unfortunately happened during the war—citizens being killed not by the enemy but by our allies: Rotterdam and Nijmegen underwent the same fate in 1943 and 1944 by American bombers.*]

ISSUE 6 — APRIL 1, 1945

[Translator's Note: *In this issue and the next there is a lot of news received from confrères in the Enschede area, in the East of the country. This mail must have been sent weeks before and taken a long time before it was received by the editor. On that same day, April 1, on Easter Sunday of 1945, Enschede was secured and liberated by Canadian troops.*]

HAPPY EASTER! On this feast day of glad resurrection, this day devoted to the pure remembrance of Christ's glorious resurrection, let us be intimately convinced of the knowledge of our own glorious resurrection, once and forever with him. For we will rise. Flames from the air may deform and hurt our bodies, but we shall rise. Hunger, fear, and dull reluctance may consume us, but we will rise. Human suffering ascending high around us and taking away our views may alarm and startle us, but the [promised resurrection] keeps radiating through us.

Today is just a single [period of twenty-four hours], but tomorrow we will be reborn splendidly to a new life. So . . . have a blessed and happy Easter, a glorious resurrection.

That Spiritan who quietly does his duty far away in Saint Pierre and Miquelon; that Spiritan who holds out as far as in the southernmost section of the African continent, he will rise again. That pioneer grown grey, who only seems to breathe for the sake of transferring the torch to younger ones, he, too, will rise. That confrère who is marching tired and astonished in grey soldier's dress among smoking ruins, he will rise. And he who is plodding, breathing heavily in a factory or a camp, he, too, will rise.

Those confrères who today wake up full of homesickness, with strange people, who feel hunger gnawing, who stand by helpless as members of their own family and their possessions perish, they all will rise again, cheering.

The number of power-stations on both ends of the ocean, the communities still united, whose members wish one another Happy Easter today in many languages, they will rise and say to one another, Happy Easter, Blessed Resurrection! The Spiritan community, in which men from many nations find one another in the joy of one passion, one love, one ideal—above the disturbance of the nations—they will once more celebrate, beaming the joy of their resurrection together with the Lord.

Of one heart and one soul are those many Spiritans—Germans and Canadians, Irish and English, Poles and Frenchmen, Portuguese and Dutchmen, Africans and Americans. All will rise and in joy sing one song.

Blessed Resurrection, that [lets us remember] the holy founders and the deceased members of our congregation, who have already preceded us gloriously to eternal life.

Blessed Resurrection, a greeting that will also be said after this eventful century, by those to whom we, belonging to this victorious congregation, will at our decease pass on the torch.

Happy Easter, Blessed Resurrection, to all Spiritans who wander here and there, scattered but not beaten, in their small plot of our harassed country, having for an external bond only this simple bulletin through which we wish them all a really happy Easter.

Adrian van Kaam, Editor

ISSUE 7 - APRIL 7, 1945

Dear Confrères:

Fortunately, we receive so many pleasant letters that it is no longer possible to reply to all of them, except to say thanks. The writers can be assured that their letters were real surprises, appreciated side by side with the many other surprises that usually happen on a farm, such as my being called to go downstairs to assist in repairing and readying a bicycle!

First of all, let me offer some explanation for our confrères in the part of the Netherlands beyond the Ijssel.

[Translator's Note: *This was the Eastern part—which at the time of this issue, was already liberated; it is doubtful if Adrian's confrères ever received this bulletin.*]

After the second issue (the first consisting of only sixty copies), there was a period without any news from them, so they might have become convinced that the Spiritan bulletin had already gone broke. Then suddenly they got the news that there was a third issue, which however was nowhere to be found. Next they received a fourth one, then the third and fifth issues came together. It is not Frater Hans van de Bijllardt's intention at all to continue his administration in this way. On the contrary, his zeal and care are unquestioned; the explanation lies somewhere else. Frater Gerard van der Zalm had the staggering ingeniousness to lose both his stock of bread and all of the bulletins during his "safari" across the Ijssel River—an involuntary disservice, which is nothing compared to his benevolent and disinterested assistance in regard to our bulletin. A few weeks later, a curate from Schoonhoven (*a small town East of Rotterdam*), so famous and dear to many of us from references to it in our lessons in physics and Bible studies, wrote: "Yesterday somebody brought me a briefcase with a series of issues of CUAU, together with a parcel of letters and some victuals. I think it was found near Utrecht. I will try to get the mail to Utrecht and, insofar as necessary, get a car with the food supply across the Ijssel to the North. I have distributed the food I found among hungry people. I will keep the bag and issues of your magazine. . ."

Father de Lange will certainly be surprised and satisfied to hear how the hungry at Schoonhoven have been fed from the provisions of one of those students to whom he used to defend so superbly his birthplace...

Frater N. van Veen, who came here from Rotterdam searching for food—he walked because he had no bicycle—could use in this case the bike of a confrère from The Hague, who was ill because he ate too much (ironic as this may seem). He returned the copies the same day. They were then transported across the Ijssel by car that night.

Next I want to point out in the light of a kind remark by one of our good Brothers that they are, of course, included in the title of "confrère," which literally means "a fellow brother." This Spiritan community bulletin belongs as much to them as to the other members of the Congregation. They live in the cordial prayers, thoughts, and feelings of us all. We also know for sure and with joy that we, too, benefit from a great and continuous share in their prayers. We would be deeply grateful if they also contributed to our correspondence section.

At last, the office for post and telegrams in Nieuwkoop can be reached by phone. A message from Gemert or from other confrères in the South—whether it is sent by the Red Cross or any other organization—can be dictated to our Father Pouw, who lives there, or mostly to the postmaster himself when our Deputy Superiors are absent due to their laudable and zealous parish work.

[Translator's Note: *There was no direct mail between the occupied and the liberated parts of the country, although some sporadic contact was still possible through the Red Cross.*]

One remark as regards expenses: Dear fathers and fraters, let us know if you would be able to make available in some abundance money for promotion, which, after all, was given for the maintenance of everyone, also for those confrères who have already let us know or will let us know of financial problems, such as doctor's bills that need to be paid along the way. One heart and one soul is a motto that also applies to the common carrying of each other's financial burdens, no matter how scattered our confrères are.

Adrian van Kaam, Editor

ISSUE 8 - APRIL 14, 1945

[Translator's Note: *During a raid, Adrian's sister Bep, who was staying at the same farm, which was raided and searched, was taken prisoner. As the memoirs reveal, by means of an appeal to the local German commander and by means of a written letter of protest, Adrian managed to free her from any blame—in German eyes—and to get her released. One Holy Ghost Father tells about a simple poor woman to whom he administered Extreme Unction before she died. She had lost both legs by an exploding mine. She said to him: "Father, Jesus has felt pain too. He now gives me strength."*]

Dear Confrères:

Almost daily our collection of news from contributions and reactions to former issues continues to grow. More often than not these [communications] were written some time ago but have arrived only now, yielding a varied but valuable archive, at once fascinating to us and important for future generations, living in more balanced times and in a quieter community. How surprised they will be when reading about the experiences of their scattered predecessors. This abundance makes it necessary to print our "non-periodic bulletin," at first appearing as the copy arrived, now on the average of once a week. In nearly all letters we receive, there are enthusiastic words of thanks for everyone who makes this repeated appearance possible, also materially by their contributions. We also got some messages from members of other congregations, who want to try to start a similar bulletin while showing their enthusiasm for this Spiritan initiative.

A special word of thanks, on behalf of all of us, goes to our printer, with whom it is so pleasant to collaborate. In spite of the present circumstances, filled with technical and other moment by moment problems, hardly any of us could suspect, he tries with much devotion to satisfy the difficult demands and even at times the merest suggestions of the editors. The fact is that in circumstances in which most people ignore such tasks or achieve them only after making fabulous promises, three skilled workers spend several days in composing this bulletin with an [astonishing] accuracy. The work they do has become so dear to us that it should receive our fullest appreciation and never be forgotten by us.

Adrian van Kaam, Editor

ISSUE 9 — APRIL 21, 1945

[Translator's Note: *Among the usual news, this issue also mentions the gift of the Swedish Red Cross to the Dutch population. In March every person was given one loaf of bread and some butter by Sweden. It was not enough to survive, but we who benefited from it will never forget this gift.*]

Dear Confrères:

Will we celebrate Ascension Day or our May 11th pilgrimage or at least Pentecost with solemnities in our chapel? Will we be together cheerfully in a well-provided refectory? Will we walk in a beautiful springlike park? Will we meet in a cozy recreation hall? Or will we have only this bulletin to bind our thoughts and feelings to one another? We know these past eight months have deprived us of much optimism and have given us at least a conviction that there are unmet desires that may try our patience for a long time to come.

To stay on the safe side, it is best that we prepare these feast days as if they were not to take place inside our monastery-castle but in this [nondescript] bulletin only. In the atmosphere of CUAU, this commitment will be successful to the degree that greater numbers of you, each in his own way, express the spontaneous responses aroused in you by days such as these. The more choices, the more beautiful and captivating the diversity we can offer in each issue, the more it will manifest our collective sense of celebration. I invite those who have so far enjoyed this common spiritual exchange, but who have not yet tried to make a permanently enriching contribution to it, to now consider doing so. Please write a short reflection on the occasion of one of the aforementioned days. It would provide a welcome gift for all. Especially contributions anticipating a possible peace issue would be more than welcome.

Adrian van Kaam, Editor

ISSUE 10 - APRIL 28, 1945

[Translator's Note: *This issue again mentions that Father Pouw, Superior at Nieuwkoop, considers Adrian the editor of CUAU just as he was chairman of the SOOS at Gemert before this time. Contact with the members in the Eastern provinces was no longer possible as they had already been liberated. It appears that a second German member of the Congregation, Frater Hinter, also in military service in the Netherlands, could no longer be reached and presumably had been taken a prisoner of war by the Allies. Frater Martin Wilson had been arrested by the Germans for cutting trees after the 8:00 P.M. curfew time but had been released again.*]

Dear Confrères:

Thanks to the new member of the CUAU crew, Frater N. van Veen from Rotterdam, who has been put in charge of [expediting delivery], it has become possible in principle to make sure this weekly issue will also reach the readers on time. Frater van Veen will see to it that in every possible way the necessary copies will be in the hands of some member of the Spiritans scattered throughout Holland (that is to say in the Western provinces only, since they are still under German occupation).

All confrères in these centers can count on the fact that the first receiver will at once take the trouble to transport these issues further without leaving them lying around negligently for another time, remembering that others look forward to their weekly bulletin as impatiently and anxiously as we do.

Adrian van Kaam, Editor

ISSUE 11 - MAY 5, 1945

[Translator's Note: *On the night of May 4, the Germans in Denmark, North Western Germany, and the Netherlands surrendered. As far as the Netherlands was concerned, this fact became official two days later, but the fifth of May became the day of liberation. Under the CUAU logo, it now said: "A publication in a free country." During the last week of the German occupation, the Allies forced the enemy to allow food drops to relieve the hunger of the Dutch population.*]

Dear Confrères:

WE ARE FREE. *Deo gratias*. Our people are free again, God be thanked. We are relieved from all the pressure laid upon us. Untied, we walk gladly through our wide, open country. The constraint is gone, and we feel clear, unrestrained, and relaxed, like the glistening lakes and ditches, the green rows of pastures, where the last remaining cattle belonging to a joyful people, and no longer liable to be taken away, are grazing under the May sunshine.

We are free. Why does this word—once only moderately imposing—now possess such a magical sound, such an elevated splendor, moving and captivating us irresistibly? It is because this newly obtained freedom stands out so starkly against the nightmare of pressure and ruin through which all our senses had to pass, against the horrors piled up in our consciousness. Exactly against the black background of these memories there shines the whiteness of freedom. How it surprises and moves us! Only in the piercing antithesis of contrast can we express the renewed relaxation our nation enjoys inwardly. Only in the outlining of contrasts can this reality be clearly known and fully lived.

In the light of the word "freedom," I see again in front of me the man, full of worry, whose guest I was allowed to be in a country house on the lakes; I hear his voice relating how shaken he was by the hostile grip the enemy had on his possessions. Now that anxiety will be calmed down, that fear in his voice will be quieted. *Deo gratias*. Thanks be to God. We are free.

I see again that fearful Jewish man sitting beside me, downstairs in the farmer's room, pondering and fingering my cord and tassel, reporting in a voice full of suffering what happened to his family. Then, with one knock on the door, he disappeared nervously into the next room.

Now he can stay where he was and with a quiet smile enjoy every visit. Thank God. We have all been liberated.

I see, too, a pale, and tired person sitting in the farmer's armchair. He is a lawyer who left the camp crippled and who becomes white as a sheet if he hears a footstep on the path in the yard. From now on he may remain unmoved, even when he hears the sound of a [stranger's] steps, for we are free.

Remembering our small village circle, where so many intellectuals hid, I suddenly taste again, in the bitter words of their debates, how desperately homesick they were for normal life. That young liberal Protestant minister, who reasons with me about Saint Augustine and Emanuel Kant, but cannot refrain from mixing these remarks with a word about this ghastly situation, he, too, is free.

I recall that attentive medical student, who had to exchange the quiet atmosphere of her room at Leyden for domestic life on a farm. Now again there is the opportunity for her to develop the gifts God gave her. Thanks be to God. She is free.

There he is in my memory—that bachelor of arts and psychology, who regularly came out of his hiding place to continue discussion of his analysis of Thijm (a Dutch Catholic writer in the 19th century), but who every time has to condense his reflection since he has to think more of his home than of his work. Now he will probably be able to get his doctorate, for we are free.

And then there was Leo Boekraad, the talented poet who had escaped from a concentration camp and who, from hiding, wrote such simple and melodious verses for our bulletin. Today he may put his name under his work without trembling. His volumes will be published again without fear. He can resume his task of writing and publishing without anxiety, for he is free.

The wildness and strangeness of this period [can hardly be expressed]. Allied weapons are thrown down in the polders. Clouds of parachute silk are hidden under the roof of our small farm. *Feldgendarmerie* (German police), caught in the agony of flight, behave recklessly. By night, after another wild day—under the smiling eyes of the unbelieving lawyer and the quiet brave Jew—I watch as the diligent hands of women and girls cut and divide the bulging pieces of a parachute, for this silk now serves a pious purpose: it is to become a chasuble for the frater (*perhaps Adrian himself*) who, after this chaotic hour, hopes to be God's priest. The skilled women have already made four clean cinctures from the loosened parachute cords. Tonight their work no longer needs to be done secretly and cautiously, since we are free.

[I'll not soon forget] the townsman with a hunted look, who came with a nervous smile to ask my help because that day he had been ordered [by the resistance] to kill a man for the first time. He needed to share the revolting bloody report with ["a man of the cloth"]. For him, too, this time is past. *Deo Gratias*. We are free.

The wild, strange times [prior to our liberation] continue to haunt me. With the farmer and his daughter you crouch in the field along the edge of the ditch. Above you a lonely sparrow-hawk screeches. In front of you cows graze contentedly. The farmer dozes off, with a bit of straw in the corner of his mouth. The daughter stares in tense fear across the polder to the far-off house, waiting to see if grey uniforms worn by the searchers will appear. [The terror they evoked] will not happen again. We are truly free.

And, then, who can forget the journeys to the damaged city? Joyless we walk amidst the stench of decomposition. We see neighbors and their children in treeless, broken streets. [Translator's Note: *Every tree on every road had been cut down since this was the only fuel to be had that winter.*] I still see their wan faces, their bodies, lean to the bones, the dullness in their sunken eyes. . .Here is a people dying, a nation of wrecks. . .your own people. . .but, thanks be to God, we are free. Their eyes will shine again and their cheeks will be full of color.

Yes, we are free. The risky letters of confrères need no longer be put in that slot or in that beam. Our houses will no longer be searched, [our privacy violated]. Each one of us can extend this list of memories and make it much more weighty. Each must find a way to make this experience his own, with whatever variations of names and persons are needed. Everybody has suffered the reality of unfreedom in multiple and intense ways, together with the nation we have come to love so much in spite of its faults.

Thank God, we are now free. And, thank God, we fathers and fraters have become really free only today. Had we managed to reach Gemert (that is to say, by last September, 1944), we would have been liberated sooner, but we could not have freed our families from the hunger menacing them. That we could do so tirelessly is our real joy and victory. Fortunately, there were many people who reached a supply center in the country. They could go and live there, collecting [food] quietly and, when necessary, putting up members of their family in town along with some newly found friends. Thanks be to God, they honored the many other town-dwellers, who were not so lucky, and who every day indefatigably could only find small stocks at a time, travelling often on hopelessly old wrecks of bicycles because, unavoidably, it took so much time and equipment to cycle up and down the country. They also had to care for brothers and sisters whom they could not put up so easily with the farmers. Honor them please! In difficult circumstances they kept on trying to alleviate the hunger of the families for which they felt responsible, at least to some degree.

Our prayer is that we may soon return to the well-ordered ranks of our Congregation, knowing by these events that we are connected more strongly than ever with the tough, well-controlled nature of our people. May we now enrich our Spiritan community supernaturally by growing in joyful asceticism and similar inborn natural virtues. May we mitigate the vices that we have also inherited from our ancestors and the national environment . . . Only then may we arouse, peacefully but irresistibly, admiration in every continent for the country that raised us, for the nation that fed and freed us. Then we shall be most valuable for our congregation and our country. In the same way every person is most valuable when he or she supernaturalizes their good talents and powers and allows them to mature as fully as possible. By the same token, one is least valuable when one's community foolishly suppresses or ignores the natural good talent God gave us all. For we were subjected for five years by tyrants of a foreign nation to this blasphemous attack on what the sovereign God put in a human being. We ourselves are members of a fraternal community that, with men of other nations, will do missionary work among a foreign race, [evangelizing] them in Christ. May we never commit a similar stupidity or crime (on a smaller scale) toward those for whom we work nor to those who work for us. May this [respect for uniqueness] be our sensible, thoughtful, and communal response.

The minimum of the possible greatness of this nation does not lie only in hoarsely shouting hoorays behind a flag or in flaunting freedom with buttons and bows or with exuberant leaping through the streets or with smoking an English cigarette! [Translator's Note: *All these were expressions of joy on a national feast day. Especially English cigarettes were a luxury in 1945, after five years of absence of practically all tobacco, a commodity often used in lieu of payment.*]

May the Mother of all people in whose month [of May] this happiness comes to us, give us the courage to model this greatness, which is first of all a moral greatness in our renewed and purified personalities. In this hour this [renewal] is our first duty as Spiritans and as Dutchmen.

Adrian van Kaam, Editor

ISSUE 12 — MAY 20, 1945

[Translator's Note: *This issue relates a lot of what happened to several communities and individual members. One frater, Joop Hogema, was wounded the day the Canadians entered Amsterdam when a few Germans shot at the crowd that was waiting at the main square. Others had been forced to feed on tulip bulbs during the last year. One student lived with his family in a small village that was taken by the Allies; on that very same day he saw his chance and managed to go to Gemert on foot—just in time, for the next day the Germans re-took the village. There is news from the Spiritan communities themselves as well as two articles by Adrian in this issue.*]

Dear Confrères:

More and more we discover through many letters that the number of readers who are now confrères is much larger than that of our own confrères themselves. In some places the custom of passing on uncensored reading matter was also largely applied to CUAU. One of these interested people is the well-known Professor Magister Doctor C. Friethoff, O.P., who teaches Thomistic philosophy at Amsterdam Municipal University.

It is a source of our special gratitude and sincere appreciation that this renowned theologian is willing to enrich this Pentecost issue with his clear article about the mission of the Holy Spirit. We think there is no better way to wish our confrères a Blessed Pentecost than by uniting with Professor Friethoff's wish for our Congregation: that it, and this includes all of us, may cooperate with all our strength with this elevated mission of the Divine Envoy. How good it is of our amiable Consolator, that his congregation, which on May 20, the feast of Pentecost, together with its mission may, on this date, 242 years later, still exist after a war that shook it vehemently. What a beautiful and simple monument of God's merciful love this is!

Our bulletin will continue as long as possible during this time of our being so scattered, but it may be less frequent owing to more difficult circumstances. The new correspondence address is:

Frater A. van Kaam
Alberdinck Thijmstraat 8
Den Haag

If possible, despatch service will go on as usual, and local help will be most welcome.

Adrian van Kaam, Editor

POSTSCRIPT

Thinking I could no longer deny my confrères the news which I received only tonight, from our Spiritan communities, I met with our printer at 10:00 P.M. to see if he, in spite of his overloaded schedule with orders for "orange" (to accommodate celebrations everywhere since *orange* is the national color of the Netherlands) [could help me]. Contrary to our former arrangement, I asked if he could extend the Pentecost issue, which was already being prepared, to a double-sized edition. To achieve this goal our three good compositors would have to work many extra hours. I promised each of them twenty English cigarettes if they could manage this extra work with due diligence.

Please help me to fulfill this promise. Let every Spiritan, at the next cigarette rationing, entrust one of them to the confrère who usually distributes our bulletin. I ask only for one cigarette for these helpers and faithful friends.

With this appeal I gladly and thankfully finish the nightly preparation for press of the copy I have been waiting to publish for these last three long months. . ..It is now 2:30 A.M.. . .Everything has been well arranged. Soon, at the first light of dawn, the compositors will start their difficult work. . .How good God is! That is the motto on one of the walls of our Gemert castle. In the old Dutch spelling it translates: "So good is God."

Do not all of these plans seem to be a tender token of the love of the Consolator to whom we are dedicated so unconditionally?

[Translator's Note: *There was an extra issue, unnumbered, on May 23, with a call from the Provincial Superior, Father Vogel, to commemorate the silver jubilee of the Superior General on May 30, if at all possible. The Spiritans who had been in Nieuwkoop and its surroundings arranged a celebration in that village. On Pentecost they had managed to celebrate this feast not far from Nieuwkoop, thanks to one Father, who had become liaison-officer with the Allies and had a car at his disposal, enabling him to transport quite a few of them.*]

ISSUE 13 — JUNE 6, 1945

[Translator's Note: *In this issue it is mentioned casually that Adrian had had at some time the chore of working in the refectory at Gemert. Special mention should also be made of the thanks the scattered Spiritans said to their confrères and superiors in the South, where there had been no famine to speak of, for the packages of food that the latter had sent them.*]

Dear Readers:

This word is for those who do not belong to our Congregation and yet who were eager readers of our bulletin, indeed I would almost say, spontaneous supporters. They considered our bulletin to be more than a typical expression of our inner and intimate community life, one which they had hardly expected. [In it they found] answers to questions they asked often. During the last months of the occupation, they surpassed in number our own confrères.

This group of interested outsiders was quite varied. It included members of a working class district in town, where CUAU was passed on from house to house through unpainted kitchen transoms, echoing the shrill voice of a neighbor's wife: "It was like reading a novel, sir. You were always looking out for that monastery at Gemert. Issue Twelve had a happy ending. You all found one another." That was what some of these people told us.

The professor, too, who received the bulletin in his study always said the same thing: "Well, there is that illegal flyer again." A healthy fellow from the underground forces read it quickly in between two jobs. He was especially aware of the reports of the adventures of our Limburg confrères. (*Limburg was the province from which many inhabitants were evacuated.*) Another reader was the patient, who slowly "digested" every good thought. He was suffering from hunger, but he said he could find more optimism in our correspondence section than on the radio.

Then there was the woman whose body was scorched with painful cancer and who kept asking impatiently when the next CUAU was to appear. Another reader was the spry young teacher who read every word to her blind sister, including our appeal for gifts. In many quiet, respectable presbyteries, the bulletin was as welcome as it was by those curious farmers and their wives. Reading it regularly were junior seminarians, scattered everywhere as well as several students at the universities that had been closed down by the Germans. (Non-Catholics were also numbered among our readers.) One was a fervent collector of illegal pamphlets, who called CUAU one of the most positive press products of the time of the occupation. Another would define the congregation in this light as an imposing world-concern. Several nuns savored the bulletin appreciatively, without criticism. Their first demand, continuously repeated but due to the circumstances continuously rejected, was: "Why can't I receive it personally if I am willing to pay for it." Sometimes this desire to pay was willingly met, but the other friendly desire [for regular delivery] except in two special cases, was not Why not?

First of all, our bulletin "sailed under" innocent-looking colors, being named "just a correspondence contact among monasteries." Next, we received an unexpected warning by a prominent resistance worker about it and also a hint of the same by a friendly lawyer who had applied himself, without much success, to defending some other unfortunate publishers. These factors made us unrelentingly careful also toward kindly interested people [like the nuns]. The enterprise, risky in itself, would have become even more dangerous. Now we had at some point to defend the editor's statement, written under the logo of CUAU, with the awareness that any mistake in this regard would only end in a prohibition to publish. Even so, a second proposal referred to a possible continuation of CUAU, also for these outside readers. One was a relative of a confrère who was the spokesman of many others: "Actually, we had never had such a good idea of the life and thinking of our boys. Through CUAU we have come closer to them than ever, and we would like this more intimate acquaintance to be continued in some way."

A university student wrote: "You strengthen and renew yourself spontaneously by such a bulletin. It is an honest log of sound Christian reactions of young men to the adversities in their own and our lives. We, the laity, should enjoy permanently this news of the splendidly vital inner life of a religious community and of their balance, so full of equanimity in suffering, a [grace] they obtained by faith and their stable monastic traditions."

A spirited young writer wrote: "There is courage and life in such a congregation of pioneers. Keep carrying these treasures in a new language [all can understand]. This will evoke enthusiasm in all young people. We want to see that our religious can think and feel religiously without ulterior or worldly motives."

We thank you all for this appreciation, but we can neither assure nor promise these interested people a possible continuation of CUAU. If anyone wants to keep contact with our congregation and its works, a special magazine is being published for this purpose from our formation house at Weert: *De Bode van de Heilige Geest* (*Messenger of the Holy Spirit*).

Finally, what has done us a lot of good was the devout interest that grew in some people for our Venerable Father Francis Libermann. It does us good when outsiders say that at this appalling juncture there was a rare, almost magical radiation of peace, quiet, and courage in suffering in those spiritual thoughts of his that were published regularly in our bulletin.

Some people wanted to know more about this quiet spiritualized person, whose death only served to increase veneration for his modesty. We want to meet this desire by mentioning some reading matter on the Venerable Libermann at the end of this article. We ask all of you, dear readers, to transform your friendliness into a cordial prayer in order that we may become holy priests.

Adrian van Kaam, Editor

[Translator's Note: *Some books (in Dutch) on Libermann are then mentioned, all of them available at Gemert.*]

ISSUE 14 — JULY 5, 1945

[The Final Publication of CUAU]

[Translator's Note: *This issue mentions the meeting at Nieuwkoop of the confrères to celebrate their General Superior's jubilee. Adrian took part in the preparations, dressed in blue overalls. The Provincial Superior, Father Vogel, had somehow managed to send some cigars. Both he and Father Strick, then Superior at Gemert, wrote appreciative articles about CUAU in this issue which finds Adrian's article not at the beginning but at the end.*]

A WORD OF THANKS AND AN EPILOGUE

Such was the custom after every evening meal. A word of thanks and an epilogue was the traditional end of a SOOS meeting with an outline of its achievements. So the same should follow here.

First, let me offer a word of thanks to our good benefactors. In the first place the De Vette and Groenendijk families enabled us to stay here and work; they accepted and even promoted with a smile every visit in connection with this project. The De Vette family, in particular on May 30, extended their hospitality to eighty-six persons, aided by Auntie Ka's excellent cooking. Later on, the J. Verhaar family gave our sick confrère a chance to recover. The D. Nieuwenhuizen family fed our frater-distributor so well that according to his last calculation he was able to cover 2100 kilometres (1,300 miles), delivering newspapers, soliciting financial and other support, and enabling correspondence among many confrères.

These families provided the basis for all of our CUAU work. We thank you so much! And let us not forget Mr. Middelkoop and his assistants, none of whom are Catholic, yet all of whom enthusiastically, diligently, and unselfishly took care of *Cor Unum* as if it were their own bulletin, even when this work was risky, when there was little food, when there were problems acquiring paper, and when they had to do a lot of extra labor for us. Their share in this success is particularly great. Thank you very much!

The Sisters of Saint Ursula at Nieuwveen and the kind fisheries at Nieuwkoop were contacted by Father Pouw late in May for a certain intention. The good farmers and their wives at Nieuwkoop-Noord, De Meije, and Zevenhoven, where, around the same time, the fraters turned up with their carrier tricycles, shared their festive programs and their joyful conversations. They gave all the confrères a splendid day. We thank you so much!

Our gratitude extends to the many other helpers, who unselfishly cooperated by laying out gas-lights, by offering accommodations, by lending us chairs, crockery, a statue of Mary, many bales of straw, a house organ, acetylene lamps, barges, sailing and rowing-boats, and making their expertise in sailing available. When, at the castle at Gemert, [items of value] had to be carried here and there and other things had to be removed in the inner courtyard, the Fathers were aghast whispering to themselves, "The fraters are having a social evening, aren't they?" Here, too, the "victims" of this event accepted the "peaceful looting" without dismay. Our thanks goes to them, too.

Then, of course, we thank all our dear confrères, who so splendidly and enthusiastically made this bulletin exist and kept it alive by their articles and letters, by their monetary and other gifts. The confrères made the meeting on the evening of May 30 a marvelous success by their lectures and songs, their recitations and other contributions. "And now it is over," said Nico, after we had been trying to get a lift, waving to Allied cars for an hour and a half near Bodegraven (*a small town near Nieuwkoop*) on the highway from Utrecht to The Hague, until one jeep picked us up and drove us to The Hague within half an hour.

"It is over," we felt—our being independent among and with the people. It is finished—the bulletin that has become so dear to us. And that's fine. Most important, what grew among us was a special spirit and atmosphere [of love and cooperation] in the midst of oppression and separation. [I will never forget] that typical editor's office atmosphere, a mentality, completely of its own, that was born in those difficult months. Sympathizing with people in this distressful period and in these ravaged surroundings, we could not escape from the impression these circumstances made on us. How thankful it makes us when we see in all the articles we received how these circumstances—which unsettled countless people—were understood and appreciated religiously by our confrères, who knew, often unconsciously, that these formation years were full of grace.

What a splendid and realistic optimism we find in all these articles and letters! This optimism prevailed amidst the darkest reality. It was balanced and enlightened by the sense of a transcendental Reality, just as real as the [dark nights we endured]. That pull upwards at the end of all articles, even from those who knew best how to fathom the bare facts, was never lacking. Ours was no longer a shallow, student-like optimism but the reasoned cheerfulness of a mature, matter-of-fact man.

The mood and the attention [of our bulletin] had to be turned toward the tragedy of a nation that was starving around us. How selflessly everybody knew how to solve this realistic, earthly experience in a supernatural way by demonstrating, often unwittingly in CUAU, how they themselves lived *in* but were not lived *by* their time.

This atmosphere of vitality, this strong sense of community, was most touching to outsiders. It was an atmosphere of manly-religious, realistically serious, who lived their beliefs spontaneously in their articles, letters, and talks.

Will we still understand [the effects of this time] when we will have regained the carefree boyish atmosphere of our training years in religious life? Will we recall this subdued view on the world through the mild colors of a stained-glass monastery window? Immersed in the flood of religious-like words in the environs of people, events and things, will we no longer need to consider intensely, consciously, and explicitly the boon [this winter has been] to us and our religious community life? Or will we become what Van Duinkerken describes in his introduction to *Cantica Graduum* by Willem Smulders?

> "What has a seminarian got to tell us? He is among his own books and professors, his mood is subject to the levelling-out in a small community of fellow students, who will not tolerate any uncommonness. Nature is given him in weekly rations on controlled walkways; he only knows human nature in cursory meetings in which he remains naïve."

[Translator's Note: *Anton van Duinkerken and Father Willem Smulders, a priest, were writers in those years.*]

Will we not be surprised to the contrary, that we knew how to write complete articles without the trite jokes one sees on commemorative plates? Amidst professors, canon law books, and many other important matters, will not some things appear strange to us, especially when our life once again becomes simplified by a slow, carefree movement between cell, chapel, and classroom?

This independent togetherness among and with the people is over. Finished is our taking part in the social struggle for life. We distance ourselves now from the heartbeat of society; we repatriate to this life between the walls, without material cares or social problems. We close this war bulletin, this journal of unexpected exploration among a nation that almost perished.

One thing we certainly take with us from these days, which our monastic predecessors, the pious knights after their laborious journeys chiselled joyfully in their coat-of-arms and above their gates, is the motto: "So good is God." [Etching it on our hearts], as it is carved into one of the walls at Gemert, enables us to thankfully finish our journey too.

Adrian van Kaam, Editor

[Translator's Note: *And so, some time in the summer of 1945 Adrian and his confrères were on their way back to Gemert. After completing his last year of theology, he would finally be ordained to the priesthood on July 21, 1946. The prayer inscribed in Dutch on his ordination card is.*]

> In de gedachtenis
> Aan zijn dood en berrizenis
> Offeren wij u dus
> Dit brood en deze kelk
> En danken u
> Dat gij ons waardig hebt gekeurd
> Voor U te staan en voor U
> Het priesterlijk ambt te vervullen.

The English translation is:

> In memory
> Of his death and resurrection
> We offer you
> This bread and this chalice
> And we thank you
> That you have deigned us worthy
> To stand before you and for you
> To fulfill this priestly office. Amen.

Appendix 4

Poetry of My Crucifying Epiphany

by
Adrian van Kaam

(Transcribed and Edited by Doctor Susan Muto)

[Editor's Note: *These moving words came to birth in August and September of* 2006 *when I sat with Father van Kaam in his residence at the Little Sisters of the Poor and transcribed what became his "last words" to us in English and in Dutch. When Father worked on these twelve poems, his physiological condition was such that while analytical work had become more or less impossible, his poetic capacity soared. It was as if left brain weakening led to right brain creativity. Working with him line by line on this poetry represented for me the flowering of our spiritual friendship and the understanding we had developed over more than forty years of colleagueship. Where one task ended, namely, the crafting of our formation theology, the culminating truth of his life and mine started anew thanks to the "music of eternity."*]

I.

INGETOGENHEID

Humble Submission to the Holy

Eternal Word,
bathed in mystery
that heals my broken heart
and sweetly calls me home
to God's unspeakable love.

Incarnate Word,
harmonized with heart divine
that stirs my deepest longing,
beyond what mind can tell
in reverence and wonder.

Saving Word,
granting lasting consolation,
in sorrow, sin, and loss,
let me bow and kiss
your all embracing cross.

Mystical Word,
spoken by God himself
directly moving the pure core
of divine intimacy
to be united with my poverty.

Hidden Word,
beyond human understanding
whose meaning God himself
may light up from time to time,
revealing his glory.

II.

INGETOGEN

Abandonment to the All-Pervading Mystery

Lord,
grant me the gift
of inner contemplation
of epiphanic radiation
that elevates my humble pleas
to hushed intimacy
with the Trinity.

Spirit of light and truth,
in revelation you are
the animator
of all that is created,
the transformator
of everyday simplicity
into music, song, and poetry.

Call me in your own way
to serve God's reign
on earth as in heaven with heart and mind
loosened by the leaven of your presence
from chains of externality
fracturing the beauty of creation.

Shy person of the Trinity,
shake me to the foundations
of my complacency.
Explode my interiority
with the fire of your love
leading me gently
to where you want me to be.

Open me, Holy Spirit,
to every expansion
of faith and reason
possible in the seasons
of my personal and worldly history.
Take me from immature familiarity
to oneness with your mystery.

Lord,
on this journey inward
from quiet prayer
to ineffable ecstasy
be with me
in consolation and aridity,
for, without you, I am nothing.

III.

PER CRUCEM AD LUCEM

Through the Cross to the Light

O suffering Christ
whose sacrifice
turned death to life,
stir up in hearts
grown cold with indifference
waves of compassion
for your crucifixion.

You ask us
from the bitter wood:
what could awaken
our willingness to share
with you the wrenching
pain that gained
our salvation?

Sad as you must have been,
scarred and bruised by sin
you did not show it.
Roughness called forth
your tender forgiveness,
insults your blessings,
lashes your love.

Teach us to imprint
your cross on our soul.
Let your grace inundate
the dark space where we feel
lost and alone until you call
us home from this night
into the radiance of your light.

IV.

GAUDEAMUS OMNES IN DOMINO

Let Us All Rejoice in the Lord

Joy lifting
joy elevating
joy raising
hearts weighed
with sorrow
to the Lord,
our gentle Savior.
You are so good
you take away our sins,
you give us in return
a pure soul.

Deepest originality
of joy
in the Trinity.
Father, Son, and Holy Spirit
living so joyfully
and letting us
share this gift
at your holy bidding.

Our inner life
is a sharing
in your own glory!
O joyful feeling,
no human joy
can compare
with this ecstasy.

Nothing is perfect,
but in this valley
of tears, God consoles
his suffering children
with touches of joy
with love overflowing.
So rejoice in the Lord:
all divine joy
comes from God alone.
You teach us
Christ crucified

to rejoice in agony.
When we are brought low,
you let joy overflow
beyond what reason
can grasp or words evoke.

Your joy, O Lord,
deepens love
beyond anything we do,
achieve, control.
It simply flows
from the heart
fastening us
day by day
to new depths of ecstasy,
in the love you bear
for all people
everywhere.

V.

GENADE VAN BIJSTAND

In the Embrace of God's Grace

Breath of God
balmy as west wind
wafting through trees
softening with warm breeze
my busy soul.

Help me
with embracing grace
to sense a deepening
beyond fear and anxiety,
beyond pain and aridity,
a deepening plunging me
into intimacy
with the heart
of the Trinity.

Protect me
with your strengthening arm
from the confusing blight,
the heinous harm
of sin, from Satan's
evil power,
deflating hope,
destroying faith,
defeating love.

Deepen daily
my waning trust
in your forgiving mercy,
in your radiating goodness
on my behalf.

Grant me the grace
of insight when I feel upset.
Let me not forget
your endless outpouring
of redemptive graces
enkindling hope,
enlivening faith,
enflaming love.

VI.

QUIA AMORE LANGUEO

I Am Pining for Love

I am pining
for your love, O Lord,
for without you
my life slowly empties
of your presence and I am left
like a well
with no refreshing
source of rain divine.

Who am I
that you grant me
the privilege
of meeting you
personally?

Who am I
that you let
me sing
this melody of love
to you alone?

Who am I
that you come to me
when I am lonely,
filling my soul
with celestial meaning
that will follow me
for all eternity?

Tears flow freely
from my eyes
evoked in waves
of adoration,
welling up from the mystery
of God's grace in me.

The longing in every
pining soul comes
to a crescendo
in the awareness
of its own spiritual

essence in the presence
of pure love,
descending from above.

VII.

JOY IN THE DYING

Lord, let me behold
the last beautiful
moment of my life
in this world.
Earthly life shows
its face to me
and I rejoice
benevolently.
Your preparation
of my poor heart
and soul for this moment
evokes thanks
in my whole being
whose hard edges
you have refined.

Thank you, Lord of life,
for granting me
amidst this strife
a final consolation,
quelling the last
traces of my anxiety,
letting none of it
be left in me.

Overwhelming every fiber
of my being is a feeling
of pure joy.
In gratefulness you allow me
to grow still, to contemplate
life's beauty, to move
into the depths of this good-bye
to my beloved earth,
to enter the kairos time
of eternal ecstasy.

Thank you, my Beloved,
for this—the greatest
of all gifts—to relinquish
fear and ready myself
to receive you fully.

Now—by your grace—

I forget about anxiety
and insecurity. I ready
my poverty for the
irresistible joy of eternity.
Let us go hand and hand
into the clouds
of endless beauty,
to that place
of unspeakable grace
where you await me
for all of eternity.

Like an excited child
I dare to sing
this hymn of welcome
to Sister Death.
How often we shall
repeat this song
when we are together
in heaven.

Joy, joy, joy.
My spirit waits upon
your loving presence,
as we dance with enthusiasm
in a tender embrace.
I sing a song of welcome
to your invitation. You
have made my child-like
soul full of sweet elation,
and I thank you for this meditation.

Being somber about my end
is not necessary.
I long to see your face
amidst choirs
of singing angels
in the presence
of everyone I have ever loved.
With palms waving in their hands,
they will welcome me,
and together we will absorb
the goodness of the Lord.
Shed from us like dead skin
will be the "what if's" of

shadowy doubts that signify
the last remnants
of the devil in us.
We shall radiate
our true form, the wholeness
of spirit that is the best
that can happen to us
poor pilgrims on the way
to our true home.
How lovely holy dying really is.

How I long to hear you
whisper words of gentle
consolation: My child,
take heart. I am so
happy with your soul.
Your time has come
in accordance with my will.
Enter the gates my Father
has opened to you. Come in
and be freed
from the ravages of sin,
come in to the place
in Father's house
I have reserved for you
from the beginning,
before you came to be.
Amen.

VIII.

GOD'S DICTATION THROUGH ME

When parts of me
life used to guarantee
fade away like dust
into the twilight of my life
poetry comes and rescues me
from culminating despair
and useless lethargy.
The miracle is that
God himself communicates
to me his own
inspiring and reflective
wonder and once again
I am made one
with him intimately,
ready to communicate
to listeners willing
to pause with me
and sing of your
awesome power
to bring
from this dying
new life. It starts
to flow through me
in movements forecasting
a suddenly restored
hand full of nerve cells
celebrating divine inspirations
once so cruelly silenced by
this tragic incapacity.

This intimacy
of the Godhead
finds entrance in me
restoring fingers once numbed
by pain that now
by God's grace
 are mine again.
Thank you for this undeserved
regeneration of muscles
gone limp as wet leaves.

Thank you for these
useless appendages
now bent and twisted
out of shape,
the sorrowful recipients
of crosses not to be
taken away. And yet
you let me converse
with the Divine Source
of cosmic and human poetry,
freed by faith to say:
O God, how lovely you are
to give me these words and phrases,
composed by an invisible hand
full of love and urgent proclamation.

Thank you, Dear Formator,
for what I could never
do by myself alone.
No longer am I on my own,
You have done this deed
in, with, and through me.
Truly, you, not I, are
the living reservoir of poetry.
I am like a copy machine,
transcribing your awe-filled
dictation, offering a message
of hope and charity
to a dead and dreary
world drowning in its own
claim to power.

I am a little pen
held in the hand
of a mighty God,
who works in me
with deep joy,
reverence, and humility,
moving my weak and fragile
fingers and senses to be
the instruments God uses
to invigorate my once opaque
mind and faltering heart.

Poetry of My Crucifying Epiphany

Day after day I experience
an accumulation
of inspiration enmeshed
in an often weary soul,
witnessing a reanimation
of sweet contemplation.
Imagine being so foolish
as to think I could transcribe
such a conversation
with the Source of all wonder!
Yet with this limping hand
I become the victim of divine
inspiration, to whose written
invitation I have no choice
but to surrender
in humble supplication.

Without hesitation, I consent
to become an instrument
of God's dictation.

IX.

NON TURBETUR COR VESTRUM

Let Not Your Heart Be Troubled or Afraid

Roaming every street
heads bowed in defeat,
voiceless victims seek
not to be so weak,
troubled and afraid,
so overly weighed
by sadness and sin
we may never win
that lasting reprieve
reason can't conceive.
Caught in such vices
faith alone suffices.

Your smile relieves stress,
you offer us rest
from condemnation,
an invitation
not to be upset
with little hope left.
We plead shamelessly
for divine mercy.
You look lovingly
at our unity,
consenting to bleed
for souls in dire need
of being redeemed
from people who deal
with others in cruel,
crass, uncordial ways,
shortening their days.

Frozen hearts, lying ploys
kill and bury joy
forcing us to pray
with passion today:
Let our hearts not be
stirred up anxiously.
Why be so afraid?
You've already paid

on your saving cross
for each human loss.
Your hanging there lets
us feel fresh droplets
of mercy that release
the blessed ministry
of gentility,
offering relief
that shatters our grief
as year by year
love casts out all fear.

X.

O CRUX AVE SPES UNICA

O Cross, You are Our Only Hope

Beam of bloodied brutality,
scandalous scar on humanity,
no one can grasp the scope
of your suffering:
how can it be
that on this splintered wood
hangs our only hope?
To appreciate your cross
we need to accept every loss
on life's embattled way.
We have no say.
All we can do
is trust in you.
We are like trapeze artists
hanging between time and eternity,
here today, gone tomorrow,
dancing across our fragile rope
in the childlike conviction
that your cross
is our only hope.
Plunging suddenly into valleys of tears
shaking with unspeakable fears,
we dare to proclaim
the freeing power of love.
You gained everything
below and above
by climbing upon the cross
that is now our only hope.

XI.

NUNC, TANDEM NUNC

Now, Only Now

Now, only now,
have I beheld
in every epiphany
your loving intimacy.

Now, only now,
can I listen
as angelic voices sing
your praises everlasting.

Now, only now,
have I been touched
by the wounded, bleeding hand
that redeems our sinful land.

Now, only now,
have I tasted
the sweet bread, the blessed wine
that signifies love divine.

Now, only now,
have I inhaled
the ritual incensing
announcing your swift coming.

Now, only now,
has intellect
left behind its need to know
and in faith begun to grow.

Now, only now,
has memory
shed shadows of near despair
and been renewed by your care.

Now, only now,
has my free will
abandoned its stubborn pride,
only in you to abide.

Now, only now,
has my poor heart
sought you as never before
becoming an open door.

Now, only now,
has my weak mind
dared to ask, even to grasp
the one truth that always lasts.

Now, only now,
has my spirit
soared aloft to freedom's height
bathed in epiphanic light.

Now, only now,
is my praying
drawn to depths in you alone
on the road to my real home.

XII.

AEQUO ANIMA

Serenity of Soul

Glowing star of serenity,
gift that draws my being
deep into a mystery
whose splendor and beauty
soars beyond human ingenuity.

Mystical Spirit of serenity,
radiating from the Trinity,
You call me in humility
to dwell intimately
with you for all eternity.

Holy balm of serenity,
healing broken humanity,
restore my sensitivity,
my loving gentility,
by your divine affectivity.

Everlasting beam of serenity,
allow me to see
with the clarity of docility
your light outflowing
in an unending epiphany.

Soaring power of serenity,
secret of peaceful inclusivity,
awaken in me the silencing
that lets me hear the symphony
of voices celebrating my dignity.

Divine depth of serenity,
answer my transcendent longing
to live in lasting harmony
freed from divisive exclusivity
by the blessing of your incarnate intimacy.

Lovely grace of serenity,
banishing doubt and anxiety,
fill me finally with tranquility,
with holy equanimity,
readying me to join you in glory.

Appendix 5

Biographical and Bibliographical Review

DATE	EVENT
October 26, 1862	Adrianus van Kaam, born at Halsteren in southwest Holland. Grandfather of Adrian van Kaam.
	Julia de Kock. Particulars unknown. Grandmother of Adrian van Kaam.
January 18, 1892	Elisabeth Johanna Franke, born in The Hague. Mother of Adrian van Kaam. Died on September 29, 1972.
February 9, 1896	Charles Louis van Kaam, born at Uitgeest, a village North of Haarlem. Profession: Streetcar conductor. Father of Adrian van Kaam. Died on December 24, 1974.
January 8, 1919	Elisabeth Johanna Franke and Charles Louis van Kaam married in The Hague.
April 19, 1920	Adrianus Leonardus van Kaam born in The Hague.
July 17, 1925	Elisabeth Julia van Kaam, born in The Hague. Sister of Adrian van Kaam. Married to J. A. Van Gemert on September 9, 1951. Two children, Han and Lisette.
April 7, 1930	Julia Elizabeth van Kaam born in The Hague. Sister of Adrian van Kaam. Married to A. M. Schellekens on June 24, 1954. Two children, Ton and Loek.

DATE	EVENT
September, 1933– July 1939	Gymnasium — Weert, Holland, following elementary education at Saint Joseph School in The Hague.
August 1939– August 1940	Entered the Novitiate of the Holy Ghost Order in Gennep.
July 17, 1937	Leonarda Jacoba van Kaam born in The Hague. Sister of Adrian van Kaam. Married to J. A. Van Leeuwen on July 29, 1958. Three children: Charles, Huub, and Elise. Died July 22, 1988.
August, 1940	First Profession in the religious life, Gemert, Holland.
September 1940– July, 1947	Seven years of study of Philosophy and Theology at the Senior Seminary in Gemert (Graduation Cum Laude). Interrupted by the Hunger Winter of 1944–1945.
September, 1943	Perpetual Vows in the Religious Life, Gemert, Holland.
1945	*Cor Unum et Anima Una* ("One Heart and One Soul"). Underground bulletin for students hiding during the occupation of the Netherlands by the Nazis. "The Social Psychology of the Student Society," written by Adrian van Kaam for students hiding during the occupation published in *Cor Unum et Anima Una*. Other articles in the same bulletin include: "Easter in War" and "We Are Free: The Psychology of Occupation and Liberation." "Christmas Eve in Ravaged Holland." A Christmas play presented seven times illegally by boys and and girls from the village and the polders of Nieuwkoop, Holland. Published by Middelkoop Press in Nieuwkoop.
July 21, 1946	Ordination to the Priesthood.

DATE	EVENT
1947–1950	After ordination to priesthood, teacher of logic, philosophical and experiential psychology, and philosophical anthropology at the senior seminary of the Holy Ghost Fathers in Gemert, Holland.
May 1948– August 1949	Study of psychiatry at the mental hospital Huize Padua in Boekel, Holland under Doctor A. Severijnen, Psychiatrist and Superintendent of the Hospital.
1949–1952	Psychological consultant of the Dutch Life Schools for Young Adults in offices, mills and factories in Holland. These life schools aimed at the integration of the dynamic principles of religion and psychology through a series of courses on various subjects preparing girls between seventeen and twenty-five for their vocational and marital life. Worked with Doctor Maria Schouwenaars, governmental supervisor of education in Belgium and founder of the *Mater Amabilis* schools.
1950–1951	Study of the Psychology of Personality and Education at the Hoogveld Institute, an affiliation of the University of Nijmegen, Holland.
1951–1952	Study (Psychological Analysis of a Religious Personality) of 1,800 letters of Francis Libermann, son of a rabbi of Saverne, who suffered from necrosis, epilepsy, and suicidal tendencies. This study resulted in a Dutch biography of 630 pages titled *The Jew of Saverne*.

Biographical and Bibliographical Review 419

DATE	EVENT
1950	A series of seven articles in *Beatrijs: A Weekly for Women* on psychological problems of adolescents and older women. "The Religious Moral Significance of the Social Workers in the Family." Van Nunen Publishers, Eindhoven, Holland. "The Religious and Moral Significance of the Social Workers in the Family." Reportbook of the Congress of Social Workers for Families, Valkenburg, Holland.
1951–1953	A series of seventeen articles in *Verbum*, the scientific Dutch monthly for religious education about psychological aspects of the religious education of adolescent girls and their impact on religious education.
1953	"A Reflection upon the Duty of European Youth with Respect to the Under–developed Regions of the Earth. "Dutch Periodical for Teachers and Educators" (DUX.)" "The Struggle of the Church Militant. A Discussion with the Editors of DUX about the Psychological Attitude of the Faithful in the Modern World." "The First Orphan of Libermann"in *Africa Christo*. "The Strongest Story in the History of the World: The Significance of the Holy Ghost in the Psychological Life of the Faithful" in *Africa Christo*.

DATE	EVENT
1954	"Christ, the Keystone of the Family: The Psychology of the Family Life and the Figure of Christ as an Answer to its Psychological Needs." "The Spiritual and Psychological Backgrounds of Religious Education in the *Mater Amabilis* School and Their Integration in the Structure of this Educational System." "Father Libermann, a Convert Jew: A Message for Our Time" in *Africa Christo*. "The Technically Trained Religious in Service of the World Mission" in *Africa Christo*. "The Venerable Libermann: A Psychological Study of the Life of a Jew, Suffering from the Epilepsy, Who Became the Founder of a Religious Order." Editorship of *Africa Christo*, the Periodical of the Dutch Province of the Holy Ghost Fathers. Editorship and Psychological Supervisor of a Series of Secondary School Readers for Grade Schools in the Netherlands.

DATE	EVENT
October 1952–July 1954	Continuation of the study of Psychology of Personality and Education at the Dutch Study Center, Culemborg, Holland. The Dutch M.O. Degree in Educational Psychology was granted after acceptance of the M.O. dissertation: "The Psychological and Religious Backgrounds of the Preparation for Life in the Schools (The Dutch Life Schools for Girls Between the Ages of 17 and 25) and Their Integration in the Structure of These Schools." Counselor in the Dutch Governmental Psychological Observation Center for Juvenile Delinquents, Kamp Overberg, at Veenendaal, Holland. Psychological supervision of a series of school–readers and educational pictures used for religious education in the Dutch elementary schools. Contribution of thirty articles to various scientific magazines in Holland concerning the integration of religious principles and the principles of psychology into the life preparation of girls between the ages of 17 and 25 in companies, mills, and factories.
1954–1956	Study of Psychology at Case Western Reserve University, Cleveland, Ohio, USA. Passed comprehensive exams for the PhD degree with the honorable mention of having obtained the highest quality points of the PhD candidates for psychology, who took the PhD exam.
1956–1957	Training in psychotherapy under Carl Rogers at the University of Chicago and under Doctor Rudolph Dreikurs at the Alfred Adler Institute in Chicago. Observer in group therapy session of Recovery, Inc., Chicago.

Appendix 5

DATE	EVENT
1957–Summer	Special studies in personality theory at Brandeis University under Professors Maslow, Goldstein, and Angyall.
1957–September	Instructor in Psychology at Duquesne University and at Mercy Hospital, Pittsburgh, PA.
1958	Granted the PhD in Psychology by Case Western Reserve University after the acceptance of his dissertation on: "The Experience of Really Feeling Understood by a Person: A Phenomenological Study of the Necessary and Sufficient Constituents of this Experience as Described by 365 Subjects in Chicago and Pittsburgh."
1958–1959	Invited by Brandeis University to take over for the academic year the courses of Doctor Abraham Maslow, Chairman of the Department of Psychology, during his sabbatical leave. Lecture series for the Psychiatric and Psychological Staff of the Metropolitan State Hospital in Waltham, MA.
1958–May	Elected as a Board Member of the Council of the American Association of Existential Psychology and Psychiatry, New York.
1958–November	Appointed Consulting Editor to the Editorial Staff of the *Journal of Individual Psychology*.
1959–1960	Assistant Professor of Psychology at Duquesne University. Invited as lecturer to Brandeis University, Boston College, Harvard University, Penn State University, and various clinics and mental hospitals.
1959	English version of the biography, *A Light to the Gentiles*, published by Duquesne University Press.

DATE	EVENT
1960–May	Appointed member of the National Board of Advisors of the non-sectarian Religion in Education Foundation, Pasadena, CA.
1961–September	Appointed Editor of the *American Review of Existential Psychology and Psychiatry*. Promoted to Associate Professor of Psychology at Duquesne University.
1963–April	Founder and First Director of Duquesne's Institute of Man. Appointed Consulting Editor of the *Journal of Humanistic Psychology*.
1963–July	Guest lecturer at Heidelberg University, Germany, and the University of Oslo, Norway.
1964	*Religion and Personality*, Prentice-Hall, Inc. On the best seller list since August, 1964. Also translated into several foreign languages.
1965	Founder and Editor of the monthly magazine, *Envoy* and the scholarly journal, *Humanitas*.
September 1965	Founder and Director of Duquesne's academic program entitled *Religion and Personality* for persons appointed to leading positions in the formation of religious (leading to an MA in Religion and Personality). This program would become the basis for a separate institute devoted to ongoing formation and formative spirituality.
November 1965	Promoted to Full Professor at Duquesne University.
1966	*Personality Fulfillment in the Spiritual Life*, Dimension Books; *Existential Foundations of Psychology*, Duquesne University Press.
1966–Summer	Visiting Professor – Psychology Institute, University of Heidelberg, Germany.
1966	*The Art of Existential Counseling*, Dimension Books.

Appendix 5

DATE	EVENT
1967	*The Demon and the Dove: Personality Growth through Literature*, Duquesne University Press. *Personality Fulfillment in the Religious Life*, Dimension Books (First Edition).
1968	*The Emergent Self*, Dimension Books. Co-authors Susan Muto and Bert van Croonenberg.
1968–Summer	Lecture Tour – Hawaii, Japan, Taiwan, Thailand and the Philippines.
1969	*The Vowed Life*, Dimension Books. *The Participant Self*, Dimension Books.
1970	*On Being Involved*, Dimension Books.
1972	*On Being Yourself*, Dimension Books. *Envy and Originality*, Doubleday & Company.
1974	*Spirituality and the Gentle Life*, Dimension Books.
1975	*In Search of Spiritual Identity*, Dimension Books.
1976	*Dynamics of Spiritual Self-Direction* and *The Woman at the Well*, Dimension Books.
1976–Summer	Lecture Tour – Australia and New Zealand.
1977	*Tell Me Who I Am* (Co-authored with Susan Muto, PhD), Dimension Books.
1978–1979	*Looking for Jesus* and *Living Creatively*, Dimension Books (Revised Edition of *Envy and Originality*); *Am I Living a Spiritual Life?* (Co-authored with Susan Muto, PhD), Dimension Books. Institute of Man becomes Institute of Formative Spirituality—due to the launching of the PhD program in this field. Recipient of Duquesne University's Presidential Award for Excellence in teaching.

DATE	EVENT
1979	*The Transcendent Self: Formative Spirituality of the Middle, Early and Later Years of Life*, Dimension Books. Co-founded the Epiphany Association in Pittsburgh, Pennsylvania, with Susan Muto, PhD.
1980	*Humanitas* becomes *Studies in Formative Spirituality*. Editor, Adrian van Kaam; co-editor, Doctor Susan Muto. *Practicing the Prayer of Presence* (Co-authored with Susan Muto, PhD), Dimension Books. *Religion and Personality*, Dimension Books. Revised Edition. Director Emeritus of the Institute of Formative Spirituality. and Professor of Foundational Life Formation. Appointment of Executive Director, Doctor Susan A. Muto, to Director.
1982	First William C. Bier Award recipient from Division 36, Psychologists Interested in Religious Issues, of the American Psychological Association for notable contributions to and applications of the Psychology of Religion. *The Mystery of Transforming Love*, Dimension Books. *The Demon and the Dove*. Washington, DC: Catholic University Press of America (Reprint). *Creative Formation of Life and World*. Washington, DC: Catholic University Press of America. (Co-editor).

DATE	EVENT
1983	*Foundations for Personality Study: An Adrian van Kaam Reader*, Denville, NJ: Dimension Books. *Fundamental Formation*. Formative Spirituality Series. Volume I. New York: Crossroad/Continuum.
1985	*Human Formation*. Formative Spirituality Series. Volume II. New York, NY: Crossroad/Continuum. *The Roots of Christian Joy*, Dimension Books.
1986	*Formation of the Human Heart*. Formative Spirituality Series. Volume III. New York: Crossroad/Continuum.
1987	*Scientific Formation*. Formative Spirituality Series. Volume IV. New York: Crossroad/Continuum.
1987–1989	Coordinator and Co-Leader with Doctor Susan Muto, in 1989, under the auspices of the Epiphany Association, of the PDTC, Professional Development Training Course, for the United States Navy Chaplain Corps.
1989	*Songs for Every Season*. Petersham, MA: St. Bede's Publications. Co-authored with Susan Muto. *Commitment: Key to Christian Maturity*. Mahwah, NJ: Paulist Press. Co-authored with Susan Muto.

DATE	EVENT
1990	*Music of Eternity*. Notre Dame, IN: Ave Maria Press. "Existential Psychology as a Comprehensive Theory of Personality," in *Studies in Existential Psychology and Psychiatry*. Seattle, WA. "Formative Spirituality," in the *Dictionary of Pastoral Care and Counseling*. Nashville, TN: Abingdon Press. "Readings in Existential Psychology and Psychiatry" in *Readings of Existential Psychology and Psychiatry*. Ed. Keith Hoeller. Seattle, WA.
1991	*The Transcendent Self: Formative Spirituality of the Middle, Early and Late Years of Life*. Pittsburgh, PA: Epiphany Books. (Reprint). *Commitment: Key to Christian Maturity, A Workbook and Guide*. Mahwah, NJ: Paulist Press. Co-authored with Susan Muto. (Second edition). *Religion and Personality*. Pittsburgh, PA: Epiphany Books. (Reprint). *Formation Guide for Becoming Spiritually Mature*. Pittsburgh, PA: Epiphany Association. Co-author with Susan Muto.
1992	*Traditional Formation*. Formative Spirituality Series. Volume V. New York: Crossroad/Continuum.

DATE	EVENT
1993	Dallas University institutes the yearly *Adrian van Kaam Honor Award* for the outstanding psychology student of the year. *The Power of Appreciation: A New Approach To Personal and Relational Healing*. New York: Crossroad/Continuum. Co-authored with Susan Muto. *Practicing the Prayer of Presence*. Williston Park, New York: Resurrection Press. Co-authored with Susan Muto. *The Woman at the Well*. Pittsburgh, PA: Epiphany Books. (Reprint). *Stress and the Search for Happiness: A New Challenge for Christian Spirituality*. New York: Resurrection Press. Co-authored with Susan Muto. *Harnessing Stress: A Spiritual Quest*. New York: Resurrection Press. Co-authored with Susan Muto. *Healthy and Holy Under Stress: A Royal Road to Wise Living*. New York: Resurrection Press. Co-authored with Susan Muto.
1994	Doctor (*Honoris Causa*) of Christian Letters, Franciscan University of Steubenville, Ohio. *Divine Guidance: Seeking to Find and Follow the Will of God*. Ann Arbor, MI: Servant Publications. Co-authored with Susan Muto.

DATE	EVENT
1995	*Transcendent Formation.* Formative Spirituality Series. Volume VI. New York: Crossroad Publishing.

Transcendence Therapy. Formative Spirituality Series. Volume VII. New York: Crossroad Publishing.

Stress and the Search for Happiness: A New Challenge for Christian Spirituality. Philippine Edition. Resurrection Press.

Practicing the Prayer of Presence. St. Paul's. Philippine Edition. Resurrection Press.

Harnessing Stress: A Spiritual Quest. Resurrection Press. Philippine Edition.

Healthy and Holy Under Stress: A Royal Road to Wise Living. Philippine Edition. Resurrection Press.

Foreword to *van Kaam's Formation Science/ Formative Spirituality and Religious Education in Asia* by William Garvey, F.S.C., Manilla: De la Salle University. |
| 1995 to date | *Epiphany International: The Journal of Formation Science, Anthropology, and Theology.* Co-Editor, Susan Muto. |

DATE	EVENT
1996	*The Commandments: Ten Ways to a Happy Life and a Healthy Soul.* Ann Arbor, MI: Servant Publications. Co-Authored with Susan Muto. *Tell Me Who I Am.* Chinese Edition. Taipei, Taiwan: Kuang-chi Press. *The Tender Farewell of Jesus: Meditations on Chapter 17 of John's Gospel.* New York, NY: New City Press.
1997	*The Woman's Guide to the Catechism of the Catholic Church.* Ann Arbor, MI: Servant Publications. Co-authored with Susan Muto.
1998	*Ten Ways to a Happy Life and a Healthy Soul.* Philippine Edition. Ann Arbor, MI: Servant Publication. Co-authored with Susan Muto. *Epiphany Manual on the Art and Discipline of Formation-in-Common.* Pittsburgh, PA: Epiphany Books. Co-authored with Susan Muto.
2002	*The Emergent Self.* Pittsburgh, PA, Epiphany Books. Co-authored with Susan Muto.
2004	*Foundations of Christian Formation.* Formation Theology Series. Volume One. Pittsburgh: PA: Epiphany Books, 2004. Co-authored with Susan Muto.
2005	*Christian Articulation of the Mystery.* Formation Theology Series. Volume Two. Pittsburgh, PA: Epiphany Books. Co-authored with Susan Muto.
2006	*Formation of the Christian Heart.* Formation Theology Series. Volume Three. Pittsburgh, PA: Epiphany Books. Co-authored with Susan Muto.

DATE	EVENT
2007	*Living Our Faith and Formation Tradition.* Formation Theology Series. Volume Four. Pittsburgh, PA: Epiphany Books. Co-authored with Susan Muto.
November 17, 2007	Death of Adrian van Kaam. Burial at Queen of Heaven Cemetery on November 24, 2007.
April 19, 2008	Blessing of his headstone in the United States and of his memorial stone in Holland at the burial ground at Gemert Seminary.

www.ingramcontent.com/pod-product-compliance
Lightning Source LLC
Chambersburg PA
CBHW070300010526
44108CB00039B/1275